# DATE DUE

BRODART, CO.                    Cat. No. 23-221-003

# An Army of Women

RECONFIGURING AMERICAN POLITICAL HISTORY

Ronald P. Formisano, Paul Bourke, Donald DeBats, Paula M. Baker,
Series Editors

# AN

# ARMY

## OF

# WOMEN

⊰ GENDER AND POLITICS IN GILDED AGE KANSAS ⊱

## MICHAEL LEWIS GOLDBERG

THE JOHNS HOPKINS UNIVERSITY PRESS

BALTIMORE AND LONDON

© 1997 The Johns Hopkins University Press
All rights reserved. Published 1997
Printed in the United States of America on acid-free recycled paper
06  05  04  03  02  01  00  99  98  97     5  4  3  2  1

The Johns Hopkins University Press
2715 North Charles Street
Baltimore, Maryland 21218-4319
The Johns Hopkins Press Ltd., London

Design by Christine Taylor
Composition by Wilsted & Taylor

Library of Congress Cataloging-in-Publication Data
will be found at the end of this book.
A catalog record for this book is available from the British Library.

ISBN 0-8018-5562-4

To my parents,

Esther and Irving Goldberg,

for their love, support, and inspiration

# Contents

## ACKNOWLEDGMENTS

The extraordinary collection of the Kansas State Historical Society and the generous, knowledgeable, and friendly support of its staff first drew me to explore politics and culture in Gilded Age Kansas, and I have appreciated both from this study's beginnings as a graduate research paper to its present form. MariJo Buhle's *Women and American Socialism* first drew me to the Woman Movement in Kansas, while Lawrence Goodwyn's study of the Populists' "democratic promise" first inspired me to explore Populism. Although I have come to disagree with many of his conclusions as they relate to Kansas, I am indebted to the vision and passion of his work.

A number of teachers have had a formative impact on my own career as a scholar and teacher. At the University of California, Santa Cruz, Buchannan Sharp's courses on British history made me appreciate the challenge of complex historical analysis. Marge Frantz and Jack Schaar inspired me with their commitment to teaching, their insistence on intellectual integrity, and their ongoing struggle with issues that matter. Had I never met them, I doubt that I would have gone on to graduate school. At Yale, Howard Lamar's encyclopedic knowledge of Western history and his timely praise during moments of doubt were a great help. My work with Jean-Christophe Agnew opened up my understanding of cultural processes. Bill Cronon has added immeasurably to my intellectual growth as a scholar, teacher, and writer. Nancy Cott, my dissertation advisor, has been a supportive and insightful mentor throughout this project, and her scholarly work has shaped much of my thinking on gender and politics.

My fellow graduate students at Yale did much to improve the dissertation on which this book is based. Reeve Huston, Susan Johnson, Amy Green, Kim Phillips, Yvette Huginnie, and Karen Sawislak provided valuable insight in the project's early stages. Two friends from graduate school deserve special mention for their help (and patience) through multiple drafts. In innumerable ways, Jenny Price has made this book a far more enjoyable experience for the reader than it might have been, and Bryant Simon has offered valuable critiques of earlier drafts while unselfishly sharing his own ideas about politics and culture. I eagerly await both of their upcoming books. My colleagues at the University of Washington-Bothell have created an intellectually stimulating atmosphere that has encouraged me to broaden my perspective and to take intellectual risks.

Melanie Gustafson began with a kind letter about my work and ended up providing me with a complete critique of my manuscript. Her understanding of the historiography of gender and politics was a great help to me. Paula Baker has read through several versions of the manuscript, and her insights have pushed the book's analytical reach several steps forward. My editor at the Johns Hopkins University Press, Bob Brugger, has kept my work focused on its central themes, and my copyeditor, Irma Garlick, has done an impressive job of steering me away from most—though not all—of my bad writing habits. The book has been much improved by her contributions.

Parts of this study appeared in another form as "Non-Partisan and All-Partisan: Rethinking Woman Suffrage and Party Politics in Gilded-Age Kansas" in the *Western History Quarterly*, where it was strengthened by the suggestions of coeditor Anne Butler. Before its publication in the *WHQ*, the article was reviewed by a number of scholars, and I am especially thankful for the insights of Ellen DuBois and Jacqueline Hall. A well-timed summer research grant from the National Endowment for the Humanities enabled me to spend several crucial months in Kansas completing the research for this book. Neil Basen provided me with a number of newspaper clippings on Annie Diggs and Mary Lease.

My family has been a constant source of support and love throughout the project. My brother and sister, Robert and Beth, have always been available to provide comfort or a sympathetic ear. My parents, Irving and Esther Goldberg, have lived lives that I deeply respect and have supported me without question and without condition all my life. I dedicate this book to them with all my love. Finally, having Elizabeth de Forest share my life has made me understand that any obstacle placed in my path does nothing to diminish the fact that I am the most fortunate person on earth.

# An Army of Women

# INTRODUCTION

## GENDER, POLITICS, AND POWER

The "Year of the Woman"—1992—has come and gone, leaving us with far more women in political office than before, and far too few. Pundits have analyzed the victories and defeats of women candidates, but they remain unsure about the lessons learned. During the 1992 campaign the mainstream media praised the U.S. Senate campaign of Washington State's Patty Murray, welcoming her "Mom in Tennis Shoes" theme as a challenge to the male-dominated Senate. Because the media focused on domestic issues and family concerns during the campaign, Murray's "Mom" image played well in the press. Once she had won the office, however, commentators berated her for spending too much time with her family and not enough with her constituents.[1] As I write this introduction, issues of crime and immigration restriction have taken center stage. Suddenly, Murray's image seems as much a liability as an advantage—can she convince voters that "Mom" is tough enough? For Murray, society's expectations abut what it means to be both a woman and a senator may prove a double-edged sword.

Political observers seldom concern themselves with the amount of time a male senator spends with his family: presumably enough to complete the obligatory family portrait for the campaign suffices. Instead, the media, along with

1

rival politicians, may question whether a candidate is sufficiently "manly." During the 1988 presidential campaign, *Newsweek* magazine featured a cover photo of Vice President George Bush grasping the wheel of his power boat and grimacing into the wind and spray. Hovering above this man who would be president, like a dark cloud on the horizon, were the boldly lettered words THE WIMP FACTOR. The big question—was he or wasn't he?—was debated at length.[2] Four years later, presidential contender Ross Perot charged Bush with igniting the Persian Gulf War in order to "prove his manhood."

Bush's critics substituted insinuations about his supposed effeminacy for the more substantial (but less viscerally effective) claim that he lacked convictions, forthrightness, and will power. Label Bush a "wimp" and people take notice. *Wimp* conjures up visions of the helpless nerd being humiliated by the school-yard bully, or the henpecked husband meekly submitting to his wife's will. Is this the sort of man you want negotiating with the Soviets? Even more threatening, *wimp* brings to mind *sissy*, which is just one short step away from the dreaded charge of homosexuality. Although Bush boasted the standard trappings of American masculinity, including a large family, a distinguished war record, and the captaincy of his college baseball squad, he constantly had to reassert his masculinity.

As Murray's and Bush's experiences show, the meanings we attach to gendered symbols are neither static, predictable, nor easily deciphered. Our ideas and assumptions about gender are embedded in our everyday experiences; they constitute a central part of how we define ourselves. These concepts are part of our written and spoken language, but they also include physical symbols as well: a football, a doll, a bag of pork rinds. Together they make up the discourse that we use to communicate our ideas and assumptions about gender; about the roles men and women play, the sexual identities they maintain, the relations they negotiate daily.

Political actors use this discourse because so many people assume gender expectations to be natural or common sense. But claims such as "That's just the way women are" and "Boys will be boys" are in fact freighted with cultural meanings. When public figures use gendered political discourse, voters often accept these basic assumptions without examining them. But political actors themselves are sometimes unaware of the multiple and shifting meanings within this discourse. They are often unable to control or predict just how gendered discourse will eventually play out in public. Sometimes, political actors employ strategies and tactics shaped by gender assumptions without realizing how those assumptions have influenced their politics.

Individuals, organizations, and institutions struggle constantly to define the terms of this discourse, and as with political conflicts, these battles are contests over power. Indeed, because gender and politics are so closely connected, a contest over one is often a contest over both. Those with greater access to public forums have a far better chance of controlling the debate. Ultimately, the winners wield considerable power in determining the politics we practice and the rules by which we live.

Following the Civil War, women began participating en masse in state and local electoral politics in order to have a say in fashioning and enforcing these rules, and these activists helped to change the way women and men thought about gender and politics and about each other. Led by the national Women's Christian Temperance Union, the National American Woman Suffrage Association, and a variety of service, charitable, and professional organizations, this "Woman Movement," as it was called, sought to reform male-dominated politics through women's participation. Activists in the Woman Movement believed that they could enter politics as equals with men and transform it into a nurturing, moral institution free of corruption and insensitivity to women's issues. During this period, rural people—first in the Patrons of Husbandry and then in the National Farmers' Alliance and the Populist Party—created organizations that promoted a political role for women while demanding a more democratic and economically egalitarian society.[3] The organizations encouraged women members to read, talk about, and understand the full range of economic and political issues. Beyond their duties as citizens-in-training, women were also the social organizers of the movement, the glue that held atomized and socially fractured farm communities together.

In challenging mainstream ideas about gender and politics, Woman Movement and agrarian reformers wrestled with some of the same complications about gender and politics that political actors face today: how to harness the seductive power of gendered political discourse without succumbing to its hidden liabilities. Reformers constantly had to reorient their approach according to whether their agenda was part of a local, state, or national movement; they had to consider the ever shifting demands of the moment. Gendered meanings that might resonate with like-minded folk could shift when presented to a more heterogeneous audience. Practices that challenged gender norms make sense in one context but appear inappropriate or ineffective in another. Activists' ideas and assumptions about gender helped to determine their ideologies, tactics, and strategies, the fate of their movements, and their impact on American politics.

The general outline of the story I tell here is not new. Historians have long battled over competing interpretations of the Populist movement. Their coverage of the Woman Movement has a less contentious but still extensive historiography.[4] By viewing these familiar stories through a gendered lens, however, I have tried to reappraise both the movements themselves and Gilded Age politics in general. My hope is that this study will pose a new set of questions about the way gender and politics intersect in American culture.

By focusing on gender, I do not mean to suggest that other causative factors such as economics, partisanship, race, or religion have no place in an understanding of Gilded Age politics. Rather, I argue that gender relations shape and are shaped by these and other forces. I have not found gender to be the only or even the primary explanatory factor; my argument is that one cannot understand these activists or their movements without integrating gender into their story.

I have set my study in Kansas, which in 1887 the *New York Times* declared "the great experimental ground of the nation."[5] Today's Kansas has an (undeserved) image as a conservative, drab place, perhaps perpetuated by stark black-and-white shots of the Kansas plains in the film *The Wizard of Oz*. In fact, the *Oz* in technicolor would be the fitting medium for portraying Gilded Age Kansas. During that period, the state was home to reformers, "cranks," and agitators of all kinds. Established in the crucible of "Bleeding Kansas," the fratricidal guerilla war that served as prelude to the Civil War, the state witnessed the nation's first (failed) statewide suffrage campaign, the first (successful) constitutional prohibition against alcohol, and the first state legislation allowing women to vote in municipal elections. Kansas was a leading state in the national agrarian movements of the late nineteenth century. It even had a thriving free love movement with a newspaper entitled *Lucifer the Light Bearer*.[6]

Easterners would often gaze westward toward Kansas, transfixed by the outsized events that seemed to be taking place there. Besides the intermittent political upheavals, Kansans endured devastating droughts, grasshopper invasions, record blizzards, and infamous cyclones. The economic climate was just as volatile, with booms and busts of dizzying proportions. The railroad-stop cow towns of Wichita, Abilene, and Dodge City were renowned for their loose and lawless ways.

In part, the hyperbole of the Eastern press fueled public fascination with the state: Bleeding Kansas wasn't all that bloody, other Great Plains states had their share of environmental disasters, and Dodge City's wild ways were both short lived and atypical of Kansas towns. These images of Kansas were not pure invention, of course, but the reality was much more subtle than the outsized portraits in contemporary books, newspapers, and magazines. Further, the "radicalism" of Kansas was of a particular kind, limited in part to an influential minority. At times this political radicalism would spread like a contagion, gripping people in an evangelistic fervor of commitment, a "pentecost of politics."[7]

Political actors in Kansas operated within a specific political context, a particular history and culture, but they were inevitably influenced by the national mainstream culture as well. Any woman or man who aspired to middle-class respectability in Gilded Age America was expected to abide by the accepted rules of mainstream gender behavior. Historians trace the roots of this discourse to a genre of literature that prescribed the ideal roles for women and men. Developed by ministers, essayists, and writers (including some women) in the Northeast during the late eighteenth and early nineteenth century, this ideology codified the notion that women and men occupied "proper spheres" in society.[8] A central tenet of this ideology was that women were morally superior to men. Women, designated as society's moral guardians, were obligated to fulfill this social role as wives and mothers. Most middle-class Americans agreed that this exalted domesticity was a woman's highest calling, her truest vocation, and her means of doing the greatest good. Women were to maintain the spiritual foundations of society within the "private sphere" of the home, raising upright children and providing a restful haven for men. Men, for their part, were expected to brave the nasty and brutish "public sphere" and to provide their families with adequate financial support.

While supposedly describing an all-encompassing manhood and womanhood, these tenets grew out of middle-class concerns about the newly industrializing urban economy. Where once all family members directly contributed to the household economy through weaving, canning, candle making, and the like, urban middle-class women's contributions were now of a less obviously productive nature. Families experienced an increasingly clear demarcation between work and home as more men began working farther from where they lived. The ethic of domesticity attempted to compensate women for any perceived loss of status or power by enshrining their position in the home and articulating its importance to society.[9]

Whereas ministers, editors, and politicians drew on this ideal in their public pronouncements, the reality of gender relations in Gilded Age America was much more complex. Different subcultures within the national culture interpreted the basic prescriptions in different ways. Some groups, such as the German-Russian immigrants who settled in central Kansas, rejected them outright. Few individuals lived their lives by abstract societal code; rather, women and men appropriated, interpreted, and fought over the symbols and defini-

5

tions of mainstream gender discourse during their daily interactions.[10] Gilded
Age Kansas thus provides a wonderful laboratory in which to study the ways
political organizations and actors negotiated a national gendered discourse
within a local context.

The Kansas Woman Movement first gained prominence in the 1879 prohibition amendment campaign. By organizing around the issue of the enforcement
of prohibition, the Kansas Women's Christian Temperance Union steadily
gained influence in state and local politics throughout the 1880s. During that
decade, the temperance organization and the Kansas Equal Suffrage Association created a loose coalition of women's groups which shared a distinctive political language, ideology, and a set of tactics. In 1887 women activists drew
on this political culture to gain Kansas women the right to vote in municipal
elections. In 1892, one hundred years before the "Year of the Woman," Kansas
suffragists declared a "War of the Women," promising that every suffragist
would "gird the armor of war . . . and not stop until the women of Kansas obtain the full rights of citizenship."[11]

As the Woman Movement gained strength in the late 1880s, another reform
movement arose which changed the way Kansans thought about gender and
politics. In 1888 the Southern Farmers' Alliance, a predecessor to the National
Farmers' Alliance, sent organizers north to Kansas and found a receptive audience among the economically depressed and politically disenfranchised farmers there. Two years later the Alliance joined with other Kansas reform groups
to form the Populist Party, which directly challenged the status quo for electoral power in the state. In 1892 the Populist Party captured the governor's office and control of the State Senate and declared the establishment of the first
"people's government in the United States."[12]

Both the Woman Movement and the Populists had to confront the power of
the Republican Party, which had ruled Kansas since it achieved statehood. The
Republican leadership wielded its political power to dictate policy, acquire
and distribute government resources, and shape political discourse. Like those
in the Woman Movement and among the populists, Republican leaders were
part of a culture that shaped ideas about politics and gender. Unlike these two
reform movements, however, the G.O.P. leadership controlled enormous resources that gave it a huge advantage in determining who would have a share
of political power in Kansas. Further, Republican political and gender discourse dominated American culture.

Activists in the Woman Movement also drew on mainstream gender discourse, but they refashioned it to fit their alternative political culture. Embracing the notion of morally superior womanhood, women reformers promoted
the ideal of a monolithic, Christian, and nonpartisan political sisterhood that

6

transcended the corrupt and bitterly partisan world of male politics. As the movement kicked off its war of women, a prominent women's paper declared, "the Democrats will . . . oppose the suffrage amendment. The Republicans will stake their issue on the . . . downfall of the state under Populist rule. The Populists will hold to the issue of land, money, and transportation. They will all be drowned . . . *by the vast army of women.*"[13] Women united would carry the suffrage amendment on their own. But as the political context shifted, women activists had an increasingly difficult time adjusting their meanings and methods to the needs of the moment.

Women activists successfully employed this vision to organize urban Anglo middle-class women to the cause. By proclaiming the existence of a *Woman Movement*, its members claimed to represent the entire sex.[14] To be accepted into the ranks, however, one needed to be "respectable"—wear the proper clothing, have the proper manners, attend the proper church. Although these requirements made the movement more acceptable to male political elites, they presented obstacles to organizing women outside of the urban Anglo middle class.

Although women activists positioned themselves within the boundaries of middle-class respectability, most men were leery of participation in politics by women. For men the challenge of women in politics went beyond the question of woman suffrage; far more worrisome were the vast changes in the relations between women and men which the vote might bring. Many men believed that the hitherto male dominion of electoral politics was threatened. What would become of the clubby, boozy, and masculine world of partisan politics if women invaded en masse? Would political campaigns come to resemble church socials, or would politics remain unchanged while "dragging women into the muck," as many antisuffragists warned? Either way, things just wouldn't be the same.

The Farmers' Alliance leadership challenged the manly images of mainstream partisan politics with a nonpartisan, moralistic, and mixed-gender political culture that embraced the metaphor of family. This gender-inclusive political ideal resonated with farm families in central Kansas, where the isolated homestead meant the social and economic interdependence of all its members. But the Alliance based this egalitarian vision of politics on the structures and assumptions of the patriarchal farm family. Alliance women and men were constantly negotiating the contradictions between these two ideals. As with the Woman Movement, the Alliance's attitudes about gender influenced their approach to nonpartisanship, moralism, and women's participation in electoral politics.

Politically active Kansans were products of specific cultures, which were made up of the "complex whole" of life. These interrelated components included economic and environmental conditions; values, traditions, beliefs, and myths; ideologies and assumptions; political and social institutions; arts and entertainment; and the material artifacts of everyday existence. Yet while Kansans were shaped by culture, they were not its prisoners. Their culture defined the limits of what was possible and what was likely to change; it did not pull a voting lever or the trigger of a gun. The specific skills, ambitions, egos, and resentments of politically active Kansans ultimately determined the state's political history. This study is most interested in the choices people did and did not make within these boundaries and what became of their efforts to transcend them.

# ONE

# ⊰ MYTHS AND REALITIES ⊱

## THE CULTURAL ORIGINS OF KANSAS POLITICS

Two myths dominated the cultural imaginations of most Kansans, and the Republican Party put both to good use. Like most myths, these had a basis in real experiences. Over time, however, those who controlled the telling of the stories—Republican editors, politicians, and ministers—dropped certain facts and added or embellished others, shaping their stories to fit their party's needs. The stories were not weakened by the transition into myth; indeed, as the metaphors became embedded in people's daily language, the mythic history wielded as much influence over people's lives as the reality of past events.

The first myth, shared by most Americans, held that the frontier West was a place of renewal, freedom, and boundless opportunity. It held that by heading west, a man could escape the defeats and disappointments of his past and prove his manhood by exhibiting enough tenacity, strength of character, and sheer hard work to subdue the wilderness and gain economic and political independence. Here was land aplenty, and good land too. Here was the answer to the threat of "wage slavery" and economic instability; here was the promise of America fulfilled.[1]

The frontier myth had a role for women as well, although it was a decidedly supporting role. Men could not conquer the wilderness alone, for without women they slipped into barbarism and became uncivilized. Women provided the domesticating influence, ensuring the founding of schools, churches, museums, and opera houses. For men, the frontier myth offered individual opportunity; for women, it suggested community obligation.[2] For both, it shaped their reasons for heading west and their reactions to what they found there.

The idea of an ever expanding frontier embodied the American belief in inevitable and unlimited progress, in the ideals of "challenge, struggle, and mastery."[3] The frontier was the place where white settlers could act out the drama of Manifest Destiny. Whites were simultaneously vanquishing an "inferior" race while ensuring their own economic security. Because of the boundless opportunity of the frontier, settlers were ensuring the replication of middle-class society in the West. Yet while the frontier myth spoke of unlimited possibilities and optimism, the reality contained many stories of defeat and failure.

The second myth was Kansas's alone. Yankee Kansans believed their state's founding was a profoundly moral act, the triumph of freedom and progress over the barbarity of slavery. Northerners who had rushed to settle Kansas in the years before the Civil War had done so to halt the expansion of slavery. Aided by the newly formed Republican Party, Free State settlers had suffered like martyrs at the hands of Southern proslavers, whose marauding ways had inspired the national epithet *Bleeding Kansas*. But in the end, through the perseverance of the Free Staters and the will of God, the righteous triumphed and were rewarded. The lesson of this story, oft repeated, was that Kansans, compared with their relatively benighted counterparts in other states, now possessed a certain moral superiority.

Like the myth of the frontier, this idealized view of the founding of Kansas would be buffeted by reality now and again. But both stories demonstrated a remarkable staying power that was helped along by those interested in maintaining them. The Woman Movement and the Populists would challenge some parts of the myths while adapting others for their own use. In either case, the myths greatly affected the way Kansans thought about and practiced politics.

## The Martyred State and Other Tales

The myth of Bleeding Kansas provided one version of the state's founding. A more accurate account would acknowledge that the settlement of Kansas was less a campaign of Southerners against Northerners and more an invasion of whites against the tribal people who lived there. Some had already been driven from their native lands in the East, and all had been promised the territory that would become Kansas. None had much of a chance before the combined onslaught of so many interests eager to civilize the area. The expansionists included people desperate for greater economic opportunity, politicians worried about providing a "safety valve" for disgruntled urban workers, land speculators looking for quick profits, and businessmen eager to expand their markets. The engines driving these interests—literally—were the railroad corporations, whose tracks and trains made expansion possible. All could draw on the logic of "Manifest Destiny" to justify conquering Indian lands. Adherents of this doctrine held that it was White America's mission to spread across the continent and beyond, subduing these lands in the name of democracy, liberty, and most importantly free enterprise. To these people, settlement of Kansas was inevitable.

The economic and ideological incentives were already well established when Congress passed the Kansas-Nebraska Act in 1854. The act repealed the Missouri Compromise, which had restricted slavery west of the thirty-sixth parallel. The Kansas-Nebraska Act instead mandated that the slavery question be answered by the new (white) inhabitants. Sen. Stephen Douglas, Illinois Democrat and an ardent expansionist, hoped that the concept of "popular sovereignty" would persuade Southerners, most of whom were Democrats, to support the bill. At the same time, he believed the act's democratic process would quell most of the Northern opposition. Douglas also had his eye on the Democratic presidential nomination and believed that this "reasonable" approach would ensure continued peace for the country while providing him with favorable national publicity.[4] Douglas eventually secured the Democratic nomination, but Kansas proved a much more intractable problem.

Although Northern antislavery advocates were eager to settle Western lands, they denounced the bill as a sellout to the "slave power." New England investors quickly organized antislavery emigration companies that pledged to keep Kansas free. They also hoped that, while fighting the good fight, they would also realize large profits.[5] The emigration companies generated much more publicity than invested capital, however. The great majority of Northern settlers came not from New England but from Ohio, Indiana, and Illinois.[6] They were drawn to Kansas not as part of an antislavery crusade but simply in the hopes of bettering their economic condition by establishing farms or businesses. Northern and Southern newspaper accounts, however, focused on the New Englanders' antislavery rhetoric and the violent response of Missouri "Border Ruffians."[7]

Southerners responded by declaring, essentially, that Kansas would be "slave" or else would not be. Few Missourians were willing to risk their slaves by settling in a territory that might eventually abolish slavery. Yet proslavers

were also unwilling to abandon the struggle. Unable to mount a legal challenge to the incoming Northerners, Missourians crossed into Kansas to raid
Free State settlements and to vote illegally (and often) in territorial elections.
Free Staters quickly responded in kind, armed with "Beecher's Bibles." These
donations from the Northeast—Sharp's rifles—were shipped to Kansas after
Congregationalist minister Lyman Beecher declared that such instruments
would be the most effective method of persuasion given the circumstances.[8]

Although the violence in Kansas was sporadic and often fueled by personal
vendettas, inflammatory news reports fanned fears both in the state and
around the nation. Antislavery Northerners appropriated the battle cry of
Bleeding Kansas for the newly formed Republican Party, which pledged to halt
the spread of slavery at all costs. In the public imagination, the settlement of
Kansas became something more than another successful episode of American
expansionism. Antislavery advocates cast the "martyred state" in a morally
righteous glow and claimed the Free Staters' ultimate victory represented the
triumph of liberty and human betterment over the dark forces of injustice.[9]

Beyond the small minority of seriously committed abolitionists, however,
most Northern settlers in Kansas were as vigorously antiblack as they were antislavery. Free Staters made these sentiments clear during their 1859 convention with a resolution that stated, "the best interests of Kansas require a population of free white men, and . . . in our state organization we are in favor of
stringent laws excluding all Negroes, bond or free, from the territory."[10] The
convention eventually rejected the resolution only after some delegates
warned that it would hurt Kansas's chance of entry into the Union. The debate
made clear that the moral battle over Bleeding Kansas had less to do with free-
ing blacks than with maintaining the supremacy of white Northern "free
labor."[11]

Whether sincerely abolitionist or simply antiblack, Free Staters saw the Republican Party as the best hope for restricting slavery in Kansas. When the
Civil War broke out, Free Staters embraced the Republicans as defenders of the
Union and viewed Democrats as rebels and traitors. When Northerners
gained control of Kansas, the Republican Party emerged both dominant and
morally sanctioned. The experiences of Kansans during the war cemented the
Republicans' position even further.

Yankee Kansas had been fighting the Civil War since 1855. Small wonder,
then, that Kansans contributed a greater proportion of its population to the
Union cause than any other state. Eventually this commitment would be translated into the greatest per capita death toll in the North. Although Kansans
fought few real battles within the state's borders, the guerrilla raid that deci-

mated the town of Lawrence became an enduring symbol for Union—and thus Republican—sympathizers. On 21 August 1863 the notorious William Quantrill and three hundred irregular troops swept into Lawrence at dawn. Quantrill, a leading Border Ruffian before the war, had sworn he would wipe out the hated center of Free State activity. Notified by spies that Lawrence was undefended and its citizens unarmed, the raiders rampaged through the town at will, shooting all men on sight, many of them in the back as they fled from burning buildings. Over 150 were killed by the time the Confederates rode out of town, leaving most of the buildings in ruins and all of them sacked or plundered.[12]

For Republicans, Quantrill's raid served as the perfect example of Democratic barbarism and as a justification for continued Republican dominance of state politics. Republican politicians would make these stories a staple of their Fourth of July orations, followed by a recitation of the "local boys" who had fallen during the war. The politicians would then urge citizens to "vote as they shot," condemning the Democrats as rebels and worse. Of course, after a time the cry would be to "vote as your father shot," but this worked nearly as well.

"Waving the bloody shirt," as this tactic became known, was practiced by Southern Democrats as well as Northern Republicans and became their most useful weapon for squashing meaningful political debate.[13] With politicians adroitly weaving these memories into their rhetoric, the two parties used the "bloody shirt" to circumvent discussions of the new role of corporations in politics, the unequal economic system, and other sticky questions. Kansas became as solid for the Republican Party as the "Solid South" was for the Democrats. Twenty-five years after the guns were silenced, Populists would struggle against this powerful legacy.[14]

The legacy of the Civil War created opportunities as well as obstacles for reformers. Because the Republican Party had opposed slavery, its leaders could present themselves as progressive and enlightened. True, most Republican politicians' progressivism extended merely to their earnest support of capitalist expansion unfettered by government regulation. Economic progress, they believed, would fuel social progress. Some of the most influential leaders in Kansas, however, had come there firmly committed to abolitionism and social reform. These women and men led the liberal Republican wing of the party, and pushed for a variety of reforms. Because they were overrepresented in the legislature, they were often able to pass laws that did not have support among the populace.[15]

This well-placed liberal support gave women's rights activists an opening for their efforts to influence the state's new constitution. Led by Clarina Nichols, they established a legacy from which Woman Movement activists would draw in the 1880s. Nichols was an experienced organizer and lobbyist, having directed reform drives in Vermont and New York before settling in Kansas. During the Free State convention of 1859, she led a small, well-organized group of women who requested that the convention strike the word *male* from the voter qualification clause. Not surprisingly, the delegates, all of whom were men, did not accept this simple yet profound challenge to their power, and they kept the gender qualification in the constitution.

Woman suffragists persisted, however, noting that women had played a crucial role in the drama of Bleeding Kansas, running farms and businesses for men who were away fighting or who had been killed. Women had sacrificed as much as the men, they insisted, proving that Republican politicians were not the only ones who could make use of the myth of Bleeding Kansas. Recognizing the validity of the women's claims, the convention granted Kansas women the most liberal property and divorce laws of any state at that time.[16] Also, as a sort of compensation for the loss of state suffrage, the delegates bestowed on women the right to vote in school elections.[17] Even these limited reforms may have been ahead of the times. Kansas voters would soon have their say on matters of reform, and the results would reveal much about the nature of Kansas politics.

In 1867, Kansas Republican leaders chose opportunism over racism and submitted a constitutional amendment to the voters authorizing "Negro male suffrage." While some of the liberal Republican legislators had idealistic motives, all Republicans were aware of the amendment's practical advantages. Although few African-Americans lived in Kansas at the time, Republicans expected that all would support their "liberators." To most Republican leaders, the plan was a convenient way to enhance the state's progressive image while increasing their party's already substantial majority.[18]

This comfortable arrangement was upset when Sam Wood, a renegade Republican legislator, outmaneuvered party leaders and amended the Negro male suffrage bill to include woman suffrage. Wood had gained prominence in the party with his role in the Free State struggle and notoriety with his radical political views and shady land deals.[19] Because of the latter characteristics, his influence in the legislature was limited, but his command of parliamentary procedure was impressive. With an odd coalition of liberal Republicans and conservative Democrats, Wood preserved the woman suffrage amendment despite repeated attempts by Republican leaders to dislodge it. The Democrats supported it for the same reason that the Republican leadership opposed it—both believed that voters would reject black suffrage if it was linked to woman suffrage. When Republicans realized that the Negro suffrage amendment could be saved only if woman suffrage were retained, they agreed to pass both measures provided each would be presented to the voters as separate amendments. With this compromise in place, the legislature finally approved the bill.

Having acquiesced to Wood's machinations, the Kansas Republican leadership set out to undermine the women's cause. After the state Republican committee voted to endorse only Negro male suffrage, it dispatched speakers who promoted African-American rights while deriding woman suffrage. Some Republicans eventually formed the Anti–Female Suffrage Committee with strong ties to the central committee. The great majority of prominent national Republican politicians and editors were either openly hostile to or silent about the women's amendment, usually repeating the claims made by their Kansas counterparts about the overriding importance of Negro suffrage.[20]

The Republicans' official position presented national suffrage leaders with a difficult quandary. Most of these women and men, including Susan B. Anthony, Elizabeth Cady Stanton, Lucy Stone, and Henry Blackwell, had been prominent abolitionists before the war. They had formed the American Equal Rights Association (AERA) to advance the cause of both women's and freed slaves' rights. As abolitionists, they had supported the G.O.P. since its origins. After the war these reformers had allied themselves with the Radical Republicans in Congress, who favored shattering the power of Southern whites and promoting the cause of Southern blacks. Equal rights activists had come to expect that the Republican Party would be the vehicle for both causes.[21]

National AERA leaders, upon hearing that the Kansas legislature was submitting both woman and black suffrage to the voters, fully expected the Republicans to offer unconditional support to both amendments. AERA leaders embraced the notion of Kansas as a radical state. Anthony, who had spent a year there after the war, was especially confident of victory, viewing Kansas as "the historic ground when Liberty fought her first victorious battles with Slavery and consecrated that soil forever to the freedom of the black race." Because of this, she believed, "There was never a more hopeful interest concentrated on the legislation of any singular state." Anthony also expected the support of her cousin D. R. Anthony, the editor of the Leavenworth *Times*. A self-proclaimed radical who had promised to "shake things up" in Kansas, "D.R." proved to be a disappointment to suffragists. Already displaying his keen ability to shift with the prevailing political winds, D. R. Anthony only endorsed woman suffrage on the final day of the campaign.[22] Given AERA's preconceptions, the shock of its members and their disappointment at the Republican Party's "treachery" was profound.

By late summer the woman suffrage campaign had collapsed for lack of support and funds. Stanton and Anthony returned to Kansas in September, however, ready to do battle for the women's amendment and against the Republicans. The two began to shift their efforts toward recruiting Democrats, some of whom were willing to work for woman suffrage to embarrass the Republicans. Stanton and Anthony then engaged the services of George Francis Train, who was as vociferous a supporter of women's rights as he was a denigrator of African-Americans and Republicans. The flamboyant and egotistical Train— he was considering a "one man campaign for the presidency"—made racism and anti-Republicanism the focus of his efforts, which, to the horror of most AERA members, were warmly embraced by Stanton and Anthony.[23]

Although Train's racism gave weight to the Republican charge that woman suffrage was part of a plot by Democrats to defeat Negro suffrage, it was his anti-Republicanism that generated the greatest political backlash. In a state that was just two years removed from the emotional trauma of the Civil War— and was 75 percent Republican—such a strategy had little chance of success. But then, Republican opposition to the measure had probably doomed it from the beginning. In November both amendments were overwhelmingly defeated; of the fifty thousand votes cast, Negro suffrage gained just two thousand more than woman suffrage.[24] Kansas voters apparently were not the soldiers of liberalism that many national reformers had supposed.

Train's tactics had less effect on the vote total than on the future of woman suffrage in Kansas and the nation. The Kansas campaign became the prism through which suffragists viewed post–Civil War equal rights reform. Here the activists entered the campaign as a single body and left it refracted in a variety of directions. Following the campaign, Stanton and Anthony created the first truly woman-centered organization in America, unshackled by commitments and alliances with other causes. "For the first time," they recalled later, "[we] saw as never before that only from woman's standpoint could the battle be successfully fought, and victory secured. . . . [S]tanding alone we learned our power; we repudiated men's councils forevermore." Because "men regarded [women] as his . . . inferior, his slave, their interests must be antagonistic."[25] From this point on, Stanton and Anthony would not abide by the rules of men's politics.

The flip side of this ethos of gender solidarity and independence was that Stanton and Anthony "learned from Train how to transform white women's racism into a kind of sex pride, a technique which they were later to turn to in building the woman suffrage movement."[26] Stanton and Anthony's racism was in keeping with the growing intolerance of the post–Civil War period.[27] In moving their racial ideology closer to that of the mainstream, they greatly improved the standing of woman suffrage in white America. Racism and elitism became ingrained in the language and ideology of the Woman Movement, providing women activists the means to draw Anglo middle-class people to women reformers' causes. Stanton and Anthony continued this approach when they refused to support the Fifteenth Amendment because it gave black men, but not women, the vote. The ensuing fight over the issue divided AERA into two competing organizations, the National Woman Suffrage Association and the American Woman Suffrage Association.[28]

Stanton and Anthony had embraced the myth of radical Kansas and fully expected the state to follow its destiny. How else to understand their belief that Sam Wood's subterfuge would result in the wholesale support by the state's Republicans?[29] Kansas Republicans had shown no previous inclination to embrace woman suffrage as a party issue; most were outraged by Wood's perceived treachery. Despite these unfavorable indications, the two reformers felt so betrayed by the Republicans that they took up with a man who could deliver the strongest rebuke possible to the G.O.P. Given their faith in the ideal of the martyred state, their strategy is perhaps understandable, if not laudable.[30] But in attacking the Republicans so bitterly, they also helped discredit the cause of woman suffrage among Kansas Republicans.

Stanton and Anthony had a national vision and agenda; they were little concerned with the niceties of state politics.[31] While the Kansas campaign gave them the impetus to form the National Woman Suffrage Association, it devastated the Kansas suffrage movement. The state organization disbanded and did not reappear until 1884. By then broad forces had reshaped both the cultural context and the demography of the state in such a way as to make woman suffrage a viable issue again. The developing cultures of Kansas would provide the basic ingredients for both the Woman Movement and Populism in the 1880s and 1890s.

## ECONOMICS, THE FARM FAMILY, AND THE MYTH OF THE FRONTIER

If Yankee Kansans had their founding myth, all settlers—Southerners as well as Northerners—subscribed to an older, even more enduring one. Euro-Americans had looked westward for economic opportunity from the time of early settlement, when the frontier meant the backwoods of Pennsylvania, Virginia, and the Carolinas. After the American Revolution, Thomas Jefferson added a political imperative to the frontier: the West would provide the land necessary for all hard-working American men to become independent yeomen farmers. Jefferson believed that land ownership could act as a counter to the threat of permanent "wage slavery," arguing that "the small land owners are the most precious part of the state." Drawing from classical writers, Jefferson argued that the farmer was naturally virtuous because of the purity of his occupation and his connection to nature. While Jefferson recognized that industrialization was necessary to maintain America's independence from Europe, he believed that the frontier ensured a steady supply of virtuous farmers to counteract the "natural" corruption of the cities.[32]

The settlers who poured into Kansas following the Civil War fervently embraced the myth of the frontier. They came west for many of the same reasons as their predecessors: dreams of new opportunities, new beginnings, independence, a better way of life. But these newcomers arrived with something different as well: the belief that the U.S. government would provide them with the basic means to achieve economic success. The Homestead Act of 1862 promised 160 acres of Western land for a nominal fee to any man (or widow or "spinster") who would stake a claim and improve it for five years. Anyone willing to work hard enough to make the land pay would thus be able to secure lifelong economic security, political autonomy, and standing in a community—the Jeffersonian ideal come to life. All the prospective settlers had to do was master the new frontier of the Great Plains that stretched before them, fifty million acres of opportunity.[33]

For most settlers conditions on the Plains presented numerous obstacles to fulfilling the promise of the frontier myth. The Homestead Act promised cheap land to those willing to stay and work on it. Unfortunately, Congress had given the best lands to railroad corporations, while speculators had subverted the intent of the law and gobbled up much of the rest.[34] The lands that remained, advertised as Edenic, often appeared more like a purgatory to those unfamiliar with the environment. Although the Union Pacific Railway Company claimed, "Nature seems to have provided protection and food for men and beast; all that is required is diligent labor and economy to ensure an early reward," the costs of settling the Plains were far more than sweat and personal hard labor. Farmers soon discovered that capital—ready cash—was imperative for survival yet difficult to acquire.[35] The culture of central Kansas was in many ways the product of people's constant negotiations between the myth and the reality of life on the Plains.

The new railroad corporations and banking houses that had grown after the Civil War had a very large stake in maintaining the myth of the frontier. The railroads profited from Western expansion in a number of ways: state and national government land grants as inducements to develop rail lines; state and local bond issues to finance lines; passenger traffic to the new settlements; and merchandise shipped to and crops and livestock shipped from the new settlements. The railroads did not want farmers to fail: their long-term viability depended on continued settlement. But because the railroads' overriding concern was immediate profits, they focused on bringing west the maximum number of settlers as quickly as possible. Since truthful accounts of conditions in central Kansas would have done little to forward this goal, truth became the first casualty in the campaign to settle the Plains.[36]

Central Kansas was a fertile and prolific paradise, a land of mild winters and balmy summers. That, anyway, was the portrait painted in myriad brochures, posters, magazines, and advertisements. Railroad corporations, abetted by land speculation companies, blanketed the East with "boomer literature" that trumpeted the many advantages of these "new" lands. While all the Plains states had their boosters, those who extolled Kansas were particularly extravagant.[37] The National Land Company was no more or less accurate than other propagandists: "One of the strongest inducements which Kansas holds out to intending settlers is the general salubrity of its climate. . . . The winter season is dry, with clear skies and pure, bracing air. Dr. Griswald, of Ohio, says, 'There is a peculiar atmosphere in Kansas, whether purer, drier, or containing more oxygen I cannot say, but it has an exhilarating effect on the system. It might be called champaign air.'"[38] In fact, such propaganda might be called champagne literature: easy to swallow, it induced intensive short-term euphoria and a sense of possibility. Drink enough of such stuff and the result was a more long-term delusion, "Kansas fever."

Kansas fever swept through whole counties in the Northern states, particularly in Illinois, Indiana, Ohio, and Pennsylvania. Railroads and speculators were not the sole carriers of this condition, however: official state agencies in Kansas also worked to spread the contagion. Hundreds of reports bearing the state's imprimatur repeated the assertions of the boomer literature, often employing impressive scientific jargon that lent the material a gloss of expertise.[39] Those who had caught the fever desperately needed others to succumb to its lure. They sent back boomer-style letters to their old hometown papers, extolling the virtues of their new-found land even in the midst of environmental and economic hardships.[40] Only by continually adding to central Kansas's population could its proponents claim their township was booming and thus ignore the distortions and outright lies that had brought people there. The constant infusion of new blood would keep the region healthy—at least for a while.

These men, of course, did not see themselves as victims of a fever. They be-

Kansas Fever reaches epidemic proportions: the Garden City Land Office in 1885. *Kansas State Historical Society*

lieved they possessed a vision that more timid folks simply could not imagine.[41] Though the vision may have been distorted, their quest for respect, for a better way of life for their families, should be taken seriously. Further, the economic pressures on them were certainly real. More and more farmers of the "Old Northwest" were being forced into tenantry, and the roller coaster economy made business failures endemic.[42] They were not lunatics or simpletons; rather, they were responding to societal expectations that America—and the frontier—provided all hard-working men with the basic resources to succeed. They were so eager, in fact, that they generally accepted "paradise" as it was offered to them. When they arrived at their new home, they were often unprepared for what they found.

Middle-class women shared men's concerns about achieving a respectable and comfortable position in society, but they did not have to carry the onus of failure. Further, they tended to have more of an emotional attachment than men had to their communities and were thus less eager to pack up and head west. Women were expected to be loving, nurturing wives and mothers, not providers, whatever the reality. Further, women had developed networks with kin and neighbors through their churches and social clubs and were often loath to give up this "female world."[43] Married women thus rarely initiated emigration.[44] Once husbands suggested the move, however, women responded in a number of ways. Of those women who moved to Kansas, most seemed to have accepted the task. Many grew to relish their new life and the challenge it brought. Others went grudgingly, remained unhappy, and urged a return back East whenever possible. Some women probably persuaded their husbands to forgo the journey.[45]

Women settlers' apprehensions would hardly have been assuaged when they crossed into the Plains from the well-watered, forested hills of eastern Kansas. When in eastern Kansas, they would have noticed little in the landscape different from their native Illinois, Indiana, or Ohio, the states of origin of the great majority of Kansas settlers. Crossing from Missouri, they found hickory, oak, and walnut forests along with recognizable soil conditions. Most importantly, there was adequate rainfall for the crops that settlers were used to raising. For these farm people, the environment behaved predictably. But by 1870, new immigrants were finding land relatively expensive and less readily available in eastern Kansas, so they kept their wagons rolling, eventually entering the land of shortgrass and bison, and stepped into another world. It was a world that had its own logic, its own rules; it was not one that easily accommodated the frontier myth.[46]

The first thing newcomers tended to notice about central Kansas was the relative absence of trees. Many settlers had assumed that local timber would provide building material, food, shelter, and scenery. One woman, upon arriving in central Kansas, summed up the situation succinctly. "Why, there isn't even a thing one can *hide behind!*"[47] The settlers, forced to use the resources at hand, fashioned their homes out of blocks of tough prairie sod and heated their houses with buffalo chips.[48] Such ingenuity was indeed impressive; unfortunately for the settlers, the sod and the lack of trees were signs of another environmental condition to which settlers adapted much less easily.[49]

The short buffalo grass that covered the Plains was a survivor—it maintained a tough, complex root system close to the surface in order to make maximum use of a minimal resource: water. Central Kansas received on average 40 percent less rain than eastern Kansas. Worse, rainfall varied widely over space and time. Rain could appear suddenly in a devastating downpour that did more harm than good, or it could come not at all for several years. Conversely, the area could see a number of wet years when rains equaled those of the humid East. During such times, boomer literature almost described the actual conditions of central Kansas. For those who arrived during these favorable but temporary periods, their rendezvous with reality was even more unsettling than for those who entered the state during droughts.[50]

Settlers eventually discovered that what they had purchased did not correspond to what had been advertised. Rather than adjust to this new reality, however, most refused to accept that climatic instability, especially periodic drought, would forever be a part of their life.[51] Instead, they placed their faith in technology, hard work, and divine destiny to conquer the Plains. If settling the Plains was a tale of heroism, it was also a tale of tragedy. Perhaps the two were inseparable; perhaps only the settlers' cultural blinders kept them from surrendering and moving on.

The effects of a drought came slowly, shriveling up the heads of corn or wheat even as farmers swore that rain was in the air. More sudden and terrifying were the myriad other environmental disasters that visited central Kansas. Hailstorms with projectiles an inch in diameter could appear suddenly amid seemingly mild weather and flatten a promising field of crops. More deadly were the prairie fires, caused when one of the many lightning storms ignited the drought-desiccated grasslands. Most people had a firebreak around their property, but the speed and ferocity of the flames could overcome the line of desperate women and men equipped only with buckets and dampened bed sheets. Inez Bridsell remembered the terror of watching an approaching fire: "I had been silently praying and I knew my brother had too. People may think they can live without God in these days but no one tired to in those early days."[52]

In addition to fire and hail, settlers had to face the threat of blizzards, flash floods, cyclones, and hot winds—winds so fierce that they could shrivel crops in a day. Any of these conditions could suddenly reverse the fortunes of a farm family on the Plains. And with few close neighbors, great distances to town, and rudimentary community welfare arrangements, settlers beset by environmental disasters could expect little significant economic relief, medical help, or emotional comfort. With each disaster, people drew upon their faith in God to provide them with the strength to continue. All the while, they looked desperately for ways to bring some stability into their lives.[53]

Perhaps nothing so disturbed farm people's faith and security as the grasshopper invasion of 1874.[54] With the suddenness of a thunderclap, a downpour of tiny "hoppers" would fall from the sky, blotting out the sun. Descending on the wheat crop, they would soon strip the fields, stalks and all. Then they would move on to the garden, fast devouring the protective covering of sacks, blankets, tablecloths—anything that could be grabbed to protect the precious vegetables. But the hoppers devoured almost any organic material in sight, including, on occasion, the clothes off one's back. Harnesses were eaten and rake handles destroyed. Even after the hoppers moved on, their bitter legacy remained: chickens that had gorged on hoppers smelled so strongly of the insect that they were inedible; the water was so befouled that the stock refused to drink. Every day came another reminder of the fragility of settlers' lives and their dependence on a fickle and seemingly malicious environment.[55]

For a few years the grasshopper invasion turned the vision of Kansas as Eden on its head. A national depression coincided with the "terrible seventies" in Kansas to limit immigration to the state, since little money was available to finance journeys and land acquisitions. But by the late seventies, a few wet years, higher crop prices, and a stronger national economy created a small economic boom in central Kansas, and soon the paeans to a prosperous and prolific Kansas were rolling unabated off presses across the country.[56] The hoppers may have given farm people a sense of their vulnerability, but this seems only to have intensified their belief in sudden salvation when the good times returned. This boom-or-bust psychology would play an important role in the fate of political movements throughout the next twenty-five years.

Good environmental conditions meant little if favorable economic conditions did not prevail as well. Although boomer literature made no mention of the economic system, the conditions that had helped limit settlers' opportunities back East were still very much with them. Whereas humans could exert little control over the environment (however hard they tried), certain people had a much greater power to determine the course of the economy.

In Gilded Age America, corporate elites, financiers, and politicians exercised enormous influence over the national and international economy. These men were not part of a secret conspiracy, as some reformers of the time claimed. Rather, they were a loose network of like-minded gentlemen intent on amassing as large a fortune as possible at the expense of whoever had less power than they. These "captains of industry" were not averse to exploiting their peers if circumstances warranted it. Indeed, they embraced the ideology of social Darwinism, proclaiming that those who triumphed in the vicious arena of capitalism were naturally selected to lead. As John D. Rockefeller pontificated, "The growth of a large business is merely the survival of the fittest, the working out of a law of nature and a law of God."[57]

The farmer and the capitalist, though in some ways worlds apart, were in fact intimately connected, much to the farmer's discomfort. In 1873, a series of international and national events set off a domino effect that eventually tumbled into Kansas. A panic on the Vienna stock exchange caused European investors to sell off U.S. railroad stock; this cast doubt upon the stocks, which had been enjoying a speculative boom. The deflated stocks in turn caused the collapse of the influential banking house of Jay Cooke and Company, which had invested heavily in the Northern Pacific Railroad. Finally, Cooke's sudden dissolution sparked a panic on the already shaky New York stock exchange, which touched off a national depression known as the Panic of 1873.[58] Crop prices tumbled, while railroad corporations, desperate for capital, raised their rates. Mortgage companies demanded payment of debts and increased their interest rates to counter the loss of investment capital and sudden instability of their loans to farmers. When farm people combined these costs with those of the environmental disasters of the period, the result was a calculus of misery.

The periodic depressions and panics, like the hoppers and the droughts, forced settlers to confront the stark reality of their dependence on outside forces. Kansans raised a tremendous amount of wheat, but they could not raise much capital. The railroad corporations that grew after the Civil War had huge capitalization requirements, which accelerated the centralization of financial resources. Since the Civil War, U.S. government policy had further restricted the availability of capital by contracting the amounts and types of currency to be used as legal tender. Economic reformers claimed these policies were a boon to large bond holders and lenders but discriminated against small debtors such as farmers.[59]

Farmers could choose which crops to grow, but they had to accept the prices set by the Chicago commodities market. The market's intricate rules and its basis in theoretical futures made traders' price manipulations, legal and otherwise, a commonplace occurrence. Whereas traders could hold on to their products until prices rose, farmers had to take what was offered at harvest time, when the market was glutted. Further, elevator operators were not averse to mislabeling farmers' wheat at a lower grade—and thus a lower price—if they could get away with it.[60] Elevator operators also profited from exclusive contracts with particular railroads which allowed the operators to charge artificially high prices for storage. Farmers also had to accept railroad rates that were often proportionally higher for Plains farmers than those in the East.[61] In Kansas, railroads, particularly the Santa Fe, circumvented reformers' attempts at regulation by simply buying off the majority of the legislature.[62] Agrarian reformers made the railroads, grain dealers, and financiers the central villains in their critique of the American political and economic system, providing farm men with an explanation of how they had lost control of their economic lives and of their nation.

Perhaps the most constant reminder of farm people's lack of autonomy was the mortgage. It rose seemingly indomitable, the great obstacle to a farm family's economic security.[63] Some farmers did come to Kansas with enough money to buy land, seed, and implements free and clear and then demonstrated enough skill and had enough luck to stay out of debt, but they were a minority. More often, they arrived in Kansas desperate for cash, having spent most of their money on the expensive journey west. Others came with some reserves but soon slipped into debt, gambling mortgages against new machinery or more land in the hope that these investments would soon pay for themselves.[64]

Yet most farmers took on a mortgage more or less willingly, depending on the economic and environmental conditions at the time. Without it, they believed that they would never be able to achieve the kind of success portrayed in the propaganda that had brought them west. If their land was already fully mortgaged, they would have to take out chattel mortgages on their stock or equipment, often at extremely high rates of interest. Because farmers most desperately needed loans during hard times, when mortgage rates were especially high and investors' cash scarce, they had to accept the most onerous lending conditions when they could least afford them.

The basic economic and social unit of a Kansas farm was the family. The cultural prescriptions that shaped the family in turn shaped the work and the play of its members. Most Kansans were Anglo-Americans born in the United States and accepted mainstream assumptions about gender roles. When farm people determined who in the family made the business decisions, who worked at what jobs, and who organized the family's leisure time, they did so within the boundaries of what was considered normal and what was not. And these decisions, in turn, influenced their response to the politics of the period.

While most husbands and wives shared dreams of prosperity, they often had different priorities. Women tended to oppose actions that risked home and farm. Many farm women were suspicious of rapid expansion based on highly optimistic forecasts. Men were more likely to favor acquiring additional land, whether for more crop acreage or for speculative purposes; they were much more likely to desire new machinery and implements.[65]

Just as immigration propagandists exploited (and reinforced) men's success ethos in order to encourage settlement, farm implement dealers became purveyors of quick-fix promises once the immigrant settled in Kansas. One farmer, who had refused to buy into these manufactured dreams, observed,

If the farmer would only let the overpolite patent right agent alone and not be a party to help fasten upon some community a patent plow attachment

25

or some combination of machinery that will, to use the agent's own words, "Certainly revolutionize the labor of the farm and save untold millions to the farmer." How much better it would be if our farmers would weigh well the subject of purchasing farm machinery before engaging in an enterprise of that kind, and then only making such purchases as are absolutely necessary . . . , and not because it is "fashionable" to purchase machinery.[66]

The new plow, harrow, binder, or reaper became the magical weapon that would enable farmers to conquer the recalcitrant Plains. For many farmers the latest model was proof not only of their own optimism but also of their current status and thus of their manhood. Whatever the actual condition of the farm, the farmer could ride atop his new harvester and proclaim his success to all who passed by.[67] Once the inevitable bad luck arrived, however, the newly purchased machinery would be transformed into an oppressive burden. Then the once glittering plow or seed drill would lie rusting in the yard, having proved unable to pay for itself, its maintenance, or its interest payments.

Many farm men saw expenditures for the fields, whether for machinery, seed, fertilizer, land, or labor, as necessary to the success of the farm enterprise. Some new machinery enabled farmers to harvest their crop more efficiently and avoid the various natural disasters that could strike at any time and wipe out a season's work. Other machinery allowed the farmer to plant and harvest more extensively.[68] For farm men, the fields, considered the traditional sphere of men, represented the business sector of the farm. Farm men tended to favor reinvesting available cash in the fields rather than purchasing items for the home, viewing such improvements as a luxury. While men could spend large sums on new machinery, "home economy" newspaper articles were constantly instructing women to economize and make do.[69]

Farm women believed that the home, which included the garden and the yard, deserved its fair share of the family's available resources. The farmhouse was not simply for shelter and comfort; it was also a center of production for both home use and sale. Farm women and their "workers"—their children—were responsible for dairy products, clothing, poultry and eggs, and produce, to name just the principal goods. Many of the items that women desired, such as better washtubs, sewing machines, and butter churns, could save both time and money. The *Western Farmer,* noting this irony, observed, "The farmer who neglects to provide the necessary apparatus to handle milk and its products on the farm is ever grumbling because [of] the price received." The writer admonished farmers to rearrange their economic priorities and find less fault with their wives' butter-making skills.[70]

In the cash-poor Plains, women produced goods that at times generated as

A Kansas farm family at home. Women and older child tend to domestic duties while the man reclines. *Kansas State Historical Society*

much profit as the crops and cost much less to produce. During hard times, women's efforts could provide the major source of cash as well as satisfying the family's basic needs. Further, farm women provided the services—washing, cleaning, child care—necessary to all families.[71] Besides their many responsibilities around the home, they often lent a hand in the fields during busy times.[72] Many took on these tasks with enthusiasm—or at least looked back fondly on them in their memoirs.[73]

Greater responsibility, however, does not automatically convert to greater power in the family.[74] Although most farm men understood the crucial role women played in running a successful operation, they did not usually grant their wives more decision-making power because of it. Available evidence suggests that while some husbands may have taken their wives' counsels seriously, most expected to have the final say about issues regarding the farm's finances. Further, if a woman did disagree with her husband, she did so in private, so that the man's prerogatives would not appear to be in question. In most farm families, the husband's judgment ultimately determined the economic fate of the family, even if his opinions differed from his wife's.[75]

Most farm men wanted to provide their wives and children with proper clothing, educate their daughters, and buy labor-saving devices for the home; to accomplish these goals a farmer believed he had to expand his operation and generate greater profits. To keep women and children from working the fields, men needed to purchase more machinery and labor. But since these investments often meant more debt and risk, they in no way ensured farm men the ability to spend money on domestic items in the future. Ironically, farm men's attempts to fulfill their role as providers necessitated a strategy that many women opposed.

In part, women feared taking financial risks because it threatened to destroy the tenuous social ties they were developing in their new home. A woman's initial view of Plains community life was often as disappointing as her search for greenery—transplanting old networks in the cultural environment of the Plains proved as difficult as transplanting hickory or oak in the natural environment. Each new economic or environmental disaster drove out another set of possible friends and neighbors, to be replaced by others with an equally vulnerable existence.

Despite these difficulties, women still took the lead in organizing social events whenever possible. These events dominated women's memoirs along with births, deaths, and marriages. Picnics and dances were the favorites, arranged to celebrate particular holidays—most notably the Forth of July—or whenever anyone was willing to spend the time and energy needed to "bring it off." Inez Bridsell recalled that the dances were a bit of heaven. "I can remember how exciting it all seemed—the music of the fiddlers, the old-fashioned calls, and our sober, hard working neighbors brightening up and forgetting their troubles for a while."[76]

Although women were the organizers, men were no less enthusiastic about such activities, which were made all the more enjoyable, no doubt, by the fact that they had to do little of the work involved. Men particularly liked the debating clubs that would meet occasionally to discuss various political, social, religious, or literary topics. Though men took the lead, these debates were still family events: another chance for families to meet and gossip, for young women and men who were so inclined to eye one another and maneuver their attentions toward likely possibilities. Not all social events were homegrown: traveling shows, lecturers, and circuses appeared periodically, and farm families flocked to them. Such attractions provided farm people with a chance to enjoy a sense of community, however brief.[77] When the Farmers' Alliance came to Kansas, organizers would look to these events as a means of bringing people together.

While the assorted trapeze artists, tightrope walkers, thespians, and elocutionists were welcome diversions, they could not match the appeal of the solitary, often ragged, and occasionally illiterate circuit preacher. Melissa Moore recalled, "Whenever there was the privilege of church, everyone for miles around would yoke up the oxen and go. We often went three miles for a night meeting and would find ox teams standing all around the school house." Church, of course, was not an institution or a specific building or even a specific day but, rather, an impromptu event. Nor did it matter which denomination the circuit preacher represented, for settlers felt that it "made no difference who preached or what he preached, or when he preached, we all went and got, I trust, some good from the meeting."[78] "Going to meeting" provided not only a sense of community but spiritual sustenance as well. If the hoppers, prairie fires, hailstorms, and other environmental disasters might bring settlers to question God's intentions, the circuit preacher could find in the Bible a way to understand their plight. And he could interpret their tribulations as preparation for a future reward, whether in this world or the next.

Established churches made slow inroads in the rural Plains, largely because many areas could not afford to maintain a permanent clergyman. For the same reason, most religious organizations did not care to service these areas.[79] Only the Methodists developed an organized system of rotating preachers to bring the gospel to the hinterland. Their circuit riders enabled the Methodists to become the leading denomination in Kansas largely by default.[80] Their influence in Kansas politics would become apparent with the campaign for prohibition in 1879–80. And the religious beliefs and customs of rural central Kansans would shape the style and content of the Populist uprising.

Anglo-American Protestants, who constituted 85 percent of Kansas's population during the late nineteenth century, shaped the state's mainstream culture. But German and German-Russian immigrants made up the largest minority group in Kansas and brought with them a different set of cultural values.[81] They faced the same environment and economic system as Anglo farmers, but often with different results. In part these variations can be traced to the German-Americans' ideas about gender, which contrasted dramatically with those of the Anglos. The differences in turn helped produce a very different family structure, farming strategy, and community organization.

Most German immigrants had been farmers in their native country and were hoping to continue the tradition for themselves and their progeny by acquiring land in America. Anglo settlers tended to include many nonfarmers who saw farming as a way to improve their economic condition, not necessarily to sustain a way of life. The historian John Ise, with a touch of German ethnic pride, noted that among the settlers "were men of every imaginable calling: ... dentists, druggists, merchants, lawyers, shoemakers, printers, cowboys, and horse thieves. A few of them combined a half dozen or more of these various vocations, and some, especially among the German and Swiss, really wanted to farm."[82] For many Americans, Kansas was the next stop in a lifelong attempt to discover the secret of economic security; for the German-Russians, it represented their chance to sustain religious and cultural traditions.

German women's role and status in the farm family was quite unlike that of their Anglo counterparts. Most first-generation German families held little doubt about the source of all authority: women and children were expected to treat men as true patriarchs. The state constitution allowed women to own land through inheritance or outright purchase. Most German-Americans, however, believed that only men should control property. They saw women's land ownership simply as a way to risk losing land to another family if the woman should marry (or remarry). Then, by custom, the husband would control the land, even if by law it remained the woman's property.[83]

German and Anglo families also had different views of the role of children. American family size had been shrinking steadily in the nineteenth century as children's education and employment shifted. As children began to work less and spend more time in school (and thus to cost more), large families became an economic burden. Further, during the nineteenth century, Anglo women's increasing power within the family may have enabled them to demand or negotiate with their husbands for smaller families.[84] Germans, however, still saw children as crucial contributors to the family economy.

Where Anglos viewed educated daughters as status symbols, Germans believed that educating women was wasteful. German husbands valued their wives for producing and caring for a large family, as well as for working uncomplainingly at a variety of jobs. Most Germans saw no shame in women working in the fields when necessary. Indeed, all members of the family were expected to contribute their maximum effort to the farm's—and community's—success. Germans were thus able to "substitute labor for capital, which allowed them to weather the boom and bust cycles."[85]

Anglos were particularly sensitive about hiring out their daughters as domestics in town, a job they identified with "lowly" blacks or Irish. Germans had no such qualms, for hired-out daughters provided badly needed money while costing nothing to house or educate. Once a hired girl married another German (as her parents expected her to do), she became in essence the hired girl of the groom's family until such time as her husband decided to establish his own farm.[86]

A modern observer, applying today's feminist standards, might judge the German woman to be hopelessly oppressed compared to her relatively liberated Anglo counterpart. Yet German women were contributing to the long-term security of the farm and to their way of life. Anglo women had a much greater chance of losing all they had built. If their farm failed, their family would have to join the rural exodus to the city, without a home, friends, or job skills. Contemporary Anglo observers, such as the editor of the *Hays Sentinel*, viewed German women condescendingly, noting that the German-Russians were "strong, healthy-looking animals, and seem capable of any work, especially the women."[87] Behavior perceived as barbaric and animal-like by Anglos, however, ensured German women's economic stability even as the culture's customs restricted their choices.

The Germans' communalism—setting aside common lands for grazing and gardening, sharing farm machinery, and maintaining community welfare systems—kept families and farms intact during hard times. Those settlements with religious missions were especially cooperative, since sustaining the community was their highest priority. Anglos, of course, were not without a code of neighborliness and often offered help to nearby families in need. But such aid was informal and erratic and could not compare to the Germans' extensive support network. For Anglos the highest priority was the success of the individual family rather than the community. In fact, perhaps the most important source of support during hard times came not from the neighborhood but from members of the extended family back East.[88]

Because German immigrants rejected strategies of high risk and debt, they had less need of public charity during economic downturns. Instead, Germans tended to be suspicious of mortgages, choosing labor-intensive over capital-intensive methods. Unburdened by mainstream American notions of male success, German men tended to place less importance on the need to acquire the latest model of harvester or binder. Further, they maintained a diversified crop and livestock production that emphasized self-sufficiency. Anglos tended to concentrate on a single cash crop that would produce high yields and thus high returns—but also higher risk. They were especially likely to abandon self-sufficiency strategies during boom times, when they believed a few productive years with a single, high-yielding cash crop could generate enough capital to pay off all their debts.[89] It was a dangerous gamble but an understandable one given the culture of which they were a part.

The Germans' strategy was hardly without its own costs. Like many strongly patriarchal communities, Germans, especially women and children, paid a price in terms of individual aspirations and beliefs. While most German immigrants may have been willing—in fact proud—to make such sacrifices, most Anglos were not. When Anglo farmers were faced with economic disaster, they did not hunt for any deficiencies in their culture. Instead, they looked to the corrupt and unjust political and economic system and decided they must reform it to save their way of life. Yet Farmers' Alliance organizers realized that farm people would have to change many of their cultural attitudes as well. The organizers would have to instill a sense of communalism to temper the fierce individualism of Anglo farmers. For although most Anglos may not have admitted it, they in fact had something to learn from their German neighbors about living in an unforgiving land.

## FARM AND TOWN: COMPETING VISIONS

The phrase *worlds apart* usually denotes cultural difference rather than actual physical space. Certainly Anglos and first-generation German immigrants seemed to exist in different cultural worlds, even though they may have inhabited the same township. Although the Anglo and German farm families appeared to share little, they in fact had things in common with each other that their counterparts in the city did not experience. Anglos and Germans who lived side by side in Ellis County understood the drastic effects of the environment, the economic interrelationship of family members, and the interdependence with one's neighbors in a way that town folk did not. The worlds of farm and town represented a cultural divide that ethnic ties could not erase.[90]

When farm people went into town to buy supplies, sell farm products, or attend an occasional meeting, they were aware of the many possible social pratfalls. Because the nearest village was often more than a hard day's wagon ride away, many farm children did not venture into town until they were in their teens. Farm women, who came into town less often than men, felt particularly awkward about town ways; many would glance anxiously at the latest fashions sported by town women, painfully aware of the perceived deficiencies of their patched and faded dresses. Farm men had a number of places to socialize when in town, such as the saloon and the livery stable. Farm women had no such sanctuary; most felt uncomfortable in these male-dominated spaces and felt unwelcomed there.[91]

Despite these difficulties, farm people appreciated many of the opportunities that a town had to offer. Even the smallest burg could boast such wonders as sweet shops, ice cream parlors, hotels, and general stores offering goods and services unknown on the farm. The clothes, language, manners, knowledge, material conditions—in a hundred ways the town dweller represented the advances of industrializing America and the promise of a better life. Even as farm people waxed eloquent about the moral superiority of life on the farm and of the independence and pride of ownership farming could (theoretically) bring, they were often envious of town life.

Farm people were well aware of the lure of the city. They were especially concerned about their children, who had not chosen farm life but had been born to it. Agrarian newspapers constantly aired the refrain "How do we keep our children down on the farm once they've seen the bright lights of the city?" The answer, in most cases, was to teach youngsters the superiority of farm life over town ways.[92] Beyond the promises of modern civilization, farm people saw in the town the threat to an agrarian culture.

Town dwellers rarely did anything to ease farm people's discomfort with urban sophistication. They used derisive nicknames such as *hayseeds* and *clodhoppers* to denigrate both the occupation of farming and the farmers' lack of social graces.[93] But townspeople's sense of superiority was more than simply a way to affirm their psychological status in society. Those who controlled the local institutions of power had an economic and political incentive for their condescending attitude toward farm people.

Before the Civil War, the agrarian frontier myth had remained a prominent feature in mainstream political culture, a source of great pride for farmers. During the Gilded Age, however, the business elite exchanged this rural ideal for one more to their liking. Propagators of the agrarian frontier myth usually presented farming not merely as an economic opportunity but also as a noble enterprise. These writers portrayed the yeoman farmer as the backbone of American democracy; with his economic independence and insulation from the wicked ways of the city, he was the perfect citizen. To whatever degree this Jeffersonian ideal had been true—or was even believed—those who manufactured mainstream ideology in Gilded Age America through newspapers, magazines, sermons, and lectures no longer espoused it. Instead, these cultural mediators replaced the farmer with the entrepreneur as the hero of the updated frontier myth, a scenario much more to the liking of the urban middle class.[94]

In Gilded Age America, the urban middle class saw the businessman, not the farmer, as the ideal citizen. Practical, rational, forward looking, optimistic, and most importantly, successful—these were the characteristics needed to run a government in the ever expanding, tumultuous Gilded Age. A typical newspaper endorsement of a Kansas town council candidate read: "In the first ward, Mr. William Morrison of the firm Morrison Brothers, who own the planing mill, and are putting up a three story brick hotel, is the nominee for the long term, and Ed Tyler, a real estate agent and a good man, who has considerable interests in the city. . . . With these two . . . the first ward is taken care of."[95] A list of the two candidates' business concerns was sufficient to demonstrate that these men were "candidates of the first caliber."

To the businessman, of course, this new calculation made perfect sense. Eugene Ware, a prominent lawyer, philanthropist, and aspiring poet in Fort Scott, Kansas, presented the irrefutable case for the dominance of businessmen in "A Corn Poem."

> *Old Business is the monarch. He rules both*
> *The opulence of nations and their growth.*
> *He builds their cities and he paves their streets*
> *He feeds their army and equips their fleets*
> *Kings are his puppets, and his arms alone*
> *Contain the muscle that can prop up the throne.*[96]

Businessmen with a liberal bent believed that commercial expansion produced social reform; conservatives believed it ensured social stability. Both saw criticism of urban business practices and policies as attacks not simply on their own interests but on the very foundation of the Republic.

Merchants, bankers, lawyers, professionals, and editors dominated local politics in Kansas. They provided the Grand Old Party with its officer corps, directing local campaigns and appropriating the spoils captured with every victory. Although the Democrats were nominally the "workingman's party," one would not have been able to tell this from their leadership or their policies, both of which were dominated by businessmen.

A successful businessman's belief in his natural fitness for office was reinforced after he had survived one of Kansas's periodic depressions. Immigration propaganda often encouraged town dwellers to move from the East and settle in Kansas. The railroads needed towns settled as much as they needed farmers on the land. Speculators were especially active in town promotion, often incorporating a village simply by buying up the required acreage, posting a few signs, and declaring a town site. If a railroad changed the route or decided not to extend a line to the town, those who had invested in lots or had established businesses usually had to watch their town wither away to nothing more than a few abandoned buildings. Sometimes settlers hoisted their houses on logs and literally hauled the town away.[97] To this day, Kansas is littered with ghost towns, monuments to the unbounded optimism of Western settlers and the unyielding reality they found.

The great majority of Kansas towns were based on economies of speculation. Only continued growth could sustain their ambitions, for few possessed the manufacturing concerns necessary to grow beyond an agricultural service center. In fact, their main industry was speculating—luring capital on the promise of continued growth made possible only by further speculation. The first order of business in establishing a town was to demonstrate that business was booming, no matter what the evidence to the contrary. The *Hays Sentinel* reported in 1880, "Ellsworth has organized a board of trade, and when one of the old country dames brings in a mess of butter and eggs, the distinguished body assembles in owl-like wisdom to consider the fluctuations of the market."[98]

Railroads became the virtual lifelines for such ventures. In most cases a community fought hard and bitterly with rivals to bring a railroad through town or to add another line. Throughout the seventies and eighties, Kansas experienced a bond-raising craze as towns sold municipal bonds to support railroad building schemes. A number went deeply into debt for phantom railroad lines that were promised but never built.[99] Of the lines that actually got built, many were shoddy, narrow-gauge tracks built at greatly inflated prices.[100] But if a town did not issue bonds, the railroad might change its route to a more "cooperative" village, with the usual sad results awaiting the recalcitrant community.[101] Townspeople, like farmers, had a deeply conflicted relationship with railroads.

Once the railroad actually established a line, the economic future of the village was hardly assured. Townspeople were not as directly affected by the whims of the Kansas environment as those on the farm; for them a hailstorm or searing hot winds meant discomfort, not financial disaster. But because the town economy was so dependent on business from farm people and because the speculative booms were often based on favorable farming conditions, hard times in the country meant hard times in town. A businessman, in fact, was more likely to fail than a farmer.[102] The town's speculative economy made business ownership particularly unstable. Those boosters who hoped to increase their own business by "booming" the town were in fact inviting other businesses that would eventually create too much competition.[103]

When times were hard, many farmers would protest against what they perceived to be an unfair economic system. Business leaders had a name for those men who criticized credit policies, price structures, onerous bond issues, and the like: "kickers," folks who would cry "famine" at a feast.[104] A kicker, according to town leaders, was someone who had failed because of his own mistakes and now had to blame others at as high a volume as was possible. He was about as low as a man could get—indeed, he was hardly a man.

To the businessman, the kicker was one of the greatest threats to the well-being of the community because he scared away capital. There was the booster, trying his damnedest to paint the town and region in the rosiest possible colors—to enumerate the myriad opportunities, the latest cultural feature, the new streetcar system almost certainly to be built in the very near future—and the kicker was calling it a lie. Businessmen never really argued the issue of truth, however. They cared only about the economic impact of such "scurrilous" reports on the flow of investment capital and immigrants to the town. When Populists began to critique the economy, businessmen would perceive a mass movement of kickers and react accordingly.

Town businessmen embraced an ideology of forced optimism. Where the farmer might ride the roller coaster of despair and exaltation, the businessman always had to put the best face on his situation. If his business interests collapsed, he was expected, if not to grin and bear it, then at least to grit his teeth manfully. Successful businessmen had no use for those who did not have the skills or the education to make the climb or those who made the attempt and fell by the wayside. For the businessman to acknowledge defeat meant admitting the frontier myth to be a lie and inviting economic collapse.

As with most urban middle-class men in the United States, Kansas businessmen gloried in the individual's ability to overcome adversity and succeed. Typical was the statement of a young lawyer upon his arrival in Denver in the 1870s. "Here is a vast field of workers and vast amounts of money to be gotten. If I am only equal to the contest I shall win, if weak then some other and stronger one will carry away the spoils." The frontier was waiting with riches aplenty; the only question was whether a fellow was man enough to grab it for his own. The *New York Herald*, eulogizing the industrialist Cornelius Vanderbilt in 1877, pontificated, "He had not advantages in his battle, no political, social, educational aid. It was one honest, sturdy man against the world, in the end the man won."[105] This ideal of vigorous, individualist masculinity permeated political discourse.

The image of the self-made man was essential for maintaining not only a town's prosperity but also the entire political philosophy of the businessman as model citizen. According to this ideal, if a businessman failed, his failure was his own; if he succeeded, again it was on his own terms. His success was therefore a sign of his capacity to govern—to be pragmatic, to overcome adversity, to achieve. If he blamed outside forces, he was challenging the claim that successful businessmen were especially suited to running government. If his success or failure was not his own, then any citizen could have equal claim to political power. Farm men, while under pressure to succeed economically, did not have a political stake in the notion of individual success. With the old agrarian myth one didn't have to be a well-to-do farmer to fit the model of the ideal citizen; one simply had to be a farmer. Businessmen, however, had staked their claim to supremacy on their individual skill as businessmen, and they were tied to the logic of this claim.

Those officials who dominated political offices, whether local, state, or national, enjoyed immediate practical advantages for supporting "business politics." The winners of local elections, especially those living in the county seat, controlled an extensive patronage system. Officeholders could dispense road-building, construction, sewer, and printing contracts to political allies and loyal supporters. Commissions from government bond or land sales brought in a nice income, which found its way to party stalwarts as well. National officeholders could dole out numerous plum positions, from local postmaster to foreign diplomat. Most successful politicians enjoyed the many unofficial perks of office, including graft if they were so inclined, and few were ever exposed or punished for this standard feature of Gilded Age politics. State and national leaders also enjoyed a steady flow of "gifts" from corporations, including railroad passes, stocks, and seats on corporate boards of directors.[106] Political leaders may have claimed that their success in business aided their political ability, but their political abilities, legal and otherwise, also aided their business success.

Farm people often complained that while their tax dollars flowed into town, little of that money made its way back to the countryside. Few farmers had the time, political savvy, or connections to run successfully for county office, and state office was even further out of reach. Yet many of them believed government owed them something, whether it was internal improvements, railroad regulation, or the free land promised by the Homestead Act. Farm people insisted that they had earned this help for their efforts in "taming the wilderness" and advancing the cause of civilization; they expected the government to fulfill the promises encoded in the frontier myth. During times of extreme crises, agrarian organizers would help shape these expectations into demands for radical change.

Farm people were emotionally and financially devastated by the combined effects of the Panic of 1873 and the grasshopper invasion. Faced with circumstances that seemed completely beyond their control, they turned to state and local government for help. The towns and counties, however, had neither the financial resources nor the desire to distribute relief aid. State politicians were more concerned about maintaining the flow of capital to the state than with the plight of farm people isolated on the Plains. Since most of the legislators lived in the more populous eastern section of the state, they had little experience of the effects of the hopper invasion and little incentive to soften its blows. The legislature did have other concerns, however. Lawmakers were so worried about the effect of negative publicity on Kansas immigration that they actually passed a bill changing the name of the Grasshopper River. State politicians were less productive at passing relief legislation. The governor did call a special session of the legislature, but lawmakers managed only to appropriate the funds required to pay them for meeting.[107] Although the state allowed counties to issue bonds to support local poor relief, these areas were so badly off that few invested in such risky propositions. The credulity of Eastern investors could stretch only so far.

The state's main contribution was to provide numerous forms for would-be recipients to fill out in order to prevent fraud. The legislature hoped to discourage the needy from expecting such handouts in the future, thereby destroying their work ethic. Ironically, most of the fraud was perpetrated by bogus relief agents who combed the country in search of contributions that went no farther than their own pockets. Although the U.S. Army, private agencies, and individuals provided significant relief, it was not enough to keep thousands of recent settlers from fleeing "back East." Despite the Kansas legislature's valiant effort to preserve the myth of prosperous Kansas—in fact partly because of their efforts—the economy of central Kansas collapsed, and immigration and investments did not increase significantly until the late 1870s.[108]

Farm people were infuriated with state politicians' unwillingness to accept the reality of conditions on the Plains.[109] Stung by the callous attitude of their government "servants," farmers in Smith County issued a circular declaring, "Forced by the illiberal and narrow spirit of the legislature to look outside the state for assistance we had reason to expect would be afforded by our own citizens, [we] make this appeal to all benevolent persons, who may learn of our distress."[110] Together with the legislature's response to the previous year's economic collapse, the hopper crisis gave impetus to an agrarian reform movement, the Grange, that was rolling westward from the Midwest.

The Granger movement's founders were not farmers at all but U.S. government clerks living in Washington, D.C. Yet many of them, including the president, Oliver Kelley, had grown up on farms and hoped to enrich the social, cultural, and educational aspects of farmers' lives: that is, to bring some of the benefits of the city to the farm. Only when the Grange's organizers discovered that economic and political issues could attract large numbers of farm people to the organization did they openly criticize the status quo. Concentrating its wrath on the railroads, grain elevator operators, and the credit system, the Grange mobilized large numbers of farm people in the Midwest and Plains.

Kansas and Nebraska experienced particularly sudden growth and for a time led the nation in number of granges per capita. In 1874, Kansas had a local grange for every eighty-eight people engaged in farming, and three-quarters of the farming population joined the organization.[111]

The Grange's political program, which emphasized railroad regulation, an expanded system of credit, and an attack on monopolies, addressed some of the most basic concerns of Kansas farmers during a time of economic hardship. After 1876, however, membership fell off as quickly as it had grown three years earlier. Yet during this time, the Kansas Grange managed to disturb the relative peace of the Republican Party, which would not be seriously challenged again until the Populist revolt in 1890.[112]

The Grange created a unique political culture that combined features from fraternal lodges, churches, literary and debate clubs, and political organizations. Hoping to bring together isolated farm families, it strengthened farmers' sense of community by binding neighbors together with secret rituals borrowed from the Masons. The Grange's meetings, picnics, and other gatherings helped fill the need for social interaction among farmers while its emphasis on education provided them with a variety of reading materials and a broader outlook on life. The Grange's cooperative stores gave farmers not only a discount on supplies but also some control of their economic destiny. Organizers gained the confidence of farm people and instilled in them the optimism necessary to challenge the political system.

Central to the Grange's political culture was its recognition of the importance of the family, and of women in particular, in the economic and social life of the farm. Rather than forming an agrarian version of a male fraternal organization like the Masons, the Grange allowed women to join on an equal basis with men. In order to receive a charter, a local grange needed nine female for every thirteen male prospective members. Much of women's work was sex specific—organizing picnics, for instance—in ways that replicated gender relations in the farm family. Yet women also served as officers and as delegates to the national organization and participated in the debates that were an integral part of the local meetings. The Kansas Grange further underscored its commitment to women as political equals by supporting woman suffrage from 1874 onward.[113]

Although the Grange's attitude toward women was far in advance of that of most political organizations, its basic understanding of gender relations stayed within the mainstream. With almost all of the leadership positions assumed by men, women's decision-making power in the organization was limited.[114] Yet while in some ways supporting the gender expectations of the mainstream, the Grange also helped subvert conventional assumptions about gender relations and politics in Gilded Age America. When Farmers' Alliance organizers came to Kansas, they brought this legacy with them.

Before the Granger movement embraced partisan politics in 1874, reformers across the country had joined to take on the conservatives who controlled both parties. In Kansas, where G.O.P. liberals joined with Democrats, the reform party did little better than the Democrats usually did. Nationally in 1872 the Liberal Republican candidate, Horace Greeley, had been vilified by both parties and soundly trounced, commenting after the election, "I hardly knew whether I was running for the Presidency or the Penitentiary."[115] On the national level, Republican and Democratic politicians viewed "bolting" a party and forming a rival organization as a treasonous offense and easily contained such attempts.

In Kansas, however, where party lines were more malleable, the Grange's entry into electoral politics in 1874 in support of the reformist Independent Party drew a majority of disgruntled Republicans who were unwilling to abandon the national party. In the face of financial depression and the legislature's cavalier approach to the grasshopper crises, the Grange was able to mobilize a large block of well-organized voters, enabling the reformers to gain majority in the Kansas House of Representatives. When the Grange collapsed, however, urban reformers were left without a base of support. Though reform parties appeared in almost every election during the next decade and a half, they never seriously threatened the Republicans again until 1890.

Republicans learned to deal with appeals for reform by including, whenever appropriate, certain vaguely worded planks in their platform which addressed popular issues. In 1876, when challenged by the Greenback Party, the Republican platform proclaimed that the G.O.P. was "the surest hope of reform [for all] to whom 'Reform' is something more than an empty name."[116] Without the pressure from a viable third party, however, the G.O.P. was able to ignore such high-flown rhetoric and get on with business. To these Republican leaders, reform was indeed an empty name, but they were quite willing to use the ideal, when needed, as a pacifier for otherwise disgruntled party members.

With the economic boom of the 1880s, party regulars no longer saw the need to be so accommodating of reformers. Republican leaders purged from the party those who spoke out against its economic policies, supported a reform party, or tried to liberalize the G.O.P. Only on social issues such as prohibition and woman suffrage did the Republican leadership allow some dissent, and even those issues became instruments of party strategy through an enforced party line. Increasingly, Republican politicians were expected to act as soldiers in a well-organized army.[117]

The Republican leadership was bound together by political, business, and fraternal ties, and it utilized an established system of reciprocity to keep allies from straying to another's camp. The letters of Eugene Ware document the many informal arrangements between various candidates and their camps to ensure support at the party conventions and before elections. C. S. Finder, the editor of the Lawrence *Evening Tribune*, wrote to Ware to suggest a scheme to dump an increasingly unpopular candidate. Finder asked, "Can you bring [the] Bourbon County [delegation] with you?" and then intimated that his paper would support Ware as an alternative candidate. Other letter writers offered or reported similar deals.[118] Such horse trading was in keeping with these men's view of politics as a practical matter run on sound business principles.

For most mainstream politicians, politics was not an occupation for the faint of heart or the ineffectually pious—in other words, not for women or third-party men. No, politics was a war, and only men brave enough and tough enough to survive would benefit by the system. In the memorable words of Kansas's U.S. Senator John J. Ingalls: "The purification of politics is an iridescent dream. . . . Politics is a battle for supremacy. Parties are the armies. The decalogue and the golden rule have no place in a political campaign. . . . To defeat the antagonist and expel the party in power is the purpose. The republicans and democrats are as irreconcilably opposed to each other as were Grant and Lee in the Wilderness. They use ballots instead of guns, but . . . the result [is] the same."[119] Ingalls went farther than many politicians were willing to admit publicly. But his belief that power, not morality, was paramount in politics was the guiding principle of most Republican and Democratic politicians. Their language was far removed from the Woman Movement's moralist Christian discourse. To play men's games, women had to speak men's language—or at least, figure out a way to translate it.

For many men after the Civil War, electoral politics had become a male world of comradeship and ritual. Partisanship was less about specific issues and more about ethnic, class, and regional loyalties. Politicians cemented these ties with patronage and reinforced them with elaborate events where party bosses would "treat" their followers. Election Day was not a place for a respectable woman. It was a time when the culture of the saloon hit the streets with a bang: banners, brass bands, and parades; rousing, maudlin oratory liberally sprinkled with spicy stories; free cigars, free barbecue, and of course, barrels of free whiskey and beer lubricating the voters' path to the voting booth. Election Day offered men the opportunity to catch up on old acquaintances, hear the latest gossip, tell a few dirty jokes, and talk politics. These raucous, fraternal extravaganzas, hosted by Republican and Democratic bosses, gave new meaning to the idea of a two-party system.[120]

The competing worlds of middle-class women's and men's politics can be traced in part to urban women's and men's separate social, work, and political experiences. Beginning in the early nineteenth century, many women from the newly forming middle class had begun fashioning a "female world of love and ritual." Reacting to their growing separation from the supposedly male sphere of business and politics, middle-class women came together first for social, then for charitable, and then for political purposes. These relationships became the foundation for the growing number of women's organizations before the Civil War.[121] When middle-class women moved to towns in Kansas, they quickly recreated the strong women's networks in which they had participated back East. A town of two thousand boasted an impressive array of sex-segregated organizations, including such groups as the Sunday Service Club and Daisy Society for women and the Odd Fellows and Masons for men.[122]

Kansas farm people had neither the separate homosocial worlds nor the sharp divide between work and home that urban women and men experienced. Farm people viewed churchgoing as a family event and religion as a source of support and guidance for both women and men. In town, church was a building, an institution ruled over by men but attended by women. Many men, while paying lip service to the importance of Christianity (as well as agreeing to pay the dues of membership), gladly ceded to women the moral responsibilities attached to churchgoing. Women, for their part, could then take moral service as their distinct calling.[123]

Women-dominated religious organizations and male-only fraternal orders often viewed each other with suspicion. Fraternal lodges celebrated their exclusion of women and developed elaborate rituals meant to counter what members perceived as a growing feminization of society in general and Protestantism in particular. Church leaders, for their part, blamed fraternal groups for "emasculating" the churches by encouraging men to abandon them for the lodges, leaving a women-dominated institution. "Are not the young and middle-aged men in secret fraternities, and not in the army of Jesus?" demanded a representative of the National Christian Association, an aggressively evangelical organization.[124] Although it hoped to convince middle-class men that time spent in the Christian "army" was a manly endeavor, the association's ire was misdirected. Men had been abandoning the Protestant church in America since the early nineteenth century because of long-term economic and cultural changes. Women had remade the church in their image, and it would take more than a public relations campaign to reverse that trend.

Kansas women began to establish church and social organizations soon after the first towns were settled. These organizations offered emotional support to their members in a new, unstable, and often threatening environment.

Women's clubs allowed members to differentiate social classes within a developing town, enabling middle-class women to identify themselves as "respectable." The clubs empowered their members to challenge male activities, such as gambling, patronizing prostitution, and drinking, which most directly threatened women. When the women worked to create schools, churches, and charitable organizations or organized to close down saloons and brothels, they were fighting to establish a way of life agreeable to both their class and their gender.[125]

Most middle-class men supported women's "civilizing" activities that helped to build up the town: a new church or school was something that any booster would be happy to crow about. However, when boom turned to bust and people were suffering, the priorities of men and women town leaders could head off in different directions. During the grasshopper crisis, while state legislators struggled manfully to ignore the problem, women's charitable organizations such as the Woman's Relief Corps played an important role in collecting and administering aid. In Wichita, after the Ladies Aid Society solicited contributions from outside the state, many business leaders complained that these efforts were hindering immigration and scaring away capital. The women's group responded: "It is absolutely true . . . that there are families in the country whose only safety from starvation lies in the charity of the people . . . , that women and children have no shoes and stockings. . . . To those who, like doubting Thomases will not believe, we propose to furnish transportation into the country and let them see for themselves."[126] The Ladies Aid spokeswoman then presented the town leaders with a basic moral equation: "As far as injury to the concerned by the circulating of the truth, will it hurt the country as much to help these people in their need, as to let one man or woman die of cold or starvation?"

In this instance, both women and men were drawing their language from society's expectations about gender roles. Women were told that they were to be the moral educators, the redeemers. They and their homes were the antidote to the heartless, dog-eat-dog world of business and politics. Men, on the other hand, were encouraged to strive for personal financial achievement, although not simply for self-aggrandizement. When a man succeeded, then his family succeeded; when his family succeeded, then society was strengthened. Middle-class women and men had access to a gender ideology that legitimated their approach to civic duty. Yet while the ideology of domesticity had been constructed to maintain gender harmony along with male domination, its internal logic set in motion inherent contradictions. Women wishing to challenge areas of men's dominance could draw on these contradictions to undermine male power.[127]

43

As white middle-class women gained political influence in Kansas throughout the 1880s, African-American men lost ground. Black political leaders embraced the rhetoric of practical politics, espoused the values of the white middle class, and were loyal Republicans. Despite their playing by the rules, the G.O.P. refused to grant them anything but the most meager of concessions. Black editors often argued that white Republicans shared many of the racist attitudes of other Gilded Age whites, and while this was no doubt true, it doesn't explain the G.O.P.'s motives. In 1867, the party leadership demonstrated its ability to ignore its racist proclivities for more practical concerns. Had black voters supported another party, they might have received more attention from the G.O.P. Unfortunately, few African-Americans saw the Democrats—the party of slavery, in their minds—as a viable option. And until a third party gained enough strength to challenge the G.O.P. seriously, black leaders saw little advantage in throwing their support to the reformers.

Beyond these obstacles, black leaders remained loyal to the G.O.P. because the party best represented their ideological perspective. Although black middle-class men tended to have smaller incomes and lower-status jobs than their white counterparts, African-Americans faced greater obstacles in achieving even limited success. Black leaders warmly embraced the ethos of the self-made man but grafted on this ideal the experience of being black in a racist culture. A black man who gained middle-class status helped not only himself but also his race. This ideal "Race Man," by practicing thrift, cleanliness, honesty, and gentility and seeking constant self-improvement, would serve as an example to whites of the true nature of African-Americans. His efforts would in turn make it easier for others of his race to succeed.[128]

Black leaders generally supported the G.O.P.'s probusiness, antilabor policies but included a constant demand for more opportunities for black men. Since most unions excluded African-Americans, they were more interested in gaining a larger share of government jobs and improving their children's educational opportunities than in supporting broad movements for economic justice. "All we ask our white brethren is the chance to prove ourselves capable—nothing more, nothing less," insisted one black editor. As with white business leaders, the black elite had little patience with failure. "Remember that in Kansas everybody must work or starve," warned the *Colored Citizen*. "This is a great state for the energetic and industrious, but a fearful one for the idle or lazy."[129]

In 1880, when African-Americans constituted nearly 5 percent of the state vote and appeared to be a rapidly growing population, the G.O.P. grudgingly delivered on some black demands. But black migration to Kansas peaked after

1880 with the conclusion of the Exodus, a campaign by Southern African-Americans to encourage migration to Kansas. Although the organizers had promised paradise, African-American migrants found the same environmental conditions that disillusioned white settlers had experienced. Although most African-American migrants had planned to take up farming in all-black townships, their lack of capital and inexperience with the Plains environment forced most of them into the cities. As the discouraging news reached the South, African-American migration slowed to a trickle, and black influence with the G.O.P. withered along with it.[130]

African-American editors might have gained additional political leverage by encouraging the growing politicization of black women. During the 1880s, middle-class black women began to develop temperance and suffrage organizations of their own. At times allied with white-dominated groups such as the Women's Christian Temperance Union (WCTU) and the Kansas Equal Suffrage Association and at times separate (but always segregated), these groups gave black women the same opportunity as whites to develop political skills such as debating and fund raising. The African-American press, however, largely ignored these efforts, instead urging black women to be "natural conservators of decency and morality" in order to help "uplift the race."[131] African-American editors were happy to report the doings of the Ladies Sewing Circle of St. John's African Methodist Episcopal Church, the Young Ladies Charitable Union, the Ladies of Queen Esther's Court, and other black women's social and benevolent organizations.[132] Editors saw these groups as befitting the "natural role" of women, a view that owed much to the cult of domesticity as seen through the lens of "race progress." In fact, Kansas black newspapers often simply reprinted "women's columns" from white wire services, with their class and racial biases intact.[133]

Not all middle-class men, black or white, adhered to the language and ideology of business politics. Those who championed reform through the third-party movements often employed an emotional, moral language that appealed to the listener's sense of right and wrong rather than to a sense of tradition or desire for efficiency. Some of these men had tasted economic failure and refused to exonerate the system, as their fellow businessmen insisted. Others were financially successful but did not accept the conditions that oppressed the less fortunate.[134] Whatever the reason, they chose to step outside the mainstream in order to remake it. While Republican papers treated black leaders with benign neglect, the G.O.P. heaped vitriolic abuse on those who dared attack the sanctity of the two-party system.

During the 1880s, the Prohibition Party proved to be the greatest threat to

Kansas Republicans and thus the most frequent target of abuse. Prohibitionists pledged to battle against the curse of alcohol, believing that "the Gospel of Christ is the substance of all reform." Their political language and tactics were almost indistinguishable from those of women activists, a point that Republican editors made repeatedly. Prohibitionists would form the core of organizers who joined with women to expunge the "terrible thralldom of intemperance" from Kansas in 1879.[135] This campaign to pass a state constitutional prohibition amendment would bring together women and men, and farm and town, to a degree unparalleled in Kansas history. The results would come to dominate Kansas politics nearly as much as the bloody shirt and change the way Kansans perceived women's role in the political arena.

## THE PROHIBITION AMENDMENT CAMPAIGN:
### THE POLITICS OF REVIVALISM

Between August 14 and 26, 1879, nearly one hundred thousand people gathered at Bismarck Grove near Lawrence to hear speaker after speaker condemn the sin of intemperance and, most particularly, the sin of alcohol. One hundred thousand women, men, and children—equal to 10 percent of the population of Kansas—had come together for the launching of the campaign to pass the first state constitutional prohibition amendment in the nation. Banish the liquor trade, they were told, and you banish poverty, sin, labor strife, political corruption, and brutality against women, among other social ills. In essence, to prohibit alcohol was to usher in the Christian millennium, when all would be brothers and sisters in the family of God.[136]

The twelve-day National Temperance Camp Meeting sponsored by the Kansas State Temperance Union and the National Christian Temperance Union was revivalism on a grand scale. Part church meeting, part country fair, and part social event, it was the perfect Kansas happening. Besides the temperance-related activities, those attending could enjoy "such attractions as the petrified man, the fat lady, and the Chinese juggler," as well as shooting galleries and lemonade stands. The meeting even had the enthusiastic support of the Kansas Pacific Railroad and the city fathers of Lawrence, who, as the historian Robert Bader reports, "both . . . appreciated the immigration possibilities inherent in promoting the camp meeting and in presenting a thriving image to the outside world. A Lawrence paper suggested that the town's citizens pile sand at strategic locations on their property, so as to produce for unsuspecting visitors an appearance of business activity."[137] Business, after all, was still business.

Prelude to an amendment campaign: the righteous assemble at a prohibition
camp meeting at Bismarck Grove, Kansas, in 1878. *Kansas State Historical Society*

Given such a seemingly absurd mix of evangelical zealotry, carnival atmo-spherics, and hucksterism, it would be easy to dismiss the Temperance Camp Meeting as simply a shuck, a twelve-day peddling of political and moral patent medicine guaranteed to cure all social ills. Or the meeting might be seen as just another example of a group of religious fanatics attempting to impose their will on the rest of the country. Certainly that was the belief of a number of con-temporaries, especially among groups such as the Irish, the Germans, and white Southerners, who believed drinking (at least for men) was a healthy so-cial activity.

But the Gilded Age temperance movement cannot be pigeonholed as simply a reactionary, illiberal force in American politics. The Prohibition Party's plat-form in 1869 called for woman suffrage, direct election of senators, and an in-come tax, all of which were radical proposals for their time. By the 1890s, the Prohibition Party would be echoing all of the Populists' demands, including the nationalization of transportation, banking, and communication indus-tries. Some temperance organizations admitted African-Americans on an equal basis, an extraordinary policy during the virulently racist Gilded Age.[138] And however wrong the prohibitionists may have been in their choice of a cure, they did not invent the ills caused by alcohol, tobacco, gambling, and other forms of "intemperance"—what today we would call addiction. While many prohibitionist activists held strong class and ethnic prejudices, these re-pressive motives did not negate the existence of very real problems. Prohibi-tionist reformers—and reformers they were—should not be lumped together with those who simply strove to maintain the economic and political status quo.

The Kansas temperance movement had a profound effect on women's par-ticipation in state politics. Women had engaged in antisaloon actions as early as 1856, when twelve Lawrence women, armed with "axes, hatchets, and ham-mers, or whatever they could best use for the purpose," attacked a log cabin saloon and "spilled every drop of liquor they could find." Less spectacularly, women often took the lead in lobbying the legislature about state liquor laws. The Independent Order of Good Templars, which admitted women on an equal basis with men, was the leading temperance organization in the state. By 1879, women made up nearly one-third of the membership. One year earlier, women from the Good Templars helped form the Kansas WCTU, which be-came the leading group for prohibition enforcement during the 1880s. Because temperance was so closely tied to the Protestant churches, women could claim that activism was simply an extension of church work.

The Methodists set the stage for the prohibition amendment by bringing

48

their revivalist tactics to the cause of temperance. During the mid-1870s, Francis Murphy, a converted Methodist and reformed alcoholic, had been a leading revivalist in the abstinence movement back East. In 1877, Amanda Way, a Kansas resident and itinerant Methodist lay preacher, brought the Murphy Movement back to her state. An officer of the national Good Templars, Way proved to be both an extraordinary revivalist and organizer. Along with other Good Templars, she scoured the countryside for those who could be persuaded to sign the Murphy Movement's total abstinence pledge cards. The favorite tactic of temperance activists was to announce a revival meeting and then call on the converted to sign the pledge. Not surprisingly, rural folk were especially enthusiastic. By the time the campaign ended in the summer of 1878, temperance activists reported that two hundred thousand pledges—representing one-quarter of the state's population—had been signed.[139]

With Kansas still smoldering from the past year's revivalism, temperance activists moved to convert the temporary antialcohol sentiment into something more permanent. Joshua Detwiler, a young businessman, proposed a novel idea: rather than pressure the legislature for a state law, temperance activists should install prohibition in the state constitution. Instead of depending on the legislature to make this momentous decision, the activists would appeal to the voters in a statewide election. Still elated by their recent successes throughout Kansas, the Good Templars' convention overwhelmingly approved the idea.

Although many did not expect the bill enabling the special election for the amendment to pass the legislature, it received numerous votes from fence-sitters. These politicians were not particularly enamored of prohibition, but "a vote against prohibition might not be fully understood by the home folks. For those planted firmly on the fence, one feature of the proposal, the referendum, seemed especially attractive: the matter was too important for mere politicians, so let the People decide."[140] The bill passed the House by one vote over the necessary two-thirds, and only after proamendment legislators had directed the sergeant at arms to haul in recalcitrant members who were hiding in their offices to avoid the vote.

The vote provided a perfect example for both proponents and opponents of women's involvement in politics. The deciding vote was cast by a newlywed representative, George Greever, whose wife, Margaret Newland Greever, persuaded him to switch his vote to a yes at the last minute. Though Greever, a Democrat from a heavily antiprohibitionist Wyandotte County district, was defeated in the next election, Margaret Greever later recalled, "It was the proudest moment of my life."[141] For antiprohibitionist Democrats, Greever's influence on her husband was a clear sign of the insidious influence that women would have on politics.

Although most observers gave the amendment only a slight chance of passing, proamendment forces entered the campaign with several advantages. The opposition remained overconfident and never mounted a serious, well-organized campaign. Unlike the suffragists in the 1867 amendment campaign, prohibitionists were not kept busy answering objections. Further, the Republican Party provided at least nominal support. The Republican governor, John St. John, gave the amendment a good deal more than that. St. John had been a zealous temperance activist when elected governor in 1878, but he hadn't done much to advertise this. In 1879, however, he came out of the prohibition closet, stating, "I was governor but I couldn't stay out of the fight."[142] With the Republican Party went the influential Republican press. The proamendment campaign also had the vigorous support of the Protestant churches, led by the Methodists, who declared, "Let Governor St. John count on this division of his army, equipped and drilled, waiting for orders." Such lockstep conformity no doubt heartened prohibition activists. At the same time, such proclamations reinforced the fears of opponents, particularly Catholics, who charged that the amendment would restrict religious and personal freedom.

The proamendment forces had a number of other factors in their favor. The Kansas State Temperance Union, with St. John as president, proved to be effective at organizing grass-roots support. Temperance activists were able to call on such outside luminaries as Frances Willard, the president of the national WCTU. One of the best-known and -loved women of the period, she drew an enormous crowd when she spoke in Topeka.[143] The campaign represented, in effect, the right reform at the right time.

Such good timing, of course, was not simply a matter of fate. Prohibition organizers successfully utilized the cultural resources that were available while transcending the restrictions imposed by the lack of other resources, such as money. One strategy pursued by Drusilla Wilson, the president of the Kansas WCTU and a veteran of the Woman's Crusade, deserves special mention. Rather than attempt to mobilize the yet inchoate WCTU, Wilson chose to canvas the state herself; she and her husband, age sixty-four and seventy respectively, traveled over three thousand miles while giving "more than three hundred public lectures and dozens of talks. . . . Working the rural school houses and village churches, they kept to the backroads, avoiding the railroad towns to which temperance workers tended to gravitate."[144] When the votes were counted, rural townships voted overwhelmingly for the amendment.

Prohibition proved to be an issue that bridged the cultural gap between small-town middle class and Anglo farm people. Besides Way's efforts, proamendment organizers apparently tried to encourage participation from the country as well as the town. The campaign rallies became exuberant festivals amenable to all involved. At one such rally in Nemaha County,

> An exuberant crowd, swollen by a large influx from the adjacent counties, participated in the day long activities. The celebration began in the morning with a street parade "a half mile in length," featuring local temperance societies, whose brilliant banners and badges made "an imposing spectacle." The principal speaker, the nationally prominent Iowa lawyer J. Ellen Foster, "completely captivated" her audience with a talk "full of strength, force and pathos." . . . In the afternoon she spoke to the children, who were called forward. . . . In the evening a mass meeting, "packed to overflowing," convened in the largest hall in town. The crowd of townspeople and farmers heard Foster speak for a third time.[145]

By creating a family event emphasizing communal spectacle and participation, organizers allowed farm people to enter the town on their own terms, to feel included rather than ridiculed. The camp meeting atmosphere enabled farm people to form an emotional community with their counterparts in town, using a discourse and milieu in which both could be comfortable.

Prohibition also brought Anglo farm and middle-class town people together by excluding others. Those who tended to oppose the amendment represented groups whom Anglo farmers and the middle class already distrusted. Anglos' suspicions about Germans and their culture were confirmed when the great majority of German men opposed the amendment. The larger towns and cities also rejected it, the greatest opposition coming from working-class men. Farm and town could join together in condemning urban places as teeming in poverty, iniquity, and strife. And where city dwellers might look at the hinterlands and see backward yokels, town and farm folk could claim temperance, honesty, and adherence to Christian values. For middling-class Anglos from farms and small towns, prohibition proved a useful device for heaping various "others" onto one discredited pile.

The prohibition amendment passed, but not by much. Although the measure achieved only a 4 percent majority, its impact on Kansas culture and politics created a snowball effect that made repeal unlikely. As the prohibition cause gained strength in the state, enforcement proved increasingly difficult, engendering corruption and contempt for the law. Enforcement became a central and contentious issue in local politics, with the WCTU leading the call for stiff fines and jail sentences for violators. In fact, the WCTU emerged as the premier temperance—and women's—organization in the state by organizing around the issue.

For prohibitionists, the new law was the opening salvo in what they hoped would be the last battle for the redemption of the state, the final struggle in the war that began with Bleeding Kansas, or so the story went. Governor St. John, in his 1881 message to the legislature, sermonized, "We now look to the future, not forgetting that it was here on our soil where the first blow was given that finally resulted in the emancipation of a race from slavery. We have now determined upon a second emancipation, which shall free not only the body but the soul of man. Now, as in the past, the civilized world watches Kansas, and anxiously awaits the results."[146]

By the mid-1880s, many Republican politicians who rejected prohibition in principle, and certainly in practice, became aware of the political possibilities of pro-prohibitionist rhetoric. Yankee (and thus Republican) Kansans had associated Southern-born (Democratic) Kansans with drinking since the days of Bleeding Kansas, when "rum-soaked" Border Ruffians raided Free State towns. (No mention was ever made of rum-soaked Jayhawkers.) For Yankee prohibitionists fighting to keep "Rebel" liquor from entering Kansas through the Missouri River border towns, the Civil War was being fought all over again. Prohibitionists simply replaced the sin of slavery with the sin of alcohol. Once again, politicians put the myth of martyred Kansas to good use.

The amendment and subsequent enforcement policies created two Kansases based on old antagonisms: one wet and one dry. The "wet lands" consisted of several scattered outposts. The most populous was the strip along the northeastern border anchored by the cities of Leavenworth and Atchison. Leavenworth, the center of proslavery activities during the days of Bleeding Kansas, had long been the focus of hatred for Yankee Kansans.[147] Kansas City, divided from its counterpart in Missouri by only a political boundary line, replicated that metropolis's fondness for saloons. Kansas City, Kansas, was by far the most heterogeneous city in the state, and that alone was anathema to Anglo prohibitionists. Cow towns such as Wichita had everything that the eager sinner desired and earnest reformer detested: saloons, prostitution, and gambling, among other iniquities. They made for colorful press reports back East, but Kansas prohibitionists didn't care much for such color. They demanded social purity and proudly wore the white ribbon to symbolize it; their desire for moral homogeneity corresponded with their fears of cultural heterogeneity.[148]

Throughout the eighties, state officials, aided by a few intrepid locals, made occasional forays against the flagrant noncompliance by the wet cities and towns. Most of these attempts were rebuffed by the sheer indifference or hostility of local officials and local juries. Occasionally, wets supplemented this strategy with threatened and actual crowd violence against enforcers. Prohibitionist legislators responded by passing progressively tougher and more centralized enforcement laws, culminating in 1885 with the Metropolitan Police Act, which set up a commission to control a state-sponsored police squad charged with enforcing prohibition. The commission attempted to usurp local prerogatives in several cities, with varying degrees of success.[149]

In smaller, more homogeneous towns, the enforcement activities varied with the power of prohibition supporters. Some towns were able to reduce the availability of alcohol to a mere trickle. Prohibitionists banished "joints" while keeping a watchful eye on pharmacies, where alcohol could still be procured for "medicinal" purposes.[150] In other towns legal and political battles raged throughout the period, although lax enforcement often prevailed. Since Republicans largely controlled the small towns, Republican officeholders received most of the graft.

Support for the prohibitionists' enforcement efforts increased during the eighties, thanks in part to the influx of like-minded settlers to the state. The number of church members belonging to evangelical Protestant sects rose nearly 150 percent during this time, while the numbers of Catholics and German Lutherans increased hardly at all. These groups, traditionally the most hostile to prohibition, generally gave Kansas a wide berth and headed instead to less pietistic states such as Nebraska. While German Kansans (and others concerned with increasing immigration to the state) bitterly attacked prohibition for inducing this trend, prohibition supporters contended that "Kansas has never lost a citizen she cared to keep, because she has scourged the saloons out of the holy temple of her homes and institutions."[151] Evangelical prohibitionists' hostility toward alcohol meshed nicely with their distrust of Catholics and foreigners.

Prohibitionists were fortunate that their enforcement efforts coincided with an unprecedented economic boom of the mid-1880s. As long as it lasted, prohibitionists were able to get a respectful hearing from Republican politicians, and the state government continued to support strict enforcement. Prohibitionists proudly noted that economic prosperity arose with the amendment. It was a very effective argument—for a while.

## THE BOOM

The boom rolled onto the Plains in 1883 amid word of higher crop prices, plentiful rainfall, and a strong national economy. It gathered force suddenly, a mass of euphoria exploding out of a foundation of solid good news. Prices for both town lots and farmland began rising as new settlers and speculators streamed in to grab a piece of this latest El Dorado. At the same time, the usual suspects—the railroads, land companies, and the newspapers—were firing up the propaganda machinery, making past claims appear almost sober in comparison. No doubt they found the effects of their work rewarding. Between 1885 and 1887 the population of central Kansas rose by more than one-fourth while that of western Kansas increased by nearly two-thirds. Some farmland values shot up an astounding 1,000 percent to over $150 an acre, and still the hopeful poured into the state.[152]

It made good economic sense to buy 160 acres at ten dollars an acre when one talked to others who had done the same and paid off all their debts in two years. Here at last seemed the fulfillment of the frontier myth: two years of hard work and a family owned their own farm, free and clear. It made a lot less sense, however, to pay ten times that much, unless one intended to sell out in a year or two, after land values rose still higher. Many, in fact, came to Kansas expressly for that purpose and lost or gained depending on how early they got into the game and how late they got out. Others sincerely hoped that Kansas would be their last stop, the place where they would finally achieve economic security and independence. But whether for speculation or cultivation, land bought at over one hundred dollars an acre almost surely meant a huge mortgage for the purchaser. The fact that the numbers didn't add up, especially after crop prices began falling in the mid-1880s, seemed to have little effect on newcomers.[153]

New settlers were hardly alone in being swept up in the excitement. Kansas farmers who had arrived before the boom took part in it in several ways. Some speculated on town lots or on additional land, hoping either to sell out soon for a quick profit or to expand their cash crop acreage. Others, sure that good times had come at last, took out additional loans to pay for improvements on the farm. In general, Anglo farmers shifted even further away from the type of mixed agriculture that would increase their self-sufficiency, choosing to put greater amounts of time and money into producing one or two cash crops. Some of the more conservative farmers castigated neighbors for their chronic myopia and warned of leaner times in the future. But jeremiads about the evils of unnecessary debt were largely ignored as many farmers grabbed for the brass ring of economic success. Those who offered the mortgages had dreams of their own, for a Kansas mortgage was seen as a sure thing by investors back East. This brought mortgage rates down and increased the availability of credit. For farmers, the easy credit made the ring shine all the brighter and the distance seem even closer.[154]

During the "high boom," Kansans' belief in what was possible, in the promise of the future, was nearly unbounded—some would say unhinged. Leading the stampede were the editors of the local papers, who strove mightily to outdo their competitors in hyperbole and naïveté. The exhortation of the *Belle Plain News* editor was typical of efforts to "boom the boom." "Do not be afraid of going into debt," he insisted. "Spend money for the city's betterment as free as water. . . . Let the bugaboo of high taxes be nursed by old women. Do all you can for Belle Plain regardless of money, and let the increase in population and wealth take care of the taxes. Double, treble, quadruple our expenditures, . . . and Belle Plain will boom."[155]

And spend they did. Fifteen towns bought complete streetcar systems, though few had any need for them. Garden City voted bonds for a railway system, then agreed to underwrite "an electric light plant, a water works, a sewer system, and a natural gas plant." Tiny Ness City, with a population of less than a thousand, "planned a $25,000 waterworks and a street railway." Villages pointed to such improvements as proof of impressive growth, and the prices of town lots continued to rise as long as newcomers kept arriving. One couldn't touch a lot in Great Bend for under five thousand dollars; in Wichita a prime location went for upward of thirty thousand dollars.[156] Each new purchase and new arrival brought more money to the towns. The towns did continue to boom, but also managed to amass huge municipal debts.

Those who pointed out the folly of it all were easily dismissed as kickers. Critics complained that money was being wasted on unnecessary projects, that railroad lines were being overbuilt and undercapitalized, and that Kansas was leading the nation in indebtedness. The boomer was unfazed by such gloomy pronouncements. He could answer them by running off a string of statistics demonstrating growth and could point to a hundred success stories. For the boomer, the state's motto, *Ad astra per aspera* (To the stars through difficulties), said it all: after passing through the grim seventies, surely Kansas was now heaven bound. Most Kansans saw their sudden prosperity as the natural result of hard work and perseverance; some added providence to the list and reckoned God was smiling on the lives of those who had purged Demon Rum from their land. But the emotional high that Kansans had caught from the boom was derived from events quite out of their control. Clarity of vision had a very limited range in boom-time Kansas, however; next to wheat and corn, optimism became the leading natural resource of the state, and it was equally capable of creating wealth—in the short term.

Looking at the history of Kansas, one might come to assume that bust followed boom as inevitably as winter followed harvest time. Most Kansans, neither blessed by our hindsight nor particularly interested in honest foresight, believed no such thing. To their minds nothing followed a boom except more boom, the reward and final redemption for enduring the hard times. When the boom collapsed, so too did many Kansans' faith in the future. Their disillusionment provided Farmers' Alliance organizers the opportunity to offer something new to believe in.

The Alliance's political culture fulfilled Kansan Anglo farm people's needs in other ways as well: their love of religiosity, their resentment of town and city folk, their desire for economic independence, their expectation of government support, and their belief in the natural superiority of their way of life. For farm men the Alliance asserted the manly credentials of farmers over businessmen and explained that farm men's economic problems were the result of societal injustice, not individual failure. The Alliance gave farm women an opportunity to recreate a network on the Plains while imbuing their role in the family with political meaning. When the Kansas Farmers' Alliance grew exponentially in 1889 and 1890, many farm people saw the movement as a political boom that would suddenly, and permanently, reverse the ailing fortunes of their families and communities.

While most farm people ignored politics during the 1880s, the new prosperity coupled with the passage of the prohibition amendment helped spur the development of an urban women's political culture in Kansas. During this period, the state's urban middle class expanded rapidly, providing women activists with a huge pool of potential converts. Prohibition, meanwhile, enabled women activists to organize around the issue of enforcement, providing a direct link between temperance activities and political action. From there, activists had to make only a small step to reach the suffrage issue. As one prohibitionist legislator proclaimed, "Kansas stands in the vanguard of progress; the state, which took the first step in prohibiting the sale of intoxicating liquors as a beverage, will take one step higher, in advance of her sister States, and give women the vote."[157] For Woman Movement activists and their supporters, "Liberal Kansas" appeared poised to fulfill its promise at last.

# TWO

# ⊰ "AT HOME AMONG YOU" ⊱

## THE RISE OF THE KANSAS WOMAN MOVEMENT

When the Kansas Women's Christian Temperance Union (WCTU) held its first meeting in 1879, there existed no state woman suffrage association and little sense that middle-class women as a group could influence electoral politics. Ten years later, when a unified Woman Movement routed the Kansas legislature's attempt to lower the age of consent, both the Kansas Equal Suffrage Association (KESA) and the notion of women's political power were well established. Between these two milestones, urban Anglo middle-class women in Kansas created a political counterculture. Taking their cue from women's organizations in the East, the newly created Woman Movement developed a form of politics founded on evangelical Protestant and domestic middle-class values. This "respectable" political culture enabled Woman Movement activists to recruit their core constituency with ever increasing success during the 1880s. Throughout the decade, the Woman Movement rarely had the need, or the desire, to stray far beyond these carefully circumscribed boundaries. The political culture it created and sustained served it well, and by the end of the decade it had a number of political victories to its credit. Most importantly, the Republican leadership acknowledged its growing power and courted its support.

Activists in the Kansas Woman Movement faced a balancing act of sorts. They needed to appropriate respectable social activities and convert them— or subvert them—into political activities while maintaining their respectability. One of the earliest meeting places for middle-class women was the parlor, where they could take part in a socially sanctioned activity, afternoon tea, while conducting everything from missionary society meetings to literary clubs to moral reform associations. Originating largely from women's church activities, these endeavors provided women with the skills necessary for active citizenship, including facilitating and participating in meetings, electing officers, recruiting members, voting, and raising money. The Protestant church and the middle-class parlor were female-identified "free social spaces" where women developed self-confidence away from the dominating presence of men.[1]

But free social spaces are never entirely free of the dominant culture.[2] As Nancy Cott has noted, the "bonds of womanhood" established by nineteenth-century women's groups "had a dual potential: to encourage women's independence and self-definition within a supportive community, and to accommodate them to a limited, clerically defined role."[3] These social spaces were not free in another sense: as a product of a particular culture, they served to reinforce the identity of the group while excluding others. Those who entered were expected to conform to the social norms—the rules—of the place. These rules, a Woman Movement activist might have explained, were simple: one needed only to be "respectable."

The Woman Movement succeeded in Kansas by providing urban Anglo middle-class women a place they could call their own. Their goal was to "civilize" their state and town, to tame the wild ways of all those who did not accept their definition of respectability, including certain middle-class men. Activists sought to uplift "lower" orders while maintaining and reaffirming middle-class values. In theory, anyone willing to embrace their notion of respectability would be welcomed into their cause. Yet women reformers also expected initiates to wear the badges of respectability, including proper clothes, language, and manners. Such distinctions did not need to be stated: the parlor served as a convenient barrier to entry, helping to maintain a homogenous political culture.

Activists of the Woman Movement hoped to infuse the political parties with respectable values by word and deed. They sought to banish all forms of political bribery, chicanery, and patronage, all types of voter apathy and ignorance. Many women activists, however, were not quite sure whether their loyalty lay with their party or with the movement. When the interests of the two coincided, all was well. But when they diverged, women activists had to confront the dissonance between their vision of a nonpartisan political sisterhood and the reality of party politics in Kansas. As the Woman Movement developed, activists found themselves making choices about who was and was not to be included in their movement and whether their movement could be involved with partisan politics.

## THE IDEAL OF POLITICAL SISTERHOOD: ELITISM AND ITS USES

Racism and nativism have been constant presences throughout American history; only the ebb and flow of their intensity has changed. During the Gilded Age, middle-class Anglo-Americans exhibited a range of prejudices notable for their virulence and brutality. Their contempt extended to African-Americans, Chinese, Catholics, Jews, and Eastern and Southern European immigrants. The middle class also fostered a growing distrust of "the laboring class." These suspicions grew with the violent strikes of 1877 and reached a near hysterical pitch after the Haymarket Riot of 1888.

Most Woman Movement activists shared these opinions, which influenced their approach to reform. The members of the WCTU and KESA held nativist, racist, and classist beliefs that shaped their organizing efforts among "their own kind" as well as their relationship with other groups. Yet while the WCTU and KESA had overlapping memberships and beliefs, they diverged in their ideology, strategy, and purpose. KESA often made use of the fears of the Anglo middle class to further suffragists' claims of respectability. While the WCTU was hardly free of these prejudices, many of its members struggled with the issue of how to claim an all-inclusive sisterhood made up of one class of women.

Although the national suffrage movement had its roots in abolitionism, KESA members tended to be much less sensitive to the needs of Afro-American women than were temperance women. Most suffragists had drifted away from racial tolerance, to the extent that many felt no connection to past efforts for black civil rights. Elizabeth Cady Stanton exhibited an almost visceral sense of betrayal in her later writings, suggesting that reformers had loosed "ignorant" blacks among the American electorate while denying educated Anglo-American women the vote. Kansas suffragists often used similar arguments, claiming that since only the "best" women would go to the polls, they would offset the "ignorant" male voters. Yet Kansas suffragists usually excluded blacks from their lists of undesirables.

Kansas suffragists favored a benign racism that might be labeled "maternalistic"—they believed in their duty to enlighten and raise up those beneath them.[4] When making the case for woman suffrage, Kansas suffragists constantly appropriated their state's role in helping free the slaves. One woman suffrage paper in Kansas, drawing on twenty-five years of Republican rhetoric, intoned, "This will never be a free nation so long as mothers are slaves. You can't raise free men from slave mothers."[5] Laura Johns, in her 1887 presidential address to the KESA convention, placed woman suffrage firmly within the myth of "Progressive Kansas" when she declared,

> From the time this wild prairie land bloomed out of the unknown into the blossoming, coveted Territory, and through the long "free soil" struggle into Statehood; through the battle fierce for the emancipation of the black man from slavery to the white master, and from the emancipation of all men from slavery to King Alcohol; through . . . the labors abundant for all reforms looking toward the elevation of our sex and humanity, have the women of Kansas, with grand courage, strength and faith, ever with the uplifted glance, borne their large part.[6]

In choosing to make use of this powerful tradition, suffragists effectively avoided using overt racism as a tactic.

Some suffragists believed that African-Americans, whom reformers had already "saved" once, could again be redeemed and made into acceptable citizens. Johns challenged the argument that blacks had not responded properly to citizenship by noting that white women had not all been model voters when first given municipal woman suffrage. In fact, she noted, no group of Americans, whatever their station or race, could claim an unblemished record as citizens—and certainly not men, who had produced so many corrupt, apathetic, and incompetent governments.[7]

KESA also had political reasons for not accenting racist arguments for woman suffrage. As Johns noted in her 1889 convention address, blacks constituted the largest non-Anglo group in Kansas, with 5 percent of the population. As most of them were concentrated in the large cities and towns, they were potentially crucial swing votes in municipal elections. Yet while Johns called for greater efforts to "work among the colored people," KESA did little to reach black women or men.[8] By 1890, KESA, which organized separate "colored" chapters, had only three active black locals in the state.

By repeating the code word *best* like a litany, suffragists hoped to convince the middle class that they not only were of "their own kind," but represented the cream of respectable society. This approach certainly had an effect on John

McDonald, editor of the *Western School Journal*. At the 1891 KESA convention, McDonald admitted that he had come to Kansas an anti–woman suffragist but had been converted after realizing that "it was the best women, the best mothers, wives, and housekeepers, who were for woman suffrage."[9]

Suffragists were fond of noting that women voters were inevitably the most refined, charming, and best-dressed women in town, as if the act of voting lent one an air of sophistication not unlike the latest fashion. Such comments served not only as an argument for woman suffrage but also as an inducement to join this elite sisterhood. For although KESA worked with women's charitable, literary, and social clubs while organizing suffrage campaigns, it was also competing with these organizations for the time, money, and commitment of middle-class women. Since many middle-class Kansans viewed KESA as a radical movement outside the mainstream, woman suffrage needed to appear not only respectable but fashionable as well.

The fixation of suffrage supporters on their own feminine qualities had as much to do with gender relations as with elitism and was in part a response to comments that suffragists were all "long haired men and short haired women, the unsexed of both sexes."[10] Such claims tapped a deep fear in men that political activity would forever alter women's "basic nature." Suffrage supporters attempted to soothe men's concerns by stressing their femininity and rejecting charges of mannishness. One, hoping no doubt to soften the forbidding image of Susan B. Anthony, reported, "Miss Susan B. Anthony dresses in black satin marveileux, stylishly made, with ruching at throat and wrists. Her hair is parted in the middle and combed down plain and smooth Quaker fashion. She is anything but 'women's rights' looking." One historian of the movement relates that for an upcoming suffrage fair, Laura Johns "urged [women] to bring . . . any article that would prove that voting in municipal elections had not unsexed them."[11] Of course only those who could afford the latest fashions would have been able to respond to Johns's call. In order to maintain a feminine image, it helped to have the money to dress the part.

Unlike KESA, temperance activists never had to counter charges that "debased" women would take part in their activities. With their foundation in the Protestant church, WCTU members rarely needed to claim that only the best women belonged to their organization. At bottom, because the WCTU was an evangelical organization dedicated to bringing others into the family of Christ, inclusiveness carried a moral imperative for some members and muted the elitism of others.

While the WCTU's agenda called for its members to bring outsiders into the fold, it was unclear what the nature of the relationship might be. In Kansas, temperance activists showed a much greater willingness to proselytize than to organize the foreign born.[12] Mary Day, state superintendent of the Work Among Foreigners Department, reported, "The census of 1880 tells us we have in our state more than 110,000 *foreign-born* citizens. The success of our work depends *largely* on the influence we have over them."[13] An earlier superintendent noted that the problem with "foreigners"—particularly Germans—was that they were, well, foreign. Beyond their proclivity to drink beer, their adherence to their own culture also upset her and other temperance reformers. The superintendent observed, "This class of our citizens—for citizens they are, with full powers of self-government . . . —have brought with them languages and customs peculiar to their fatherland." Since immigrants' citizenship was inevitable, the most pressing concern was "How shall they become Americanized and not endanger our free institutions?" "They must be enlightened," the superintendent insisted, "or laws inimical to our best interest will be the result of their enfranchisement."[14]

While both KESA and the WCTU viewed immigrants as a threat, each organization proposed different remedies. KESA argued that a quick infusion of Anglo women's votes would do the trick; the WCTU offered to convert foreigners into good Americans. Whether German immigrants appreciated such differences is doubtful, and most German-born men remained adamantly opposed to both woman suffrage and prohibition throughout the nineteenth century.

Many temperance workers believed it their duty to save African-Americans, as well. Echoing Johns's claims, a local superintendent of the Work Among Coloreds Department argued that slavery had robbed blacks "of the ages of culture and education that has been thrown around us; if we had no better advantages than they, could we do better?" The writer prefaced her remarks by asking, "Is there not some woman in every town where there are colored women that will gladly help to lead and teach these women that have so recently come out of bondage and ignorance?"[15] Despite the benevolent racism, the writer at least indicated a willingness to include black women in the WCTU's work.

Some temperance activists went beyond maternalistic concerns for African-Americans and embraced an egalitarianism that was quite radical for its time. Mrs. L. B. Smith, a former WCTU president, instructed temperance activists interested in working with black people: "First in importance is to *forget* the *distinction of race;* make them feel that while you want to benefit them, you want them to be—not mere recipients of favors, but helpers and allies in this cause, filling their quota of good character to the sum total of national life;

thus their self-respect and interest will be awakened." Lillie Hillard, a county superintendent, reminded WCTU members that all temperance activists, not just those in the Work Among Coloreds Department, should strive to include African-Americans. She claimed, with a pointed qualifier, that she was "sure the superintendents of various lines of work—many of them—would gladly extend their work, regardless of the color line."[16] She closed by reminding her readers that "our work is for God, and home, and *humanity*—not for any particular sex, or color, or nationality."

Such exhortations made it clear that while racism remained strong within the organization, pleas for racial tolerance and equality also had a place in the WCTU's political discourse. There were numerous reports of Anglo women in Kansas enthusiastically giving their time and money to black fund-raising efforts, apparently free of attached strings. White temperance activists also aided black WCTU members in their attempt to build a Home for the Aged and Orphaned in Leavenworth. The facility, which the African-American community needed desperately, proved to be an immensely successful organizing tool for black WCTU chapters.[17] Such projects enabled African-Americans to shape their WCTU chapter to the needs of the community rather than simply fulfill the agenda of white reformers.

Many white temperance activists realized their missionary efforts to save their black sisters were making little headway. To remedy this, they encouraged the work of black WCTU members "among their own kind." In 1888, the WCTU hired Naomi Anderson of Wichita as an organizer and instructed her to "carry the gospel of temperance to her own race."[18] Lest any Anglo temperance activists challenge Anderson's credentials while organizing, Fanny Rastall, president of the WCTU, felt compelled to amend this announcement with the declaration that Anderson was a WCTU member in good standing. Like the slave narratives before the Civil War, black activists needed white validation to gain credibility outside the Afro-American community.

Frances Harper, an Afro-American reformer who served as the national superintendent of the Work Among Coloreds Department, managed to recruit black temperance activists while making small steps to improve the racial tolerance of white activists. A former abolitionist and strong suffragist, Harper had turned to temperance work in the 1880s. Constantly touring the country, she provided a stirring role model for African-American women interested in temperance reform. Harper, who had a considerable reputation as a writer and orator, attracted large crowds of both blacks and whites to her Kansas talks. Her lectures were among the few integrated public events in the state, encouraging whatever racial tolerance existed among Anglos at the time.[19]

The black community had a decidedly mixed reaction to the WCTU's efforts. Black ministers, editors, and other members of the middle class provided the most support, but even here one finds ambivalence toward temperance activists. Black editors and ministers preached the gospel of "race progress," which included a condemnation of African-Americans who drank extensively, or whose antisocial behavior could be traced to drink. But leaders also believed that white officials had enforced prohibition unfairly by consistently raiding black "joints" while ignoring the more ostentatious white "clubs."[20] African-American leaders were interested in moral suasion and uplift; they were not in favor of filling the jails with black men and city coffers with fines from the meager wages of black families.[21]

Black editors praised the WCTU's religious and benevolent efforts, and black women's part in this, while reserving judgment about the organization's political activities.[22] But the African-American press showed little support for, and some hostility toward, the idea of women's involvement in politics, particularly for black women. Since suffrage organizations did not have the WCTU's benevolent activities to recommend them—and were elitist to boot—black newspapers ignored or criticized them. Their editors believed that such forays into the political realm would only distract black women from the reality that white people had forced upon them. One writer began his article by placing black women on a pedestal: "This race has produced some of the grandest women that the finger of creation ever touched—women whose accomplishments enrich the history of the race and bedeck the cities of the continent." Despite these glowing exceptions, however, "a majority of our girls must be taught trades to sew, cook, wash, printing, telegraphy, etc. Girls, put off those triangle bonnets, silk dresses, double-jointed rings, go to work, be useful, and educate yourself."[23] Black women leaders such as Ida B. Wells and Frances Harper were not to serve as role models; rather, like stars in the sky, their position in society was to be admired but never attained.

Black women in Kansas were not so willing to concede their helplessness. Their letters to the *American Citizen,* always printed without comment, reveal their interest in municipal suffrage and their belief that black women could use the vote to help "improve the race." Several women noted that the new municipal woman suffrage law would enable African-Americans to "banish the saloon, the bane of our people." One woman urged the Republican Party to adopt a woman suffrage platform: "so that the greatest and highest good may result from the right of franchise, let all . . . join heart and hand against the one great social evil in our land, and abolish the liquor traffic."[24] Black middle-class women saw alcohol as an immediate threat to their family and race. Whereas black editors tended to view the liquor question in terms of race progress alone, many Black women, like other women, had known or experienced the emotional or physical violence of drunken husbands, fathers, and acquaintances.

Although numerous African-American women wrote to their newspapers in support of woman suffrage, they always began with a reference to race progress. The letter writers shared the black middle-class values espoused by the newspapers. These women also believed that the threat posed by racist America—including lynching—took precedence over the suffrage issue. Unlike white suffragists, they did not compare women's disenfranchisement with slavery, a comparison African-Americans would have found ridiculous. They eschewed talk of solidarity with other groups of women, focusing their arguments for woman suffrage on its positive impact on blacks as a race.

While black women acknowledged the need for race solidarity, they sometimes exhibited exasperation, in a sardonic tone, at having to downplay their interest in women's rights issues. Anna Smith, from Valley Falls, Kansas, began her letter respectfully, praising the *American Citizen*, the Republican Party, and efforts at race progress. She concluded, however: "Am also in sympathy with the Woman's Suffrage question, and long to see the day when the ladies will have the same privileges at the polls that the men now have. We, the women, would like to elect some of the noble and qualified men of our race. . . . Yet as we are not allowed, we gracefully submit to our lot, and hope ye lords will perform the duty well."[25] With her elaborate bow to "the lords of creation," Smith was acknowledging women's subordination while attempting to deflate men's pretensions. Although black women chose their mixed-gender group over their gender-specific causes, just how "gracefully" they did so will never be known.

Middle-class black women's support for suffrage and temperance, despite the ambivalence of black men and Anglo women activists, points to the shifting fault lines of Kansas politics. African-American women supported these causes because they believed woman suffrage and prohibition would help their race and promote the status of women within the black community. Further, they could connect with Anglo-dominated women's organizations, particularly the WCTU, in a way that immigrant women could not.

Black and Anglo women shared a common language and religion, as well as a common nationality. Blacks, after all, were born on the same American soil as Anglos, however much whites might have liked to deny this. Some African-Americans tried to take advantage of this shared heritage by embracing the nativist rhetoric of Anglos. Frances Harper, after noting that African-

Americans were never found among bomb-throwing—and "foreign"—anarchists, pledged blacks' fealty to the American flag thus: "every *American-born* child shall be able to read upon its folds liberty for all and chains for none."[26] Further, middle-class black women adhered to the basic tenets of the ideal of domesticity, as well as some of the same values. Anglo women activists could consider their black sisters to be respectable, if not quite equal.

While some WCTU members overcame the most vile racist assumptions of their culture, most of them were unable to surmount the cultural and geographic barriers that separated them from their "sisters on the farm." Farm women in Kansas were overwhelmingly Anglo and Protestant and shared the Woman Movement's middle-class values of frugality, hard work, restraint, and "purity." In fact, because of economic necessity, farm women probably practiced these values to a greater degree than urban women. What most farm women lacked, however, were "town ways." They rarely acquired the manners and language of those raised in urban areas, who had access to the latest styles and trends of the nation's metropolitan centers.

The distance between farm and town was not merely cultural, of course; most farm women would have had to travel many miles to attend suffrage or temperance meetings, most of which took place in town. Since going into town was usually a luxury, few could afford to take the time needed to attend. Nor might a farm woman's husband think highly of such a trip, with so much work to be done, though no doubt he saw his own excursions to attend political conventions and meetings as the fulfillment of his duty as a citizen.

One answer to these barriers would have been for Woman Movement activists to organize farm women into country chapters, just as they had helped establish separate "colored" locals. This strategy was in fact proposed by a number of leaders, including Laura Johns, who noted in 1887: "The organization of our auxiliaries is too much confined to the cities. Three fourths of our population is in the country, and our few country clubs are among the best and the brightest; therefore we should this year see to it that school districts receive more attention than heretofore."[27] Despite such suggestions, neither KESA nor the WCTU did much to organize or encourage farm women. Perhaps the WCTU should have created a Department for Work among Farm People. But since temperance activists categorized Kansas rural folk as part of the mainstream, the WCTU saw no point in saving them.

Laura Johns was right in identifying the potential support among farm women and men. The Grange had wholeheartedly endorsed woman suffrage and encouraged women's participation in the organization's activities and its local leadership. Rural townships had far surpassed urban centers in their support of the prohibition amendment. In fact, the prohibitionists' strategy of organizing the rural districts, as well as creating social spaces in town meetings amenable to farm people's culture, contributed significantly to the amendment's narrow victory. Yet even as the Farmers' Alliance began to organize in 1888, Woman Movement activists made no move to tap this potential and increasingly well-organized source of support. Although suffrage activists would have been startled to discover it, many were less able to travel the cultural distance between farm and town than to cross the divide that separated middle-class black and white women.

## A Separate Place: Building the Woman Movement

The Woman Movement's insistence on respectability created an imposing barrier to entry. To those on the outside peering in, this respectable fortress must have seemed rather cold, unwelcoming, and forbidding. But the same walls helped create a safe, nurturing, and familiar environment for those inside. For the respectable few, part of the charm of the movement's gatherings was knowing that they had passed muster, that they had been accepted into a self-selected group of energetic, like-minded, and like-cultured, women. The sites of these gatherings bespoke their sensibilities of gender, class, race, ethnicity, geography, and religion.

For many Anglo middle-class women, the parlor and the church were the only places where they could even imagine themselves entering—even tiptoeing—into the realm of politics. Experienced Woman Movement activists referred to these meetings as "drawing room work." Here a woman could take her first hesitant steps into the political arena, comforted by the presence of like-minded women eager to coach and encourage their neophyte sister. No men stood in the background ready to chortle over a mispronounced word or a misunderstood parliamentary procedure; no husband or brother to correct a halting opinion. The meetings were run under Robert's Rules of Order and were guided by the golden rule—Do unto others as you would have them do unto you. To activists this was not an empty cliché: it was meant as the watchword of the movement, and they expected that all women would follow its basic precept.

From these intimate gatherings, women could move on to more demanding events, including local, district, and state conventions. The larger and more important the convention, the more activists valued a command of Robert's Rules over strict adherence to the golden rule. Woman Movement organizations believed that all members should learn the skills necessary to participate in a political debate. Only then could they hold their own in a nominating convention filled with men only too willing to use their cultural prerogatives to their advantage; only then could they become active, engaged, and effective citizens.

Men, after all, were used to getting the last word; they were partial to getting the first word as well. Women needed to overcome men's basic assumptions about women in politics: that men knew best, that women should accede to men's wishes, that women were not expected to show men up. Johns, in her 1887 KESA address, commended Woman Movement activists for quickly gaining a command of these complex rules. "To-day we have many women who are able parliamentarians," she noted, taking care to highlight the example of Fanny Rastall. She also found "among [Women's Relief Corps] women knowledge of parliamentary tactics that challenges admiration and commands respect. In our own auxiliaries our women are displaying an equal aptness with our brothers in learning and displaying the rules that govern assemblies and expedite the business of the same."[28] If women were to transform politics, they would first have to learn the ground rules set down by those in power.

Parliamentary rules were just the first step in a woman's political education. She also needed to acquire enough information on political and economic matters to have something worthwhile to say once she had the floor. A "suffrage society should be a school for [its members'] development, and in a new direction," Johns maintained. "There are other organizations in which they may learn domestic economy; let them here learn political economy. Elsewhere they may learn about the perturbations of the planets; let them learn the interaction of parties. I think it is safe to say that more women know about the solar system than about the Constitution of the United States." Woman Movement organizations could be the stepping stones for women wishing to move from concerns of the home to concerns of the world. "Suffrage societies ought to stir women to do more thinking for themselves, to arrive at their own conclusions from their own study of conditions and measures, principles and movements. Women want more self-determination."[29] For Johns, simply winning the suffrage without proper education would be meaningless, merely piling more ignorance upon ignorance.

If women were to learn about "the science of government," they needed to have access to material that had heretofore been considered outside their realm of interest. Both the WCTU and KESA saw to it that their members were well provided with reams of literature addressing everything from dress reform to the tariff question to the role of cabinet ministers, as well as temperance and woman suffrage issues. "Feel the intellectual pulse of an organization and it will tell its true condition," Fanny Rastall lectured the 1887 WCTU convention. "The best thing to prescribe is a nourishing mental diet. No well-read, well-informed Union ever failed in interest or in effort. Those organizations that take and read papers and documents prepared for our especial use most correctly measure their value, and desire to provide others with the same privileges."[30] The Kansas WCTU began publishing its own paper, *Our Messenger,* in 1886, and it also made use of the national WCTU's *Union Signal.* KESA maintained a column in the Western-oriented *Women's Tribune,* published in Omaha, and urged suffragists to take the nationally distributed *Women's Journal* along with other "progressive" magazines.[31] The WCTU was also able to persuade a number of local newspapers to carry occasional "temperance columns" to spread the good word to both members and potential supporters.

Having acquired the basic facts, women now needed to learn about the unofficial lessons of politics. The golden rule was fine for the parlor, but in the rough-and-tumble electoral arena, it did not afford much insight into the workings of government. As Johns warned her audience, women had to be aware of "the tactics of the rounders, strikers, and bosses, the contemplation of which with the mal-administration of municipal affairs, disgusts the majority of women and cheapens the ballot in their estimation. There is something not in the books for women to learn—it is that which comes with experience and observation."[32]

Several years earlier, Johns had indicated that such lessons would be difficult for both the leadership and rank and file. "Those of us who have served this organization have found no beaten path, and we had no previous experience," Johns confessed. "We have had to learn our work doing it, and the lessons thus learned have sometimes been costly and painful. We were like generals undertaking, without knowledge of military tactics and short of munitions, to lead a great but undisciplined force uphill, against a well *manned* and strongly provisioned citadel."[33] The battle lines had been drawn, and the Woman Movement had drawn them. As Johns's pun and her military metaphor indicate, women reformers were fighting a war against an enemy who had managed to acquire superior intellectual skills through the trick of culture. Women lacked the experience that had been denied them by men, so now they must drill constantly if they were eventually to triumph. Little wonder, then, that some men feared an upheaval of gender relations.

The Woman Movement was not all business, although its detractors liked to depict its members as killjoys, unsmiling shrews, and "senile old ladies."[34] Rather, both the WCTU and KESA realized that providing entertainment was as important as promoting spiritual and intellectual growth. The WCTU had an added incentive, for they needed to present Kansas men with an alternative to the saloon and the bawdy theater. Temperance activists sponsored numerous dances and socials where thirst could be slaked by bounteous supplies of lemonade and ice cream, but no beer.[35] Whether in fact men saw these elevated diversions as a substitute for dancing girls and booze is highly unlikely, but the WCTU's events did serve as a way to attract the middle class in a nonthreatening atmosphere. In many ways, these affairs helped bridge the gap between the WCTU's vision of a political sisterhood and its commitment to preserving the heterosexual institution of the family.

The WCTU's Young Woman's Christian Temperance Unions, known as Ys, were particularly active in organizing social events that replicated the standard heterosocial gatherings for young people at the time. Perhaps unique to farm states was the "corn social," with a bill of fare that featured "corn mush and milk, hulled corn, canned corn, corn meal gems, cornstarch cake with popcorns on top" and a program that included readings of Whittier's "Corn Song" and "The Huskers" and " 'Popping Corn' in a hundred selections."[36] Such was the stuff of small-town life in Kansas, and the Y's "pumpkin pie socials" and "Japanese weddings" proved to be effective for drawing in new members, raising money, and handing out temperance literature. The Ys lent the temperance movement a much-needed sense of play and youthful enthusiasm that leavened the sometimes forbidding image of crusading WCTU members. The Ys were yet another dimension that the WCTU could offer prospective members.

In order to educate women properly in the art of political warfare, the Woman Movement first had to attract potential members. The parlor meetings served this purpose and worked particularly well with upper-class women who preferred a refined setting in which to experience their political conversion. For more middle-class tastes, both the WCTU and KESA organized mass meetings to attract the curious. The WCTU was more apt to use churches, while KESA usually rented the town hall or opera house. In either case, meetings were labeled "lectures" and were promoted much as were the traveling lyceums and chautauquas that crisscrossed America at the time. Middle-class Kansans saw such events as cultured entertainment and were especially likely to attend if the featured speaker was a well-known figure such as Susan B. Anthony or Frances Willard. Often activists used these events to raise money as well as consciousness.[37]

All the different activities—the tea parties, the mass meetings, the socials, and the discussion groups—helped to build the two organizations by bits and pieces. A few potential converts here, a few new members there, the movement's fortunes rose slowly, at times imperceptibly, creeping forward at an ice cream social in Moundridge, a suffrage lecture in Hays. At the annual conventions, the organizations were able to take stock and to glory in the combined achievements for the year. Among an ever growing cadre of like-minded activists, women could reinforce their faltering convictions or flagging energies by listening to the various triumphs being touted by the assembled delegates. Although men occasionally spoke at KESA meetings, both conventions were dominated by women acting as delegates, speakers, and chairpersons. These gatherings were celebrations of women's ability to organize and expedite large-scale political events. The WCTU conventions were particularly demanding, with all the state's departments, officers, and districts reporting their successes and failures. Despite the crowded schedule, delegates attended committee meetings, debated resolutions, and designed and ratified a plan of work for the coming year. Business matters were interspersed with delegates joining together in spirited songs, surrounded by political banners, flowers, and brightly colored bunting.[38]

Those who attended the conventions were repaid by witnessing their vision of political sisterhood come to life. Here political, forceful women were the norm; here woman suffrage and prohibition were not controversial beliefs but basic foundations of one's political ideology. Everywhere one looked, declared the Burlingame WCTU president, were "sisters [we] have met on other like occasions, whose faces have become familiar to us and whose names as dear as household words, and [newcomers] . . . who will henceforth be no strangers to us." Fanny Rastall captured the intensity of feeling created by the Woman Movement's political culture in her 1891 presidential address: "I realize I am at home once more among you; that I am with women who know and trust me and whom I know and trust; women who have united their efforts with mine for years to accomplish a purpose we deemed of the greatest of importance and won victories and met discouragements in its pursuit. [T]hese trials and conflicts have bound us closely together, and though separated in the future, our lives in the past have so entered into the life of each other that we cannot forget if we could."[39] The Woman Movement offered its members not only the opportunity to effect meaningful change in the world but also the chance to share in its emotionally fulfilling community of women.

The intense love of one's fellow crusaders was a powerful motivating force, but unfortunately it did not pay the bills. Women activists constantly worried about raising sufficient funds to keep their organization operating. In all the Woman Movement's undertakings, the business of soliciting contributions and collecting dues took up a substantial amount of time. KESA was so hard pressed for cash during its early years that Bertha Ellsworth, the sole state organizer, was forced to split her time between talking about the cause to potential members and selling the reform-oriented books that brought in her only income. This plan might have succeeded, except "that financial gain and hunting up suffragists do not uniformly lie in the same channel, and one is either in danger of sacrificing the municipal suffrage petition and the long personal interviews, which I have found most affecting in inducing women to take an active part in the suffrage work; or, on the other hand, in giving to the suffrage work the thorough attention and tact it demands, one is apt to find they have made no money. I made that discovery with unpleasant frequency."[40]

Since both KESA and the WCTU depended on paid organizers to create new chapters, state officers frequently bewailed the financial constraints that hindered their growth. The movements depended on organizers to bring together women for that first parlor or church meeting. Further, organizers needed to find a few women in each town with enough talent, commitment, and moxie to sustain the infant chapter through its first uncertain months. Identifying these local leaders was an organizer's first priority, Ellsworth explained, because, "The best, most thoughtful, reliable and valuable workers do not always come to the surface in public. Some *cannot*. One must *fish* for a knowledge of their worth and abilities through private and personal channels. But once discovered and touched with a consciousness of what they *can* and *ought* to do, how gloriously some of them develop, even into public service of the most efficient kind."[41] It was on just such a fishing expedition in Salina, Kansas, that Ellsworth discovered Laura Johns, newly transported from the East. By the time Ellsworth left the city, Johns had established Salina's first KESA chapter.

Such success stories, however, could come about only if the Woman Movement had the resources to support its organizers, and for much of the time it did not. The constant scramble for cash suggests middle-class women's lack of control over their families' finances. Despite both organizations' solidly middle-class membership, state and local treasurers constantly, though gently, admonished members to pay their dues of between fifty cents and a dollar a year. One may infer that there were a number of husbands who tolerated their wives attending a Sunday afternoon meeting but who were fairly unenthusiastic about having to pay for the privilege.

Activists in the Woman Movement understood that men controlled the money and thus needed to be approached for contributions. Such solicitations meant breaching certain middle-class rules of etiquette. Ellsworth noted, "I had to overcome my repugnance to interviewing men on the money question on the business streets and in business hours, and . . . I met quite a number of freezing expressions of 'who are you, and what are you intruding upon my time for, anyway?' "[42] Eventually, however, she overcame her discomfort, although perhaps many of her intended targets remained somewhat nonplused. For many men, Ellsworth's solicitations were just the type of crime against nature they feared would come of woman suffrage.

Ellsworth's account gives some idea of the sacrifices demanded of the organizations' leaders, especially during the early years. Because both the WCTU and KESA got off to slow starts, it was the leadership's commitment and hard work that enabled them to reach a critical mass by the late 1880s. Many of the leaders traveled at their own expense while working full time for the cause. Some single women, like Bertha Ellsworth, lived hand to mouth, depending on their wits, the hospitality of supporters, and the occasional teaching job to sustain them. Certain married women, like Annie Diggs, supported themselves through newspaper work and lecturing. Finally, women such as Fanny Rastall were aided in their work by affluent husbands. In most cases, they took on enormous responsibility, both as leaders and as role models.

Committed, talented leadership was crucial to the Woman Movement's success. For however right the cultural conditions in Kansas may have been, the movement's achievements were not foreordained. Although the movement's members gained a sense of political empowerment, their activities placed them on the margins of what mainstream society—including many of their friends and neighbors—considered acceptable behavior. And while the movement provided women with support and companionship, other, less risky organizations offered that as well. The early years bear this out: although the Woman Movement contained the potential to succeed in Kansas, both the WCTU and KESA drifted at first. Individual leaders had to step forward and provide their members with a sense of direction and momentum.

Laura Johns and Fanny Rastall were the right women at the right time, bringing to their floundering organizations a sense of purpose and direction. More importantly, they quickly demonstrated a range of skills; they could speak and write persuasively, organize lecture tours as well as local events, lobby legislators, and raise money while keeping a careful eye on expenditures. Each displayed a canny political mind, correctly charting the prevailing political winds and shifting their organizations' strategy accordingly. During their stewardships (Johns's from 1887 to 1895, Rastall's from 1885 to 1891), KESA and the WCTU grew quickly and received increasing respect from the male political leaders of the state. Yet both women found themselves challenged by shifting political conditions at the end of their terms.

Johns, the younger of the two, had moved to Salina from Illinois, where she and her husband were schoolteachers, in 1883. After Ellsworth knocked on her front door, Johns turned her energies to reform, first as president of the Salina chapter, then as vice president (1885–86) and president (1887–95) of KESA. A committed temperance activist, she served as state superintendent of the WCTU's Department of Scientific Temperance Instruction.[43]

Rastall had moved from Milwaukee to Kansas in 1869, after marrying John Rastall the year before. In Kansas, John Rastall published the staunchly prohibitionist newspaper the Burlingame *Chronicle*. Fanny Rastall initiated her career with the Kansas WCTU with a stint as recording secretary (1881–84). Despite an initial terror of public speaking, she quickly gained confidence lecturing to WCTU members. In 1885 she was elected president of the organization, a post she held for six years, when she left to serve on the national WCTU board. Rastall balanced Johns's prohibitionist sentiments by being an early and active supporter of woman suffrage. By their example and their policies, they helped foster a shared sense of purpose between the two organizations.[44]

## Negotiating Boundaries: The WCTU and KESA in the Political Arena

While both KESA and the WCTU grew in influence and membership during the 1880s and early 1890s, they did so at different rates and at different times. In part, this may be traced to Rastall's and Johns's tenure of office: the WCTU began its ascent in 1885 and peaked in 1890, whereas KESA's greatest successes came between 1887 and 1894. But Johns's and Rastall's years of leadership also coincided with a political context that provided each organization with particular opportunities. Although they shared many features, the WCTU and KESA diverged in important ways and experienced different relationships with the political parties of the state and the nation.

During the 1880s, the national WCTU became the preeminent women's organization in America. Its rise coincided with the growth of the Prohibition Party, whose vote total grew markedly during the decade. For many Anglo middle-class women and men, prohibition was the answer to the many social disturbances they were witnessing. The middle class was particularly worried by the widespread, often violent strikes by working-class Americans, many of

"She came and saw and conquered":
Frances Willard, president of the
national WCTU. *Kansas State
Historical Society*

whom were recent immigrants. These conflicts led many in the Anglo middle
class to look for a panacea that would return order to the Republic, and prohibition seemed to fit the bill.[45]

Middle-class women had their own reasons for distrusting alcohol. They
were excluded from the saloon and from much social drinking, and yet they
were often helpless against the effects of male drunkenness and alcoholism.
The national WCTU, founded in 1874, offered women the opportunity to
combine their Protestant evangelism, worries about alcohol, and desire to reform society. The organization grew slowly but steadily during its first six
years. It took the vision and personality of Frances Willard, however, to shape
its concerns into an effective program.

Willard became national WCTU president in 1879, wresting control of the
organization from the more conservative Annie Wittenmyer. Constantly traveling, Willard devoted most of her time to writing, speaking, and organizing.
Through these efforts she became one of the best known and loved women of

the period, attracting both members and money wherever she went. Historian Ruth Bordin has written that Willard "was more than liked, she was loved, she was adored. Her intense, almost sexual attractiveness to members of her own sex was a major factor in her success. Women competed for her favors and cherished some intimate moment with her as they would a male lover."[46] Kansas women were no less susceptible to Willard's persona. One local admirer noted during the 1879 prohibition amendment campaign: "Well, Miss Willard 'came and saw and conquered,' and this is the feeling of the whole community. We can have but a meagre conception of what her power is by reading about it, or hearing of it from others; we must see and know her to understand what she is. As for our women, she left us all in a state of perfect infatuation. When I think of her and all the wonderful good she is doing, my heart warms and glows, and I feel almost a reverent admiration for her. . . . And I pray that God will preserve her health and prolong her days of usefulness, for verily there is, in all the world, but one *Frances Willard*."[47]

Much as Willard's charisma played a part in the national WCTU's growth, her "Do Everything" program was the real basis for the organization's success. As the name implied, Willard urged the organization to look beyond the narrow confines of temperance and to "make the world . . . HOMELIKE"—to bring the characteristics associated with the middle-class home to society at large. In Kansas, such calls to middle-class reform and Christian missionary work met a receptive audience. By 1890 the Kansas WCTU had thirty-three departments, including those for "Social Purity," "Peace," "Work among Railroad Men," "Sabbath Enforcement," and "Legislative and Franchise Work."[48] The range of interests encompassed by the WCTU enabled it to attract women who would have normally shied away from explicit political activity. Such women, however, were quite comfortable with the Department of Mercy. For some, these rather tame departments were but stepping stones to petition signing and participation in municipal politics. Even women who were content in their "Flower Work" aided the WCTU's political agenda by signing a petition, voting in municipal elections, and contributing dues to the state organization.

The varied work of the Kansas WCTU suggests that the members' perspective is not easily identifiable by modern standards. Neither entirely liberal nor conservative, they are also unrecognizable as modern feminists. Some members were in the front ranks of the woman suffrage cause, while others were busy working to close an "obscene" production of *Fanny Hill*. *Our Messenger* simultaneously demanded that government enforce Sabbath observance and decried government policy toward American Indians.[49]

The organization's aims were at the same time broadly humanitarian and aggressively authoritarian. Some WCTU members fought for prison reform, urging that "prisoners be treated like men, not brutes"; others protested war, declaring, "War is wrong; a huge, black, evil thing, and no amount of sophistry can ever make it right in the sight of our Heavenly Master."[50] Simultaneously, many of the organization's activities were aimed at imposing its view of social purity on the rest of the nation. Yet the WCTU did not see such undertakings as contradictory: all were part of its broad vision of women-centered reform. One could trace the path from the Gilded Age WCTU to Phyllis Schlafly's anti–Equal Rights Amendment brigades as easily as to modern-day feminists.

KESA began its existence with few of the advantages enjoyed by the WCTU. Suffragists did have some celebrities of their own, but none could match the drawing power—or the respectability—of Frances Willard. The suffragists' closest contender was Susan B. Anthony, but she brought with her a number of drawbacks. The Kansas Republican leadership never forgot or forgave Stanton and Anthony's "traitorous" alliance with George Train in 1867, and thus her influence with the G.O.P. old guard was limited. Further, the questionable political judgment she displayed in 1867 appears to have been a constant in her career; though a powerful speaker, she was a myopic tactician. Often she allowed her (usually justified) moral outrage at the machinations of male politicians to cloud her understanding of state and local politics. In fact, Anthony was sometimes too powerful a speaker, lacing her talks with witty, sarcastic attacks on prominent state and local politicians who opposed suffrage. These remarks, which greatly amused her audience, did little to increase her popularity among Republican leaders.[51]

Anthony, however, had a much more difficult task than Willard. Willard represented a respectable movement and enjoyed a substantial middle-class base of support among both women and men. Anthony was battling for a cause that had limited appeal at the time and was particularly threatening to men. She saw herself as an agitator for suffrage, drawing attention to her cause in the hopes that such a strategy would aid the long-term goal of a national woman suffrage amendment to the constitution.[52]

Local suffrage leaders had more immediate concerns. They needed to build a grass-roots movement that addressed the cultural needs of middle-class women in Kansas while gaining influence with political leaders. KESA could not offer the diversity of programs available to the WCTU. Instead it had one long-term goal, state woman suffrage, and a number of intermediate steps, including school bond and municipal woman suffrage. The WCTU's enthusiastic support for woman suffrage was both a help and a hindrance to KESA. Without the WCTU's influence and organizing efforts, passage of the municipal woman suffrage bill would have been impossible. Yet the WCTU, with its powerful enforcement issue, tended to overshadow suffragists' efforts to interest women in the larger suffrage issue. KESA assumed a position of authority in Kansas only after the Populist Party had shaken up state politics.

The two organizations' ideologies were similar enough that they never clashed over policies. Yet each maintained a different ideological focus that, for all their similarities, allowed women a choice of perspectives. All Woman Movement members shared the belief that woman was a moral, nurturing creature whereas man was in most cases either amoral and acquisitive or debased and cunning. Activists in the Woman Movement were quite clear as to who was responsible for the notoriously impure state of the nation and world. Eve may have handed the apple over to Adam, but from that point on he and his male descendants had made a mess of things.[53] But while the WCTU employed men as a metaphorical replacement for debauchery, selfishness, and other "male" traits, KESA approached the "problem" of men more pragmatically.

For the WCTU, men were rarely individuals but were rather an aggregate entity badly in need of moral instruction. Rastall, speaking at the 1886 convention, noted that men were the ones who fought prohibition, and for two reasons. "Either men want to drink intoxicants, or they are connected directly or remotely with the traffic from a financial stand point."[54] Men were the enemy because they took advantage of the opportunity to sin; they controlled the businesses, the government, the police force—all the official institutions of power. Having erred, now they had to be saved.

KESA shared some of these assumptions about men, faulting them for most of the ills of society. Like the WCTU, suffragists charged men with corruption, whether it be of politics or of innocent women. "Did you ever know a fallen woman," queried the *Kansas Suffrage* newspaper, "who hadn't been helped to her fall by some man?"[55] But the two organizations put these insights to very different uses. The WCTU's conventions were paeans to the power of righteous women over unrighteous men. Occasionally, individual men were praised either for embracing evangelical Christianity and forsaking the bottle or for being longtime supporters of prohibition. While WCTU members recognized that there were "good" men—including, presumably, their own husbands—the sex as a whole was suspect. "We must prove all men," warned Rastall, "and hold to those who are true."[56] On the other hand, all women were presumed innocent. Prostitutes were fallen women, those who had been seduced from their natural state of grace. In the eyes of the WCTU, evil dressed in pants.

KESA was more interested in winning men's support for woman suffrage than in saving their souls. Both groups pushed for woman suffrage, but the WCTU tended to view the franchise primarily as the means to better prohibition enforcement. Thanks to the prohibition amendment, the WCTU had the law on its side and demanded that men uphold it. KESA, however, was trying to change the law, and hence it spent more time considering how to approach and persuade men to support their cause than did the WCTU.

Suffragists came to believe that because men as a group had little sense of morality, they needed to be addressed in their own political language. Men, explained Laura Johns to the 1890 KESA convention, had a very different perspective from that of women. Men tolerated corrupt government because of "the absorption of men in business and professions making them apathetic to other matters; . . . the fact that there's money for the corruptionists who form the ring, and none for the honest advocates of good government. What a pity that work for a principle hasn't money in it! If there were 'boodle' on the side of fair play, decency and good order, would not these have more support?"[57] Women, by contrast, "had a higher standard of administrative efficiency, . . . sincerity [and] character in candidates" because they had an "enthusiasm and . . . spirit of helpfulness, a thoughtfulness and knowledge . . . born of faith in the right and ultimate triumph."

In order to persuade men to support woman suffrage, Johns believed it was necessary to resort to "the lower ground of expediency, when we would fain make our demand upon our *right*." The problem was that "The age is demanding results. The commercial spirit of the world is saying to us, 'What have you to offer?' The politician is asking, 'to which party will women give their strength, if we give them the ballot? and how many votes will they take?' The financier and the manufacturer are inquiring as to what effect women's enfranchisement will have upon wages and upon the industries. Rather than ask, 'is it right,' men [demand], 'what will the world get for it?' and until we have something to trade for our liberty I fancy we'll remain in political thralldom."[58] Johns realized that to win men's votes, suffragists would have to deal—in both senses of the word—with the dominant political culture. At KESA conventions, speakers tended to favor arguments accenting the natural right of women to be voters. When addressing men, however, particularly in the 1893–94 suffrage campaign, they turned to whatever tactic they felt was most effective at the time.

The WCTU suffered from no such confusion about tactics. Its speakers and

writers projected their arguments in unwavering, moralistic terms and left little room for Republican politicians to maneuver when it came to the issue of
prohibition enforcement. Since most politicians valued their ability to stick
their fingers in the air and point in the direction of the prevailing political
wind, the WCTU's inflexibility was a bit trying. Because the Republicans officially supported prohibition, however, few could condemn the organization
outright.

A number of politicians did remark on the danger of "over-zealousness,"
especially when a local officeholder felt he was getting undue heat from "the
ladies."[59] Rastall, a particularly vocal opponent of appeasement, noted that
the WCTU in Kansas had not gained the approval of those in power. "It takes
more courage to do our work in Kansas than in any State in the union," she
claimed. "Because we are not satisfied with present conditions we are misunderstood, called ingrates, traitors."[60] Many political leaders expected the
WCTU to play by the rules of men's political culture. Its members, however,
were writing rules of their own.

Even before municipal woman suffrage enabled the WCTU to take the bat-
tlefield as voters, the prohibition enforcement issue galvanized the organization to challenge the local judicial system. Indeed, while Rastall's fervent support of the "Do Everything" policy attracted women to the organization, it
was the local campaigns against the neighborhood joint that brought temperance women notoriety and political influence. By the mid-1880s, Kansas politicians and editors generally acknowledged the WCTU as the leading reason
for the ever growing success of prohibition enforcement. Kansas Attorney
General Simeon Bradford, in office from 1885 to 1888, called the organization
the backbone of the prohibition movement, having clearly succeeded the now
foundering Kansas State Temperance Union. Bradford acknowledged pri-
vately that WCTU representatives had "discussed their views quite fully with
me, and I found their views to be much more practical and sensible than the
men."[61]

Practical and sensible they were—and to Kansas "wets," downright scary.
State Republican leaders were content to make resolutions condemning the
"rum-soaked Democrats." The WCTU, meanwhile, was busy organizing local
forays against whoever dared to peddle alcohol to the townsfolk. It was particularly effective in the small towns, where it often organized a number of "leading (male) citizens" to head the assault.[62] Unlike the Women's Crusades of the
1870s, the Kansas WCTU's campaigns had the law on their side. Temperance
women could rely on the power of the courts to back up their efforts at moral
suasion—provided, of course, that local judges and police officers were made

to understand that their jobs would be in jeopardy if they did not take swift action. Local officials who proved recalcitrant, whether because of bribery, ideological objections, or their own drinking proclivities, could be voted out of office or reported to the state attorney general and risk jail themselves. After the passage of municipal suffrage, such electoral threats were rendered much more potent.

The WCTU's ongoing victories against liquor dealers and the corresponding public humiliation of these men set it apart from other women's organizations. It did not merely petition or lobby or plead, although its members could be quite effective in these areas. More ominously for men, women activists threatened to send them to jail. In a time when women's legal relationship to men was often that of helpless victim, such an obvious show of power was impressive.

Once prohibitionists had closed most of the small-town saloons, the WCTU turned its attention to those druggists who were selling alcohol as medicine and sent a number of formerly respectable middle-class merchants to prison.[63] When the U.S. Supreme Court ruled that liquor mailed from out of state could be resold in its "original packages" (o.p.), the WCTU took on this new challenge as well. In one town, *Our Messenger* reported, "The women of Olathe have taken the initiative and called a citizens' meeting to prevent the o.p. vendor from getting a foothold there. Mrs. J. P. St. John was called to preside. Many prominent citizens declared that they would have none of him, and that he must go, peacefully if he will, forcibly if he must."[64] Many women may have felt that joining such a posse meant transgressing far beyond the boundaries of decent womanhood. Others, however, found such opportunities, especially when sanctified by the local church and elites, to be a fine antidote to the political helplessness of "women's sphere."

For these women, prohibition was not a "symbolic crusade" but a practical response to a real threat.[65] Drunkenness and alcoholism were genuine problems in Gilded Age America and remain so today.[66] Women and children were often the victims of alcohol abuse, yet men were predominantly the drinkers. Drinking had moved from being a custom shared among family members in the eighteenth century to being a male ritual in the nineteenth. The saloon was a man's world; the dance hall girls and prostitutes were exceptions that proved the rule. Thus male patrons received all the benefits of the institution. Wives and daughters, however, had to pay the emotional, physical, and economic costs that often accompanied alcohol abuse.[67]

Only recently have we begun to understand the deep psychological wounds that alcoholics inflict on their families. Although we should avoid directly transferring the current vogue for "codependency" onto the Gilded Age, we can still assume that family members of alcoholics experienced feelings of helplessness, betrayal, and self-blame. The diaries of Martha Shaw Farnsworth of Kansas provide a window into the mind of an Anglo middle-class woman during this period.

Farnsworth married John Shaw in 1887 and soon after learned he was "addicted to drink." After Shaw attended his "beer parties," Farnsworth reported that he became insanely jealous, ill tempered, and physically abusive. Despite this, Farnsworth continually professed her love for him, even while excoriating the "influence of drink." She referred to alcohol as a malevolent, and seductive, third party. Unable to confront her husband about his addiction—her few attempts ended in violence—she was forced to lead a double life. One day she reported, "The Browns and us went to a Re-submission [of the prohibition amendment] meeting at the State House this evening. . . . *Oh I hate the thought of Re-Submission and liquor,* but for the sake of peace, I must go to such meetings with my husband, who is *fond of his Beer.*"[68] Eventually Shaw died of consumption and the effects of his drinking, which he continued despite his illness. Farnsworth remarried but remained haunted by her earlier relationship.

WCTU members did not have to experience such tragedies firsthand, for the knowledge of these situations could serve as potent examples of the evils of drink. In fact, victims of alcoholic husbands may have chosen to avoid the WCTU. Many, like Farnsworth, may have been afraid of their husbands' wrath or mortified with shame. Women came across drunken men often enough in the street for them to serve as constant reminders of the "curse of alcohol."[69] WCTU members projected on such scenes fears about their own sons and husbands and swore to protect them from such a fate.

If alcohol abuse was not a chimera, neither was prohibition an effective solution. Prohibitionists took a real problem and, quite literally, demonized it, equating alcohol with Satan and blaming it for all society's ills. Even though Frances Willard and other national WCTU leaders eventually came to believe that poverty was a cause of drinking, Kansas WCTU members seemed convinced that only the complete eradication of alcohol would transform workers into prosperous middle-class citizens.[70] The bogeyman of Demon Rum enabled WCTU members—many of whom were aware of the social injustice that permeated Gilded Age society—to ignore difficult (and radical) proposals to reform the nation by seizing on a single, simple panacea.

The WCTU, like other prohibitionists, was opposed not merely to drunkenness and alcoholism but to any alcoholic consumption. Temperance women viewed all forms of alcohol as temptations that inevitably led down the road to ruin. The organization even believed sacramental wine provided an inducement to sin and urged clergymen to replace the offending beverage with grape juice. In this way they hoped to assure that God's holy temple would not be sullied by Satan's brew.

Rather than the moderation that *temperance* implied, prohibitionists sought to purge all that could defile the body. Laura Johns, in her role as superintendent of Scientific Temperance Instruction, warned that students must be taught "the fact that science had indisputably established beyond question, that the use of alcoholic beverages at all is an abuse of the human system in exactly the proportion to the amount taken. . . . Children in our schools do not need to be reformed . . . but they need to be formed." Teachers, most of whom were women, needed "to teach the danger of forming this awful, insidious, inexorable appetite."[71] To purge such "foreign elements" from the body was to purify mind and soul; to purify the individual was to cleanse society, to rid it of all that was deemed undesirable. The WCTU's fear of impurity applied equally to alcohol and immigrants. Both the drinker and the "foreign masses" could be saved, but they would have to be molded in the image of God—or at least the WCTU's white Anglo middle-class version of the divine.

Temperance activists assumed their religious beliefs to be the singular truth, and those who did not accept this were, wittingly or not, Satan's helpers. Opposing the forces of evil were "the batteries of the WCTU, [which] will never be silenced until He who called and enlisted us in this grand army of the Republic gives us our discharge."[72] This philosophy did not provide any easy justification for the exigencies of practical politics.

WCTU members embraced the spiritual power they found in Christ's gospel and converted it into political energy. "The evangelistic work is indeed the foundation of all our efforts," Fanny Rastall told the 1885 convention. "If it were not for the strength gained from Bible study and prayer, how long would courage last? How long could we face a frowning world? Without the comforting assurances that Christ is able to save to the utter most, what would we offer to fallen humanity? With faith in our invisible leader, we can dare and do these things from which human nature instinctively shrinks."[73] Christ's presence could be experienced as a motivating force in itself, energizing women to challenge those perceived as sinning against His word—primarily, that is, men.[74] For Kansas women who felt such a calling, the WCTU enabled them to transform this spiritual energy into the concrete works of the organization's many departments.

Although most leaders of the Woman Movement subscribed to some form of Protestant belief, KESA's religious pronouncements were far less zealous than the WCTU's. Instead, KESA members tended to use Christian imagery as part of their political language. Drawing upon biblical stories for political allegories, they attempted to prove the biblical basis for woman suffrage.[75] At the 1891 convention, KESA even made this official policy, proclaiming, "That women ought to study the Bible and investigate all doctrines for themselves, and that it is a Christian duty to work for complete emancipation of women."[76] Such attempts at religious logic had their dangers, however, since antisuffragists could point to equally compelling passages in the Bible to support their cause.

Some KESA members, such as Annie Diggs, stood well outside mainstream conceptions of Protestant theology. Diggs had been active in a variety of women-centered reform groups since the early 1880s and had been a particularly effective prohibition leader. At the same time, Diggs, a self-described "Universalist-Unitarian" and "free thinker," became well known for her attacks on mainstream Protestant theology, particularly its male leadership.[77] Because she had long worked for both woman suffrage and prohibition, however, the WCTU tolerated her apostasies, and she was warmly welcomed at its events.[78]

Woman Movement activists who supported mainstream religiosity were more concerned that others share their vision of moral politics, political sisterhood, and respectability than that they subscribe to a particular Protestant theology. The movement's barriers may have kept the majority of Kansas women at arm's length, but it also enabled those ensconced within to create a homogenous solidarity. Shielded from other women with different cultural backgrounds and political agendas, the movement was able to coalesce by the late 1880s. Its cohesiveness enabled it to mount a successful campaign for the municipal woman suffrage bill, which in turn gave it a certain measure of power in reform politics.

But the Woman Movement's social cohesiveness masked a deep division within the ranks that no amount of sisterly rhetoric could hide. For, much as women valued their ideal of a nonpartisan, morally superior political sisterhood, most of them held intense loyalties to a political party and a corresponding ideology. At times the two agendas coincided, but when they did not, they threatened to tear apart both the movement's political sisterhood and the moral authority that this idealized vision helped create.

But the practical results of this vision were neither inevitable nor unchanging. Those working in the movement chose the degree to which they would implement it, or challenge it, or amend it. If the vision of a monolithic political sisterhood was a fiction, then women activists were largely the authors. The vision, the culture, and the changing context made some choices more likely than others, but the individual players involved made decisions within these constraints and chose partisan or nonpartisan strategies and exclusive or inclusive strategies to fit their political needs. Sometimes they chose well; other times they did not.

# THREE

## ⇥ THE WOMAN MOVEMENT TRIUMPHANT ⇤

When a small band of women formed the Kansas Equal Suffrage Association (KESA) in 1884, the Women's Christian Temperance Union (WCTU) greeted the new organization cordially if not enthusiastically. In Kansas, reformers had linked the issues of woman suffrage and prohibition since the amendment campaign in 1879. But although the two organizations shared a number of concerns, their future cooperation was not assured. In a number of other states, the temperance and suffrage societies shared little except mutual suspicion. In Kansas the WCTU's and KESA's commonalities provided the basis for cordiality, but there were enough differences to preclude a closer working relationship.

Whereas Laura Johns and Fanny Rastall helped steer the two organizations toward a common course, Helen Gougar, a suffragist and prohibitionist from Indiana, served as the catalyst. Gougar's timely visit to Kansas in 1884, coupled with her experience in Indiana politics, set the Kansas Woman Movement on its triumphant journey toward municipal woman suffrage in 1887. Municipal woman suffrage altered the movement's ideas about what was possible in Kansas politics and gave its members a new sense of themselves as political beings; it drew the WCTU and KESA together in a well-organized campaign and demonstrated the efficacy of working together. And it gave Helen Gougar a chance to practice a broad-based, multiethnic municipal electoral campaign that provided woman activists with a glimpse of politics beyond the comfortable walls of Anglo middle-class culture.

But municipal suffrage also created certain expectations among the Republican legislators who voted for the bill, expectations that had little to do with the Woman Movement's agenda. And municipal suffrage gave Kansas men a glimpse of women's new political power without granting women full political equality. If the majority of men found the new reality of empowered, politically active women acceptable, then all would be well for the future of woman suffrage in the state. But if men found the experience unsettling, they would register their discomfort when asked their opinion at the ballot box. Finally, although municipal woman suffrage gave women activists the opportunity to live out their vision of moral, nonpartisan politics in local campaigns, it exacerbated women's already intense partisan battles at the state level.

## THE CAMPAIGN FOR MUNICIPAL SUFFRAGE

When suffragists formed KESA in 1884, they had no particular reason to make municipal suffrage their main focus. At their first convention, delegates passed a resolution demanding municipal, state, and presidential suffrage in no particular order. No state had yet granted women municipal suffrage, but a few had passed presidential or state suffrage. Helen Gougar, however, had no interest in beseeching the state's electorate to bestow suffrage on women, which would have been necessary for state or presidential suffrage. Gougar, a leading temperance and suffrage activist in Indiana, had learned that lesson the hard way. Having recently led a campaign in her home state to elect prosuffrage (and Republican) candidates to the state legislature—and failed miserably—she knew the dangers of relying on men to support woman suffrage once they were hidden away in the privacy of the voting booth. Municipal suffrage was another story altogether: the Kansas constitution clearly gave the legislature control over who voted in local elections.

The Indiana campaign had been an emotional and often nasty battle. Once the dust had cleared, the Democrats controlled the legislature while Gougar merely salvaged her reputation, winning a five-thousand-dollar libel suit for character defamation. The campaign had left her physically and emotionally battered; some said the experience had turned her hair white. No doubt hoping to renew her faith by spreading her gospel of woman-centered reform, Gougar set off later that year on a fourteen-month nationwide lecture tour.

Perhaps she was also looking for a strategically superior battleground for her crusade. Like the settlers streaming in, Gougar saw Kansas as a state eager for progress and unshackled by tradition—a new frontier for reform.[1]

As it turned out, woman suffrage in Kansas was badly in need of a Helen Gougar. On her first day in Topeka, she found a dispirited group of women attempting to organize a state Equal Suffrage Association. They had arrived at the Capitol from throughout Kansas, anxious yet hopeful, only to be met by a chilly local reception and equally dampening weather. The would-be delegates had come expecting to find other like-minded women streaming into the city answering the call to battle like the Minutemen of old. Instead, just half a dozen had arrived, with little experience in addressing large audiences or organizing a statewide movement. Gougar's arrival helped cast off the "wet blanket that fell upon [the] enthusiasm and expectations" of the slightly bewildered delegates. She led the little group to the empty State Senate chamber, where the suffragists felt overwhelmed and intimidated by the imposing room. But as a future KESA secretary, Bertha Ellsworth, later recalled, "we were not long doomed to loneliness." Gougar, elected president of the convention, delivered several rousing speeches, and by "the late evening the Senate chamber was overflowing."[2]

Having established her reputation with the KESA membership, Gougar convinced the leadership of the wisdom of lobbying for municipal suffrage. Gougar, who had extensive legal experience, drafted a municipal suffrage bill giving women the right to vote in incorporated towns and cities.[3] After her experience in Indiana, Gougar viewed the Republicans' seemingly impervious lock on the Kansas legislature as a godsend: suffragists could depend on liberal Republicans to introduce the bill and shepherd it through the legislative committees. Most importantly, the campaign would bypass the need for the type of costly, exhausting electoral campaign that Gougar had experienced in Indiana.[4]

The members of KESA knew that they had little hope of winning the campaign by themselves. Johns looked to her allies in the WCTU to provide the necessary troops and additional political influence. As an officer in both organizations, she was well placed to bring the WCTU into the fray. Although the Kansas WCTU had officially supported suffrage since 1880, Rastall was more inclined to fight for all forms of suffrage equally. At Susan B. Anthony's urging, however, Rastall switched the WCTU's focus from presidential to municipal suffrage. The smaller but more activist KESA was now joined by the larger and better organized WCTU, and the new coalition strengthened both organizations without threatening either.[5]

Led by Helen Gougar, who was designated "Generalissimo by reason of her previous large experience," the women established a two-pronged attack. Each year their forces, led by the general and her able lieutenants, returned to the statehouse to lay siege (albeit decorously) to that citadel of male power. Meanwhile, Johns, Ellsworth, and others (including Annie Diggs, soon to be a noted Populist), continued to drum up grass-roots support from a growing list of supporters. The WCTU used the Methodist-style camp meetings that had been so effective during the prohibition amendment campaign, while KESA organized district conventions, bringing in Anthony, Clara Colby, Lucy Stone, Julia Ward Howe, and other out-of-state luminaries, as well as "local talent at all points." The WCTU's disciplined workers were particularly adept at circulating petitions, one of the few political weapons for women which society sanctioned; over ten thousand signatures were eventually collected.[6]

Gougar and the KESA leadership made their calculations amid a shifting political landscape in Kansas. The Republican Party, having survived the Greenback revolt of the 1870s, appeared once again to have reasserted control of Kansas politics. But in 1882 the G.O.P. gubernatorial candidate lost the election to a Democrat. To any Kansas Republican Party regular, this was a phenomenon as astounding as a blizzard in July. In fact, while seasoned Kansans accepted the most extreme perversities of nature, they had come to expect a certain consistency in their politics. Unlike the mysteries of Kansas weather, the cause of this unnatural disaster was all too easy to understand: Gov. John St. John, Republican hero of the Prohibition campaign, had run for an unprecedented third term and had been soundly trounced. St. John claimed that his decision to run was based on the urgent appeals of the temperance forces, who wanted a strong supporter of prohibition to push for rigid enforcement. Further, he could point to his record as an able, honest administrator and a tireless booster for Kansas, activities that most Kansans admired. But St. John had also attracted a healthy collection of political enemies, and his attempt to become Kansas's first third-term governor brought his disparate detractors out into the open.[7]

St. John's role in the prohibition campaign made him a national hero of the temperance movement, but in Kansas his zealous support of stricter enforcement was beginning to wear thin for many Republicans. These men either were antiprohibition to begin with or, more importantly, were antienforcement: They had no "kick" against prohibition as long as the state remained "reasonable" in its anti-alcohol efforts; that is, as long as lip service would suffice. This policy allowed towns seized with the temperance fit to keep things dry as cotton while less fusty folks allowed discreet—and well-controlled—

"joints" to survive. This arrangement was particularly convenient for those Germans who remained Republicans but were vehemently opposed to prohibition, and to woman suffrage.[8] St. John embraced both causes and spoke of little else on the campaign stump. The Democratic candidate, George Glick, a wealthy railroad lawyer, inveighed as often in the opposite direction, maintaining that the campaign was about whether men were men and women were women—two categories that Glick and his supporters held to be immutable. Denouncing enforcement methods because "no man with a spark of manhood or honor in him would inform on another who sold him intoxicating liquor," he declared that woman suffrage would "drag our mothers and sisters into this political damnation."[9]

But beneath the uproar over prohibition and suffrage lay other issues at least as important. Some Republicans objected to St. John's presumption in trying to break the unwritten rule limiting a governor to two terms. Others chafed at the strident moralism of his rhetoric, which often seemed more fitting for a Methodist camp meeting or a WCTU convention than for the manly arena of partisan politics. Some Republicans wondered aloud whether St. John wasn't taking his last name too literally. And then there were powerful rivals within the state Republican Party such as U.S. Senator John J. Ingalls, a political and cultural conservative who objected to St. John's reformism and worried about his ambitions for the U.S. Senate. To complete St. John's troubles, the popular ex-governor, Charles Robinson, attracted many liberal Republican votes by running on the Greenback-Labor ticket. These liabilities appear to have been at least as responsible for St. John's defeat as his prohibition–woman suffrage positions, for the state legislature stayed firmly Republican, and many of the representatives were strong prohibitionists.[10]

If Republicans were unhappy about St. John's botched candidacy, they were apoplectic when their erstwhile standard bearer agreed to run as the national Prohibition Party's candidate for president. Concentrating his campaign in key states, he managed to draw enough votes in New York from Republican James Blaine to throw the election to his Democratic opponent, Grover Cleveland. At a time when men held up strict adherence to partisan politics as proof of one's manhood and sense of honor, St. John's devotion to a party of ministers, "longhairs," "cranks," and women must have appeared as treachery against both his party and his gender. Across the country his burning effigy illuminated the livid faces of Republicans frustrated with losing the White House for the first time since the Civil War. In Kansas, the legislature changed the now offensive name of St. John County to Logan. Ironically, St. John's defeat was in some ways a gain for Kansas prohibitionists, for the debacle convinced G.O.P. leaders that Republican prohibitionists could be a serious threat to party unity.[11] Yet the politicians also understood that the strident, self-righteous tone and narrow focus of a St. John could not win elections.

The Republicans' response was a time-honored and effective one: coopt the opposition. For the next several years the G.O.P.-dominated legislature passed a number of laws strengthening prohibition enforcement at both the state and local levels. Much of the pressure for these reforms originated with the WCTU, and some Republican leaders began to view women activists as allies against antiprohibition and antisuffrage Democrats. Hence, when the woman suffragists introduced their municipal suffrage bill in 1885, they found some willing listeners among the Republicans.[12]

Although some Republican legislators were sincerely prosuffrage, the majority appeared to be more interested in the potential political assets and liabilities of the bill. In 1886, some of these Republicans raised a third-party scare, claiming the bill was a "coup" by "St. John's lieutenants" and women activists to control local politics for the Prohibition Party. Immediately, the bill was conveniently buried in the calendar. Republicans, with ugly visions of 1882 dancing in their heads, were probably more concerned about the upcoming state election than about a supposed cabal of insidious "drys." Party strategists desperately wanted to avoid forcing Governor Martin to decide between vetoing and signing the bill.[13]

One year later the G.O.P. leadership found even more prohibition supporters in the legislature, increased pressure by the women activists, and no election worries. With these changed conditions, Republicans recognized the prospect of cleaning up in the local elections by granting women municipal suffrage. Taking advantage of the favorable political atmosphere, Sen. R. W. Blue and House Speaker A. W. Smith, influential prosuffrage legislators, guided the bill quickly through the committees. Democrats well understood the partisan motivations behind the G.O.P.'s sudden support of woman suffrage. They sneered that the bill was simply a devil's bargain among the prohibitionists, the WCTU, the Methodist Church, and the Republicans, a rather intricate conspiracy theory that was not all that far fetched. Although probably no explicit compacts were made, the Republicans did appear to be the only true champions of prohibition, while the WCTU openly appealed to the Methodist Church for help during the election. Suffragists had focused almost all their lobbying efforts on Republicans, believing they would be more receptive than Democrats. Republicans, for their part, believed that women would automatically grace their deliverers with a substantial block of votes. After all, had they not proved themselves to be the party that championed morality?[14] Women activists, however, had a different vision of moral politics, and it did not always have Republican officeholders in it.

## PURIFYING THE CESSPOOL: THE PROMISE AND CONSEQUENCES OF MORAL POLITICS

The legislative debate leading up to the bill's passage gave both sides an opportunity to lay out existing dogma about women and politics. When the measure came to the floor for a vote, the main question was not whether the bill would pass, but in what form and by how large a majority. Despite the obvious partisan nature of the fight, legislators generally avoided outright references to party issues. Although a few telling shots about "blind obedience to party" did make their way into the debate, both sides embraced the higher ground, sticking to the moral issues raised by the bill.[15]

Prosuffrage legislators offered a wide array of justifications for suffrage, most of which had been used by the Woman Movement. Several asserted that women's competence and intelligence compared favorably to men's; Republican Senator Donnell noted, "The time was when the department clerks at Washington were all men; to-day a large proportion are women, and they give the best of satisfaction." Others claimed the bill to be a matter of simple justice, since women had earned the right with their sacrifices during the pioneer period and the Civil War. Representative McCammon demanded, "[Did not] women . . . do as much as men during the great struggle of 1860–64?" The most frequent argument utilized by prosuffragists linked woman suffrage to the "inevitable step in the progress of the nation."[16] Woman, that great civilizing force, would stride to the front of the Parade of Progress and lead the vanguard to the millennium. The bill was not about such mundane matters as partisan politics; it was about Enlightenment and Redemption.

The Democrats had their own ideas about Woman and Progress, and they were decidedly less optimistic. "Women would purify politics just as you would purify a green stagnant pond by pouring in a few gallons of fresh spring water." Politics was irredeemable; women could stay unsullied only by remaining in and maintaining the last bastion of godliness, the home. The dangers were readily apparent to the Democratic representative from Leavenworth, who demanded of his peers whether "you would like your wife to be in a jury room with eleven of the average jurymen of today. . . . I call to mind the happy face of my aged mother, and I have too much respect for her to imagine her down in the cesspool of politics." He then asked one young legislator whether he "would like to take for his wife a young woman lawyer, not pure and undefiled, but fresh from a divorce suit, with all its degrading accomplishments." Another legislator "opposed the bill in the interests of the home" and cited the rising divorce rate to prove women's imminent moral collapse.[17] If women were corrupted, could civilization as these men knew it be far behind? Apparently not.

Prosuffragists responded by asserting that woman suffrage, far from destroying the home, would in fact strengthen it. Mr. Coleman, Republican from Nemaha, responded to such attacks by asking whether "the husband can spend his time late at night in wild carousals and then come home with the expectation that his wife had been exerting her influence to bring up their offspring as good and honest children, while he has been spending a night in immorality and debauchery." Echoing a basic assumption of the Woman Movement, he argued: "[Antisuffragists] say that women should not be dragged into the cesspool of politics; if politics are so degraded, there should be something done to purify and elevate politics. Some purifying influence should be injected into the politics of our country. I believe that woman is the Hercules who will reform the politics of to-day. Will it drag her down? Never!"[18] Helen Gougar could not have said it better.

The municipal suffrage bill passed by an overwhelming majority in both chambers of the legislature. In the House, where the vote was ninety-one in favor to twenty-two against, just three Democrats voted for the bill, while only five Republicans opposed it. Jubilant women activists, watching the vote tally from the gallery, let out an exultant cheer when the count was recorded. They showered supportive legislators with praise and their particular champions with flowers.[19]

Given the margin of victory, the impressive Republican support of the bill, and the prosuffragist legislators' professed unswerving dedication to "moral politics," we might reasonably expect, as many newspapers predicted, that full suffrage would be the next "inevitable step in the progress of the nation." This particular march of progress, however, had a long and difficult road ahead of it. Hitherto unseen obstacles began to materialize two months after passage of the bill, when Kansas women participated in their first municipal suffrage election. These warning signs made it clear that women's and men's political assumptions were at times farther apart than the legislators' words might have led observers to believe.

In many local elections women simply reinforced the Republican majority, but in others the new voters challenged both male political culture and male political power. Most G.O.P. legislators had voted for the measure because they believed that women would vote Republican. While the bill awaited Gov. John Martin's signature, he received numerous letters from women urging him to sign it because "you will receive from every woman in Kansas gratitude that words can fail to express."[20] For the governor and his fellow Republicans, a vote for the local G.O.P. slate was all that was necessary in the way of thanks. In the past, women and men had performed their public activities apart. Now the political actors and actresses were sharing the same stage, but they were still reading from different scripts.

On the very evening when the House passed the bill, woman suffrage workers gathered together to decide how best to harvest the fruits of victory. In less than two months, women would get their first chance to vote in a Kansas municipal election, and the activists were determined that it would not be business as usual. In the short time available, they developed a set of tactics and strategies that newspapers came to identify as "women's politics." Drawing from their experience in the WCTU and KESA, women leaders extended their own political culture into the male-dominated electoral arena.

In some instances, women activists challenged the ruling Republicans and created enmity among erstwhile allies; in other cases, particularly in the large cities, the Woman Movement's politics dovetailed with the Republican agenda, prompting the Democrats to claim that women voters were helpless pawns of the domineering Republicans. Not surprisingly, the newspapers in towns where the editor's party had suffered because of women's votes didn't much care for the manner in which women conducted politics or for the people they tried to elect. Behind editors' sincere statements about the proper ways to practice politics lay one indisputable fact: women's politics were objectionable only when women did not support the editor's choice of candidate. Whereas gender relations shaped men's criticism of women's politics, politicians and editors were most concerned about maintaining political power. The degree to which women challenged men's political power determined their reaction to municipal woman suffrage.

Woman suffragists wasted no time introducing their perspective into Kansas politics. The day after the legislative vote, they drafted a circular containing "information deemed necessary to the new voters." Soon thereafter, they sent over 50,000 copies to 283 cities and asked local activists to distribute them. The circular attempted to inject the direct concerns of women into the local races, asking prospective women voters: "Do you wish to have all dramshops, gambling dens, and houses of prostitution closed in your city? Do you not wish to have your . . . schoolhouses made wholesome places for your children? Do you not wish to have livestock kept from roaming your streets, breaking your walks and invading your gardens? Do you not wish to have your money spent as prudently as possible?" This quasi–direct mail approach connected a centralized state organization with disciplined local chapters, creating a system of political activism which circumvented the traditional parties. Suffrage workers enlisted the services of sympathetic Protestant ministers, who donated meeting space and made proclamations from their pulpits. The WCTU appealed directly to the Methodists for support in encouraging women to vote for "moral" candidates.[21]

Activists in the Woman Movement also utilized local newspapers wherever possible. The regular WCTU columns were full of election advice, while the news sections often carried special appeals by Gougar, Rastall, and Willard. These appeals, which were basically press releases, communicated three basic themes. Each declared a Christian crusade against, in Gougar's words, "the three corrupting elements of social and political life—the saloon, the brothel, and [the] gambling den." Rastall implored women, "For Christ's sake and for humanity's sake, lift up your voices and urge the use of this proper and now legal method of aiding to bring nearer Christ's reign on earth." But if the millennium beckoned to the dedicated and fearless warrior, then near apocalypse threatened the faint hearted and weak willed: "If you fail in doing your whole duty at the present crisis, the vicious elements of society will rejoice."[22]

Beyond these moral and spiritual imperatives lay more earthly concerns: how politicians across the country would be influenced by the nature and number of women's votes. Gougar warned that "the eyes of the country will be concentrated on your action under this new order of things." Willard, aware that this "awesome responsibility" was being bestowed upon many women who were still intimidated by the thought of transgressing into the male sphere of politics, declared: "Most of us did not seek this power, many of us have feared and dreaded it. *But it has come.* The clear-cut issue is, *Shall men who will close the saloons and keep them closed be placed in power?* . . . We dare not disregard these sacred interests; *we will vote for God and home and native land.*"[23] Gougar, Rastall, and Willard's collective message was clear—women could protect their families by redeeming local politics. To accomplish this goal, they needed to eschew petty partisanship and embrace social and political purity.

At first, Woman Movement leaders did not specify what women should do beyond voting, but local women's groups quickly began improvising. Some women attended Republican or nonpartisan "citizens" conventions and attempted to nominate their candidates through these channels. Other women held "women's caucuses" when they were dissatisfied with the nominees whom the two parties offered. Led by the WCTU, these women nominated "women's tickets," which usually consisted of men. Occasionally, women would be nominated, and in a few cases all-women slates were selected.[24]

In almost every case where women were actively involved, prohibition enforcement became a central issue of the campaign. When women were given official Republican party sanction, good feelings abounded between the ruling party and the women voters. At such times, Republican leaders considered woman suffrage a clear example of the type of moral, progressive reform that would make Kansas the banner state of the nation. When women's votes did change an election's outcome, it more often resulted in a Republican loss. When that happened, concerns about morality, progress, and all that took a back seat to the straightforward business of partisan politics.[25]

Aside from ministers, there were few groups of men in Kansas as supportive of woman suffrage as Republican editors. Their usual enthusiasm for politicized women, however, did not extend to those who dared to vote against Republicans. Most editors in towns where women challenged the G.O.P. exhibited deep reservations about the "new element" in politics. In Fort Scott, the editor of the *Daily Monitor* felt impelled to elucidate "HOW WOMEN SHOULD VOTE." "The *Monitor* is in receipt of a communication from a very estimable lady of this city, which endeavors to lay down a few general rules for the guidance of the female voters. First, she admonishes them to vote for the right; to select good men regardless of party. Secondly, she asserts that the Republican party is no more entitled to consideration for the passage of the municipal suffrage bill than any other party; that it was not a party measure, etc.; in fact advocates a general scattering all along the line." The editor made clear that such logic had no place in the electoral arena. He assured his readers that those women who insisted on nonpartisanship "have much to learn of the science of government before they can become helpful, intelligent voters."[26]

The editor then went on to instruct the new voters properly. The Republicans, he explained patiently, were the sole deliverers of women's political emancipation. But beyond the case for simple gratitude, he stressed that nonpartisanship was not an option—that would contradict the "scientific" imperatives of politics.

As to voting regardless of party, the ladies must understand that party organization is absolutely essential to accomplish any good in politics. There must be political parties, having certain and well-defined policies of government, or chaos will result. The women must identify themselves with one party or the other, and be loyal to their creed when adopted. They must endeavor to mold the sentiment of their party to the advocacy of the best measures, and in this way they can and will accomplish great good. But should they adopt the policy advocated by our fair correspondent, they will be like broken reeds, which no one can lean on.[27]

The objective, scientific truth was clear: politics was impossible outside the two-party system. Obviously, the ladies had let their emotions get the better of their senses. Only after the majority of Fort Scott women supported the Republican slate did the *Monitor* proclaim municipal woman suffrage a "grand success."

Women's threat to the established order of partisan politics did not always have such a happy ending for Republicans. In Garden City, women backed the Democratic candidates, rejecting the Republican slate, which was widely believed to control the city's "whiskey ring." Naturally, the Republican *Daily Sentinel* was appalled. "Yes, it was a great Democratic victory," groused the editor, "but, unfortunately, the Democrats can't be held responsible for it. The new element in politics worked early, late and earnestly for the mugwump ticket yesterday, and many of them made use of methods which were anything but commendable."[28] Not surprisingly, the Democrats praised "the ladies" and excoriated "the whisky ring." To these Democrats, woman suffrage and prohibition seemed a very good thing indeed. For both editors, what mattered most was controlling local politics and the benefits this entailed. Woman suffrage was simply a means toward this end or a hindrance.

For many women, however, moral purity was the only acceptable end for political power. They were quite willing to repudiate "bad men" on a party's ticket, scratching off the name of the official candidate and replacing it with their own choice. As the Osawatomie *Gaslight* gleefully reported, "And scratch! How they did scratch! They scratched many a man that itched for office and tore his prospects into tatters."[29] To the *Gaslight*, an independent paper and thus no stranger to the charge of unmanly nonpartisanship, the situation was loaded with irony and humor. To the erstwhile officeholders, however, it was no laughing matter.

The Republicans who were challenged argued that the issue was not temperance or morality—naturally, they were as right on the prohibition issue as any upstanding member of the community. The bottom line of politics was economic, however, and as the *Emporia Evening News* explained, "The ladies, if they intend to take part in politics hereafter, will find that when they make an issue it will be necessary to find a cause for making such issue, as the voters— male and female—as a rule, will not cast their votes in direct opposition to their own best interests, not even to please four or five of a dozen would-be leaders."[30] The editor found such machinations by a clique of women offensive to his moral sensibilities, although he made no mention of the Republican "courthouse ring" at issue in the election.

The editor insisted that women's sense of morality must not interfere with her family's financial well-being. "The ladies who headed the movement of

Tuesday last will have to learn," he argued, "that every good husband has just about as much influence over his wife as said wife has over him; and that the probabilities are that when said husband's business interests conflict with those of an electioneering committee, sent out as against him and his interests, he may possibly argue the matter with his wife in such a manner that she will plainly see that it would not be in the line of her duty to assist in causing dissension that might possibly result in financial loss to the city, or interfere with the progress of her husband's business, and thus become a drawback to his prosperity, instead of a helpmeet."[31] This stern lecture, addressed to the town's middle-class residents, made clear that business was to come before morality. It also assumed that men would "naturally" champion the former and women the latter and that the woman who continued to support moral issues over economic ones would in effect be challenging her family's economic interest. By choosing idealistic morality over practical business sense, she would be violating her sacred duty to protect her children by hindering her husband's business pursuits. Suddenly, it seemed, there was some confusion about just who were the "best men." For Woman Movement activists, the "best men" were proenforcement and anticorruption; for most Republican leaders, "the best" invariably meant "Republican." The two did not always coincide.

The situation put the WCTU in a difficult bind. Men as a class appeared failures at providing moral leadership: they had passed a prohibition law and then refused to enforce it; they had allowed graft and dishonesty to flourish in local politics. Women could work to save men's souls, and thus increase the number of good men, but this was a slow process. Women needed to identify and promote the morally upright men and propel them into office. Olive Bray, superintendent of the Franchise Department, urged her sisters to "find in our legislative men pure in private life, honest in political life. . . . men of ability, who have faith in our cause, and through them make known our wants."[32] The problem, as Laura Johns wrote in *Our Messenger,* was that "we have so few desirable men left on earth with enough public spirit to accept of these offices for the sake of public welfare."[33] Johns counseled WCTU members to be satisfied with the best that was available.

The losers in the municipal elections most keenly felt the women activists' injection of "purity" and nonpartisanship into Kansas politics. All men, however, experienced the effect of women's political participation on male political culture. Men's reactions to these changes were decidedly mixed. The manly art of politics had certain unwritten rules, and those who took part were expected to follow them. The presence of women in general, and the actions of

Woman Movement leaders in particular, struck at the heart of long-established codes of behavior.

Before municipal woman suffrage, men's party loyalties and political morality were relatively simple: if you were a Democrat, Republicans were dirty scoundrels, and if you were a Republican, Democrats were low-down, lying curs. There was a certain symmetrical beauty to this arrangement which kept campaigns from being too intellectually taxing. Third-party efforts such as that of the Greenbackers, with their challenge to the hegemony of the two-party system and their insistence on messy issues such as economic reform, were kept outside the political mainstream and treated with contempt. Besides, they almost never managed to get themselves elected. Real men, after all, achieved political power.

Into this cozy male world stormed the women. Suddenly, men who thought they had achieved a modicum of respectability through elected office were being branded with a variety of moralistic condemnations by society's recognized civilizers. Women's methods appeared perfectly logical—to women. If they were morally superior (and didn't everyone agree about that?), then they were right and those men who disagreed were wrong. Not surprisingly, quite a few men did not accept this reasoning, even though they might agree with the fundamental assumption of women's moral superiority. Even male supporters of woman suffrage felt compelled to instruct women in yet another area of their "inexperience." One editor explained, "The experiment has been tried and it seems to be a success. . . . The ladies, as might be expected, have a few things to learn. They have to learn, for example, . . . that a ticket gotten on the basis of a single idea is seldom successful. And they have to learn that under certain circumstances other people may, perhaps, vote differently from the way they do, and yet remain respectable members of society and, possibly, Christians."[34] Women had transformed religious-based morality into a political weapon, but it was not an officially recognized weapon of those who made the political rules.

Some men were no more happy with women's organizing tactics than with their use of morality. Activists in the Woman Movement were excellent grass-roots organizers, and they brought these skills with them into electoral politics. Men cried "foul" to many of these efforts, again claiming a breach of the rules. Some felt that such devices as the Woman Movement's use of the circulars and newspaper appeals amounted to unfair influence at best and political brainwashing at worst. Some objected to women's attempts to round up prospective supporters and convey them to the polls. One paper reported that "The WCTU commissioned carriages with their motto 'For God and Home and Native Land' and 'Hurrah for Kansas.' It was a new feature in politics, and one which quite a number of the male sex did not take to kindly."[35]

Given the many creative incentives politicians had invented to induce men to vote for them, women's canvassing appears fairly benign. Men, however, were not used to competing for votes with women, and they much resented this infringement on their traditional turf. Some editors were particularly upset with women's unseemly aggressiveness. One paper, after sharply criticizing the tactics of the "new element," reported darkly: "A well-dressed lady in a carriage passed along Fulton Street and drew up beside a walking man and asked if he had voted. He replied he had not. He was invited to take a seat in the carriage, which invitation he accepted and he was at once driven to the polls."[36] A *lady* giving a *stranger* a ride in her *carriage*—what next! To the writer, this woman had clearly transgressed the boundaries of acceptable social and political behavior.

Men's concerns about the effects of politics on women's morals went beyond objections to particular incidents. During the debate over the woman suffrage bill, legislators argued whether the cesspool of politics would defile women or else drive away the "best" women, leaving only "degraded" women to vote.[37] Supporters of suffrage rarely missed an opportunity to demonstrate that despite woman's newfound political right, she was still the paragon of grace, selflessness, goodness, and charm. The *Ashland Republican-Herald* testified: "When election day came last week many of the best and noblest and purest women in Kansas went to the polls, and not one of them is any the worse for it. Not one of them has lost any self-respect, or any respect to those whose respect is worth having."[38] Another paper made clear that, contrary to earlier worries, women voters were conforming to male expectations of femininity. "Up to date over one hundred and fifty fair maidens have registered, and in looking over the books it is an astonishing fact to see how few short-haired women have registered," it reported. "And nearly all the women will actually tell their age, too; now and then one fibs."[39]

On one hand, this supporter was attempting to validate women voters by dissociating them from those women who would dare transgress the strict borders between men and women. Short hair was men's hair, after all, an alteration that rendered the willful woman unworthy of serious consideration as either a woman or a voter. The editor was also placing women in what he considered to be their proper social role: as vain, harmless creatures. His twinkly-eyed comment would no doubt have drawn an appreciative chuckle from most men (and a number of women as well), helping to make woman suffrage a painless pill to swallow. But the condescending tone and content, endemic to so many men's remarks about women's participation in politics, made clear that women were expected to conform to male notions of proper politics and proper behavior.

If Republicans wanted the best women to predominate at the polls, the polls would have to be cleaned up, toned down—in a word, "domesticated." The lawmakers accomplished this quite easily. Just before the election they passed a bill forbidding all forms of electioneering within one hundred feet of the polling place. Suffrage activists did not ask for this new legislation. Rather, the bill evolved out of the logic of the legislators' arguments concerning the threats to women's purity.

The bill wrought a dramatic change in the character of most local elections. Most Republican editors enthusiastically applauded the changes. The editor of the *Lawrence Tribune* echoed the sentiments of most of his G.O.P. colleagues: "What a different spectacle was presented today from the old-time elections, where men who never drank at other times got drunk; fights were constantly occurring; the polls were surrounded by jostling crowds of rough and intoxicated men, disputing in angry words the personal character and family history of candidates, [and] a large extra police force was necessary to keep the polls safe and partially decent. Now, a chalk mark suffices without an officer to keep a space of fifty feet reserved for those who are voting and are ready to vote. Then the wives dreaded the coming home at night of their excited, and perhaps drunken, husbands; now husband and wife drive in their carriage, or walk to the polls, and together quietly deposit their ballots and depart."[40] Though this picture of saloon madness turned domestic bliss may have been overstated—hyperbole not being unknown to Kansas editors—municipal woman suffrage clearly had a profound effect on the ritual of male political culture in Kansas.

Tellingly, many editors gave credit for these changes to the "ladies" and not to the law, claiming, "It is universally admitted that the presence of ladies everywhere else has an effect for the good. Conventions, political gatherings, courts, and celebrations are always freer from vulgarity and debasing influence when attended by women. It will be so at the polls."[41] Because women were acting in their traditional role, Republican editors accepted this form of women's influence on politics. But although the writer confidently reported that women's positive effect on politics was "universally admitted," was this vision of politics shared by most men?

A good number of Kansas men opposed drinking and the accompanying culture of the saloon. A majority of them had, after all, voted to abolish the sale of alcohol in 1879.[42] Yet most had either participated in the raucous Election Day celebrations or else condoned them—why else would such celebrations continue during state and national elections in November? Further, there had been no organized opposition to these rituals before or after municipal woman suffrage. Finally, one may assume that Democrats were no more boisterous than Republicans, or surely the Republicans would have used this as political ammunition. In fact, the domesticating effect of the electioneering law was the unintended outcome of some men's desire to protect women from other men's actions, a desire born of a fear of sullying middle- and upper-class women's moral purity.

Republican editors and other upright folk may have applauded the sanitizing of local elections, but many other men ruefully acknowledged the observation of a Democratic paper in Medicine Lodge that the "woman's caucus on Thursday was rather a dry affair; no cigars, buttonholes, nor bottles. The few men who were present came out spitting cotton as they never did before. Ladies need have no fear in attending the polls on Monday; men are generally godless critters, but they will respect a woman, even when voting."[43] Men would go along with this infringement on their prerogatives—it was the law after all—but they did not have to like it. No doubt many felt that they had lost a much-looked-forward-to day of dirty jokes and free cigars, not to mention the rare opportunity of slaking a powerful thirst in this very dry state. Kansas men were suddenly confronted with the grim possibility that elections, those twice-yearly, heretofore publicly-sanctioned stag parties, were no longer going to be any fun.

Although the presence of women at the polls directly threatened the rituals of men's political culture, Kansas men's fears of municipal suffrage went beyond the political. Men had more general concerns about how women and men would relate to each other after women lost their political innocence. More concretely, they worried about getting fed.

On Election Day, the specter of the cold supper stared many a man in the face. The complaint that a man would be forced to dine on leftovers or nothing at all because of his wife's voting seemed a bit small minded to prosuffragists. Municipal elections in Kansas came but once a year, and a trip to the polls took no more than thirty minutes, if that. Prosuffrage editors tried to make light of the complaint: "The ladies have voted, and, surprising though it may be to some of the croakers, the world wags merrily on its accustomed course. Nobody had to eat cold victuals as a consequence, and the baby and the housework received their usual amount of attention just the same."[44] Despite the evidence that men in fact were getting fed and that women were attending to their domestic duties, men continued to voice these complaints during other debates about woman suffrage.

Editors were right to chide men for acting like "poor, helpless husbands," unable to prepare a meal in the unlikely event that their wives did not.[45] Even within the gender expectations of Victorian America, the position seemed a bit selfish. Rather than taking this complaint literally, however, one might speculate on its deeper cause. The opening phrase of the editor's comment is instructive: the world as men had come to know and appreciate it had not turned upside down. Women, prosuffrage editors assured their male readership, would continue to cook, clean, tend the baby, and perform the myriad other service functions expected of a wife. Men's fears about woman suffrage went beyond the prospect of a cold supper. At bottom lay their uncertainty about maintaining the many prerogatives they enjoyed in marriage.

Divorce represented the ultimate destruction of the domestic world. Another of men's objections to municipal woman suffrage was that it would cause domestic dissension and ultimately lead to the destruction of the family. Their worry was that husband and wife would fall to bickering over candidates and issues, introducing strife where domestic bliss had once thrived.[46] Prosuffrage editors often noted that although husbands and wives voted different tickets, they were on amicable terms.[47] Only occasionally did papers report the minor disagreements, tense moments, or hidden grievances that came out of the new experience of a man's vote being canceled out by that of his wife. Yet we can assume that married women experienced a range of reactions to their new right—from that of men who embraced woman suffrage to that of men who opposed it with violence. Now that women were voting citizens, with a political culture and program at times at odds with men, the new disagreements would add to the changing shape of gender relations in Kansas.

Men's fears about women's newfound political power did not often find their way into newspapers. The suspicions regarding cold suppers and cottondry elections which lurked within the hearts of men were not the sort of thing a respectable fellow complained about in print; better to stick to arguments about women's purity. Most of the evidence comes from those refuting the charges. Yet these fears would continue to surface in other woman suffrage campaigns. Given the Woman Movement's program, such concerns are not surprising. Women activists struggled to convince men that women would transform and purify politics, and men's political culture, but that men shouldn't feel threatened by the changes. It was a difficult point to sell.

Despite some men's underlying uncertainties about municipal suffrage, newspaper editors generally declared this "experiment" a grand success.

Woman suffrage offered order, respectability, sobriety, and cleanliness to the political process—traits that any progressive editor admired. As long as women did not challenge established interests, editors gave woman suffrage their warm support. One wonders, however, how Republican legislators felt about the outcome of the elections. Clearly they had expected to benefit from the newly enfranchised voters. But in the small towns throughout Kansas, the women's vote in the city elections either reinforced the Republican majority or, less frequently, provided a serious challenge to Republican officeholders. The result was hardly an overwhelming success for the Republican Party.

There was at least one exception to this state of things, however, and it merits a closer look. In the Democratic stronghold of Leavenworth, women voters became the phalanx for Republicans bent on closing the saloons and ousting the Democrats. In the Leavenworth campaign, the Republicans' greatest hopes and the Democrats' deepest fears were realized. We might expect that this battle would take on bitter class and ethnic overtones. The scenario seems to promise a classic struggle between the Republican Yankee majority of Kansas and the alliance of outsiders—Southerners, workers, the foreign born— who gave the Democrats one of their few majorities in the state. To some extent this is true, but the exceptions to the rule provide us with a better understanding of the choices available to Woman Movement activists. The woman of the hour, once again, was Helen Gougar. Rather than helping establish an elite subculture, as she had done in 1884, she instead worked in Leavenworth to expand the boundaries of respectability.

## THE BATTLE OF LEAVENWORTH: WHOSE VICTORY?

Leavenworth was the most hated town in Kansas, at least for Republicans. The city had its competitors, of course: Republicans cast a disapproving eye on Wichita, Kansas City, and Dodge City as well. But none combined so many elements that were anathema to so many Republicans as did Leavenworth. It had been the proslavery capital during the days of Bleeding Kansas and had served as a command post for Southern Border Ruffians. The triumph of the Free Staters and the defeat of the Confederacy had done little to bring Leavenworth into line with the rest of Kansas. The city's leaders remained committed to the Democratic party and opposed to prohibition. Not only did the town serve as a convenient entry point for Southern bootleg whisky, but the saloons ran openly, paying regular "fines" that amounted to licenses. Some of the saloons mimicked the gaudy liquor palaces of Chicago and offered services to elite clientele ranging from hot meals to prostitution. For working men there were neighborhood taverns, and for the poor there were basement joints. The city never achieved the national notoriety of Dodge City, it is true. But though Leavenworth may have had fewer shoot-outs than the famed cow town, it had more saloons.[48]

To Kansas Republicans, the Leavenworth city fathers were as much rebels as the ruffians who had sacked Lawrence over twenty years before. Republicans' indignation over Leavenworth's flagrant disregard for prohibition probably equaled the affront they felt at the Democratic Party's two-to-one majority in city elections. Republicans, who saw themselves as law-abiding citizens, decided to use state law against the scoundrels. Leavenworth became one of the first targets of the commission formed by the Metropolitan Police Act.[49] At least one Republican legislator believed women voters could be recruited to fight the scofflaws; during the debate on the bill, Senator Blue had declared that "municipal woman suffrage would help to wipe out the saloons—even in the city of Leavenworth."[50]

Republicans in Leavenworth convened shortly after the suffrage bill's passage and decided to do just that. Led by the *Leavenworth Times* editor, D. R. Anthony, the town's leading Republicans formed a Law and Order League to fight the good fight in the upcoming city election. Anthony's conversion to the suffrage cause had been as sudden as his conversion in the 1867 amendment campaign. As late as 1885, he had vigorously opposed both municipal woman suffrage and prohibition. With the bill a reality and victory over the hated Democrats a possibility, Anthony suddenly saw the light.[51]

The *Times* made no bones about who was running the show—the Law and Order League's founders read like a who's who of Leavenworth elite. "Every manufacturing interest was represented. The most prominent merchants of the city were there. Prominent bankers and leading capitalists were in attendance, while hundreds of business men and citizens occupied seats in the crowded balcony."[52] Though the *Times* was no doubt employing typical Kansas hyperbole—the Democrats claimed a number of elites for their side—it was clear that the Law and Order League was not meant as an egalitarian organization. The men and women who led it mapped out a strategy that called for canvassing houses in the more affluent wards, "selecting only those who were known to favor Law and Order."[53]

Helen Gougar rode into Leavenworth and changed all that. To Democrats, her sudden arrival took on the tenor of an invasion. More than once the Democratic paper, the *Standard,* referred to her as a "foreign presence."[54] Taking command of the forces of law and order, she quickly reformulated their basic strategy. Gougar had long argued for a more inclusive reform movement. As early as 1882 she had insisted, "Most great reform has its origins with the poor and lowly."[55] In Leavenworth, she was able to put this thinking to the test.

Gougar reasoned that however comfortable her fellow reformers were with "their own kind," their efforts would be futile unless they captured some of the Democrats' constituency. She insisted that the campaign must appeal to workers and foreign-born immigrants; it also had to galvanize the black community, whose members could be expected to vote Republican if they felt there was any hope of victory. Speaking to a group of elite supporters, she instructed, "Ladies, let German, Irish, Polish, white, colored, temperance, and anti-temperance all be invited to register. We want the knowledge of the facts for future use among our women, as their work will only begin when the votes are counted out. If they are not for law and order then the near future must see them converted through your efforts."[56] For Gougar this campaign went beyond simply closing down the saloons. Hers was a battle for the hearts and minds of Kansans, the opening front in the crusade to use municipal suffrage to transform the state into a bastion of woman-centered reform.

Gougar wasted little time before assuming control of the drive. Rather than attempt to convert people by "saving" them, she stressed her audience's concerns and interests. Her tactics were ingenious, and her organization was thorough and efficient. She attracted Irish voters by giving talks in their neighborhoods on the Irish Land League's struggle against British oppression.[57] She directed her efforts at Germans through the local churches, using an interpreter to reach the women.[58] She approached workers through the Knights of Labor, whose leaders had generally supported temperance measures. Having made the acquaintance of the organization's leaders in her national reform work, she made overtures to the local leadership. She soon had speakers from the Knights taking part in the campaign. Gathering crowds in front of the Knights' lodges, Gougar would lecture on the "labor problem" and the plight of working men and women, always accentuating the role of alcohol.[59] Her affiliation with the Knights of Labor gave her credibility in working-class neighborhoods, especially among the women there. Finally, knowing the key to organizing black support lay with the churches, Gougar reached out to black ministers, who offered their support. She appeared to be assembling an astonishing coalition, the likes of which had never been seen in Kansas.

While Gougar was busy building bridges, D. R. Anthony was having trouble abandoning his elitist position. Although a column entitled "Mrs. Gougar's Work" described Gougar's forays into various parts of town, Anthony continued to focus on the actions of "the best" men and women in the city. Nor did the *Standard* let its readership forget Anthony's perspective or his past positions toward workers. In one story it reprinted excerpts from his antilabor editorials for the past few years. By late March the paper was referring to the Democratic candidates as "the labor ticket." Apparently, however, none of these candidates was particularly familiar with manual labor.[60]

Despite Anthony's elitism and the *Standard*'s appeals to class solidarity, Gougar appeared to be making inroads on once inviolate Democratic territory. With Gougar's army of organizers spreading through the city, the Democratic leadership must have felt overwhelmed and outmatched. Long accustomed to relying on "treating," vote buying, and party loyalty, they simply could not match Gougar's grass-roots organizing strategy. At once desperate and defensive, their responses to her campaign were akin to those of a man caught in an avalanche, with similar effect.

Part of the Democrats' problem was that they were so obviously corrupt, at least in regard to the prohibition law. The Law and Order League had an unmuddled issue to rally their forces around, for the saloons were clearly open and flourishing. The Democrats could not directly defend the saloon, because with the Metropolitan Police commission breathing down their necks they had to demonstrate at least minimal support of enforcement. If they failed, they might not only lose the election but also end up in jail. They were thus forced to use code words, imploring citizens to "keep the city as it always has been—prosperous and friendly."[61] They also kept a steady fire trained on Gougar, implying that she was a hired mercenary who cared nothing for the fate of the city.

The Democrats at first tried to finesse the question of the saloon, promising that all drinking establishments would close on Sunday and would not serve minors or inebriated soldiers.[62] They also tried the tested method of intimidation, using mobs to frighten people bringing complaints against saloons. Increased pressure from the Metropolitan Police commission and the state legislature, however, forced the Democrats to try a more subtle strategy of appeasement.[63] With few other options, Mayor Neely, who was running for another term, boldly tried winning over "the ladies" with a pledge to close all the saloons at once and forever.[64] The saloons did indeed close for a short while before the election, but most citizens saw this sudden change of heart as more a result of Neely's desperation than of his dedication to temperance.

The Democratic leaders realized that their biggest problem in the upcoming election was "the new element." Women represented a huge pool of voters who appeared to be immune to the Democrats' traditional methods. Further, Democratic leaders were uncomfortable about organizing a Democratic women's group, no doubt because of their—and their male constituency's—

philosophical opposition to woman suffrage. Gougar's work among working-class women thus went unchallenged.

Although Anglo middle- and upper-class women led the fight for prohibition, some working-class women responded favorably to Gougar's appeals.[65] These women left no record revealing what drew them to her campaign, but a general knowledge of working-class conditions at the time allows room for speculation. A working-class woman had good reason to oppose the saloon, for she could be economically devastated by an alcoholic husband. An alcoholic father was a threat to those closest to him—the combination of his power within the family and his economic powerlessness in the economic world could lead to a ruinous cycle of violence and destitution. Even casual drinking would have strained the poverty-level income of most working-class families. The saloon was a man's special privilege, but the costs were often paid by the entire family.

When all else failed, the Democrats produced one last secret weapon: they hired a reporter from the *New York World* as a character assassin. The reporter concocted a story that Gougar had impugned the morals of upper-class women in Leavenworth. After the story ran in the *World*, the *Standard* immediately reprinted it. Gougar, however, had seen this kind of thing in Indiana and moved quickly to counter any damage. She had the reporter arrested for slander, and though he escaped jail on a technicality, the judge decided in favor of Gougar. The *Times* rushed out an edition that proclaimed her innocence and explained how the ruse had been worked. Apparently the Democratic ploy did little damage to Gougar's reputation. Her charismatic appeal, tied to a strong grass-roots network and undergirded by community institutions, was not easily negated.

Election day dawned, and Gougar's army moved through the city with a well-organized get-out-the-vote drive. When the day ended, the forces of law and order claimed victory, though not always the office: Neely squeaked by with a 16-vote majority out of 6,000 votes cast. His margin of victory came in a last-minute surge of "discovered" votes, which even by the *Standard*'s account sounded fraudulent. In the council races, however, the Law and Order League's "Citizens'" slate captured every seat. It was also elected to all but two of the school board positions.[66] In all the wards, the women voters appeared to provide the Republicans' majority, polling, 2,467 of the 6,437 total votes and voting overwhelmingly for the Citizens' ticket. In the largely black sixth ward, women gave the league's ticket a majority of 356, whereas the G.O.P.'s majority was 48 among men. The biggest surprise was in the working-class wards, where support for the Republicans increased dramatically, along with the number of voters. The two corresponding increases strongly suggest that most of the new Republican votes came from women, a conclusion to which the *Standard* bitterly assented.[67]

At the league's celebration party, Gougar was surrounded by delegations from the black community, the WCTU, and the Knights of Labor, as well as an entourage of elites. Her speech highlighted the work of black women and men during the campaign. Upon conclusion of her talk, she was presented with a silver platter by her "staunchest friends . . . the Knights of Labor."[68] Looking out at the integrated crowd of workers and business people, black and whites, Helen Gougar might have sensed that this was the beginning of a new era in Kansas, and perhaps in the nation. Looking back, how momentous that overcast day in 1884 must have seemed to her, when her efforts on behalf of KESA helped put in motion the movement that had made victory possible.

But as the glow of victory began to fade, the limitations of Gougar's triumph revealed themselves. When the *New York World* charged after the election that the Law and Order League was made up of "the lower classes of women in the state," Laura Johns was quick to set them straight: "The organization of Leavenworth women was instigated, led, and formed of . . . the very best and finest women in point of culture, social position, and Christianity in the city. When they were organized into good working shape they carried the work among the colored people and foreign-born."[69] In Johns's estimation, the "lower classes" could be redeemed, but only at the hands of the "best" women. Woman Movement activists would remold their working-class sisters into the image of middle-class respectability. Unlike KESA's organization, the Law and Order League was rigidly hierarchical. Ordinary folk were given no significant place in the reform movement and thus no lasting stake. In this light, Gougar looks less like an organizer than a missionary, albeit a sensitive and effective one.

With the close of the campaign, the *Times* once again exhibited its true colors toward "the valiant working men and women." Underneath the column "congratulating our laboring men and our colored citizens on their noble stand for law and order," the paper hotly condemned strikes, claiming that they took a high toll on workers' families, and so should be avoided.[70] The story did not mention the effect of poverty-level wages or unsafe working conditions on working-class families. The new city council, for its part, did nothing for the lowly conditions of either workers in general or blacks specifically. Its neglect in these issues, however, should not have come as a surprise. Though the Law and Order League may have gotten working-class support, particularly from women, it had never claimed to be in favor of anything be-yond closing the saloons.

Both sides claimed victory in the "Battle of Leavenworth," but we should consider just who the winners and losers were. The crusaders were white and Protestant, and despite Gougar's efforts, many of her antagonists were work-ing class and foreign born. In cities such as Wichita and Kansas City, Kansas, such divisions were even starker. But this does not mean that workers or the foreign born shared power in Leavenworth's Democratic Party. Rather, the de-mography of Leavenworth's elite—their Southern origins aside—was similar to that in most Kansas cities. What the Democratic Party offered working-class men was accommodation on issues such as prohibition, woman suffrage, and religion. Gougar's army threatened to overturn that arrangement. Beyond this, however, the business of politics would remain business, regardless of who won office.

After the election, Gougar's grass-roots network proved to be a weak trans-plant. Her efforts had been as much a revival as a political campaign, and she left little of lasting value that could be sustained without her. As in a revival, the commitment of the newly converted soon faded after the circuit rider pulled up the tent stakes and rode off to the next town. The Democrats, even in their humiliation, understood this. The *Standard* consoled its followers: "The Standard does not despair. Mrs. Gougar will not be with us always."[71] The Democrats were right. Without Gougar, Leavenworth would return to the Democratic fold in 1888. Prohibition would disappear as a "live" issue, al-though the saloons would remain. After 1887 the number of women voters in Leavenworth dropped precipitously to a mere 622, far outstripping the slight decline in the women's vote throughout Kansas.[72] Gougar's victory was in fact an ambiguous one.

On April 6, 1887, nearly twenty-thousand women throughout Kansas dropped their first municipal ballots into the ballot box. Women made up over 37 percent of the total vote, a number far in excess of the estimates by even the strongest woman suffrage supporters.[73] Yet the legacy of this apparent tri-umph was ambiguous for all involved. As the Battle of Leavenworth shows, one group's fight against oppression need not substantially help another group. The Woman Movement was both an alternative political culture and a part of the mainstream: its members were oppressed as women but also con-tributed to a system that oppressed others. This dialectic relationship was cen-tral to the movement's ideology of reform and to their relationship with women whom they defined as other than "the best kind."

Both Republican and Democratic leaders could find ample reasons for criticizing the women reformers' tactics and ideology as long as male power or prerogatives were threatened. Yet these men's objections to the Woman Movement's political agenda contained a central irony, an example of the law of unintended consequences. Middle-class men had helped develop the ideology of domesticity in part to buttress male control of social power. They had assigned women an exalted status and responsibility within the home in order to help ensure their acceptance of this new code of gender relations. Now, however, women had extended the logic of this ideology—one that had been constructed to bar women from political power—in order not only to enter politics but also to lay claim to a position above men.

Yet unless women could gain some control of the institutions that dominated politics, unless their political language became part of the accepted discourse, they would remain marginalized from power. Women activists desired political power on their own terms, on the basis of their own political culture, brought about by nothing less than a revolution in the practice of politics. Male political leaders maintained, however, that political power could be had only within the context of male-defined politics. And since politicians' control of these institutions remained unchallenged, they were relatively free to ignore the demands of women beyond the local level. Following the 1887 election, the Woman Movement would have to face this tension between gaining a measure of political power and redeeming mainstream political culture.

## THE BONDS OF PARTISANSHIP

Between the 1887 municipal elections and the 1890 Populist uprising, women activists formulated a strategy that would balance their roles as outsiders and as insiders. During municipal election campaigns, they maintained their nonpartisan approach. The partnership that the WCTU and KESA had formed during the campaign to win municipal suffrage flourished after their legislative victory, allowing them to maintain an impressive display of political sisterhood. Politicians, in turn, recognized the Woman Movement's growing influence and were increasingly careful about offending them.

Members of the Woman Movement were well aware that in order to maintain their political capital, women had to keep voting. Male politicians were not acknowledging women's influence in politics because of a sudden burst of protofeminism; rather, they were doing what they were supposed to do—attract the support of voters. The impressive number of women voters in 1887 did much to counter the antisuffragist argument that women would not vote if given the chance. But leaders of the movement knew they had to maintain these levels of participation and increase them if possible. Johns, in her 1887 presidential address, insisted that voting in municipal elections "is more important than any legislative work. More important than the election of any women to office, is that the number of women's votes shall show a considerable gain over . . . 1887, and that they shall be cast for moral measures and moral men."[74]

National suffrage and temperance leaders, who hoped to use the example of Kansas in other state and national campaigns, shared Johns's concern. Just before the 1888 election, Frances Willard issued an appeal through *Our Messenger* reminding women, "You are placed before the world as an example to the flock; universal womanhood is to be judged in you; and the deliverance for which we have so long hoped and prayed is to be hastened or postponed by your decision." Anna Shaw, an officer in both the National Woman Suffrage Association and the WCTU, insisted, "All the states of the union and the nations of Europe are watching."[75] Similar calls to arms, or at least to register, appeared with regularity in *Our Messenger* and friendly newspapers from February through March.

The vigilance of women activists was well warranted, for Easterners were indeed turning their eyes to Kansas once again, wondering what strange new experiment the Sunflower State was up to now. One antisuffragist woman from Massachusetts went so far as to write Governor Martin and request voter turnout information from the last election. She was sure, she wrote, that few women would have shamed themselves and their family by voting.[76]

Although the Woman Movement's get-out-the-vote efforts bore fruit eventually, the first year's results were disappointing. And just as Johns, Willard, and others had predicted, antisuffragists in Kansas and elsewhere pounced on the results of the 1888 election to "prove" that municipal woman suffrage had failed. Kansas suffragists noted, however, that men's votes had dropped off as well that year. To the relief of suffragists, the number of women voters increased again the following year and then continued upward well into the early twentieth century.

But getting women to vote was only half the battle. As Johns had argued, women had to vote well—that is, they had to vote as Woman Movement leaders wanted them to. These women tended to see political issues as dichotomous: one was morally right or morally wrong. Since they believed that "true" women would instinctively know which was which, they expected all respectable women to vote for candidates supported by the movement.

Leaders of the Woman Movement hoped to create a women's block of voters which would force politicians to acknowledge the movement as a new force in politics. In her 1889 address, Johns celebrated men's "growing respect for [women voters'] powers. Men who had regarded women's enfranchisement with lofty scorn were now seeking—entreating the support of women voters."[77] Politicians who failed to take women activists seriously were apt to have to pay for their lack of political acumen with their jobs. In the 1888 Cimmaron election, WCTU members perceived a "failure of the men to be just to the women in joint convention." The women "then withdrew, formed a women's convention and nominated their own ticket." Not only were three of the "women's candidates" elected, but "the opposition was kept so lively as to be compelled to dispense with their refined nonsense against woman suffrage and bring their exalted wives into dangerous proximity to the polluting polls."[78] In Oskaloosa, voters elected the first all-women municipal government in the U.S. By voting as a block, activists and their allies forced antisuffrage men to repudiate their ideas about gender to support their practical political agenda —maintaining power.

When women's votes helped elect Democrats over Republicans, G.O.P. editors and politicians did not much care if the victors met the Woman Movement's exacting moral standards. They were Democrats, and that was enough proof of their depravity. Sol Miller, the editor of the Troy *Kansas Chief* and a leading Republican Party boss, routinely castigated women reformers for their continued insistence on rejecting morally suspect Republicans. He was particularly incensed at the efforts of Helen Gougar, who, he claimed, had worked against Republican candidates both in Indiana and in Kansas. "Whether Democratic Party boodle paid for it," Miller noted, "she probably knows. . . . If she should invade the state again, she might tempt the legislature to repeal the woman suffrage rights already granted." For Miller, Gougar's victory in Leavenworth was more an aberration than proof of her "usefulness," concluding that "our corner of Kansas" was better off without an "incessant squawker" like Gougar.[79]

African-American editors shared with their white counterparts a proprietary interest in those they considered "their" women. Black editors objected bitterly to the attempts of white women suffragists to organize their black sisters. Black politicians, like Woman Movement leaders, were struggling to build and control a block of voters to use as leverage when negotiating with white politicians. When women activists declared during the 1888 municipal elections that they would "take particular interest in the colored people in the coming spring election," black political leaders perceived the action as political trespassing. They were particularly incensed when the (white) WCTU superintendent of Work Among Colored Women claimed that her organization was instructing African-American women "in what offices need be filled, and the necessity of electing good temperance men." In 1889, when a WCTU committee attempted to organize black women in Leavenworth, the city's African-American newspaper responded angrily: "Thank you ladies! We know our duties as citizens, without putting yourself to any inconvenience." Turning the Woman Movement's proselytizing upside down, he suggested arranging "a committee [of black men] to confer with you in regard to your duties as citizens." Unlike the movement, he suggested, Kansas blacks had stood by the G.O.P. "We desire to see that you do for the party what we have."[80] Neither black politicians nor white women activists saw any need to ask Black women themselves which political agenda they wished to support.

African-American leaders had little choice but to follow the dictates of the Republican Party and hope that it would reward them for their loyalty. Since no party was willing to enact legislation explicitly in favor of African-Americans, they had to be content with low-level patronage jobs from state and local Republican politicians. Where black votes did matter the most, however, was in the large cities, where they sometimes made up as much as 25 percent of the vote. Here black voters could swing elections, and politicians who could deliver large blocks of these votes were valued by the ruling elite.[81]

Black political leaders never took advantage of the fact that the percentage of black women who voted in municipal elections was far greater than that of white women. In Kansas City, Kansas, for example, black women constituted one-third of the women voters, while African-Americans made up about one-quarter of the population.[82] Yet black editors and politicians made no effort to mobilize black women as voters, a strategy that would have increased their political power in the cities. As one writer put it, African-American women could best help the race by "maintaining the home and religious standards, and leaving politics to the men."[83] Rather than empower black women, African-American political leaders chose to maintain the status quo between the sexes.

Even as the Woman Movement was transformed from a loose affiliation of women's organizations into a more coherent entity, activists increasingly had to struggle with the internal contradictions of their movement which threatened to reverse the momentum toward unification. Most prominently, they had to confront their ambiguous relationship with the political parties, particularly the ruling Republicans. As women reformers proclaimed their allegiance to one or another party—or rejected the idea of partisanship altogether—fault lines began to reveal themselves and widen even as the movement's foundation appeared to be growing more solid.

The roots of the Woman Movement's policy of utilizing respectability as an organizing tool were in part the product of a racist, nativist mainstream culture. The policy, however, was not inevitable. Leaders chose the degree to which they would implement it, as Gougar's Leavenworth campaign demonstrates. If the movement's vision of a monolithic political sisterhood was a fiction, then women activists were largely the authors. The same may be said for their approach to partisan politics. They employed partisan or nonpartisan strategies as they fitted their political needs and in response to specific political contexts.

The movement's organizers could be remarkably nonpartisan during local elections, insisting that all candidates, regardless of party affiliation, conform to middle-class women's notions of morality. Even after the 1887 elections, Republican politicians continued to misunderstand these activists' refusal to conform to the rules of "business politics" and party loyalty during municipal elections. Perhaps the politicians were misled by women leaders' very different approach to state politics. Many of these same women, when gathered at their state convention, had few apparent qualms about tossing aside their moral concerns about partisanship while supporting a resolution that lionized their particular party. In such cases, they displayed a partisan zeal that might have made John J. Ingalls proud, had not the mere thought of women debating politics rendered him dyspeptic.

Both the national and Kansas WCTU conventions were the site of bitter partisan battles, largely because of the growth of the Prohibition Party during the 1880s. In 1884, Frances Willard combined her charisma and personal standing with skillful parliamentary machinations to gain the national WCTU's support for St. John's presidential candidacy. J. Ellen Foster, a well-established Iowa lawyer and prohibitionist, led the opposition. Foster, a zealous Republican, raised the nonpartisan banner largely as a convenient defense for the outnumbered G.O.P. women. Although Willard was victorious, Foster and her supporters fought back at each subsequent convention, transforming what had been grand affirmations of solidarity into snarling dogfights.[84]

In 1888, Foster delivered what she hoped would be a final, irrevocable blow to Willard's policy by forming a rival, nonpartisan WCTU. Foster, in a story featured prominently in the Topeka *Capital,* instructed her supporters, "if the crusade fire still burns on the altar of your heart, if you believe that God still has work for a women's temperance organization, then leave the party union, gather those about you who are like-minded, and form a non-partisan, non-auxiliary union, and do the blessed work as of yore."[85] Unfortunately for Foster, few women abandoned Willard and the national WCTU. Only the WCTU in Iowa, Foster's home state, adopted a nonpartisan policy.

In Kansas the battle lines were less clearly drawn, largely because of the state Republican Party's ambivalent stance toward prohibition. The Kansas WCTU had three major factions, with numerous permutations. Prohibition Party supporters, led by Fanny Rastall, made up the most powerful faction. This group was split, however, between those championing the Prohibition Party at all levels and those who favored retaining Republican allegiance to the state party. Republican temperance women were quite numerous, but they too were divided: some were strong supporters of the state party, others stood by the national as well as state G.O.P., and a third group advocated a strict nonpartisan stance. The last major faction consisted of radical nonpartisans who eschewed any support of "men's" political parties, seeing them as the basis for what was inherently wrong with the system. Finally, there were a few Democrats, but since their party was openly opposed to both prohibition and woman suffrage, they usually argued the merits of nonpartisanship.[86]

Combatants put forth equally logical yet totally opposite arguments for their cases, revealing the many fissures hidden within the WCTU's ideological foundation. Rastall reasoned that nonpartisanship meant supporting all parties that endorsed prohibition. At the national level, she maintained, the choice was obvious. "Prohibition, national prohibition, enforced prohibition is our object, toward which we move with steady eye, lured not to right or left by entreaty or threat. . . . If any party says, 'trust us, we will do it at the right time,' we answer: there is no time like the present."[87] Since the national Republicans had clearly stated that the time was indeed not yet right, Rastall felt sole support for the Prohibitionists was justified.

Among all the parties, the Prohibitionists were the only ones to incorporate fully the Christian, moral language of the Woman Movement. The 1885 Prohibition Party platform acknowledged "almighty God as the sovereign of all men, whose laws human enactments should conform to."[88] Its leaders cared little for the practical politics of Democrats and Republicans. "The question is not how long it will take to enforce [the prohibition amendment], but whether it is a good law," thundered a Prohibitionist editor. "If the answer is in the affirmative, then pass it and enforce it. . . . Have faith in God and dare to do right. . . . The man who will not vote for his principles because he is in the minority is unworthy of the name of man." Masculinity could be measured, he insisted, not by a man's fealty to his party but by his fealty to God.[89]

Republican politicians, including those who supported prohibition, had little patience for this type of talk. The *Great Bend Register,* after castigating St. John for his presidential bid and women's prominent role in it, remarked, "Yesterday was the day set apart by the National Prohibitionists as a day of fasting, humiliation, confession and prayer for the triumph of the prohibition cause. Prayer is good, fasting we never admired, but it takes votes to win on election day." The *Register* had little interest in moral politics for its own sake—that was "best left to the ladies." For Republican politicians the question was not whether a law was a good or bad one but whether it increased their chances of getting elected.

Rastall often pointed to this type of logic when explaining to her troops why the G.O.P. could not be trusted. Yet she also understood, more than Prohibitionist men, in fact, that the state Republican Party could be manipulated to support the prohibitionists' cause. During the mid-1880s she gave the state G.O.P. her qualified, cautious support, pledging "the fealty of the WCTU of Kansas . . . to the Republican Party, so long as it is loyal to prohibition." She added, however: "We should now define loyalty. The leading party papers of the State now advocate that the question be buried and prohibition be ignored hereafter in party politics." She warned that "if the Republican Party is to retain supremacy in Kansas, it must not only keep prohibition of the liquor traffic among its cardinal principles, it must give us enforced prohibition; it must name as candidates for office men who, without fear or favor, will enforce the law we so highly prize—the constitutional law for the protection of home and children."[90] With such pronouncements, Rastall and her supporters rejected all talk of political expediency. They argued that the Prohibition Party had been formed only after the two parties, particularly the Republicans, had allowed their political concerns to overwhelm their moral beliefs. Yet Rastall also understood that the power of the Republican Party in Kansas had to be considered and its partial success in supporting prohibition recognized.

Republican supporters in the WCTU drew on G.O.P. accomplishments when arguing the merits of their party. They maintained that strong Republican support from the Kansas WCTU would convince the national G.O.P. of the wisdom of a prohibition plank in their platform. Although this assumption was somewhat naïve, its corollary had more merit: the WCTU's vocal opposition to the national Republicans would probably antagonize state leaders and weaken their support for enforcement. A declaration against the national Republican Party, according to a WCTU delegate named Mrs. Taylor, would be seen as attacking "the party [that] had given us prohibition"; she "thought the sin of ingratitude was an appalling one."[91] Perhaps recognizing this, the convention endorsed the state G.O.P., but only "as long as it continues to enforce prohibition." The WCTU continued to support the national Prohibition Party, however.

This compromise position was still unacceptable to a third faction, which gained increasing favor after the WCTU's bitter debates in 1884–86.[92] These women echoed Foster's argument at the national convention in favor of non-partisanship. However, where Foster, a zealous partisan, had hoisted the non-partisan banner largely as a maneuver to bolster her weak position in the national organization, the Kansas contingent was actually antipartisan.[93] They wanted no part of male political culture at all, arguing that "it would be best to stay out of party matters altogether."[94] By 1894 these women would become more insistent that if women were to truly clean up the "dirty pool" of men's politics, they would have to eschew the temptation of men's parties.

After 1886 the partisan battles—at least the open ones—no longer dominated the WCTU's concerns. In part this was due to the trauma caused by the partisan rifts in 1884 and 1885, which caused a number of members to abandon the organization for less upsetting endeavors.[95] Rastall, usually on the offensive in her convention address, felt compelled to devote some of her 1886 speech to defending the WCTU's past political positions. But beyond these internal considerations, the organization's new stance was no doubt shaped by the collapse of the Kansas Prohibition Party, which largely disappeared after 1888. With no third party to support, the former Prohibitionists in the WCTU joined with the nonpartisans—the latter probably including some exhausted Republicans—and rejected any official endorsement.

Such a stance, however, did not cause Rastall to underplay her criticism of the Republican Party for its less-than-complete enforcement policies. Republicans, for their part, were apparently not shy about returning her volleys. In 1889, Rastall responded to these charges by counterattacking, claiming that Republicans hid behind partisanship to avoid challenges to their enforcement policies. "Should a public officer be criticized," she argued, "the cry of 'party' is raised, until we are led to wonder if one man is the party. . . . So far as I know, the WCTU of Kansas has made no assault on any party; individuals or official neglect of duty had been exposed in cases where it seemed necessary."[96] To the charge that she "hated" the Republican Party, Rastall responded that she "could not hate the Republican Party any more than I hate an erring or deceased friend."[97] Rastall left her readers to decide which of the two choices applied to the G.O.P.

In challenging the Republicans, Rastall believed the WCTU could best gain influence in state politics by playing the gadfly. By keeping pressure on the Republican Party to "do right," Rastall and the WCTU were able to secure a number of enforcement and "social purity" bills in the state legislature. Her constant criticism of the party had its risks, however, as Republican politicians' growing hostility toward her indicates. Republican WCTU supporters argued against the strategy of tweaking the lion's tail, believing that the G.O.P. would respond more favorably to praise than criticism. Further, Republican women probably wanted to prove to their party that they could deliver the WCTU's support when necessary. Yet as long as the Prohibition Party remained an active presence, Rastall's policy worked to influence Republicans considerably.

KESA had similar, though less divisive, internal struggles, the major factions consisting of Republicans, Union Laborites, and nonpartisans. At the 1887 convention, suffragists fought over whether to thank the Republicans for granting women municipal suffrage. Union Laborites argued that their party had unequivocally endorsed woman suffrage since the Greenbackers, something the G.O.P. had never done. Anna Howard Shaw, visiting from the National Woman Suffrage Association, suggested that any partisan endorsement would exclude women with party affiliations other than those on the resolution. Finally, some KESA members simply wanted nothing to do with "men's" parties. Johns, whose Republican sympathies were well known, argued forcefully for the resolution and got it passed.[98]

Although Johns's political sympathies shaped her policy, it is also true that her strategy, like Rastall's, made practical political sense. At the time, the Republicans were the only political game in town. As suffragists had learned in 1867, they would be unlikely to succeed in Kansas if the Republican Party campaigned against them. Yet however supportive Johns was of the state G.O.P., she did not let her Republican sympathies interfere with KESA's commitment to nonpartisan municipal election campaigns. Indeed, at the same convention at which she pushed the pro-Republican resolution, Johns praised the fact that during municipal elections, "party lines were almost entirely ignored, and the efforts of the women [were] directed toward the election of men pledging themselves to the enforcement of law, and the rescue of our cities from the ghastly vices that infest them."[99]

Johns continued to champion the Woman Movement's nonpartisan approach to local politics even after the Populists' challenge to Republican rule rendered the approach truly treasonous in the eyes of some state G.O.P. leaders. Johns's policy earned her the temporary enmity of Joseph Hudson, editor of the influential Topeka *Capital* and a suffrage supporter, even as she was organizing the Kansas chapter of the Republican Women's Association. Yet Johns and other Republican woman suffragists remained unrepentant about their efforts to defeat "the friends of 'King Alcohol' "—even when they were Republicans—while working to establish a formal role for women in the state G.O.P.

Because middle-class women had demonstrated the ability to affect local politics as a voting block, it made sense to activists in the Woman Movement to maintain a nonpartisan approach to municipal politics. In state politics, however, the issues of prohibition and suffrage did not sway many men, and women had no vote. Thus many women activists looked for a role in the parties to secure influence in state politics. Further, they were committed to both the ideological positions and cultural symbolism that their parties represented. Ultimately, these women could no more ignore their party-based loyalties than they could reject their gender-based beliefs.

Although Woman Movement activists openly displayed party loyalties, they were not pleased when their partisan battles received prominent newspaper coverage. Kansas editors knew news when they saw it and enjoyed playing up the novelty of women locked in fierce parliamentary combat. Further, as most Kansas editors specialized in shooting down overly bombastic or moralistic claims—except, perhaps, their own—the Woman Movement's unsisterly conduct provided instant ammunition for the press. The *Daily Commonwealth* covered the 1885 WCTU convention and reported that "whenever one of the avowed advocates of [the Democrats] rose to address the convention there was a noticeable tightening of mouths and firmer expressions on the countenances of members of the opposite party. . . . [T]he [Prohibition] party had strong advocates, notably Miss Newly and Mrs. St. John. This element was greatly feared, and a lady said to the Commonwealth man that it was a 'dangerous element in the convention.' "[100] The reporter's tone conjures up an image of the "Commonwealth man" addressing "a lady" with his tongue firmly in cheek, while nodding earnestly at her "unladylike" opinions. Without openly ridiculing his subjects, the reporter rendered an image of a mildly amusing scene where women were playing at being men.

During the 1887 municipal elections, editors had supported woman suffrage only when women had endorsed the editor's party of choice. When they crossed party lines, however, editors claimed that the "new element" had traversed enemy territory. Editors approached the Woman Movement's convention fights in much the same manner, praising an organization's nonpartisan or partisan position according to how it affected the editor's party. In 1885 the Topeka *Capital* played it both ways, praising the WCTU's rather lukewarm "encouraging" of the G.O.P. but adding ominously, "Whether more or better work should be done by the Union if it should keep aloof from all political parties is as yet a matter of opinion, and it will be settled one way or the other, as the cause of temperance or the cause of party politics shall appear to have the strongest hold upon the membership. The quiet, silent, powerful forces of Christian energy and the noisy machinery of practical politics may or may not work well together."[101] As the paper would later indicate, Christian energy went particularly well with the noisy machinery of the Republican Party. In the *Capital*'s view, however, the pairing of the WCTU with the Prohibition Party made for a calamitous—and unacceptable—racket.

The threats and imprecations tossed by editors, however unwelcome to women activists, were a strong testament to the Woman Movement's new-found political influence. As the *Capital* noted, the WCTU had become a power to be reckoned with in both local and state politics, and this was before municipal woman suffrage. After women won this limited franchise, their power was even more evident.

## "WE FELT OUR POWER": BUILDING A UNIFIED MOVEMENT

From the campaign to secure municipal woman suffrage to the 1894 state suffrage campaign, the WCTU and KESA enjoyed a symbiotic relationship that enabled them to achieve impressive victories in both state and local politics. The WCTU had supported suffrage since 1880 and had been the leading voice for women's enfranchisement in the years before KESA was formed. KESA members balanced this relationship by unswervingly supporting prohibition. If KESA harbored any free-thinking antiprohibitionists, they did not choose to express their sentiments.

By the late 1880s, the two organizations' similarities extended to both their leadership and the rank and file. Beyond Rastall's enthusiastic support for suffrage, the WCTU leadership included Susan A. Thurston, who served as state supervisor of the Franchise Department and the Topeka Equal Suffrage Association president, and her sister Olive P. Bray, editor of *Our Messenger* and a KESA member. Laura Johns served simultaneously as KESA president and the WCTU's state supervisor of the Scientific Temperance Instruction Department. Anna C. Wait, one of the founders of KESA, was a prominent member of the Prohibition Party. Reporting for *Our Messenger* about a local suffrage meeting, a KESA member wrote, "the familiar faces of so many white ribbon-ers made us feel that we were in a WCTU convention, and the list of officers elected has many names well known to our work."[102] Overall, territorial disputes between the two organizations were virtually nonexistent. At the 1891 KESA convention it was reported with approval that although the Winfield

Suffrage Society had disbanded, a strong WCTU chapter had taken its place.[103]

Besides their shared goals and membership, KESA and the WCTU also spoke the same political language, derived from their urban Anglo middle-class experience. This discourse maintained that women had a duty as Christians and citizens of the Republic to participate in politics. Espousing the vision of a monolithic political sisterhood that transcended "man-made" divisions of party and class, Woman Movement activists believed there was a single political agenda to which all women could ascribe. They utilized this fiction to organize middle-class women into a movement that connected the WCTU and KESA with a growing list of newly politicized women's groups, including the Woman's Relief Corps and the Social Science Federation.

Although few Kansans viewed the Woman's Relief Corps as a political organization, it was an early ally in the prohibition and suffrage causes. The corps was a service organization affiliated with the Grand Army of the Republic, which was made up of Union veterans. Kansas, with its unusually high number of Civil War veterans, had a correspondingly large Woman's Relief Corps, which during the 1880s provided womanpower for the WCTU's and KESA's legislative campaigns. At a huge camp meeting in 1886, *Our Messenger* reported, "On the right of the platform was a tent with 'WCTU Headquarters' in large letters on the side, and a little farther off was another tent marked 'WRC Headquarters,' for the three great women's societies, the Equal Suffrage Association, the Woman's Relief Corps, and the Woman's Christian Temperance Union, were united in carrying on this camp meeting and worked harmoniously together, each endorsing the others and mutually aiding one another."[104] These local efforts at cooperation became the basis for the growing effort by those active in the Woman Movement to build a gender-based coalition.

Although not as large as the "Big Three," the Social Science Federation served as a meeting place for some of the Woman Movement's most influential leaders.[105] A self-proclaimed progressive club, the federation's ideology predated that era, and as an early supporter of women's rights, dress reform, and a scientific approach to everything from nutrition to government, it attracted a variety of reform-minded women to its ranks. Unlike the national Social Science Association, however, the Kansas organization was constituted entirely of women.[106] Federation meetings gave women the opportunity to address a range of challenging subjects beyond the domestic boundaries sanctioned by the mainstream, although these were not neglected. Topics ranged widely, including hypnotism, airships, the Pasteur system, the electric fountain, dress reform, and Bellamy's *Looking Backward*.[107] All provided the means to self-education and the sharpening of debating skills.

The Social Science Federation was perhaps the most intellectually challenging of the many self-education clubs, modeled after Eastern counterparts, which Kansas women formed in the late nineteenth century. The most prominent organization was Western Sorosis, affiliated with the national Sorosis Club. Founded by a journalist, Jane Croly of Chicago, Sorosis served as a meeting and networking place for women professionals.[108] By 1890 women had established many other professional organizations, including the Kansas State Teachers Association.[109] Made up of educated, energetic women who were pushing the gender barriers in their own professions, these groups presented suffragists and temperance activists with potential supporters for their causes.

Although the many women's literary, social, and charitable organizations could serve as training grounds for future leaders, few of these clubs were interested in political activities. Leaders in the Woman Movement such as Johns and Rastall had little patience for these organizations, believing that they took women away from suffrage and temperance activities. "With church work they willingly wear themselves out," Johns complained. "[F]or the Y.M.C.A. or other philanthropy . . . they perform disagreeable, often menial service. They almost die for these, but for their own enfranchisement they would not let their little finger ache. So much better do women like to work for the advancement of others than for their own promotion, and for this tendency they have been so much commended, that they are by no means sure it isn't their one *raison d'etre*."[110] Despite Johns's disparaging remarks, she did also note the potential to convert these women into committed activists. All that was needed was for women's clubs to direct their work, at least in part, to a more practical purpose. And Johns, along with other Woman Movement leaders, knew just where such purposeful energies should be directed.

To this end, Johns and Rastall issued a call in 1888 "to all state organizations of women to send representatives to . . . the State Equal Suffrage Association, for the purpose of forming a Kansas Council of Women."[111] Inspired by Francis Willard's formation of the National Council of Women, the Kansas chapter brought together delegates representing the full range of women's organizations, some eighteen in all. Beyond the WCTU, KESA, Woman's Relief Corps, and the Social Science Federation, representatives arrived from Protestant missionary groups, charitable organizations, social and literary clubs, and professional associations. In the council's preamble to its constitution, the delegates declared their basic agreement about women's role in state politics.

We, women of the state of Kansas, sincerely believing that the best good of our homes and state will be advanced by our own greater unity of thought, sympathy and purpose, and that an organized movement of women will best conserve the highest good of the family and the state, do hereby band ourselves together in a confederation of workers committed to the overthrow of all forms of ignorance and injustice, and to the application of the golden rule to society, custom, and law.[112]

With one foot in the home and the other in the political arena, the Council of Women believed it could define and enact a women-centered electoral agenda.

The founders of the council made clear that the new organization would in no way dictate its program to its auxiliaries. Instead, it was to be the official formation of the unofficial network that urban Anglo women had established throughout Kansas. Its rather vague and grandiose resolution to "overthrow all forms of ignorance and injustice" was similarly a restatement of Woman Movement activists' assumption that all respectable women shared a common vision of society. Thus when the Kansas Senate in 1889 suddenly voted to drop the age of consent for girls from nineteen to thirteen, the WCTU was able to assemble the troops quickly on the side of "the women's issue." The resulting avalanche of petitions helped bury the bill in committee when it came to the House and strengthened the WCTU's reputation as a lobbyist.[113]

Johns attributed the movement's quick victory in the age of consent battle to the indirect power of municipal woman suffrage. "If we . . . ever had any doubt that even our small moiety of the suffrage would strengthen our influence for righteousness," Johns declared, "the effect of our protest at this time and the attitude of the politicians toward us would have dispelled that doubt. We felt our power and it was a new thrill which we experienced." This power, however, had been gained in a particular political context. When the context shifted, women reformers would have to reorient themselves or face being left behind.

Such victories gave the Woman Movement a sense of momentum and a sense of history. Participants could see themselves in an ever expanding army, marching inexorably onward to further the cause of all women. Each step into the political field seemed to mark another advancement, big or small. Women, united and unflinching, could successfully challenge the forces of immorality. It was a powerful fiction and an effective organizing tool, but its proponents would eventually have to confront reality.

The Council of Women stood as a monument to Rastall and Johns's vision of a political sisterhood. Its lack of Afro-American, Catholic, immigrant, or

Along with Fanny Rastall, Laura
Johns was the architect of a united
Woman Movement in Kansas. *Kansas
State Historical Society*

rural women's groups was also a symbol, and one that most Woman Movement activists approved of, mutely if not openly. The purity of the membership
established the council as a representative body of the "best" women, at least
in the eyes of its peers. Few were concerned that this exclusivist practice put
their commitment to ending injustice into question. In the eyes of Women's
Council members, respectability equaled morality. They could rationalize that
they spoke for their less fortunate sisters and that reformers' political activities
would one day enable all women to become respectable.

The Woman Movement could ignore such contradictions because those excluded made no attempt to gain entrance. Although the movement would
eventually pay a price for these policies, the cost would not be obvious to any
activists. In the meantime its elitism was central to its appeal among most
middle-class Anglos, its support from Republican politicians, and its self-
identity. When dealing with those in power, respectability paid important
short-term dividends.

Members cherished the world of the parlor, church, and lecture hall, and the political culture it produced. It spoke of a caring, informed, moral citizenry, of the golden rule and the power of sisterly affection. This way of practicing politics earned the devotion of thousands of Kansas women. Yet those who gained power from this vision did so by excluding vast areas of reality from their perception of politics. Divisions among women and men and among women themselves—persistent divisions that formed the fault lines of American culture—could not be ignored forever.

Those in the Woman Movement took on the preconditions given them by the middle-class ideology of "separate sphere" and "respectability" and shaped it to fit their needs. In doing so, they created a political culture they claimed represented an alternative to mainstream politics. Many activists, however, had not decided whether they wanted to tear the house called male politics down or to dwell inside it as equals. With the forming of the Populist Party in Kansas, that choice became ever more difficult and ever more significant for the future of the Woman Movement.

# FOUR

# ⊰ LIKE A FAMILY ⊱

## BUILDING THE ALLIANCE COMMUNITY

**A** simple law of the physics of economics: the higher the boom, the harder the fall. For Kansans the bust of 1888 was a very hard fall indeed. Once again, nature had a hand: drought returned to the Plains after nearly five years of plentiful rain. Nor did the drought come alone. When the rain dried up, the hot winds began to blow, followed, somewhat improbably, by successive blizzard-ridden winters. The drought did not have to stay long—just a year or two, enough time to shatter some hard-earned illusions. Crops failed, while prices continued the downward spiral begun in the mid-eighties. Along with shriveling the corn and winter wheat, the drought withered the confidence of all who had built the boom's precarious edifice. With no foundation to support it, those who had peddled unbounded optimism as Kansas's leading commodity could no longer find a buyer. Land values collapsed, suddenly, spectacularly. When panicked Eastern investors cut off the flow of credit and moved to secure their loans, the collapse was complete.[1]

And then came the exodus. Whole counties in Western Kansas were depopulated, leaving a cultural landscape as devastated as the "hoppers" had left the fields and gardens. The speculators and quick buck artists left first, scurrying out of the ruins in search of a newly manufactured paradise. Next went those who had come to Kansas with dreams of a new life but had arrived too late and acquired too little to justify trying to hang on. Many of these people joined the Sooners in the land rush in Oklahoma after the U.S. government repudiated yet another series of treaties and opened the erstwhile Indian Territory to settlement. Others returned "back East," "back to the wife's relations"—back to the reality of yet another failed dream. In two years the state experienced a 13 percent loss in farm population and an extraordinary 36 percent drop in the towns.[2] Most of those farmers who remained in central Kansas were left with a crushing debt, and no apparent means of paying it off.

Boom, bust, protest—it is tempting to attach this third component to the cultural cycle of nineteenth-century Kansas. For just as the hopper invasion and economic depression of 1873–74 triggered the success of the Grange, so too did the bust of '88 appear to usher in the growth of the Farmers' Alliance. Although representatives from the Southern Farmers' Alliance had begun organizing in Kansas a year earlier, they made headway only after hard times hit. By late 1888, when the Kansas State Farmers' Alliance held its first meeting, a handful of "lecturers" from Texas had signed up over five thousand new members. By the second state meeting in August 1889, delegates reported a membership of twenty-five thousand from thirty counties; nine months later, the Farmers' Alliance counted fifty-two field organizers working to create and maintain over two thousand suballiances with a total of more than one hundred thousand members.[3]

Numerous historians have pointed to central Kansas's enormous debt load—the highest in the country—to explain why that region provided the bulk of support for the Farmers' Alliance and Populist Party. But although statistics on mortgages establish the very real economic pressures felt by Kansas farmers, these figures alone do not explain how Alliance organizers and members were able to create a vibrant political culture.[4] Percentages and averages do not tell the story of why farmers, faced with economic ruin, chose to join together in weekly meetings, to read books, pamphlets, and newspapers about politics, to debate issues, to make speeches, and to present papers. Economic hardship was the catalyst, not the cause. Although the bust may have inclined Kansas farm people to look favorably on the movement, hard times alone did not create it or guarantee its success.

Alliance organizers had to convince rural people, isolated on their farms, that they were part of a national reform movement. Anglo farm people's sense of community on the Plains was transient and fractured, and organizers faced many obstacles to creating a political community among people with little experience of class or group solidarity. Once defined as a political entity, farm people needed to learn how to act as a group: to recognize shared interests, and more importantly, to trust one another's motivations and judgments. Further, they had to develop political self-respect; they needed to believe that what they said and did as political actors mattered. As Lawrence Goodwyn has written, "the people need to 'see themselves' participate in democratic forms."[5] Farm people had to be convinced that it was worth their time and effort to participate in the Alliance. There was no guarantee that given the opportunity, people would naturally choose active citizenship. Farm people's time and energy were in short supply; the Alliance needed to offer inducements that made paticipation emotionally and economically worthwhile, that made active membership a pleasure as well as a duty.

The Farmers' Alliance's program offered farm people concrete plans to challenge the corporate elite. "The people" could overcome the avaricious policies of the railroads by nationalizing them, thus removing the profit motive from what the Alliance believed should have been a common resource. This strategy would in turn eliminate the corrupt relationship between corporations and politicians and would render both more efficient and solicitous of the people's will. Organizers argued that the government, not the national banks, should be solely responsible for issuing money. With the control of the banks returned to the citizenry, the money supply could be expanded and mortgage rates lowered. In order to stabilize crop prices, the Alliance demanded that speculating in crop and livestock futures be abolished and the system of agricultural trading be tightly supervised. It also called for the government to reclaim all unused railroad lands and make them available to settlers. Once these reforms were in place, argued the Alliance, farm people would be able to compete with other classes and would then succeed or fail on their own merits.[6]

Like the Woman Movement, the Alliance presented Kansans with a vision of politics that could inspire and uplift current and potential members. Where the Woman Movement embraced a vision of women as a monolithic, morally superior group, the Alliance constructed an ideal of a "producers' republic." To create this ideal, organizers drew on an image familiar to Gilded Age reformers: "the great and noble farming and laboring class," who constituted the "middle class." Arrayed against these "producers" were the "parasites" of society—the bankers, speculators, lawyers, politicians, and the corporate elite.[7] It was not clear on which side the Alliance placed those who had traditionally considered themselves middle class, such as clerks, merchants, and other service people. Beneath the middle class (however defined) were the hopelessly poor, the wretched of the cities, people to be pitied and protected, so that all could one day have the opportunity to stand proudly in the ranks of the producers.

Alliance leaders placed the farm family at the heart of their idealized vision, using it as both a guiding metaphor and a practical model for their organizational structure. According to William Peffer, editor of the *Kansas Farmer,* "The Grange and the Alliance are families where the father's manhood, the mother's devotion, the brother's affection and the sister's love are so cultivated and developed that they reach out beyond the purview of the family circle and embrace with fraternal kindness every member of the order."[8] When using the metaphor of the family, writers equated it with trust, shared responsibility, reciprocity, and social order. And like the farm family, the Alliance offered a productive role for every member of the household. Its leaders assumed that mothers, fathers, sons, and daughters would reproduce within the Alliance organization the cooperative model of family labor found on the farm.

Farmers' Alliance leaders believed that the farm family, as the basic unit of the farm community, was the foundation for the organization's political culture. Taking their cue from the Grange, the Alliance integrated the needs and perspectives of women and children into the tactics and ideology of the organization. The result was a very different culture from the fraternal world of mainstream politics. Farmers' Alliance activists used gender-inclusive spaces to create a family-based political community. They also realized that women played a particular role in the farm family and community which made both their participation and their perspective vital to the movement.

The leaders' ideal of familial politics differed in one important respect from life on the farm: it encouraged women to have an equal political voice with men in the local suballiance. At home, a farm woman's second-class status was reinforced by her political inequality—her inability to vote and her general inequality under the law provided a clear line of demarcation between the sexes. This political imbalance reinforced societal norms about women's and men's proper roles, and the normal lines of authority. Society had clearly designated men head of the house; women were clearly their advisers.

But in the Alliance this line was removed. Although women's dues were half those men—a policy meant to encourage women's participation—women were given an equal vote in the running of the suballiance, and no other by-law used gender as a means to differentiate membership. Within the movement women and men were equal under the rules. Indeed, Alliance leaders' professions of support for this ideal suggest that the organization had a firm commitment to gender equality. But the leadership also put forth contradictory rhetoric that undermined its support of women's equal participation. The membership's negotiations and struggles within this idealized vision provide a more accurate picture of gender relations in the Alliance.

This tension between the social reality of the farm family and the utopian vision of the Alliance leadership may be found in farm women's occupational title. The term they chose to identify themselves was *farmer's wife*. Even women whose husbands had passed away and who ran the farm themselves chose that term. The unmarried woman who worked on a farm had no title at all. The meaning of *farmer's wife* is worth considering, for it embodies the essential contradictions of women's place in the movement.

At its worst, the term seems to suggest ownership, seems to link the woman to her husband, dead or alive, by the insidious possessive. And just as the possessive connected the farmer to his wife, this metaphoric tether snaked its way through the various aspects of their lives, binding a woman to "her" man, from the first inclination to head West to the decision to mortgage the farm. Even in her membership in the Alliance, a farm woman almost always joined with her husband whereas men often joined alone. But farm women—farmers' wives—did not see themselves this way. Farm women took great pride in the work that they did: they provided money for the family and brought food from the ground to the table. A farm woman was a worker, and proud of it. For her, the possessive was a sign not of dependence but of partnership, a recognition that she shared her husband's occupation.

The role of these farmers' wives in the Alliance reflects this ambivalence. The leadership sought to integrate women into the organization, to make them equal partners in the Alliance family. But although the movement stressed women's political equality with men, farm people generally agreed that men had the final word at home. In attempting to build their mixed-gender political culture, Alliance leaders would soon be faced with this basic contradiction.

## FROM THE CRADLE TO THE COURT: CREATING A MIXED-GENDER POLITICAL CULTURE

"The object of the Farmers Alliance," wrote William Peffer, "is best expressed in one word . . . EDUCATION." His notion of education, however, included far more than simply learning about the issues of the day. Rather, he and other Alliance leaders advocated "education that will reach from the cradle to the court, that will give us better homes, better schools, better politics, better legislation, and better administration of the law; education that will give us better methods in the home, on the farm, in the storeroom, in the market places; . . . education that will build up agriculture on a high, broad level, where farmers shall be in all respects abreast with the foremost men of the time."[9] Peffer believed the Alliance's program needed to include all members of the family at all points in their lives. "From the cradle to the court," from the home to politics: all forms of knowledge must be integrated. If the family was a microcosm of the country, then the family had to be transformed, "improved," and all its members remade into model citizens.

The Farmers' Alliance was not alone in celebrating the family; it was a central metaphor in mainstream American culture. And other movements, such as the Knights of Labor, encouraged women to participate in the organization. But the Alliance, following the lead of the Grange, was probably alone in using the idealized family as a model for political organization; only the Alliance envisioned a productive role for every member of the family, so that the make-up of the organization's "family" was similar to that of the farm family. Leaders were not simply fighting for a set of political demands; they were also struggling to transform rural life into a culture that was more livable, more desirable, more vibrant than it had previously been. Like the Grange, the Alliance sought to create a sense of community among farmers, a community that was at once political, social, economic, and intellectual.

The Alliance constructed a political culture that would accommodate this family-oriented agenda. The Woman Movement, concerned more with organizing and educating women, shaped its political culture to serve the needs of its membership. Members met in woman-identified spaces such as parlors and churches and infused their political language with Christian metaphors. The movement allowed women to feel comfortable in these surroundings while discouraging participation by their urban middle-class male counterparts. Party bosses, meanwhile, practiced their politics in male-identified spaces and embraced masculinist imagery. When party leaders were not practicing politics in private men's clubs or saloons, they brought the culture of the saloon into the streets.

The Farmers' Alliance openly defied the *modus operandi* of the mainstream, believing that alcohol, cigars, and bawdy humor were the product of a debased political system. The Alliance was not, however, averse to brass bands or barbecues. It blended these elements of men's politics with features that embraced the entire family. At the same time, its tactics and language often resembled the Woman Movement's, including the use of Christian metaphors and the emphasis on political education.

The Alliance provided its members with spaces to meet in which neither sex would feel uncomfortable. Almost every township had schoolhouses that served as sites for community events. Farm women had traveled to these buildings, which were sometimes no more than a long "soddy," to vote in school district elections. Sometimes a suballiance would assemble to "raise" an Alliance building, much as neighbors had gathered to "raise" a barn. And in fact, the Alliance buildings were simple structures that resembled the barns used to hold community dances. The local picnic grove, where families had met many times before, now hosted Alliance rallies. Safe and familiar, these places became the sites for building the Alliance's political community.

Farm men, women, and children were used to interacting with one another in these spaces; they knew the basic codes of behavior between men and women, children and adults. Here were places with spiritual and communal connotations, well suited to the ideal of family-oriented moral politics, places where "the belief in a Supreme Being and the acknowledgment of accountability forbids vulgar language and profanity. . . . Strict adherence will certainly elevate all our members to a higher plane of moral action. A pleasant social element naturally grows out of a conscious feeling of moral rectitude."[10] This higher standard included banning alcohol from Alliance events, an especially notable exception from the rituals of mainstream men's politics. J. Chisholm of the Roxbury Alliance proudly proclaimed, "We have a splendid grove and good water, but no original packages."[11] In such an environment farm women could at least take their first steps into the political realm at ease with their surroundings.

The Alliance maintained this mixed-gendered approach at its weekly meetings. The Southern Farmers' Alliance, like the Grange, was a secret organization; only duly initiated members could attend meetings, membership requests were examined carefully, and its charter forbade members from revealing the membership roll to outsiders. These rituals served to bind its members together, to make those accepted into the order feel different from those not of the elect. Although the secret rituals that opened and closed the meetings were drawn from the Masons, Odd Fellows, and other fraternal lodges, the main content of the meetings was quite familiar to women. A typical meeting began with an ecumenical prayer from the suballiance chaplain, a position occasionally filled by a woman, followed by a song or two and then perhaps a recitation.[12] A member might give a paper, to be followed by a discussion. The essay often dealt with political questions, although members also read papers on such subjects as "The Sin of Intemperance" and "Sound Business Practices in the Home and the Fields."[13] Meetings thus combined elements of church, literary and debating societies, and school district meetings, all of which were equally familiar to farm women and men.

The Alliance's encouragement of children's participation underscored its commitment to a familial model of politics. Children's role in late-nineteenth-century politics rarely went beyond marching proudly in campaign parades;

Alliance kids, however, played a more active role, whether singing songs, delivering a poem, or reciting the "Alliance catechism."[14] As one might imagine, these performances were greatly appreciated by the proud parents, who saw in their children the early development of model citizens. Occasionally, entire meetings would be geared toward "the young folks."[15] Children's attendance was also important because it allowed women to keep an eye on both the meeting and their young children, especially when there were no older children to act as baby-sitters.

Woman Movement activists, who celebrated the idealized family as vociferously as any others during this period, did not envision a role for children in their organizations. Even the WCTU, which spent a good deal of energy dreaming up contests, games, carnivals, and other activities to steer children toward the "righteous path," had little interest in integrating them into the weekly meetings. Woman Movement organizations existed to attract and educate women, who would then work to protect all families in society. In its scheme of things, women were at the center, protecting the children and saving the wayward men.

The differing religious practices of urban and rural Kansans provides one way of understanding the way the Alliance and the Woman Movement thought about family and politics. The congregations of urban, middle-class churches were evangelical, dominated by women, and concerned with saving the souls of straying men. In the country, the traveling preacher sought to redeem every man, woman, and child who gathered to hear him. The political cultures of the Alliance and the Woman Movement reflected these different practices. The Alliance lecturer drew on the tradition of family churchgoing. Whereas before, "going to meeting" meant packing the family in the wagon to hear the Methodist circuit rider, now the family would congregate to hear the "Alliance gospel."[16]

Although most farm people felt a deep craving for a personal connection with God, churches were few and far between and the visits of circuit riders unpredictable. In some ways, the Farmers' Alliance provided a replacement for church.[17] It was a wholly democratic institution whose "preachers" combined religious imagery with political meaning. As an Alliance editor put it, the Farmers' Alliance represented "the morals of Christ and the politics of Jefferson."[18] Another correspondent, reporting on a woman member's lecture, praised her for "handl[ing] her subject well both from a bible and financial standpoint."[19] Activists thus employed both secular and sacred sources to validate the farmers' cause while offering their members both spiritual sustenance and political education.

Alliance members believed that their acts would bring about a Christian millennium, a time when peace and justice would rule the earth. They were less interested, however, in the ultimate outcome of the millennium—Christ's return and the final Day of Judgment—than they were in the immediate, concrete results their actions would bring. Speakers used the trope of the millennium to propound the notions of chaos before order, the complete cleansing of a corrupt system, and the need for sudden change.[20] For the Alliance, *gospel* became synonymous with their ideology and program. One correspondent who attended a rally reported, "There was enthusiasm enough to spread the blessed gospel all over our beloved state and kindle the flame that shall light us on to victory."[21]

As the Farmers' Alliance began to nourish the spiritual needs of its members, farm people took to examining established churches and found them wanting. "Plus Ultra," a frequent columnist for the *Independent Free Press,* asked his readers, "Am I not correct in estimating the influence of the Farmers' Alliance for morality, temperance and self-denial co-equal with the church itself? I would not underestimate the value of the educational influence of the church, but, alas! too often the faults of its servants . . . are placed in a background of shadow."[22] The churches could serve Wall Street's mammon or the Alliance's gospel; there was no middle ground.

Alliance writers often perceived churches as citified palaces that had forgotten rural folk such as themselves. The Protestant church had played an important role in the past, but it had been corrupted. "It pretends to be the religion of Jesus Christ," one letter writer asked. "But is it?" His answer reflected both his political sympathies and his rural perspective: "Not by any means. While poverty, ignorance, and starvation walk around under the shadow of these temples of worship, a minister at $10,000 a year talks to a crowd of bankers and stock gamblers, who go out during the week and lay all kinds of schemes and devices to defraud and impoverish the people under the law." The only way to make the church more meaningful was for it to become active in the struggle for reform. "Then and not til then," he wrote, "will [ordinary people] have confidence in the professions by the church. . . . If [the church] can't do this, then the Farmers' Alliance will soon come to the front as the moral and religious education for to-day."[23]

Although not every urban Protestant church was a palatial tribute to the earning power of its congregation, Alliance members believed that those who attended church in town dressed in stylish clothes and expected others to do the same. One woman member wrote, "I for one do not enjoy riding ten miles in a lumber wagon with a calico dress to be seated in the back part of an aristocratic congregation. But perhaps I am a haughty farmer's wife."[24] Members' antagonism toward church was rooted as much in their resentment toward middle-class townspeople as in their feeling of abandonment by church leaders.

The Farmers' Alliance's religiosity brought members closer together, in part by accentuating farm people's differences with the urban middle and upper classes. The movement's religious discourse also allowed Alliance women and men, quite literally, to speak the same political language. The metaphors, images, and stories drawn from the Bible were both familiar and familial to women and men, having been shared at revival meetings, in Sunday school, and in the home. Where the Woman Movement's evangelical spirit alienated members from many mainstream politicians, the Alliance gospel bound farm women and men together.

Farmers' Alliance women and men shared more than a political language—the movement's focus on education put women on a roughly equal footing with men during suballiance meetings. Most men accepted the idea of women as educators: primary school teachers were usually women, and more importantly, mothers were expected to be moral instructors to their children. During the 1859 state constitutional convention, Kansas woman suffragists had gained the right to vote in school elections by winning the argument that education was traditionally a part of women's "sphere." Women could participate in teaching and learning the Alliance gospel while remaining within the boundaries of acceptable behavior.

In order to facilitate this education process, the Alliance produced and distributed "a perfect avalanche of literature."[25] Alliance editors joined with other like-minded newspapermen (and some women) across the country to form the National Reform Press Association in order to distribute articles, features, and letters concerning "the issues of the day." Kansas led the way with the *Kansas Farmer,* the *Advocate,* and the *Non-Conformist,* as well as over two hundred local reform papers, by far the largest number in the country. The reform press also helped disseminate such classics of American reform as Henry George's *Poverty and Progress,* Sarah Van Der Emory's *Seven Financial Conspiracies against the American People,* and Edward Bellamy's *Looking Backward,* which were published in cheap editions for as little as twenty-five cents. Along with the nationally prominent works, there were local efforts such as S. M. Scott's "Great Sub-Treasury Plan" and S. S. King's "Seed Time and Harvest."[26] Members were particularly eager for statistics, "hard facts" that could "scientifically" prove their point, so that they would not be dismissed as mere hayseeds. Sometimes entire books were devoted to this purpose.[27] Many county and local alliances built up impressive libraries, and members were instructed to "read, read, or your life is wasted."[28]

Kansas's ability to sustain so many reform papers is clear proof that Alliance members were heeding this advice. But reading alone does not automatically translate into knowledge, much less wisdom. For the Farmers' Alliance to be a successful school, it needed to promote free discussion and critical thinking. Each local and county alliance, as well as the state organization, elected a lecturer and assistant lecturer. Their job was to facilitate discussion and learning. The lecturer gave talks, distributed political tracts, and proposed topics for the following week's deliberations.[29] Women members, unused to contributing to political discussions, appreciated the advance notice because it enabled them to come to the meeting prepared to participate.[30]

The Alliance fostered the idea that its "schoolroom" encouraged free thinking rather than learning by rote. Lecturers often proposed topics of a pro-and-con nature, urging participants to "discuss them from various points of view. This the alliance can well do as it has in its membership those of all parties and beliefs."[31] The huge number of debates and resolutions recorded in the *Advocate* and *Kansas Farmer* attest to the spirited nature of the discussions during the weekly meetings. Suballiances such as the Lone Tree Alliance took great pride in announcing, "The question Resolved that National banks should be abolished was debated in a manner that would put our lawmakers to shame and a decision was reached in the affirmative."[32] In some ways, Alliance meetings gave political purpose to the debating and literary societies that farm people so enjoyed. And they allowed women along with men to become versed in the "issues of the day."

The decentralized decision-making process gave all members, women as well as men, a chance to make their voices heard. Although most policies were formulated by the leadership and passed down to the rank and file, the leadership needed the endorsement of the membership to enact the policies. In most cases, the members backed the decisions; in others the suballiances spent much time debating the issues before endorsing the program. A few times, the rank and file defeated the initiatives of the leadership, as in the case of the Kansas State Alliance's failed attempt to back the National Cooperative Exchange. A common communication from a suballiance to the *Advocate* was, "[We] have received news about the new sub-treasury plan and are now engaged in considering it."[33]

Within the movement decision-making power rarely remained in the same hands for very long. Almost the entire state leadership changed annually; local offices also circulated frequently among different people. The Alliance believed that a member's democratic education included assuming a position of responsibility. However, its decentralized organizational structure was not simply a product of the leadership's selflessness and adherence to democratic principles; members nurtured a suspicion of any who had the appearance of professional politicians. According to the editor Henry Wallace, farmers' groups had gone into politics in the past and had "fallen among thieves" but now the farmer would not be led by politicians or even editors of agricultural papers such as himself. "No outside influence can guide him," he argued. "He must lead and guide himself. The law of vigorous growth, whether in boy, girl, or man, or party, or nation, inexorably demands self-reliance and self-government."[34] For Wallace and other Alliance activists, the redeemed farmer-citizen must reclaim the government from those who had usurped it.

Alliance members believed that the "two old parties" fostered a political culture that separated the citizenry from the government. The party system engendered a network of "parasites," politicians interested only in maintaining their office and fattening their wallets. To counter this tendency, the Alliance proposed that "the office should seek the man"; that a convened delegation of citizens nominate the proper candidate without any prompting from the individual concerned. A nomination was an honor bestowed upon a worthy citizen, not a prize grabbed by the man with the quickest tongue, the flashiest clothes, or the most generous handouts at the convention. Alliance members expected to vote for "the best men irrespective of party." One correspondent wrote, "In my mind the highest type of nonpartisanship is that which leads a man to talk political morality, regardless of any party affiliations, and to vote as he talks. Any other course is not honest, and is productive of great injury to the cause of reform."[35] Rejecting party appeals thus became a moral act and a crucial step toward redeeming the Republic.

Such radical nonpartisanship facilitated women's participation in the Farmers' Alliance. Party men saw mugwumps as a neutered species, worthy only of scorn. The Alliance, however, embraced nonpartisanship as a central part of its political vision. Because it saw politics as something to be controlled not by a party but by informed, active citizens, women had a role in electoral affairs despite being denied the vote. Learning about the issues, women could offer their opinions about policies and candidates; through their local alliances they could have a part in the electoral process.

## The Farmer's Wife in the Farmers' Alliance

Despite all the attempts by leaders to create a truly democratic political culture, women and men were not equal participants in the Farmers' Alliance. Although it created a "free social space" that allowed its members to envision a new political order, it constructed this vision out of the materials present in their culture. When members made use of the structure of the farm family to create political community, they brought along with it the relatively patriarchal underpinnings of that structure.

The initial problem was getting women to join the organization. Some felt insecure about participating in politics; others were pressured by husbands or fathers to avoid such "men's work." And few women had the spare time to investigate an organization making extravagant claims. "A woman's work is never done" may be a cliché, but it was one born of hard experience. Men were therefore far more likely to attend the first few meetings than women.[36]

Many suballiances, as well as the state Alliance, moved to correct this imbalance. Their efforts paid off immediately: by 1890 women constituted approximately 30 percent of the membership. The Kansas Farmers' Alliance politicized somewhere between thirty thousand and fifty thousand farm women, an extraordinary number, especially when one considers that the Kansas Woman Movement in its entirety never reached more than eight thousand members (see table, below).

These numbers appear impressive, but they do not tell the whole story of gender relations in the Alliance. The recipe for creating a mixed-gender political culture went beyond adding some women to the mix, stirring, and then enjoying the results. The two main ingredients did not seamlessly blend together with little effort or care. Alliance members were engaging in an experiment of sorts, although few saw it that way. Perhaps they would have been better off if they had.

Despite the leadership's enthusiasm for women's participation, some men were less than thrilled to be a part of a mixed-gender political culture. Although mainstream politics had disempowered farm men, they did enjoy the transitory benefits of the nominating conventions and the raucous Election Day celebrations. As Annie Diggs noted, "politics for the farmer had been recreation, relaxation, even exhilaration. . . . But the farmers' wives participated in no such ecstasies."[37] Although most Alliance men appear to have rejected these inducements and embraced the movement's family-style political culture, there remained some holdouts who perhaps yearned for the time when politics meant a rare whoop in town. Or perhaps these men simply did not believe a woman could discuss the issues of the day intelligently; perhaps they savored the idea of an all-male gathering place, free from worries about behavior and language. Maybe, like an offending member of the Lone Tree Alliance, they wanted to be able to smoke without being asked to do so outside by a woman member.[38]

Whatever the reason, Farmers' Alliance leaders kept constant pressure on

## Women as Percentage of Total Members
## in Selected Kansas Suballiances

| Suballiance | No. of Men | No. of Women | Women as % of Total | Source |
|---|---|---|---|---|
| Berlin | 29 | 20 | 40.8 | *Kansas Farmer,* 29 July 1889 |
| Victory | 42 | 23 | 35.4 | *Kansas Farmer,* 30 October 1889 |
| Paxton | 22 | 13 | 37.1 | *Kansas Farmer,* 19 June 1890 |
| Lone Tree | 59 | 40 | 40.4 | "Lone Tree Alliance Minute Book" |
| Olpe | 39 | 10 | 20.4 | *Advocate* (Topeka), 18 June 1890 |
| Hoosier Valley | 65 | 25 | 27.8 | *Advocate* (Topeka), 28 May 1890 |
| Bethel | 51 | 33 | 39.2 | *Alliant,* 9 July 1890 |
| Rolling Home | 12 | 8 | 40.0 | *Independent Free Press,* 28 April 1892 |
| *Total* | 319 | 172 | 35.0 | |

NOTE: Figures are drawn from sampling eight suballiances and one county alliance. Samples were difficult to obtain because suballiances rarely differentiated members by sex. Of course, having access to such a small sample means that the margin for error is great. Still, the numbers are fairly consistent. Only two alliances, Olpe Alliance and Hoosier Valley Alliance, had less than 30% women. The average percentage in the suballiances listed is consistent with the Cowley County's report that its membership consisted of 1,500 men and 800 women. This figure is clearly an estimate. However, since alliances were more likely to inflate male membership numbers (because men equated with voters), the ratio of women to men is probably not inflated.

recalcitrant men. Ben Clover, the president in 1890, published a number of stern warnings to those men who excluded women from their meetings, threatening finally to revoke the charter of any suballiance that followed such a course.[39] The *Advocate,* in a stinging rebuke to these "backward men," argued, "Those farmers who regard their wives, mothers and daughters unsuitable persons to associate with themselves as members of the sub-alliance, must be descendants of a disreputable parentage—must have married into a family of questionable character, and must acknowledge themselves responsible for the perpetuation of a degenerate race." Since women had both the right and the ability to participate in the Alliance, the paper reasoned, then the only reason to bar a woman was because she was "degenerate." The *Advocate* concluded threateningly, "In view of the old maxim that evil associations are corrupting in their influence, it is a question whether such men are themselves suitable for membership."⁴⁰ The paper's free-swinging denunciation, usually reserved for defenders of the "old parties," demonstrates Alliance leaders' understanding of women's importance to the movement. Most activists in the movement would have found the idea of a male-only Alliance unthinkable. They saw such sentiments as a repudiation of the type of alternative political community they hoped to establish.

After 1890, men rarely objected to women as full, participating members of the Farmers' Alliance, at least in public. But although women no longer faced outright disapproval, they did have to deal with the cultural expectations of relations between the sexes. Men, after all, expected to have the final word; they could speak loudly and enter a debate more aggressively. Women were expected to speak "pleasingly," that is, in soft, deferential tones. Men needed to be aware that women were not used to speaking about politics in a public situation, and women had to gain confidence in their abilities and ideas. One Alliance woman reminded men: "perhaps . . . the Alliance sister . . . may often be silent when she should have taken part in the discussions, but be sure she is busy thinking and planning. Unity of thoughts and actions on the part of the brothers and sisters of the Alliance must result in good to us all."⁴¹ Men were as unused to interacting with women in a political context as women were unused to speaking in public.

Woman Movement activists were able to make their first journey into the public sphere in the calm waters of an all-woman group. Farmers' Alliance women, however, had to negotiate men's expectations about what was proper. Though no evidence survives describing this process, new arrangements between the sexes were probably broached carefully, accepted slowly. There were no doubt hurt feelings, bruised egos, and ruffled feathers.

At first, farm women had a more difficult time establishing their political identities than did their counterparts in the Woman Movement. Eventually, however, Alliance women gained a status relative to men within the organization that members of the Woman Movement would have envied. If indeed the suballiance was a schoolroom, then it taught its members more than the ideas of political reform. It was also a school for gender relations, for teaching women and men how to work together in a political movement. This was no small lesson in Gilded Age America; it would be no small lesson today.

Alliance women's increased political participation may be traced through several sources. Reform papers began reprinting talks by women on a variety of subjects, indicating both their increased participation and their suballiance's willingness to promote it. Even more importantly, farm women began to assume positions of leadership in the suballiances. In 1889, Cowley County had but one woman officer in its fifteen suballiances. By 1892, half of the suballiances had at least one woman officer, and one of these, Lydia Brookshire, was her suballiance's president.[42] Although the most common position for women was that of secretary, a number were also appointed to the crucial position of lecturer or assistant lecturer, and a lesser number attained the president's position.[43] Nor were the secretary's tasks unimportant: she recorded her suballiance's proceedings in the state or local reform press, thus giving women a chance to assume a public persona. These dispatches also set an example for other women who had held back from such public displays of political participation.

Despite these obvious gains, the percentage of local women officers—no more than ten percent—remained far below the percentage of women members in the organization. This imbalance was even more striking at the county level, where only a handful of women became officers, and none appear to have been elected county alliance president. The county alliances wielded substantial power, often shaping policy by voting resolutions and electing delegates to the Kansas Farmers' Alliance convention. Farm women thus had little access to the policy-making machinery of the organization.

On the farm, the conventional wisdom declared, the husband ruled the fields while his wife controlled the home. This division of labor and expertise was part of a larger division of power and status within the family and society. In the Farmers' Alliance, women and men replicated this division of labor to some degree: men ruled the conventions and the buying and selling cooperatives; women controlled the domestic duties. Even the women's rights supporters in the organization would have agreed that women and men were essentially different creatures, and thus naturally suited to different tasks. But in the Alliance's family ideal, women's and men's unequal status in the family was not supposed to be replicated in the movement: husband and wife were to be political equals. This uneasy fit between difference and equality established a shaky foundation on which to build a mixed-gender political culture.

Alliance leaders viewed women's special nature as a resource to be nurtured. One of the most intangible benefits of a mixed-gender meeting was that the gatherings were, quite simply, more fun than when farm men met alone. William Peffer noted: "Be sure to invite women and young people of both sexes. Let it be understood that at this first meeting there will be some good music, and see that people are not disappointed. One active young man or young woman put in charge of that matter will do the necessary work and prepare for at least two songs, one at the beginning, and the other at the end of the meeting."[44] The (male) secretary of the Neosho County Alliance was more direct: "Many ladies lent a charm to the meetings by their presence."

Such a comment should not be dismissed as frivolous. As Peffer was aware, for the Alliance to succeed, the meetings had to be enjoyable as well as informative. Since farm people were used to family entertainment, women would increase the organization's sociability as well as ensure its mission. Furthermore, farm women were needed because "the cause for which the Alliance came into being is a holy one; its purpose is to secure peaceful, happy homes and to make better men and women. It is therefore essential that the woman element, the mother nature, should make its influence felt in the order."[45]

A constant refrain heard from both sexes in the Alliance was that women should assume the same responsibilities as men.[46] Writers urged women to take part in running the local organization: to deliver a talk, to facilitate a meeting, to learn about the issues, or to recruit neighbors to join. But women were also expected to do double duty, to take on those chores usually associated with their sphere. Mrs. M. E. Clark, who later became vice president of the Alliance, urged women members that, beyond their normal responsibilities of membership, "another duty [of women] is the care of our brothers and sisters in sickness. If it be possible, visit them; offer them your sustenance, if need be in household work; be quiet and cheerful; do all the good you can while there."[47] Women, she reasoned, who were "nurturers by nature," were best suited to do the work of the mutual aid committees, which provided food, company, child care, and laundry service to invalids or the destitute. Activists could advertise these benefits as inducements to prospective members.

Since farm women were the cooks and bakers at home, they took on the task of preparing food for meetings, picnics, and benefits without a second thought. However women might have viewed this chore in the home, within the Alliance they transformed it into a political act. Leaders valued food as a symbol of farm life, as a way to raise money for the cause, and as a means of bringing people together. Newspaper accounts of meetings and picnics constantly bragged about the food available, noting both farm women's skills in preparing it and farm people's ability to provide for themselves despite the lack of cash. "The very cheapness of the products which the ladies know so well how to fashion into tempting viands," one correspondent reported, "renders such things possible even in the midst of hard times."[48] Farm people could point to such "sumptuous spreads" as proof of the superiority of their culture, emphasizing their supposed independence and self-reliance—unlike the merchants, lawyers, and politicians in town. Frances Butler, editor of the *Barton*

*Beacon*'s "Woman's Column," put the relationship of Alliance women and food in perspective when, recruiting for an upcoming event, she requested "your presence, your council, and your basket of food."[49]

Farm women also used food to earn money for the local alliance, much as their gardening and poultry raising provided much-needed cash for their families. The most common activity was the box supper, which women members made available to townspeople and visiting farmers. Although members and townspeople were often at odds politically, businessmen apparently were not averse to purchasing lunch from Alliance women.[50] Other fund-raising activities included selling goods at fairs and rallies.

Women directed the profits from these ventures toward a wide range of items for the local alliance. "The good sisters of Plum Creek Alliance got up a supper," reported one member, "the proceeds to go towards purchasing an organ. About one hundred partook of the bountiful repast and a most enjoyable time was had. The proceeds netted $20."[51] Other efforts bought books for the suballiance library, reform newspaper subscriptions for those who could not afford them, and provisions for free barbecues and picnics.[52] These events were a particularly good method of drawing in curious—or even cynical—nonmembers. Few, after all, could resist a free lunch.

Farm women's contributions enabled the Alliance to appropriate a thoroughly respectable activity such as a picnic and convert it into a subversive political act. Farm people went to camp meetings and picnics as a way of creating a little temporary community. The Alliance combined both to sustain their political community. As one announcement in the *Advocate* put it, "It's basket picnic season with a fury, doubling as an Alliance rally."[53] The picnic was part social event, part political theater, and part revival meeting. As picnic season opened in May, announcements would pop up like Kansas sunflowers, making promises such as, "Brick Alliance will have a picnic on the 5th of June. Extensive preparations are being made for a grand good time. Van B. Prather, assistant state lecturer, will deliver the address. This announcement alone should be sufficient to insure a large attendance. When, in addition, it is remembered what a farmers' picnic means in the way of social intercourse and good living, nothing more need be said. The crowd will be there."[54]

The Farmers' Alliance picnic functioned as a way both to recruit members and to maintain solidarity. If the crowd was indeed there, members could look around them and see a huge gathering of like-minded folk, cheering on speakers as they preached the Alliance gospel. Even if some of the crowd were there only in search of a well-stocked picnic basket, all could feel part of a community of farm people.

At the picnic the secrecy and rituals were abandoned, with notices requesting "all interested parties" to attend. Those who came were treated to quite a show—but a show with a purpose. May Davidson, secretary of her suballiance, reported, "Believing that the mingling of the people tends to develop a better state mentally, morally, socially and financially, the Greenfield Alliance . . . determined to celebrate its second anniversary . . . with a picnic." The "ladies of the Women's Relief Corps, who are nearly all Alliance in this county," kicked off the event by raising the American flag. "It would go a long way towards proving to our enemies that we are as loyal to the dear old stars and stripes as they," she declared. The state president of the Women's Relief Corps then followed with a speech on the importance of patriotism. Davidson noted, "The jest and repartee which flow highly from one another proved that though we daily carry a heavy load, yet we can lay it aside for a time and give ourselves up to the pleasures of the hour, thus giving and receiving fresh courage, and bringing ourselves more closely together." She concluded with the advice to others "to go and do likewise."[55] Most alliances needed no such prompting: every week the *Advocate* reported on some five or six picnics, and many more were recorded in the local papers.

By late 1889, Kansas Farmers' Alliance members had added a feature to the picnic and rally which would contribute to the quintessential image of the movement. Organizers began requesting members to meet outside town at a specific time before proceeding to the picnic.[56] When a large enough group had assembled, the line of wagons slowly made its way through town. Latecomers would arrive and extend the line even farther. It was not unusual to have five hundred wagons in a line, and some parades claimed as many as fifteen hundred wagons and seven thousand participants.[57] Families began decorating their wagons with ribbons, bunting, and a variety of banners proclaiming DEATH TO THE MONOPOLIES and THE FARMER IS ALL.[58] To round out the parade and keep everyone in step, members formed brass bands, drum and fife corps, and marching glee clubs.[59] The Alliance took the basics of the political parades of the parties, which were celebrations of masculinity, and converted them into paeans to the farm family.

Members converted their wagons into full-fledged floats, transforming them into defiant declarations of the superiority of Alliance doctrine and rural culture. Young women were often featured, representing "all that was noble and uplifted in farm life." At the "Grand Alliance Rally" in Valley Falls, "Swabville Alliance turned out with a handsomely decorated wagon upon which eight beautiful young ladies in costumes of white and blue, arranged themselves forming an artistic and lovely picture."[60] At one rally, S. M. Scott

**145**

A group of Alliance members assemble in Dickinson County to reclaim some cultural space and demand political power. *Kansas State Historical Society*

found "floats containing ladies representing the suballiances of the county," a parade 199 wagons strong—a sort of Miss Agricultural Kansas pageant.[61] Some floats were political cartoons on wheels: the Rice County rally boasted "wagons loaded with young ladies, representing the states, a corsair regiment of boys and young men, and wagon loads of children labeled 'overproduction,'" to ridicule the Republicans' claim that overproduction was causing low prices.[62]

Besides representing the political views of members, the floats also revealed the ambiguous role of women in the Alliance. Women were celebrated for their beauty and vitality, to be admired and applauded. As representatives of all that was good and pure in rural life, they were to be defended and protected. It was the boys and men who strode boldly by their sisters' sides who served as the honor guard. When the battle shifted from the Alliance to the Populist Party, this arrangement would be repeated in the rhetoric of reformers.

As Alliance parades wound their way through town, members undoubtedly felt a renewed pride and confidence. Simply looking down the long line of iridescent wagons must have imbued them with a sense of empowerment, of political possibilities. But one can imagine other emotions at work here as well.

By bringing their political culture to town in its most outsized, even outrageous form, members were reclaiming what townspeople had appropriated as their own. In the prohibition amendment campaign, organizers had been careful to use sites in which both farm people and townspeople would be comfortable. Now the Farmers' Alliance members were demanding and winning these contested terrains on their own. Within the parades, farm people did not have to worry how they spoke or dressed. They were in effect creating a rural corridor; in that cacophonous, multihued line, they were in control.

The parade inevitably made its way out to a picnic site, where the Alliance's familial political culture was in full bloom. Once there, the men and older boys erected pavilions while the women and younger children unloaded the baskets and spread the contents on communal tables. After lunch the rally began, the main speaker lecturing, exhorting, and demanding for over two hours while the crowd followed every word. The events began to assume huge proportions, with claims that upward of ten thousand attended some picnic rallies. Even if the actual numbers were half that, it would be an enormous crowd for rural Kansas, representing a population larger than that of most towns in the state. For people used to seeing nothing but the plains in all directions, the sight must indeed have been impressive. More than that, it would have been inspiring, tangible proof of the political movement they had helped form.

As Alliance leaders began calling for candidates to challenge the old parties in the late spring of 1890, some county alliances converted the picnics into mass nominating conventions.[63] The event was now a picnic, a rally, a revival, a county fair, and a political convention thrown together into a day-long celebration of rural culture. Several decades later the Kansas journalist Elizabeth Barr would remember these campaigns as

> a religious revival, a crusade, a pentecost of politics in which a tongue of flame set upon every man, and each spoke as the spirit gave him utterance. . . . The farmers, the cattle-herders, they of the long chin-whiskers, and they of the broad brimmed hats and heavy boots, had . . . heard the word and could preach the gospel of populism. . . . Women with skins tanned to parchment by the hot winds, with bony hands of toil and clad in faded calico, could talk in meeting, and could talk straight to the point. . . . The meetings grew bigger and bigger, til no buildings could be found to house the crowds which drove for miles and miles to hear the speakers who were fast gaining national fame. All day picnics were held and people by the thousands came. . . . to hear the tidings of great joy.[64]

Beyond its explicit political purpose, the campaign brought a sense of celebration to a hard-pinched land. And this too was important for the movement. One state official declared: "Let each county arrange to hold a grand demonstration or picnic in the near future, and try to get out every man, woman and child. . . . Whoop it up with an earnest enthusiasm worthy of success and success is ours."[65] There are few things so inspiring, in the short term, anyway, as a political movement's ability to throw a good party. And as long as the Alliance remained committed to its social and educational goals, women would have a role as the party givers.

## THE MIGHT OF TRUE MEN: CONFLICTING IMAGES OF MANHOOD AND SUCCESS

When Farmers' Alliance women and men negotiated gender roles and expectations, their points of reference went beyond their own Anglo farm culture. The Eastern media, which prescribed the ideal roles for all respectable women and men, was the most prominent source. But farm people also compared their own notions about gender, about masculinity and femininity, with the claims of Anglo middle-class townspeople, employing ideas about gender in the Alliance's ongoing cultural battle, now turned political. Alliance members' idealized notions about gender and family were wrapped up in their vision of their movement. When they considered townspeople as economic, political, or cultural rivals, gender and politics remained intertwined.

When Alliance members and Republican leaders argued over political and economic policy, one of the fundamental issues they wrestled with was who was to blame for the farmers' difficulties. What this debate translated into was a struggle over competing claims of manhood and success. Republican leaders implied that a farmer's financial problems were of his own making—he had simply failed at his chosen occupation and therefore failed as a "real man." Alliance members, however, challenged this charge and claimed instead a different measure of success and of masculinity.

Many members insisted that farmers were in no way responsible for their problems; that their farming practices were as effective as possible, given their economic circumstances. A number of farmers, however, had been warning their neighbors for some time that Kansans' farming practices were often outdated, inefficient, and wasteful. These "progressive farmers" were the most vocal proponents of the view that farmers had been responsible for much of their own misery. Their arguments were then used extensively by the Republican Party to criticize Alliance positions that advocated government intervention on the side of farmers.

In Kansas most progressive farmers were solidly middle class and as conservative in their politics as they were in their financial management.[66] Many appear to have come to the state free of debt and then pursued practices that

kept them that way. Progressive farmers used the latest proven scientific practices while maintaining careful economic management of the farm. In Kansas
the Farmers' Institute functioned as a meeting place for those holding such
views. When the Alliance began to organize, Farmers' Institute members offered progressive farming techniques as the proper antidote to farmers' complaints.

To progressive farmers the real problem was not the economic structure of
society but the attitude of farmers. J.C.H. Swann, a farmer and frequent contributor to the *Kansas Farmer,* argued, "After [the Civil War] we were all seized
with money-getting mania. Speculation, wild farming, and running in debt for
farms, stock of fine grades, and machinery, never once reflecting that a failure
of one or two crops would come." Following the bust farmers had allowed
themselves "to become engulfed; and these syndicates know it, and know that
your products will be sold; hence they combine against you and they ever will
until you free yourselves of debt."[67] In the eyes of these critics, debt was the
greatest sin. But excessive risk taking and high living were not the sole causes
of debt. Critics bemoaned farmers' failure to rotate and diversify crops, to col-
lect and spread manure properly, to read the agricultural journals, and to understand the special characteristics of the central Kansas environment. They
urged farmers to house machinery and livestock properly and to gather and
replant seed rather than buy it. Only by taking such precautions, they argued,
could farmers prosper.[68]

Such claims might have carried less weight if Republican sympathizers had
been the only critics. Some Alliance editors and members, however, also
pushed for improved farming practices. William Peffer, editor of the *Kansas
Farmer,* saw a better understanding of farming techniques as a central part of
the Alliance's educational program. In his pamphlet *The Way Out,* Peffer included "better farming" and "farm economy" as two of the eight changes that
needed to occur in addition to a variety of legislative action. The *Advocate*
published an article that admitted the problems caused by monopolies and the
credit system but then argued that societal reform would not help much if
farmers continued "the unnecessary purchase and wasteful care of farm machinery great and small." "No dodging," the writer insisted. "Their reckless
and inexcusable improvidence in this way alone . . . has impoverished more
farmers in Kansas than liquor, taxes, tariff, trusts, and monopolies combined. . . . It is for each individual farmer to reform himself in regard to how
much machinery he runs into debt for and then destroys."[69] Unlike J.C.H.
Swann, however, the writer called for a combination of individual and political reform.

Although Alliance editors generally supported progressive farming ideas, they were careful to point out that such individual improvements should supplement, and not replace, mass action.[70] Many members, however, were not particularly interested in being lectured about improving their operations, whether by friend or by foe. One farmer, responding to the charge of wastefulness, turned the progressive farmers' analysis on its head. "Well now, ain't that getting the cart before the horse?" he asked. "Isn't our poverty the cause of our failure to provide buildings for the proper housing of our implements and machines as well as our grain, and stock and everything else that needs housing?" A more important question was, "How are we going to get money to build sheds and barns after providing for food and clothes, and doctor bills and accidents, and taxes and interest, and school books and other essentials out of the proceeds of 13 cent corn that it cost 15 cents per bushel to raise?"[71] Many of the progressive farmers' ideas required investments of time and money to implement them—both of which were in short supply in late-1880s Kansas.

Clara Egan, an Alliance member writing in the *Kansas Farmer,* extended the idea that "it takes money to make money" in her poem, "If It Wasn't for the Mortgage." For Egan, debt caused by an unfair economic system kept farmers from progressing in numerous areas—social, cultural, and economic.

> If it wasn't for the mortgage,
>  I'd try self-improvement some;
> I'd take a dozen papers,
>  and read 'em, every one.
> I'd study modern farming
>  from a scientific view
> And keep posted up on politics,
>  as every man should do;
> But with time and money lacking,
>  I must give it up, I fear,
> Till the happy time when I can say
>  my home and farm are clear.[72]

For Egan, improved farming methods would come only with a reformed economy, which would come only with political action. She and other members saw the progressive farming debate as a smoke screen thrown up to mask the inequalities perpetrated by "the Money Power."

The Farmers' Alliance had ample evidence to prove its claim that the economic and political system was corrupt and weighted in favor of large (and usually ruthless) corporations. Further, the specific economic conditions at the time, especially the low crop prices and the difficult credit situation, made farming "hard to pay." But these claims do not address the questions of whether farmers had an important hand in their misfortunes and whether government action alone could save them.[73] As J.C.H. Swann noted, Kansas farmers were not much better at practicing improved farming during good times than during hard times. Rather, they were more reckless and inefficient when greater economic opportunities existed.

Tellingly, farm women were never the object of progressive farmers' ire. Most Kansans believed that management of the farm was in men's hands, however much women might have contributed in reality. It was no accident that Clara Egan chose a male narrator for her poem about paying the mortgage. Although Alliance members asserted that farm men were unable to practice efficient farming without money, everyone—from members to progressive farmers to Republican leaders—agreed that farm women should strive to economize in the home. Unlike the attack by progressive farmers on their fellow men, these articles on "home economies" contained suggestions, not criticisms. The articles usually acknowledged women's ability to conserve, recycle, and manage a limited amount of resources with great ingenuity. In their hands flour sacks were sewn into dresses and trousers, garden soil was carefully tended, poultry yards were cleaned, and recipes were found or invented for every edible item on the farm. Such measures were not called progressive homemaking, but just common sense.

Women may have longed to abandon such stringent economizing, especially with all the extra work it entailed, but society (and their families' welfare) demanded that they continue to scrimp and save. A popular expression of the time, "A woman can throw out with a spoon what a man makes with a shovel," might more accurately have been rendered, "A man can waste with a plow what a woman saves with a spoon." Women were not morally superior by nature; society just demanded that they act that way.

Farm men bore a different set of cultural pressures. A man who came to Kansas without adequate cash reserves was faced with the specter of yet another financial disaster, unless he struck it rich—and fast. His concentration on a single cash crop was like throwing all the chips on a single number: a few winning harvests and he could pay off the mortgage. He refused to appropriate the communal low-risk strategies of the German-Russian immigrants, for those were not his ways.

Kansas businessmen, who felt they had a pretty good idea about what it meant to "be a man," believed Alliance men were simply losers—"kickers," "cry-babies," and "calamity howlers"—who had been knocked down by their own shortcomings and now did not have the gumption to pull themselves back up. These Republican faithful were not surprised that such whiners were making noises about forming a third party, the last refuge of "long hairs" and political neuters. Criticism of Alliance farmers fitted well the standard business-oriented thinking of the Republican leadership: farmers had failed because of poor business practices. Such incompetents should not be rewarded with government subsidies and political offices.

To a businessman's thinking, if a merchant had overbought stock, allowed too much credit to customers, or built too large a building for his needs—in short, if his costs exceeded his sales—he would rightly go out of business. No one would mourn his personal failure outside his family and close friends. If enough merchants were forced to close down because of their inability to ride out hard times, fellow businessmen would not mass together and demand relief from Washington. A Kansas businessman, knowing this, saw little reason to "reform" society in order to save those he perceived as failed agricultural businessmen. When too many farmers produced too much grain, just as when too many merchants opened up an excess of stores, the businessman understood that the fault lay with the men who chose to enter a crowded field. If they could not get tough, learn to live with less, and outstay the competition, they should rightly fail. The end result, to this way of thinking, would eventually be more efficient and productive businesses and farms. And it would mean that those who succeeded did so on the basis of their own abilities, without help from anyone, as real men should.

Nothing enraged Kansas Alliance members as much as the overproduction issue. To the Farmers' Alliance, the overproduction argument was an amoral answer to a moral problem. What mattered to members was that they were getting low prices for their crops because of weak demand, while people in the cities were starving. To illustrate this point, the *Advocate* ran a series entitled "Overproduction" with short notices from papers around the country describing unemployed male workers and hungry women and children, followed by comments such as "Overproduction did it," and "Overproduction again."[74] L. L. Polk, president of the National Farmers' Alliance, presented his own moral calculus for the problem. While lecturing in Kansas, he argued, "Mr. Morrill [a Kansas Republican congressman] declared from his seat that it was overproduction. . . . If Mr. Morrill had come into the streets of Washington on a cold November morning he would have seen the children picking bits of coal out of the ash piles to warm themselves by, and morsels of food out of the heaps of garbage to satisfy their hunger. . . . As long as a single cry for bread is heard, it is underproduction and underconsumption."[75] Farmers' Alliance members and G.O.P. leaders were looking at the same situation, but they were viewing it from two very different perspectives.

Although the Alliance based its arguments with the G.O.P. on ideological differences, there was more at stake than ideas about government activism and the right of private property. Many Alliance members used these political battles to place a moral framework around the antagonisms they felt toward townspeople, particularly the merchants. For these members, the struggle was as much for status and respect as it was for economic and political justice. All were necessary for the redemption of the American farmer.

Alliance members and merchants focused on the movement's cooperative ventures as the most visible source of their disagreement. The cooperatives provided tangible proof that by joining together, farmers could help themselves financially while gaining a certain degree of economic autonomy. The Alliance's cooperative buying and selling plans enabled farm people to use volume trading to their advantage. They joined together to bulk their grain for sale, which enabled them to receive lower railroad rates and a higher price. Some alliances, if they were able to raise enough capital, invested in a cooperative elevator, thus bypassing the grain elevator operator entirely. Members paid lower prices for supplies by buying staples in bulk quantities or by establishing a cooperative store.

In Kansas, these different types of cooperative ventures proved enormously important during the Alliance's organizing drive. One suballiance in Saline County boasted, "We organized [our suballiance] about the middle of November 1889, with only 13 members, and for a while it looked as if it would die out. But a little while ago it took a boom, as soon as we commenced sending for a few goods and it leaked out that we got our goods at quite a good discount to what we are in the habit of paying at our retail places of business; so at our last meeting we numbered 54 and seven applications for admittance and we don't represent the ignorant or humdrum class of farmers either."[76] The Elk Valley Alliance, which began with nine members, credited its various cooperative efforts with pushing membership past seventy.[77] Valley Alliance in Burton County went from fifteen to one hundred members after the Alliance's state agent helped them form a cooperative store.[78] These success stories, trumpeted in the state's reform press, served as guides for other suballiances wishing both to save money and to gain members.

The cooperatives allowed farm people to feel more self-sufficient and less obliged to store owners. One farmer complained that "merchants charge too much so that they can live in luxury."[79] Farm people believed that because the numerous middlemen—the salesmen, shippers, and merchants—each demanded their share, they drove up the cost of goods. And each, claimed one Alliance correspondent, had no respect for the farmer. "[A]lliance members in this locality begin to see how they have been treated by the merchant, the grain dealer, the stock dealer, and in fact all others, who get their goods through the drummer or commission man."[80] Cooperatives enabled members to avoid most of these obstacles, or at least to place the Alliance on equal footing with the middlemen.

Many Alliance members suggested that merchants did far more harm than good. One correspondent saw them as the willing tools of the Money Power, eager to sell unnecessary machinery to farmers in order to lure them into the credit system, so that banks could then repossess the farm. The writer castigated the merchants, claiming that there were "ten merchants where there should be only one. The more merchants, the more high prices, because they all have to live."[81] In fact, the more merchants there were, the lower the prices would likely be because of the need to attract customers in an overcrowded field. Many Alliance members, however, were not overly interested in the economic plight of the merchant. In fact, one writer presented a detailed plan that promoted cooperatives explicitly in order to make merchants superfluous and depopulate the towns.[82]

Such modest proposals illustrate the depth of farmers' resentment against town dwellers, which went far beyond the price of coal or clothes. The Farmers' Alliance gave farm people the opportunity to counter the slights, real or imagined, that country folk had experienced for years. The cooperative ventures, like the parades, allowed them to reclaim cultural dignity within the town.

Although some farm people denigrated town life and its cultural and economic institutions, not all Alliance members agreed that the movement could do without the support of townspeople. Some leaders, particularly Stephen McLallin and Annie Diggs, believed that merchants should be courted, not scorned. McLallin's *Advocate* declared in 1889, "Every wise alliance man will be ready to assure the businessmen of the town and villages, that our movements is not hostile to his interest. And every far-sighted suballiance will think twice before opening a local [cooperative] store."[83] McLallin and others saw merchants as possible sources of money and influence. Diggs even equated the farmers' plight with that of the merchants, arguing, "The contest now . . . is between the industrial classes of which the agricultural class is but a section, and the moneyed powers. . . . The contest will be severe and there should be no division in the ranks. The small merchant and the small grocer are alike with the farmer the victims of an unwholesome concurrence of tendencies." Diggs urged farm people to be more sympathetic to the merchant's plight. "It is no flowery bed of ease to be in a struggle of trade," she insisted. "An overwhelmingly large percent of retail dealers fail in business; this means distress to such families as nothing short of foreclosure of the farm can bring to the farmer's family."[84]

Diggs and McLallin believed that the connections between farm and town were fairly obvious. But then, they lived in Lawrence and Topeka, respectively. Neither would have experienced a well-dressed dude's sneer, nor would they have been called "hayseed" while walking through town. And they had not directly experienced the satisfaction of gaining some control of their financial dealings through the cooperatives, as many Alliance members had.

A number of merchants echoed Diggs and McLallin, noting that the farmer and the merchant were part of the same local economy. When the Alliance first began organizing, businessmen viewed many of its efforts as positive, comparing it to the numerous business and trade associations that had sprung up in post–Civil War America.[85] Most small-town merchants realized that farmers were their most important customers. No self-respecting merchant, however, would sit around and watch himself be put out of business. A number argued that competition among businesses already forced them to offer their goods at the lowest possible prices, and that the Alliance should concentrate on bulk selling rather than buying. An editor of a Republican paper wrote, "The farmers aren't doing very well at present, but they are mistaken if they think they are the only sufferers. Let any of them offer to exchange his farm at a fair valuation for a stock of merchandise, and he will find plenty of chances to make such a trade."[86] While merchants felt equally put upon by the hard times, they had a very different idea about what the remedy should be. Natural selection, not government intervention, was the merchant's code.

The subjects of this political dialogue were almost exclusively male. When these combatants addressed each other, they did so as "merchants" and "farmers," reflecting the idea that it was the men who were in charge.[87] Such language is not surprising from urban Republicans, for it reflected their belief that economics and politics were men's domain. But the Alliance professed to be different: it recognized women as political actors. In fact, Alliance speakers and writers were far more likely to use gender-inclusive language such as *people, ladies and gentlemen,* and *brothers and sisters* than were Republicans when commenting on politcal matters. But when it came to recognizing women as economic beings, the movement rarely portrayed the "farmer's wife" as a worker responsible for the success of the farm. In the battle between the merchant and the farmer, the debates recognized neither urban nor rural women as participants. This fight was part of a larger struggle to redefine manliness. But it also reflected the patriarchal assumptions that underlay the

Alliance's egalitarian program. These assumptions would become even more apparent as the organization moved away from nonpartisanship and toward the formation of the Populist Party.

In confronting the cultural power of townspeople, Alliance members attempted to recapture the basic definitions of citizenship and manliness which urban middle-class men had appropriated. The Farmers' Alliance hoped to reassert the importance of the farmer as an actor in American politics and culture, to reinvigorate the agrarian ideal. In its attempt to reconstruct the cultural identity of farm men, however, it created a model of gender relations at odds with its expressed desire to establish farm women as active, educated citizens.

The Alliance fought the battle over images of manliness in the rhetorical arena, introducing new metaphors and symbols, or reinterpreting old ones, in letters, poems, speeches, and songs. Farm men took particular delight in appropriating the term *hayseed* for their own purposes. Just as the Alliance glorified the ideal of nonpartisanship which the main parties had derided as effeminate, so too Alliance men proudly hoisted the banner of *hayseed* aloft to celebrate rural values. They often employed a mocking tone when using the term, acknowledging the slight while turning it on its head. One correspondent to the *Industrial Free Press* noted, "Hayseed attended the County Alliance meeting and met many of his brother hayseeds there. There seems to be a kind of magnet . . . that is drawing the hayseeds together. . . . If the 'lazy lousy' hayseeds stay away from town, quit talking politics, and work like the d——l and get the necessary rain, they may have more for their masters this year than they had last."[88] By proudly proclaiming themselves members of this hayseed army, the farm men's ragged clothes, long beards, and heavy boots could become symbols of masculine power rather than of shame. Such pronouncements argued that farm men, once victimized, could regain political power, and thus their manliness, by banding together.

Some Alliance members tried to re-establish the old agrarian notion of the farmer as ideal citizen—and ideal man. The organization's collective victory would then enable natural leaders to come to the fore; success would be measured by what a man's work contributed to society rather than by how much money he made. The song "The Farmer Is the Man," one of the most ubiquitous in the Alliance repertoire, explicitly advanced this idea.

> *Oh, the farmer comes to town with his wagon broken down,*
> *but the farmer is the man who feeds them all.*

*If you'll only look and see, I think you will agree*
*that the farmer is the man who feeds them all.*

*The farmer is the man, the farmer is the man*
*Lives on credit till the fall.*
*Then they take him by the hand*
*and they lead him from the land,*
*And the merchant is the man who gets it all.*

*When the lawyer hangs around*
*While the butcher cuts a pound,*
*Oh, the farmer is the man who feeds them all.*
*When the preacher and the cook*
*Go strolling by the brook*
*Oh, the farmer is the man who feeds them all.*

*When the banker says he's broke*
*And the merchant's up in smoke,*
*They forget that it's the farmer feeds them all.*

*It would put them to the test*
*If the farmer took a rest;*
*Then they'd know that it's the farmer feeds them all.*

*The farmer is the man,*
*The farmer is the man,*
*Lives on credit till the fall—*
*With the interest rate so high*
*It's a wonder he don't die,*
*For the mortgage man's the one who gets it all.*[89]

In the song the food chain works but one way, from farmer outward. Townsmen become, like children, the dependents of the farmer. The farmer, the song claims, is the basic source of life. Yet something terribly wrong has happened: the dependents, by devious means, have managed to rob the farmer and leave him with nothing. The dependents have "unnaturally" taken on the role of masters. The farmer gets nothing in return: the food goes out, but no goods or services make their way back toward the farmer. Except for the butcher cutting the occasional pound, townsmen are not doing anything constructive. Farm men, because they produce the basic source of life, are the only truly successful men in the song.

Although the merchant and banker have temporarily emasculated the farmer, the song leaves the implicit threat that townspeople continue to live only because the farmer has agreed not to "take a rest" and starve his counterparts in town. In the Alliance's eyes, if the economic system were fair, then townsmen would be the helpless ones and farm men the ones properly in control. Such a vision stands in sharp contrast to Edward Ware's poem, which declared that since the businessman provided the motive power for the rest of civilization, he was the natural leader.

When the Alliance focused on the farm man as the central figure and crop production as the most exalted vocation possible, it pushed women to the margins as cheerleaders, helpmates, or victims. In establishing the farmers' claims to masculinity, writers ignored farm women's contributions to the farm economy and the food distribution system—and thus women's claims to citizenship.

Some members attempted to fashion a new ideal of farm manhood that balanced strength and courage with nurturance. In the poem "The Sturdy Brown Hand" by Alliance member Alice Hare, the first two stanzas present this rural vision in contrast to the mainstream conception that equated masculinity with power and monetary success.

> Perhaps there are some whose names are renowned
> But how many hands are now big and browned
> Yet know not the glory of chisel or pen
> But toil for their loved ones with the might of true men
>
> There are hearts that are noble and lives that are great
> Who know not of fame or honor of state
> For who is more noble than he that will give
> All the strength of his years that his loved ones may live?[90]

The poem then goes on to recite the standard paeans to agrarian masculinity: building the ships, breaking the land, driving back the savage. In the past, poets had heralded these triumphs as proof of national greatness. Hare, however, connected the farmers' accomplishments to his family's happiness. She saw the labor itself imbuing the farmer with nobility and greatness—a kind of labor theory of emotional value.

"The Strong Brown Hand" equates the farmer's tactile relations with land, animals, and tools to his ability to use his body to comfort his loved ones. Addressing the bride-to-be of a farm man, the author counsels:

> If his heart is as true as his strong hand is brown
> Surely no better refuge can ever be found
> In sickness he'll be the best nurse in the land
> There's the tenderest touch in the sturdy brown hand.

*If poverty comes he'll meet it halfway;*
*If death's angel carries a loved one away*
*He'll be strength in your weakness, a solace in grief*
*In his strong manly faith you will find sweet relief.*

The farmer's relationship with the earth has given him an almost feminized touch for nursing and comforting, yet one that remains "manly." The idealized Alliance man, like the Alliance itself, combined the best of both male and female characteristics without surrendering any claims to masculinity.

Throughout the poem, Hare obliquely compares the farmer's brown callused hands to the soft white hands of the townsman. If the farmer is manly, then the townsman is effeminate. If callused hands are nurturing and loving, then the hands of the townsman remain cold, insensitive, and ineffectual. Given the choice, what right-minded farm woman would not choose a sturdy "son of toil" over a hapless "paper collar"—and thus a life on the farm over one in town. For even if the farm woman's life would be one filled with hard times and tragedies, it would be far richer.

Some Alliance members linked their new cultural assertiveness to electoral struggles. One correspondent to the *Kansas Farmer,* having attended an Alliance march through town in mid-September 1889, observed, "As the delegation from the Victory Alliance passed through Girard, numbering about fifty, it made some of the citizens draw a long sigh. It made some of them feel as though there was a day not far off when they would have to come down on equal footing with the farmer."[91] For the Alliance, this "equal footing" represented a broadly cultural claim for enhanced social status as well as for political and economic power.

"From the cradle to the court" encompassed the interconnected political, economic, educational, religious, and familial components of life on the farm, and in 1889 and 1890 the Farmers' Alliance brought this vision of political community to Kansas. With its foundation in the family and the local community, the Alliance sought to create a utopian, holistic vision of a democratic, egalitarian America. This vision was well understood by the majority population of Kansas—Anglo, Protestant, and rural. The vision was a product of that culture, and as long as the Alliance organized its suballiances within the culture, the movement thrived.

The Alliance's vision held two contradictory notions of the family: the egalitarian political family and the patriarchal farm family. At first, each ideal helped to strengthen the organization. Leaders attracted thousands of farm women to the movement by promising they would be political equals with men. These women, in turn, helped politicize the communal events that brought farmers—and families—together. But the Alliance also supported the idea of man as head of the family, proving his manhood through the crucial breadwinner role. In this version of the family, the husband was the principal political actor, and his honor, his status, and his manhood were the prize to be won from the Money Power. As long as the movement stayed focused on the nonpartisan, local suballiance, these two visions coexisted.

But the Alliance was part of a dynamic political process, and its members and leaders would find themselves both directing and being swept up in that process. By the spring of 1890, many Alliance men and women believed that abandoning the nonpartisan stand was an inevitable part of that process. Most of those who embraced the new Populist Party did not think it posed a threat to the Alliance's vision of political community, which was at once more parochial and more inclusive than the new party.

Though the Populists would ultimately fail in their mission, their new strategy pushed them away from the nonpartisan, family-based agenda of the Farmers' Alliance and toward a strategy of attracting the one thing—votes—on which all parties depended. Because neither women nor children could vote in state and national elections, the party focused on men. The move to the Populist Party eventually deepened the basic contradiction in the Alliance's vision, between the politically egalitarian Alliance family and the patriarchal farm family, which would soon have its effect on the movement as a whole and on its members.

_____

# FIVE

### ⊰ "FOR BETSY AND BABIES" ⊱

#### FROM FARMERS' ALLIANCE TO POPULIST PARTY

As the Farmers' Alliance gained strength during 1889, most of its members assumed that they would work through their parties—Republican, Democratic, Prohibition, or Union Labor—to enact reform. In virtually one-party Kansas, however, the only way to achieve influence in state government was through the Republicans, and the G.O.P. leaders had declared in no uncertain terms that they would not relinquish power to the Alliance. The Republican legislature did not wish to upset its cozy relationship with the railroads or jeopardize the availability of Eastern capital. The legislature's refusal to act taught many Alliance members that they would have to challenge the ideal of nonpartisanship.

As early as mid-1889, Stephen McLallin's _Advocate_ began to argue for the transformation of the Farmers' Alliance into a political party. In response, a number of local alliances organized independent "People's" or "Farmers'" tickets for the county elections.[1] Alliance members chose the nominees at picnics that were transformed into "people's conventions." Here both women and men could question candidates about the issues that Alliance members had been reading about and discussing throughout the year. The local suballiances' experiments in grass-roots electoral democracy proved quite successful in the elections that fall. A number of Republican candidates, long used to guaranteed election results after winning their party's nomination, found their assumptions about the political status quo sorely tested.

The suballiances moved into local politics because of the ever worsening economic conditions coupled with the legislature's unwillingness to do anything constructive about them. Because the Alliance was strongest at the local and county level, and because statewide elections were a year away, the suballiances and county committees led the move toward independent political action. Few of these local organizations, however, had any concept of what could be done at the county level to tackle the national problems that the Alliance had identified. Instead, the Alliance used the county elections to register its disapproval of Republican policy and the political system that the G.O.P. and the Democrats supported. And by reminding the townsfolk that the opinions of the hinterlands mattered, members used the elections to assert their newly developed cultural pride.

As in 1873, state politicians were most worried about frightening away capital. Their belief in laissez-faire capitalism buttressed their opposition to legislation that would allow governments to aid farmers and challenge the railroads, money lenders, and grain elevator operators. When the legislature adjourned in late 1889, it had little to offer Alliance members which would justify their working within the "old parties" to reform society.[2]

The Alliance began the official hostilities by attacking the most visible symbol of Gilded Age Kansas Republicanism, U.S. Sen. John Ingalls, "the greatest Democrat skinner of them all." The Alliance could find little that he had actually done for farm people in Kansas other than his skillful ripostes to the "rum-soaked rebels of ruination." Unlike his fellow Kansas senator, Preston Plumb, Ingalls had little sense of the plight of the poor and even less inclination to do anything about it. The Alliance had been further outraged at Ingalls's contention in the New York *World* interview that "the purification of politics is an iridescent dream," an obvious affront to the Alliance's vision of moral politics.[3] In May 1890 the Alliance's county presidents' convention voted to condemn Ingalls and demand that the Republican-dominated legislature elect a senator who would represent the interests of Kansas farm people.

Farmers' Alliance leaders were soon fed up with both the G.O.P.'s tone and its utter disregard for farm people's plight. Urged on by urban reformers eager to harness the farmers' new-found political power, the Alliance leadership took the final step toward abandoning nonpartisanship. On June 12, 1890, it officially crossed the Rubicon when its delegates met in Topeka with representatives from the Knights of Labor, the Farmers' Mutual Benefit Association, the Patrons of Husbandry, and the Single Tax Association. Called by the Kansas Alliance president, Ben Clover, the meeting brought together the organizing expertise and membership lists of agrarian activists with the political savvy of longtime urban reformers. The delegates pronounced the formation of a "People's Party"—soon to be known also as the Populist Party—and embraced the National Farmers' Alliance's program, which was largely the product of past third-party platforms. The Alliance's avowedly nonpartisan political community had become a political party.

The transformation from the Farmers' Alliance into the Populist Party did not occur without a struggle from within the membership. Indeed, the Alliance did not so much evolve into the Populist Party as give birth to it. With the creation of the new party, the Alliance did not disappear; rather, it continually struggled with its identity and its relationship to the new organization. The Populist Party did not quite kill its parent, but it didn't pay much attention to it either.

Leaders had organized the Farmers' Alliance around the promise of a non-partisan political community that embraced "first, social; second, educational; third, financial; fourth, political" activities.[4] Based on the farm family and the local neighborhood, the Alliance was to be above party politics, transcending the rituals of mainstream politics and pursuing an enlightened non-partisanship that stressed morality and social and economic justice. This program enabled farm women to take an active political and social role in the movement, but its reliance on the assumptions of the idealized farm family undermined its egalitarian impulses. The Populist Party, with its need to attract voters, accentuated the male-centered aspects of the movement. Many Alliance women supported the move to a political party while decrying women's inability to participate as voters. Few women or men saw the new party as a threat to women's role in the Alliance.

While the Populist Party marginalized the role of farm women, it offered new opportunities to urban women reformers who supported the Populist agenda. Many of these women had first gained political experience in the Woman Movement's municipal suffrage campaign. They had established strong connections to the Union Labor, Prohibition, or Republican parties and understood the workings of state party organizations. The most prominent of them, Mary Lease and Annie Diggs, gained national attention. Whether or not they would be able to make common cause with Alliance farm women, however, remained to be seen.

## The Nonpartisan Party

Republican leaders who suffered losses to the "People's" tickets reacted with predictable outrage. The *Winfield Courier,* which had been feeling the heat from the Winfield-based *Non-Conformist* for several years, made no bones about Republicans' utter contempt for the Alliance "traitors," "anarchists," and "calamity howlers."[5] The very act of placing a slate in opposition to the Republicans was to them a declaration of political war.

Not all Republican papers were ready to concede such power, real or fictive, to the Farmers' Alliance. The Alliance's local victories in 1889 did disturb many Republican leaders, but they decided to kill with kindness, employing their favorite tactic of cooptation. Much of the Republican press attempted to assuage farm people's anger by agreeing that some (unnamed) reforms were necessary and by praising the Alliance's social activities as beneficial to the lives of farm people. Some, such as the *El Dorado Republican,* made clear they printed Alliance material as a matter of "good business, because we have many readers who are Alliance supporters." Others, such as the *Great Bend Register,* were even more favorable, attacking those who claimed that farmers' "bad management" was causing farm failures. Instead, the paper insisted that low prices, high shipping rates, gambling in options, and a fixed currency were to blame.[6] Many of the Alliance's G.O.P. supporters were liberal Republicans who had cheered on the Grange or had flirted with reform parties during the politically promiscuous seventies.

The G.O.P. in 1890, however, was far removed from the relatively tolerant party of the 1870s. The Republicans had long since given up the idea that a political aspirant could reject the party one year and then be welcomed back into the fold the next. The party had been steadily weeding out heterodoxy in its ranks for ten years, and it was not about to tolerate dissent while the barbarians stormed the gate. When the Alliance crossed the line from local skirmishes to all-out war, the G.O.P. closed ranks and counterattacked furiously.[7] At the front of the charge, not surprisingly, were a number of the Alliance's erstwhile Republican allies.

Suddenly, all the pleasant noises of Republican support for the Farmers' Alliance were squelched beneath an onslaught of vituperative denunciations. As with their criticism of the Woman Movement's political activity, Republicans asserted that the Alliance had crossed the boundaries of acceptable behavior. The *Topeka Capital*'s Joseph Hudson, a former Grange supporter, argued, "A large majority of the farmers of Kansas are Republicans, and while they are ready to join cooperative organizations for the mutual benefit of producers, they will not consent to being led by wild theorists who expect to cure all the ills of financial depression by defeating the Republican party."[8] The state Farmers' Alliance convention did not heed such warnings, voting to nominate proreform candidates on its own and unite with the Knights of Labor. In response the Republican press turned ón it with the fury of having been betrayed.[9]

Not surprisingly, Republican editors immediately questioned the manhood of those "deserters" who ran when times got tough. Just a few months after praising the "industrious" and "serious" farmers of the Alliance, the *El Dorado Republican* charged that all members were "kickers, whether they have much or little. They don't take care of their farms or their machinery. . . . The most zealous supporters [are] the easily discouraged, slack and indolent farmers, those who let the 'women and gals' milk the cows, cut the wood and carry the water while they, 'the lords of creation,' discuss with more or less depth of wisdom, the awful evils of the agricultural age."[10] To the *Republican*'s editor, Alliance men compounded their emasculation in numerous ways. Not only had they failed in their duty to provide for their families, but they had also covered this up by forcing "their" women to do extra work. Alliance men, meanwhile, acted more like women than men, whining and crying about troubles they themselves had created. Ironically, farm women had always performed the chores the *Republican* had listed.

Other Republican papers were equally swift in reversing their praise for the Alliance, sometimes in inverse proportion to their previous support. The *Register* now began releasing a torrent of statistics "proving" the availability of currency, the ease of mortgage payments, and the general prosperity of the state. The *Fort Scott Daily Monitor* revealed its antagonism toward the newly partisan Alliance, as well as the paper's underlying contempt for farm people, when it declared the organization should be "content [to restrict itself to] their best methods for raising cabbage [and] how many rows of corn should be on a cob." With third-party talk in the air, however, the *Monitor*'s editor felt the Alliance had gone too far: "when the farmer transcends that sphere of action and undertakes to discuss economic questions [such as] the causes that lead to the price of farm products which are now below the cost of production . . . then the Monitor will denounce the farmers' organization as breeding discontent and treason to the [R]epublican party."[11] The *Monitor*'s main objection to the Alliance was that the farm man had abandoned the "party of his fathers."

This act of political patricide, the *Monitor* made clear, would not be tolerated by "real men." Though the paper was questioning the masculinity of the Alliance "turncoats," its tone was strikingly similar to the attacks that it and other G.O.P. papers leveled against the Woman Movement's local election-eering. In both cases the Republican editors assumed a condescending, patri-archal tone, like that of a stern father castigating a wayward child. By using this approach they hoped to reassert the broad cultural prerogatives over women and farm people that the party had enjoyed for so long.

Alliance members, however, were busy creating an alternative political cul-ture that challenged Republican assumptions about manliness and power. Many members saw the idea of a new party as an extension of the political community they had established. The county election campaigns had given them a suggestion of what their new way of practicing politics might look like. Citizens joined together at mass meetings to choose the candidates, rather than having them be hand picked by an elite "ring." Women took part in these deliberations, whether voting directly for the candidate or at least joining in the debate.[12] Candidates were required to discuss "the issues of the day" intel-ligently and were chosen for their abilities—"the office seeks the man," rather than the other way around. Power emanated from the people, from the sub- and county alliances, which then instructed state leaders what to do. Eppie Winter, a frequent contributor to the *Alliant*, began her argument for a third party by acknowledging the local accomplishments of the Alliance. "The last year has revealed a great many undeniable facts and has served well to educate the people," she noted. "We have learned to think for ourselves. We alliance people of Cloud County, Kansas, have a store that was started about the first of last February. . . . We have a county organ, run by the alliance, do all our own shipping and select our shippers from our list by a vote of the people, and buy through our exchange." Although this had earned Alliance members more money, Winter asked her readers, "But how long will it last? Will it do the next generation any good? Just as soon as our work ceases, just that quick will the benefit stop unless we make use of politics and partisan politics at that."[13] Only if Alliance members achieved concrete gains would their politi-cal community be worth maintaining. Yet they would need to sustain their po-litical community if they hoped to enact political reform.

A number of Farmers' Alliance members saw the new party as a betrayal of this community. Most of those who objected to the People's Party appear to have been Republicans, which is not surprising since the G.O.P. had the most to lose. Although motivated largely by partisan concerns, Republican Alliance members identified some of the most important contradictions be-tween political community and political party.[14] Their arguments paralleled many of the same claims made by supporters of nonpartisanship in the Woman Movement.

Alliance Republicans charged that most candidates who were being chosen were old "third-party men," professional politicians who were less successful than their Democratic and Republican counterparts. Alliance Republicans drew on past arguments by such men as Henry Wallace, the agrarian editor who had warned that "the farmer must lead and guide himself." Indeed, Union Labor–affiliated candidates predominated in the 1889 county elections largely because they could offer some political experience.[15] They also came to hold important positions in the Populist Party's bureaucracy. Alliance Republicans believed that such men, once in office, would simply behave as people expected politicians to behave: they would work primarily to maintain their tenure and personally profit to the greatest degree possible. One Alliance Republican, asking "every man and every woman to . . . candidly consider this matter," warned against any politician who offered his help out of the goodness of his heart: "[D]on't you know that did we stop and carefully study . . . the reasons why these 'patriots' have so suddenly taken such an interest in us, where in the heretofore they have not known us; don't you know that did we hesitate long enough to think, we would not go? There is no one thing more needed by the agricultural classes than to do their own thinking."[16] Whatever the motivations of Alliance Republicans, their fears would become all too real after the Populists struggled to maintain their tenuous victories following the 1890 election.

Alliance Republicans also argued that the new party would cause an irrevocable split in the organization's political community by surrendering the ideals of education, familial spirit, reciprocity, and the free exchange of ideas. Some turned to the example of the Grange as proof of the pitfalls of partisanship. One man recounted, "Sixteen years ago there were in Jefferson county thirty-four subordinate Granges, with just as much enthusiasm then as there is in our thirty-five subordinate Alliances of today; their aims, objects, and purposes were for the improvement of agriculture and the elevation of the farmers, just as the objects of the Alliance are today." Instead of sticking together, however, "Party prejudices got into our ranks, dissolving our membership. . . . [W]e should in our Alliances, discuss and dissect these national issues until we gain a knowledge that will bring us nearer together; then as good Democrats, Republicans, and Prohibitionists attend our primaries [and] nominate good men in each party."[17] Like the Woman Movement's nonpartisan advocates, these Alliance members feared that party politics would rip asunder the organization's solidarity.

Although it is unclear how many Alliance members quit the organization after the creation of the Populist Party, scattered evidence suggests that most suballiances experienced some drop in membership. Such setbacks appear to have been temporary, however, for the state Farmers' Alliance continued to report increased membership throughout the year.[18] The creation of the Populist Party signified that the reformers were getting serious; that they were willing to take their fight directly to the highest centers of power in the state. Yet it also signaled that the new party was willing to sacrifice the Alliance's vision to attain power.

The Populist Party, by concentrating its efforts on the upcoming election, gave reformers a well-focused organizing tool. Beyond asking people to meet together and educate themselves on the issues, organizers issued two specific requests: renounce old party affiliations and vote the Populist ticket. They promised that a Populist victory would mean immediate economic relief and political reform. Such tactics proved enormously successful in drawing Kansans to the party. But the new emphasis on voting accompanied a shift in the Alliance's language as well as its political vision. As Election Day approached, Populist leaders became focused on mobilizing enough voters to gain control of the state government.

### "Hayseeds Like Me": Manliness, the Vote, and the Struggle for Power

With the formation of the Populist Party, the vote came to signify immediate redemption; the millennium suddenly seemed one electoral victory away. R. S. Phelps, a Populist from Miltonvale, exhorted readers to "go to work to elect the whole ticket from President on down. We can do it if our present officers do their duty, and carry out the wishes of the people, and all the combined money power can't help it. We must keep right in the middle of the road."[19] The Populist Party, by creating the middle way between Republicans and Democrats, between rich and poor, would create a new mainstream and a new middle class. In doing to, it would transform the vote into the instrument of justice and morality that the nation's forefathers had intended it to be.

Since only men could vote in statewide elections, the notion of an Alliance family shifted noticeably. Whereas the Alliance had challenged the idea that politics was a man's sphere alone, the Populist Party's new emphasis on the ballot excluded women from participation in what Populist leaders proclaimed was a citizen's most important duty.

The song "To the Polls" reflected this new way of thinking. The first verse asserts the act of voting as a male rite of redemption:

> *To the polls! to the polls! ye are serving the right;*
> *Let us follow the path that our fathers have trod,*
> *With the light of their counsel our strength to renew,*
> *Let us do with our might what our hands find to do.*[20]

The song, sung to the to the tune of "To the Work," goes on to equate manly labor with manly voting: "Voting on, voting on . . . Let us work, let us vote. . . . And labor til the vict'ry comes." From there, "To the polls" becomes a battle cry, exhorting men to march

> *To the polls! to the polls! let the hungry be fed.*
> *To the banner of life let the weary be led;*
> *In our ballot and banner our glory shall be*
> *While we herald the tidings—the people are free.*

> *To the polls! to the polls! we will rally again;*
> *We will free our dear homes from the bondman and chain.*

It was a heady call to arms, this rallying of the troops to shield the helpless and rescue the weak; it was the stuff of dime novels, wrapped up in the moral righteousness of the cause of reform. But it was not a call to which women could respond, for if the ballot was to be the movement's glory, then Alliance women could not take part in it. The new emphasis on the vote thus helped strengthen those elements in the Alliance's political culture which stressed men's redemption over women's participation.

The Union Labor Party helped lead the way in this reformulation of the Alliance's vision. Long and fruitlessly had these reformers toiled since the glory years of the middle seventies, when the Grange had joined the Liberal Republicans to gain control of the state legislature. When the Farmers' Alliance began to turn toward partisan politics, Union Laborites hoped to reconstruct the coalition from twenty-five years before. Union Labor activists viewed Alliance members as good-hearted country folk who had at last found the proper road to power through party politics. Union Labor papers did not show much understanding of the broad purposes of the Alliance, but they did recognize its potential as a source of votes. One of the leading Union Labor papers in the state, the Ottawa *Journal and Triumph,* chuckled paternalistically, "It is quite amusing to see farm organizations and their organs contend 'that there is no politics in it,' and at the same time . . . they are compelled to fall into the political ruts and follow the old well-beaten paths of the Greenback Union Labor organization. The road is already graded and macadamized, gentlemen. On it a little team has been pulling an enormous load. But with the combined help of all the farmers' and labor organizations in the state elections next fall, the old ring bosses are going to hear something drop."²¹ Although the writer had probably employed the word *ruts* simply to extend his metaphor, the term serves to underscore the ironic predicament facing the Alliance. With the Republicans unresponsive, many Alliance members believed that forming a new party was the only available avenue to meaningful reform. But in doing so, the movement accepted many of the same practices of the political parties they opposed.

The *Journal and Triumph*'s use of the term *gentleman,* as well as the writer's chummy tone, bespoke the clubbish nature of male politics. Although third-party reformers from the Greenbackers to the Union Laborites had publicly supported woman suffrage, their political culture appears to have been little more oriented toward women's participation than was that of the mainstream parties. Although in sympathy with women's rights issues, the third-party leaders were more interested in legislative programs and election battles than in educational and social activities. Ironically, the Alliance's cross-gender approach to political culture may have opened up new opportunities for women within the Union Labor organization after 1888.²²

Third-party organizations had not discouraged women's participation in the past, but neither had they been aware of women's particular needs and perspectives. Perhaps because reform-minded urban women could participate in the Woman Movement, both urban women and men saw less need to fashion a role for women within the Union Labor Party. Although old-party men claimed that third-party men were emasculated and feminized, the Union Labor Party initially was far more male oriented than the Farmers' Alliance.

Union Labor leaders revealed their male-centered approach in the language they used when addressing Alliance members. The *Journal and Triumph* tended to address men exclusively, as voters, far more than Alliance papers did. A typical exhortation to potential supporters read: "Farmers . . . do you think you live too high when you get down to eat your bread and butter three times a day? Do you think your wife is extravagant when she wears a dress that is threadbare for weeks and months, daily patching and sewing up the holes? Do you think her extravagant when she has not a decent dress or pair of shoes suitable to attend church or go into company? Brother farmers, stop and meditate."²³ Union Laborites had been patiently preparing the road to reform in expectation of fellow travelers; to these veterans, Alliance men were pilgrims in need of direction. In order to set the farmer on the right path, reformers employed the farmer's old nemesis, the male ethos of success. In the passage above are questions not asked but implied: Brother farmer, why have you let your wife be reduced to such poverty? And what are you going to do about it? Alliance supporters, both women and men, would soon be asking this question outright.

As McLallin, Diggs, Ben Clover, and other Alliance leaders agitated for a third party, numerous reformers began asking farmers questions that had long plagued them. Taking their cue from the Union Laborites, many Alliance activists decided to use farm men's guilt as an organizing tool. "There is nothing that will touch the heart of a loving father more quickly than to realize his poverty," the *Industrial Educator* assured. "As soon as he sees the wrong, he, like a true protector is ready to do anything that is just and honorable, to make amends for what has been, without doubt, mostly his fault. He finds he has listened too much to the teachings of others, who were designing friends, plotting for their own selfish ends." Alliance writers listed other sins of the Kansas farm man: he speculated in hopes of cashing in quickly, he borrowed money too easily and too often, and he neglected his family's welfare in favor of expenditures for the fields.[24] Fortunately for the disgraced farmer, he could still redeem himself morally and economically—by voting the reform ticket.

Such indictments of farm men, commonplace in reform newspapers during 1890, presented the flip side of the Alliance's attempted reclamation of the farmers' manhood. According to these Populist writers, farming could be reestablished as a manly, noble vocation only if the farmer did the right thing politically. To renounce old party ties, hoist the banner of reform, and strike with the ballot—this was the only road to redemption. Ben Clover presented the choices to the Alliance man quite plainly. "See your toil and care-worn wife as she brushes away the silent tear and then remember that for years you have outraged your manhood by casting a vote for this infamous system," he thundered. "Shall we not rise up and assert our manhood? Shall we longer remain the victims of corporate greed when we have the power within ourselves to free our homes, our families and friends from its unholy grasp?"[25] The former hayseeds could replace their role as unmanly victims—for only women and children were unable to defend themselves—while at the same time assuring themselves the economic success that had eluded them.

Clover's calls for moral redemption matched the religious overtones of the Alliance's crusade. The Populist Party, however, focused exclusively on the sins of the father: he alone had to expurgate his misdeeds in order to free his wife and children and reclaim his role as protector, while admitting his past sins. The popular protest song "The Hayseed," appropriately sung to the tune of "Save a Poor Sinner Like Me," revealed just such a tale of confession and redemption.

*I once was a tool of oppression*
*And as green as a sucker could be*
*And monopolies banded together*
*To beat a poor hayseed like me.*

.———.———.———.

*And the ticket we vote in November*
*Will be made up of hayseeds like me.*[26]

A vote for the Populist Party provided farm men with a wonderful opportunity. They could work to fight against the powers that they believed were destroying society while reinforcing their self-esteem and improving their economic condition.

Populist writers had rhetorically transformed Alliance women from active participants into passive victims. The movement had not yet abandoned its earlier ideal of women in political partnership with men, but the vision now existed alongside a seemingly contradictory one of farm men boldly fighting the good fight for "Betsy and babies."[27] Rallies, picnics, and meetings became less an end in themselves—the creation of political community—and more a means to a short-term electoral goal. A shift began, subtly, almost unconsciously, it would seem, toward the idea of Alliance women as auxiliary to the movement, an idea that fitted easily in with the notion of the farmer's wife as helpmeet.

Ironically, some Farmers' Alliance women took the lead in utilizing men's insecurity to further the Populist Party's cause. One wrote, "The joy with which a mother could greet her new-born babe is changed into a sigh of despair as she thinks that a long dreary life of servility and toil is the only legacy she can leave her child. But this shall not be. Where are the sons of free America with the blood of our Revolutionary fathers in their veins? Come to the front and stand in the ranks; not of barbaric warfare, but at the ballot box, and tell them we have found out their tricks." Another farm woman demanded of Alliance men, "As the old parties are taking the bread and butter from wife and children, and will eventually take the home, which will you do, be nonpartisan and insure the welfare of family and home, or stick to the parties?"[28] Such exhortations suggested that Populist women were not altogether sure that their men had the wherewithal to overcome the Money Power. Only by voting the nonpartisan party could farm men prove their worth and their manhood.

While Alliance women employed the notion of the male ethos of success to garner support for the Populist ticket, they often had a second agenda buried within their exhortations. Their comments to Alliance men betray annoyance,

Celebrating the masculine political ideal: the "Dauntless 98" declare "For never but by farmers' votes will farmers' wrongs be righted." *Kansas State Historical Society*

bitterness, and sometimes outright anger at the movement's new direction. With the Populist Party's emphasis on the vote, some women found it appropriate to note that men, whether farmers, politicians, or the corporate elite, had created the mess in the first place. They also observed that men had denied women the franchise while abusing their political rights by trading votes for Election-Day "treats." In demanding that their husbands or sons "arise and be men, and not be content to remain in slavery while the ballot, the most deadly weapon of warfare is still in [your] hands," Alliance women often assumed an accusatory, condescending tone. Before the movement's focus on the electoral arena, Alliance women's language had connoted solidarity and inclusion. Now some women displayed a growing sense of exclusion, noting that men were now part of a separate brotherhood, that of the voter.

Rosa Thompson, secretary of the Portis Alliance, dutifully recorded in the *Advocate* her suballiance's resolution, "We, the male members, will support Baker [the Populist candidate] for the sixth congressional district." She then added, "I would say right here that 'the females' would support the same ticket if they could get the chance."[29] Such remarks often appeared as asides to the main business of politics, as if women recognized that defeating the Money Power remained the most important task. In fact, while almost all Alliance women who wrote to the reform press supported the Populist Party, they integrated their desire to help the party with their anger over their newly lowered status. "We women could come right out and say what party it was that passed laws detrimental to our interests," wrote one exasperated supporter. "We could say that we had waited so long that we had nothing left but our votes (that is, if we had the vote) and so we must use them to defend ourselves. But you might as well shout 'scat' to a lot of wild cats as to say 'party' to a man— they would scatter just as quick. You say that women don't need to vote, for you protect their interest. From the present state of affairs it looks like you hadn't protected yourselves or us either; but I am digressing."[30] Alliance women's "digressions" pointed to the depth and complexity of emotions that many of them felt about the founding of the Populist Party. They resented men's ties to the old parties, with memories of Election-Day drunken sprees (and no doubt postelection hangovers). These women believed that farm men, in giving in to the temptations of "the party," had failed their basic contract with women.

The legitimacy of men's power in the family and in middle-class society in general rested on their ability to provide for their family. According to both Populist and Republican writers, however, farm men had proven to be political and economic failures. Why, then, should they be allowed to stay in charge?

"Even now there are hosts of men who still cling to these old rotten parties with an affection superior to that for home, and wife, and children," wrote one disgusted woman. "Give women the ballot and this nonsense would cease. Let us hear from more alliance women, not only through the press but at the meetings of the alliances. Let them try to beat a little good sense through the thick skulls of their husbands and brothers, and if this is impossible leave them at home on election day to rock the babies, while the women go to the polls and work for the good of the cause which they are enlisted."[31] These Alliance women did not want to return to the prepartisan days. Instead, they demanded to be included as equals in the fight for social justice; to be able to use "that mightiest weapon, the ballot," in the cause with which they were inextricably involved. The creation of the Populist Party made clear to Alliance women that despite the rhetoric of equality within the movement, they would remain in a supporting role without the vote. For whereas the ballot promised to return to farm men a sense of control over their lives, it reminded women of how politically helpless they would remain until they won the right to vote.

## "QUEEN MARY" AND "LITTLE ANNIE": TWO PATHS TO POLITICAL PROMINENCE

Republican editors responded to Alliance women's activities with a certain awe and deference. "It was the farmer's wives that did it," explained one paper, sounding a theme that was often repeated in the press. Perhaps Republican editors excused Farmers' Alliance women because of their adherence to traditional roles such as cooks, social organizers, and teachers. Perhaps the editors were simply following their own tradition of heaping scorn on farm men while ignoring the women. Whatever the reason, Alliance women escaped the scathing abuse directed at the political insurgents during the campaign of 1890.

Although Republican editors absolved Alliance women from the sin of trespassing socially accepted boundaries, women who took to the campaign stump were quickly branded as transgressors. Unlike the farm women in the Alliance, these women were based in large towns and cities. Most had first gained their political experience in the Woman Movement or the Union Labor Party, through which they had become acquainted with the ways and means of mainstream politics.

Republican editors routinely attacked Populist leaders as "she-men," "kickers," and "demagogues," unmanly malcontents who, having failed at business and politics, were now appealing to the basest instincts of the populace. In other words, they were failures as men. Republicans saw Populist women leaders as the opposite side of the same debased coin, masculinist women who were all too successful in the male world of politics. The journalist William Allen White, in his famous "What's the Matter with Kansas" essay, condemned the Populists for sending "three or four harpies out lecturing, telling the people that Kansas is raising hell and letting the corn go to weed."[32]

Mary Elizabeth Lease, the purported author of the statement that Kansas farmers should "raise less corn and more Hell," was the direct object of White's scorn. Lease, who came to enjoy a national reputation, represented all that Republican leaders hated and feared about Populism and its women orators. It is emblematic of the G.O.P.'s tactics that a Republican reporter had fabricated the phrase in an effort to prove Lease an anarchist while also making good copy; it is emblematic of Lease's character that she embraced the remark as her own creation.[33] Lease was constantly turning the opposition's attacks to her own advantage. She took mainstream expectations about gender and politics and placed them on their head. She gloried in her rebellion against both the political and the social status quo, and the farmers loved her all the more for it.

Born Mary Elizabeth Clyens in 1850, she had come to Kansas from Pennsylvania in 1870. Three years later she married Charles Lease, a pharmacist. They spent the next decade failing as farmers in Kansas and Texas, which left Lease with an enduring distaste for farm life. When her husband opened a pharmacy in Wichita, she enthusiastically dedicated herself to urban reform activities. She quickly moved from participation in Wichita's women's clubs to a wide range of causes. Although originally a Republican, by 1888 she had embraced the Union Labor party. Stumping in central Kansas during that year's campaign, she became renowned as a powerful speaker. She also found time to cofound the Knights of Labor newspaper, the *Colorado Workman,* and to edit the *Union Labor Press.* Lease was thus well positioned to take a leading role in the Populist uprising in 1890.[34]

During that extraordinary summer, Lease came into her own as the premier radical orator in Kansas. Her primary talents were her remarkable voice and the force of her persona. William Allen White admitted that he "had never heard a lovelier voice than Mrs. Lease's. . . . A deep, rich contralto, a singing voice that had hypnotic qualities. . . . She could recite the multiplication table and set a crowd hooting and hurrahing at her will."[35] One Republican editor similarly admired her voice but opined that "if she would expend her energies in some better channel—Salvation Army for instance—she might become a power for good."[36]

Such condescending words were the best Lease could expect from the opposition press; usually their broadsides were far uglier. The editor of the *Wellington Monitor* deployed all available weapons in his attack on her. "A miserable caricature upon womanhood, hideously ugly in feature and foul of tongue, made an ostensible political speech." After noting "the editor of this paper understands that he came in for the principal share" of abuse, he riposted:

> All we know about her is that she is hired to travel around the country by this great reform People's party, which seems to find a female blackguard a necessity in its business, spouting foul-mouthed vulgarity at $10 a night. . . . The petticoated smut-mill earns her money, but few women want to make their living that way. . . . Her venomous tongue is the only thing marketable about the old harpy, and we suppose she is justified in selling it where it commands the highest price. . . . In about a month the lantern-jawed, goggle-eyed nightmare will be put out of a job, and nobody will be the worse for the mud with which she has tried to bespatter them.[37]

The editor's allusions are telling: he likens Lease's political activities to prostitution, an occupation he implies Lease might have taken up if she had not been a "goggle-eyed nightmare." His wrath was born not merely of Lease's foray into politics, which was galling enough, but in her temerity to attack him and other "prominent citizens." Because Lease overstepped the bounds of acceptable behavior, she was denied the usual courtesies accorded to respectable women.

The *Monitor* was not alone in attacking Lease by way of her personal appearance and nonfeminine bearing. White supplemented his paean to Lease's voice by sneering, "She stood nearly six feet tall, with no figure, a thick torso, and long legs. To me, she often looked like a kangaroo pyramided up from the hips to a comparatively small head. Her skin was pasty white; her jowls were a little heavy. . . . She wore her hair in a psyche knot, always neatly combed and topped by the most ungodly hats I ever saw a woman wear. She had no sex appeal—none!"[38] One could challenge the "pudgy little editor" for tossing stones from glass houses, but such a charge would be beside the point; old-party men in Kansas were rarely attacked because of their looks and their adherence to gender norms.[39] This was reserved for those who stood outside the mainstream.

Even Lease's defenders felt impelled to defend her femininity, although the defense reads as equally damning. According to one sympathetic reporter, "Mrs. Lease is a tall woman—fully five feet nine inches, and rather slender. Her face is strong, good, not pretty, and very feminine. There is no mark of masculinity about her. She is woman all over. Her hair is a dark brown and evenly parted in the center and smoothed down at the sides with neat care. Her nose, chin and cheek bones announce themselves strongly. However, they give no sense of harshness to her face."[40] That the reporter managed to anticipate White's attack by some thirty years indicates that certain features of Lease repelled or fascinated her enemies and allies. The point of contention about her hairstyle, figure, and face was whether they conformed to contemporary notions of femininity. If detractors could establish that Lease was indeed a "man-wife," then they could add this fact to buttress their argument that she had stepped over the line of acceptable behavior.[41]

Photographs of Lease during this period reveal a tall woman with strong features and a regal bearing. As the reporter noted, she is indeed "not pretty" by contemporary cultural standards, and she has the look of a person not to be trifled with. Lease herself never objected to attacks concerning her femininity, nor did she attempt to defend herself. Indeed, she flaunted her masculine style, daring men to challenge her on their own turf. In one speech at Washaura, Kansas, Lease concluded her usual crowd-jolting speech by challenging any in the audience to controvert her. A Reverend Zibriska rose to pick up the gauntlet, perhaps feeling that any man could match a woman in a duel of political oratory. The good reverend, however, soon found himself outmatched. He opened with a slashing attack against the Populist nominee for governor, John Willits. Having completed this initial thrust, however, Zibriska was swiftly placed on the defensive. The local correspondent gleefully reported: "Mrs. Lease took the reverend gentleman in hand, placed him on the witness stand, and constituted herself the examining counsel. . . . Amid the wildest cheers from the audience Mrs. Lease completely vindicated Hon. Willits . . . and with withering sarcasm demolished the thoroughly punished, thoroughly silenced divine, who was glad to skulk out of sight and out of hearing."[42] The writer, a man, concluded, "We need more women like Mrs. Lease."

In this scene, not only did Lease take on a masculine role, but she also placed "the reverend gentleman" in a subordinate position, as a domineering husband might treat his wife. That Zibriska was probably used to women's deference and respect made such a transposition even more striking. The writer, in employing violent language to describe Lease's action, was following protocol: Populist correspondents gloried in the image of Lease as a warrior-champion of the oppressed. "With cheer and cheer," reported one correspondent, sounding more like a sportswriter than a political commentator, "did [the audience] greet her every thrust at the hellish powers that held the producers of the land by the throat."[43] Not only were Lease's supporters unconcerned about her "gender bending," but they also reveled in the idea of a woman handily dismissing those who had impugned Alliance men and Populist politi-

Little Annie and Queen Mary: Annie Diggs (*left*) and Mary Lease (*right*). *Kansas State Historical Society*

cians as unmanly failures. Whether or not Alliance men truly wanted farm women to emulate Lease would be revealed in the coming years.

Although Lease chose to put forth, even exaggerate, a masculinist persona, there was one boundary she dared not cross. Motherhood was still a sacred subject. Lease and her supporters swiftly countered any attacks on Lease's abilities as wife and mother. Republicans based their criticism on simple logic: how could one spend so much time on the hustings and still find time to rock the cradle? The *Topeka Capital* backed this up with the claim that Lease's son had been arrested for stealing a watch but was then released. The affair served as a lesson to mischievous boys, "inasmuch as his mother, who ought to be home taking care of him and keeping him out of mischief, is traipsing around the state at the expense of the farmers, bawling calamity." The charge, however, was pure fabrication, a technique not unknown to the *Capital*. The *Advocate* responded that the one arrested was in fact the son of a Republican politician, "whose father and mother are both at home to look after his morals." The true lesson, it contended, was that there was no logical connection between political activity and juvenile delinquency.[44]

In claiming that women's political participation led to bad motherhood, the

*Capital* was skating on some ideologically thin ice. The charge played into the hands of antisuffragists who made the same claim, a situation that the long-time suffrage supporter and the editor of the *Capital,* Joseph Hudson, would not have endorsed. Hudson's Republicanism, however, usually triumphed over his suffrage impulses. He thus could write off any loss to the latter cause in support of the former as the price of doing political business in Kansas. Like most Republicans, he supported woman suffrage as long as it did not interfere with the G.O.P.'s prerogatives.

In condemning Populist women orators, G.O.P. officials soon had to explain why Republican women were similarly engaged in partisan speaking tours. Most prominent among them was Laura Johns, who, as president of the Republican Women's Club, was becoming a prominent spokeswoman for her party. The *Advocate* noted that despite Johns's efforts, the Republicans had continued to heap scorn on Lease, particularly in reference to her gender. McLallin, the paper's editor, argued that if any Populist speaker insulted Johns, "the miscreant who would so demean himself would receive a swift rebuke from all true disciples of the soon-to-be-victorious party."[45] Populists, the *Advocate* made clear, placed a woman's political activities within the acceptable boundaries of her sphere.

Johns, however, was careful to play by the rules of femininity. The same could be said of Annie Diggs, who began writing and speaking for the Populists at the same time as Lease. Diggs's basic chronology was similar to Lease's. Born in 1848, she moved to Kansas from the East in the early 1870s and was married three months after Lease in 1873. Diggs's husband, a postal clerk in Lawrence, was similarly a middle-class town dweller. In all other ways, however, the two women were strikingly different. Where Lease had moved quickly from local women's clubs to state party politics, Diggs had expanded her contacts within the Woman Movement. Originally drawn to temperance work, she soon became active in the Kansas Equal Suffrage Association, the Social Science Federation, and the Unitarian Church.

Her association with the Unitarian Church led her to help establish the Kansas Liberal Union in 1881, which consisted of "spiritualists, materialists, Unitarians, Universalists, Free Religionists, Socialists, and agnostics"—in short, a who's who of middle-class fringe reform groups in Gilded Age Kansas. She lived in Boston the following year, where she was elected vice president of the Free Religious Association. During this period, she began contributing to local and New York newspapers and in 1882 published the *Kansas Liberal* with her husband. Her trip back East led to a conversion of sorts. She later recalled, "I became convinced that the reforms which we sought were after all economical rather than moral questions."[46]

When the Farmers' Alliance appeared in Kansas in the late 1880s, Diggs became an early supporter. Diggs "turned her persuasive charms on Colonel O. E. Leonard, . . . editor of the *Lawrence Journal* . . . and won his consent for an Alliance column written by herself. The day following her first article an editorial appeared disclaiming responsibility for the view that appeared in her column." Quickly gaining notoriety, Diggs's column was picked up by other papers sympathetic to the Alliance. Steven McLallin was so impressed by her work that he hired her to become associate editor for the newly established Topeka *Advocate*. This prompted the *El Dorado Republican* to smirk, " 'Wimmin don't think they just feel,' hence you will find an issue of the *Advocate* which is filled with personal abuse of Ingalls and other Republicans, [and] a claw stretched toward the editor of the *Republican*."[47] Like the *Monitor*'s editor, the head scribe at the *Republican* did not much like getting scored by a woman, and a calamity howler to boot. Tellingly, the writer condemned Diggs for her supposed feminine qualities.

The *Republican*'s negative reference to Diggs was a rarity among Republicans, however. More often the "persuasive charm" that Diggs reportedly used on the Lawrence editor mollified critics to an extent that she was spared the vitriol directed at Lease. Diggs, schooled by the Woman Movement, embraced the outward manifestations of middle-class respectability. Her physical appearance, like her manners, contrasted sharply with that of the more confrontational Lease. Standing a foot and a half shorter than "Queen Mary," "Little Annie" wore her hair in a decorative bun and possessed "eyes that sparkled." One might speculate, in fact, that Lease's and Diggs's political styles originated in part from the way society categorized their outward appearance.

These two styles greatly influenced how allies and enemies perceived the two. The *State Journal,* a Republican newspaper with conservative social and political views, noted the differences between Diggs's and Lease's approaches to politics: "Though Mrs. Diggs' name has been coupled with Mrs. Lease . . . she is, in fact, . . . an entirely different woman from her running mate. Mrs. Lease is a woman of rhetoric, Mrs. Diggs is a woman of much feeling. Mrs. Lease thinks she is a logician; Mrs. Diggs never practices self-deception of any kind. Mrs. Lease is a politician; Mrs. Diggs is a woman. When one sees Mrs. Diggs on the platform he is inclined to regret that a woman should be there; when Mrs. Lease follows he is sorry she is not a man." The passage is an interesting mixture of fact, perception, and myth. Diggs was indeed a much more perceptive thinker than Lease. The *Kansas City Star* reporter noted that Lease's "mind is untrained, and while displaying plenty of a certain sort of power, is illogical, lacks sequence and scatters like a 10-gauge gun."[48] And whereas Lease was the more powerful speaker, Diggs took on the role of political strategist. Although Diggs developed as an influential political insider—by 1900 opponents referred to her as "the Boss"—Lease was perceived as being the masculinist "politician." Given their very different personalities and approaches to politics, it is not surprising that they "disliked each other cordially."[49]

While Diggs cultivated her image as a woman of charm and grace, she was busy establishing herself as a political force to be reckoned with. The two images were inextricably entwined: only with such a façade could she have managed to maintain her influence in the Populist Party. She was as diplomatic as Lease was confrontational. Both styles had their uses, but Diggs's was more suited for the long haul. Where Lease's victories were scored in public and were usually at the expense of others, Diggs worked the sidelines. The *Barton County Beacon* credited Diggs with ensuring Peffer's election, along with the "passage of the law compelling the governor to appoint two women on every board of five persons having charge of educational or charitable institutions, besides doing a lot of other things."[50] Diggs played by the basic rules of the game, stretching and testing them. Lease refused to go along, glorying in her rebellion. Farm people may have professed love for "our little Annie," but Lease captured the spirit of revolt in 1890.

With all of the differences between Lease and Diggs, they still had more in common with each other than with most farm women. For although Lease had spent ten years on a farm, she had quickly embraced the urban cultural worldview. Her farm experience left her sympathetic to farm people's plight, but it also alienated her from rural culture. Diggs, for her part, had never lived on a farm. Neither woman made an effort to reach out to farm women or to present herself as a role model. Instead, Lease and Diggs would lead the way for a small group of urban women reformers to gain influence within the Populist Party, women who hoped to bridge the gap between the Woman Movement and the Populists. First, however, they would have to negotiate the conundrum of partisanship and political sisterhood.

The relationship between urban Populist women, the Populist Party, and the Woman Movement was just one of the many components of the complex matrix that emerged in Kansas after the summer of 1890. Kansans woke up the morning following Election Day to find the political landscape completely unsettled. The Populists had taken a large majority in the House, gaining 96 of the 125 seats. They had captured five of eight congressional offices. Although most of the Populist state officers had been defeated, it was generally believed that John Willits had been "counted out" by Republican election officials. Joseph Hudson snarled, "The people's party managers trusted for victory to the ignorance of the people, and to the shame of Kansas their confidence was not misplaced."[51] Hudson and other Republicans would soon be casting about for ways to destabilize the new coalition, none of which had much to do with political education.

As the political groups confronted one another after the election, political activists often found themselves maintaining a precarious balancing act among different loyalties and agendas. With such a varied and interconnected cast of political players in Kansas, including Farmers' Alliance members, urban and rural Populists, partisan and nonpartisan Woman Movement activists, Prohibitionists, Republicans, and Democrats—to say nothing of the various racial, ethnic, religious, and regional groups—it was not yet clear how these relationships would be resolved in the political arena of Kansas.

# SIX

## ❧ THE MATRIX OF REFORM ❧

On November 4, 1890, Kansas politics turned topsy-turvy. The G.O.P. appeared to have suffered a grievous defeat—a "Republican Waterloo," according to one paper. The Populist Party, meanwhile, seemed poised to take control of state politics by 1892. Though the Populists had failed to capture a majority of the voters, they had nearly equaled the Republicans. Since the party had been officially open for business only since June, such an accomplishment was remarkable and full of promise for the future. If nothing else, the Populists had replaced the Democrats as the major challenger to Republican rule. The Democrats had lost half their voting strength, despite the endorsement by anti-prohibitionist Republicans of the Democratic gubernatorial candidate, ex-Governor Robinson.[1] The Prohibition Party fared even worse, slipping from nearly seven thousand votes in 1888 to just over a thousand two years later.[2]

Beneath the immediate numbers, however, the Populists' position was more precarious. The estimated Populist voting coalition consisted of ex-Republicans (36%), ex-Democrats (31%), ex–Union Laborites (29%), and ex-Prohibitionists (4%). Although Populists had declared an end to old factionalisms, they would soon discover that traditional antagonisms were very much alive. The new party would also have to deal with Democratic machinations. Because the Populist victory threatened the Democrats' viability as a political party, they had the most to gain by controlling the new party. In their efforts, Democrats had one bit of tantalizing "proof" of the benefits of Populist-Democratic cooperation: both parties had nominated John Ives for attorney general, and he had been the only non-Republican to win executive office.[3]

Most observers gave the Farmers' Alliance a good portion of the credit for the Populist's triumph. The Alliance's influence was especially strong in the local and congressional races, where the Populists had been most successful. Many voters were willing to take a chance on a new politician whom they either knew or had helped select at a suballiance or county meeting. In order for the Populist Party to grow, it would need to nurture the Alliance.

If the Alliance was to remain strong, its leaders would have to work to ensure that women remained involved in the movement. And a healthy Alliance was crucial if farm women were to continue to express themselves politically. The Woman Movement had thus far left the hinterlands alone, and the Populist Party had shown itself to be more interested in male voters than disenfranchised women. The Alliance remained farm women's only opportunity for learning political skills, debating current issues, and assuming leadership roles. If the Populist Party ignored the Alliance, farm women would find it much more difficult to participate in politics.

While Alliance women faced narrowing opportunities following 1890, urban Populist women used their newfound prominence as leverage in the Kansas Equal Suffrage Association (KESA), hoping to fight for women's rights issues within the Populist Party while committing KESA to the Populist agenda. Because of the Populists' rise to power in state politics, urban Populist women expected that they would receive a corresponding number of offices within the suffrage movement. The many non-Populist factions in KESA did not take kindly to these maneuvers, however. Following the 1890 election, the old battles between Union Laborites, Republicans , and nonpartisans were reborn with renewed fury.

Although KESA faced certain dangers because of the new political alignment, it also recognized the opportunities suddenly available. Whereas Laura Johns and other KESA leaders had rejected a call for a statewide suffrage campaign in 1889, the next year's election had made this a viable possibility. The Populists, led by Mary Lease, Annie Diggs, and a number of supportive men, had persuaded the Populist leadership to indicate that they favored state woman suffrage. Many Republicans, worried that the Populists might steal all the credit if Kansas women got the vote, began to signal their support as well.

With a statewide campaign looming, however, the Woman Movement would have to rethink its strategy of creating a culturally homogeneous movement. The Woman Movement had gained both solidarity and the support of many politicians by remaining within the boundaries of respectability. These policies, however, had cut women activists off from the majority of Kansans, including farm people, African-Americans, workers, and Catholic immigrants, some of whom would be needed to pass a state constitutional amendment.

Although the Women's Christian Temperance Union (WCTU) avoided the partisan battles suffered by KESA, it still had a difficult time adjusting to the new political arrangements. After the 1890 election, the WCTU found that its once strong influence over prohibition policy had all but evaporated. The continued depression had dissipated support for prohibition, and the WCTU found itself increasingly on the defensive at the local level. As a statewide issue, prohibition was swaying fewer voters. After 1890, Fanny Rastall failed to adjust to the Populists' presence in politics. Long used to playing the Prohibitionists off the Republicans, she had trouble conceiving of politics without her old allies. The WCTU, having become comfortable with arrangements during its "golden decade," was now at a loss as to how to proceed in the "Wet Nineties."[4]

For all of the political actors involved, the early 1890s offered challenges, opportunities, confusion, potential disaster—everything, that is, except stability. All would have to face wrenching changes, compromises, and disunity. None could be certain how the upheaval would influence the gendered meanings in Kansans' political discourse. Four years later, only one group would emerge victorious from the matrix of reform.

## Negotiating the "Isms": Populism, Prohibition, and Woman Suffrage

The Populists took the most tortuous route to the final showdown. Although they might have avoided some obstacles, they came to the political arena burdened with more contradictions, expectations, and internal divisions than any other group. What is more, they had the Republicans waiting close by, ready to give a helpful shove whenever the Populists tripped themselves up. And if no Populist mishaps were imminent, the Republicans were happy to invent a few.

Kansas voters had elected Populists because they had promised concrete change. Although promises of reforming the national political and economic system had added moral force to their arguments, Populist leaders had essentially pledged immediate relief from onerous mortgages, high railroad rates, and low crop prices. They had appealed to farm men as failed breadwinners who could redeem their honor and their farm by voting for the Populist Party. Having chosen this organizing strategy, they now had to deliver the goods.

Unfortunately, Populist legislators did not have the votes, as Joseph Hudson was quick to note after the 1890 election. "While the People's Party controls the house by a very large majority," he assured his readers, "the senate is still Republican by 39 to 1, and a governor's veto also stands in the way of radical legislation of which businessmen and capitalists might have stood in dread. There is no danger of the passage of any measures which would render capital unsafe."[5] Until Populists had a crack at the Senate in 1892, nothing could be passed without Republican consent. This the Republicans would not give, unless it was for one of the milder reforms that liberal Republicans could stomach. When the Republicans did support a reform measure, they outmaneuvered the Populists and gained sponsorship of the bill, along with the credit.[6] Populists, many of whom were novices at the art of legislative manipulation, were more often than not left in the dust by their G.O.P. rivals.

Although the legislature passed few economic reforms, woman suffragists believed the new make-up of the House made passage of a woman suffrage bill possible. Hoping to avoid the bruising experience of an amendment campaign, they argued that the legislature was constitutionally empowered to grant women voting rights. Annie Diggs, heading the Farmers' Alliance's legislative committee, began a "vigorous campaign to secure full suffrage for women."[7] Diggs, assisted by Sam Wood, the suffragists' champion from the 1867 amendment campaign, persuaded Populist Rep. J. L. Soupene to introduce the bill in the House. Although it failed to gain the necessary two-thirds majority, Diggs and other Populist leaders exerted pressure on recalcitrant legislators and got the bill passed on the second try by sixty-nine votes to thirty-two. Sixty-four Populists, four Republicans, and one Democrat voted in favor; sixteen Populists, twelve Republicans, and four Democrats voted against.

The leading opponent in the debate was not a Republican, but rather the Populist Speaker of the House, Peter Percival Elder. P. P. Elder maintained a chivalric approach to gender relations which Diggs branded "a relic of the Dark Ages." But he had fought the good fight for third-party causes in Kansas for nearly twenty years, abandoning a successful career in the Republican Party which had included a stint as lieutenant governor. Because of his credentials, his word carried a good deal of weight with Populist legislators, particularly those with third-party backgrounds.

Although outmaneuvered by prosuffrage Populists, Elder did not surrender quietly. He registered a protest signed by seven other Populists, four Republicans, and four Democrats. The document read like a collected works of anti-suffragism: the objections included the threat of more domestic quarrels, the degradation of pure womanhood, and the problem of drawing to the polling booth only those of ill moral character. A new objection was that "the demand for female suffrage is largely confined to the ambitious office-seeking class, . . . and will transform them into politicians, and dangerous ones at that." Elder then added a touch of whimsy, stating, "When the laws of nature so change the female organization as to make it possible for them to sing 'bass' we shall then be quite willing for such to become a law." Only at the end did he inject a bit of practical politics, declaring, "It is a grave mistake, and an injury to both sexes and the party, to add another 'ism' to our political creed."[8]

Diggs was so incensed at Elder's flippancy, as well as his sneering comments about women activists, that she decided to do a little political muscle flexing of her own. Writing in the *Advocate,* she chastised Elder for his "coarse, boorish, ungentlemanly" comments that were "entirely devoid of that dignity that should characterize the utterance of a representative of the people and especially the speaker of the House." Going a step farther, she pronounced a political death sentence upon him: if he had "any future political aspirations he may as well abandon them. In a state where woman's influence in politics is as potent as it is in Kansas, it will be useless for any man who has so little respect for their influence, and whose allusions to the fair sex are characterized by the coarseness of this protest, to ever again become a candidate for office."[9] The response to Diggs's attack reflected the immense influence and respect she had amassed among Populists; none chose to rebuke her in print. As for Elder, Diggs's comments probably reinforced his belief about ambitious, dangerous women politicians. In any case, he apparently decided to keep his own counsel on the matter, at least publicly.

Because the suffrage bill now had to pass the Republican-dominated Senate, Diggs gave way in favor of Laura Johns. Hurrying to Topeka from her Salina home, Johns "made every possible effort" to persuade her fellow Republicans to approve the bill. Republicans, however, hid behind the somewhat dubious claim that the bill would not stand a chance in the Kansas Supreme Court, despite evidence supplied by suffragists which proved that the bill had at least a fighting chance of being declared constitutional. Among the senators were a number of longtime suffrage supporters, who normally would have voted for the bill simply as a symbolic gesture, whether unconstitutional or not. These were not normal times, however. Not wanting the "calamity party" to gain the credit for enfranchising some 250,000 new voters, the Republican leadership stonewalled the "Populist woman suffrage bill." The bill was defeated by thirty-nine votes to one.[10]

In objecting to the woman suffrage bill, P. P. Elder had buried his most effective argument against it under a barrage of sanctimonious and flippant verbiage. A number of Populists agreed with him that another "ism" would indeed split the party. The National Farmers' Alliance had thus far managed to avoid an open endorsement of woman suffrage, afraid of alienating socially conservative Southerners, immigrants, and working men. In Kansas the Populist leadership was concerned about driving away Democratic supporters: former Democrats made up nearly one-third of the Populist vote, and an additional fifty thousand remained in the old party as potential converts.

While many Kansas Democrats were opposed to woman suffrage, they were even more committed to the defeat of prohibition. In fact, many objected to woman suffrage primarily because it would aid prohibition efforts. Kansas farm people, however, were among the strongest supporters of prohibition, and Republicans were quick to exploit this possible division in the Populist coalition. The one true issue, claimed the *Topeka Capital,* was prohibition; only the G.O.P. could be trusted to enforce the law.[11] If voters abandoned the Republican Party in 1890, nothing could save the state from the reign of Demon Rum.

Prohibitionists aided the Republicans by repeatedly urging the Populists to embrace the temperance cause more actively. The WCTU attempted to establish common ground with the Populists by connecting the Farmers' Alliance's appeal to "protect our homes" with the fight against the saloon. In an exchange featured prominently in the *Capital,* the WCTU requested that the Populist Party "recognize that the greatest enemy of every home is the organized liquor traffic. . . . For the sake of your families, your desire to be free from unjust oppression and the love of your homes which you have met to protect, we earnestly urge that you speak plainly against the greatest foe, and nominate only men who are avowed opponents of the liquor traffic."[12] The WCTU's beseeching tone stands in sharp contrast to the fiery challenges Fanny Rastall had hurled at the Republicans in the late 1880s. Although Rastall was no less insistent a prohibitionist, she now had very few political cards to play; all she had left was the power of moral suasion.

Rastall herself was partly responsible for the WCTU's loss of influence in state politics. Although she could not have been expected to counteract the effects of the depression or the demise of the Prohibitionist Party, she left the WCTU rudderless in its approach to the Populists and the Farmers' Alliance. In her 1890 convention address, she made no mention of either organization. In 1891, however, she demonstrated some of her old political savvy by warning the Republicans that if they bowed to resubmissionist pressure, they would lose the support of "Christian farmers" to the "new party." As this was

Rastall's farewell address, however, she never followed up on this promising means of leveraging power. More importantly, she never instituted steps to connect with sympathetic alliances or other farmer's organizations. In 1892 the WCTU's state superintendent of the Temperance and Labor Department urged members to reach out to the Farmers' Alliance, "the largest labor organization in the state."[13] As with other such resolutions, the WCTU took few steps to implement the concept.

In appealing to the Populists' moral sense, the WCTU was at least coming to the right place. The Alliance remained the hotbed of moral politics, and its members overwhelmingly supported temperance activities. Further, the leadership had more than its share of temperance activists. John Willits, the Alliance president and Populist gubernatorial candidate, claimed that "four-fifths of the Alliance were uncompromising prohibitionists." Given farm people's level of support for the prohibition amendment in 1879, this number was perhaps not far off. Although women led the way in registering their opposition to alcohol, men joined in as well.[14] Numerous suballiances passed resolutions condemning the "liquor traffic," original packages, and resubmission.[15] The question was not whether the majority of Populists supported prohibition but whether they would make it an integral part of their reform program.

Prohibitionists had an even tougher row to hoe than woman suffragists in gaining Populist support. Woman suffrage was still an issue to be won, and thus worth fighting for; prohibition was simply something to be maintained and strengthened. Further, the saloon was not the threat to farm people that it was to the town-dwelling prohibitionist. Thus Willits, as president of the Jefferson County Alliance, supported a resolution that called for "the speedy overthrow of the liquor traffic" yet was careful to note "[we] as a party are not organized for the express purpose of prohibition."[16] A correspondent from Point View, Kansas, wrote the *Advocate*, "I have been for forty years connected with temperance societies . . . but I think if the People's Party surrender to this hobby it will cause a division and defeat."[17] Ben Clover, a longtime temperance supporter, put the distinction between personal commitment and party endorsement more bluntly, insisting, "The question uppermost right now is not whether a man shall have the right to drink or not, but whether he shall have a home or not, drunk or sober. . . . Excessive wealth on the one hand and extreme poverty on the other lead to intemperance and vice. Abolish both, and the prohibition battle is two-thirds fought."[18]

Despite such pronouncements, Populists were careful to maintain credentials as prohibitionists. Besides Peffer, Willits, and Diggs, the Populists could point to Fannie McCormick, their candidate for state superintendent of schools. McCormick, who had been an officer in the Prohibition Party and was a WCTU member in good standing, continued to preach the importance of prohibition enforcement. The *Alliant*, after citing McCormick's temperance credentials, argued, "Our resolutions may not all be written in ink, but the flesh and blood embodiment of our devotion to woman's advancement and to prohibition . . . are offered for the voters of Kansas to pass upon in the candidacy of Mrs. Fanny McCormick, of Great Bend, Kansas."[19]

Perhaps prohibitionists did pass upon the symbolism of McCormick's candidacy and voted for her, but the majority of voters simply passed. In general, the issue seemed to make no difference at all. Nor did her gender—her margin of loss was comparable to that of her male counterparts. Attorney General Ives had suspect prohibitionist credentials, yet he was the only Populist to gain state office. As a Democrat, and an antiprohibitionist to boot, Ives could be expected to give prohibition enforcement minimal attention at best. His victory came at the expense of Lyman Kellogg, a prohibitionist.[20] On the other hand, most of the successful congressional candidates were prohibition supporters. For the next ten years prohibition would remain largely a dead issue in Kansas elections. Republicans would still haul it out now and then, but it continued to have a negligible impact on state politics. Things would not change until Carrie Nation took ax to cask in Kiowa, Kansas, as the century turned.

Although Populists had consistently refused to acknowledge prohibition as a "vital issue," temperance activists still believed that the new party could be brought into line. They set their hopes on the 1891 Industrial Conference in Cincinnati, called by various reform groups to discuss formation of a national Populist Party. Frances Willard, Helen Gougar, John St. John, and other temperance leaders advanced on the Industrial Conference ready to commit their forces to the grand reform cause, if only the delegates would support it. Gougar, who had recently been well received at the National Farmers' Alliance convention in Indianapolis, proclaimed, "I find [among the Alliance delegates] a determination, deep-seated and uncompromising, to wheel the People's Party into line for Woman Suffrage and Prohibition, and don't believe there will be any flinching at the February meeting. Wouldn't it be glorious to fight in such a phalanx in 1892?"[21]

Despite Gougar's optimism and Willard's intensive lobbying and bargaining, the prohibitionists came away empty handed. The most Willard could squeeze out of the convention was a lukewarm resolution requesting the states to submit a woman suffrage referendum to the voters. Prohibition was ignored entirely in the final platform. Willard, Gougar, and St. John withdrew angrily from the convention. St. John sniffed that he had just witnessed "another whisky party born," a charge the Republican press gleefully reported despite its own party's inclusion in the denunciation.[22]

In highlighting the new party's "repudiation" of prohibition, the Republican press was particularly unsparing in its jibes at Populist women. The *Capital* reminded its readers that Annie Diggs appeared to have abandoned her prohibitionist friends. Diggs had begun her political career by opposing beer sales to University of Kansas students in the 1870s. She still hoped to fuse the concerns of the Woman Movement with the Populist Party's demands, but she had traveled a significant ideological distance from Lawrence in the 1870s.[23] She was now the adviser to prominent politicians and an important political figure in her own right. Her response to the Republican attacks indicated the philosophical changes she had undergone, as well as the distance between her former and present allies.

Diggs's rhetorical maneuverings demonstrated her new-found mastery of practical politics. During the initial committee meetings, she worked tirelessly in favor of the woman suffrage plank and vigorously supported the proposal allowing Willard, Gougar, and St. John to address the convention. Once both attempts failed, however, she put her party above her former causes. After being "besieged by questioners" following the retreat of prohibition forces from Cincinnati, Diggs revealed, "I did not expect [a prohibition plank], and hence was neither surprised nor disappointed by its omission. No person who is conversant with our cause and the purpose of our political revolution could for a moment expect that any other than the industrial and economic issues would be made vital or prominent."[24] Diggs specifically addressed Helen Gougar's contention that "the drink evil is the cause of poverty." "[P]overty is the large underlying cause of imtemperance," Diggs countered. "[M]onopoly, the concentration of wealth and power in the hands of the few, and the increasing poverty, degradation and helplessness of the many are the near evils which threaten the life of the republic. [T]here is but one course for me to pursue; that is to work with might and main for the success of a movement (I shall never *belong* to a party) whose purpose it is to avert the imminent peril to the nation and to save the homes and the liberties of common people."[25] Diggs was making a claim to continue her work as a temperance activist by fighting the Money Power. For her the "drink evil" had merely become one of many symptoms of the disease that was crippling the Republic. This difference in diagnosis made Gougar's envisioned "glorious phalanx" of prohibitionists and Populists impossible, despite their many commonalities.

Although Diggs had rejected Populist support of prohibition, she still hoped that the Kansas Populists would endorse woman suffrage. She viewed suffrage as a basic political right that deserved to be included in the Populist agenda and saw Kansas as the proper place for her party to support it. Immediately following the convention, Diggs explained that while there were compelling reasons—that is, Southern Democrats—for the national party to ignore moral issues, there were equally compelling reasons to support them back home. Kansas was full of "prohibitionists and woman suffrage advocates. When the Populists ignored [these issues] in 1890, it was all the Republicans talked about."[26] Fanny Vickery echoed this optimism, drawing on the myth of Kansas liberalism: "nationally we are willing to lay the equal suffrage plank as a sacrifice on the altar of reform for a time. [However], we have not this ignorance and prejudice to overcome in Kansas."[27]

This appraisal of Kansas's moral exceptionalism would soon be tested, however. Democrat-Populists were not the only party members who objected to endorsing woman suffrage. Although the Union Labor Party had supported it in the past, members had never had to worry about the practical implications of their stance since they rarely won office. Now, however, they were part of a movement that appeared a step away from controlling state politics. Having worked so hard and long to gain political legitimacy, Union Laborites did not want to throw away their big chance for a cause that seemed to them beside the point. The point, they reasoned, was gaining and maintaining political power so that economic and political reforms could be enacted. If woman suffrage resulted from that, most of them would be happy to support it at that time. Until then, however, they wanted no part of it.

For Populists the woman suffrage issue became a symbolic flash point for the larger issue of cooperation—"fusion"—with the Democratic Party. The election of Ives, a Democrat-Populist, had established a powerful precedent. Most former Republicans, however, rejected any such devil's bargain. They had no difficulty recognizing the Democrats as the greater of two evils, and although they had abandoned the G.O.P. temporarily, few were willing to remain Populists so that the hated Democrats could flourish. Instead, they insisted that Populists remain "in the middle of the road," maintaining their independence from both old parties. "Mid-roaders" were more likely than fusionists to have supported woman suffrage before 1890. The threat of Populist cooperation with the Democrats, however, gave mid-roaders a practical reason to endorse suffrage. Democrats were willing to set aside a good number of principles to defeat the G.O.P., but their opposition to woman suffrage was not one of them.[28]

While Populists were struggling over the question of fusion, the Democrats adroitly turned 180 degrees and fused with the Republicans in the 1891 elections. For the Democrats the maneuver was largely in response to pressure from their national committee. A Democratic congressman from Georgia explained, "If the damned Alliance, or the People's Party should carry Kansas this year, all hell can't hold the Alliancemen of the South; therefore it is necessary to break up the People's Party in Kansas, in order to preserve the solid South."[29] Republicans were also eager to quash the Populists' challenge to the "banner Republican state" before the 1892 presidential election. When the Populists won only 127 of 404 local offices, G.O.P. newspapers declared Populism finished as a force in state and national politics. The open collusion of the two old parties, however, had actually increased the Populist vote by 11 percent.

Most Populist officeholders and party functionaries remained unimpressed by this bit of good news; quite a number of them were showing symptoms of that occupational disease, self-preservation. Former Union Laborites and Democrats appeared to be the most susceptible. Because Union Laborites possessed established reform credentials, they were more likely to assume leadership in the first place. Whereas they made up only one-third of Populist voters, they constituted nearly 60 percent of the new party's legislators elected in 1892.[30] Further, the Populist central committee was dominated by former third-party members, including the chairman John Breidenthal. Breidenthal, a banker, speculator, and longtime third-party man, was also "an able exponent of practical politics and the separation of political principles from daily activities."[31] Breidenthal headed the drive to establish the Populist Party as a successful force in state politics, whatever the ideological cost.

With the Alliance's fervent support, most Populist rank and filers remained committed to the middle-of-the-road strategy. Most of the nationally known Kansas Populists—Mary Lease, Annie Diggs, U.S. Senator Peffer, *Advocate* editor McLallin, Alliance president Willits, and Congressmen Otis, Davis, Clover, and Baker—were vociferous mid-roaders.[32] Not surprisingly, all were strong woman suffrage supporters and stood by McLallin's condemnation of fusion: "better defeat than victory at such a sacrifice."[33] Unfortunately for Kansas mid-roaders, all but McLallin were scattered across the country for much of 1891 and 1892, working to build a national Populist Party. That left the fusionists to control the newly constructed party machinery.

This advantage enabled fusionists to outmaneuver the mid-roaders at the 1892 nominating conventions. Mid-roaders were further hampered by their commitment to having "the office seek the man."[34] Fusionists had no such qualms, manipulating county conventions whenever possible so that candidates acceptable to both Democrats and Populists would be nominated. Numerous times, fusionists from both parties held secret meetings and arranged elaborate deals. Such was the case in the Fifth District, where the dairy farmer John Otis lost the nomination to the physician E. V. Wharton, a "good, sound Democrat." Otis warned presciently, "These fusion candidates won't come as near being elected as the candidates who made a straight fight on the Alliance platform and depend fully on the Alliance for support."[35]

When they were unable to "cook" the county meetings, fusionists subverted its intentions by manipulating the state convention. The Democratic ex-governor George Glick, after watching the Sixth District fusion candidate be defeated by a mid-roader, opined that, although the fusionist forces would not triumph in the county convention, they would ultimately get the nomination: "It will be done by the committees later in the campaign."[36] Fusionists were beginning to make the machinations of Republican bosses Cy Leland and Sol Miller look mild in comparison.

Although the state convention proved more independent-minded than Glick or Breidenthal had hoped, fusionists were still able to nominate a state ticket that was agreeable to the Democrats. This included the gubernatorial nomination of Lorenzo Lewelling, a Wichita produce dealer and political unknown, who pledged to honor the fusion agreements. The Democrats were entirely candid about their motives, one leader stating, "The People's Party is fast becoming a part of the Democratic party and in two or three years we will have it all."[37] It remained to be seen, however, how effective these arrangements would prove at the polls.

Mid-roaders expressed outrage at the parliamentary shenanigans practiced by the fusionists. In pressing their grievances they used moralistic and religious language that placed them squarely in opposition to mainstream politics and the "practical" fusionists. "A political party is either right or wrong," preached the *Kiowa Times*. "The voting strength of a party consists of the aggregate of its members, each of whom believes that the principles of the party are right and that the principles of the opposing parties are wrong. This being the case, does there not apply with striking force the inquiry of the great apostle to the gentiles 'What consort hath Christ with Balial?' "[38] For the writer, fusion could not be reconciled with Christ's teachings. The fusionists' response was rather facile, refusing to discuss morality or ideology. "There is no fusion," reasoned one correspondent to the *Industrial Free Press*, "it's simply a cooperation, by which we propose to land the Republican Party in the soup."[39] That is to say, exactly what the mid-roaders had charged.

In fashioning their justifications, fusionists tended to look no further than the upcoming election. Mid-roaders, by contrast, took a long-term view of both the state and the national party. They believed fusion efforts dissipated the moralistic fervor that had imbued the agrarian crusade. Michael Senn, an Alliance and Populist organizer, reported that after the campaign, "I found in my campaign work many voters, especially Republicans who, while admitting the evils of monopoly and plutocracies, and the justice of our demands, have lost faith in the possibility of any reform. They believe that all men can be bought: that all will use public office for selfish purposes."[40] The *Kansas Agitator* agreed: "What started out as a great uprising of the people for reform . . . thus turns out to be a stupendous and perfectly shameless traffic for offices."[41] For many in 1890, the political millennium had seemed at hand. Now, however, the pharisees had taken control of the temple. If passion and faith had fueled the movement to victory, it could also speed it to defeat. Faith, after all, could be a fragile thing.

Senn, however, was not as despairing as the *Agitator*. Faith could be restored and the high ground recovered if only the Alliance remained strong. "We need to awaken the Alliance," he counseled. "There had been the mistaken idea that the Alliance had performed its work, that it had graduated into the People's Party. I think we all know better now."[42]

## "Something More Binding": Reclaiming the Alliance

Despite Senn's optimistic conclusion that Populists now understood the importance of the Farmers' Alliance, most Populist leaders remained blissfully ignorant. Republicans, however, were quite aware of the Alliance's role in the 1890 election. The *Kansas City Times* noted, "The local Alliances were the backbone of the movement. They met frequently, received instructions from their central officers, pledged themselves to voting the ticket, read their party literature, and acted with the precision of a machine. A sentiment and a reason were the strong springs, but there was everywhere the direction of a pervading intelligence of management."[43] Whatever the accuracy of the writer's machine metaphor, it was true that the suballiances had taken on a role akin to that of enlightened urban ward leaders. Not only did they deliver the votes and organize rallies, but they also made sure that local voters understood the issues, and thus what was at stake, in the election.[44]

Republicans gave special credit to Alliance women. The former Republican congressman William Phillips, a victim of the Populist uprising, explained that the "secret of the Alliance success is that [women] were given equal voice with the men. . . . They became thoroughly aroused, and they held men together in the cause. For my part, I don't care how soon women are given the ballot in Kansas."[45] Phillips was right in line with other politicians who had been defeated by women's efforts; such sentiments were heard from men in all parties eager to rationalize their political setbacks.

While Republicans warned against the power of politically aroused farm women, many Alliance men seemed to have conveniently forgotten the organization's earlier attempts at gender equality. Just as Alliance members struggled to regain their place in the vanguard of the agrarian reform movement, so too did women attempt to reassert their position in the organization. Both Alliance women and men would be faced with the difficult task of maintaining a nonpartisan approach to politics without being ignored in the highly charged atmosphere of Kansas politics.

Although the Populist Party threatened to undermine the Alliance's vision, the party also provided some farm women with new opportunities. After 1890 many Alliance leaders "graduated" to the People's Party.[46] A number of Alliance women responded to the sudden loss of local leaders by moving into positions of prominence in their organization. For many farm women, maintaining the Alliance meant preserving the one organization that offered them a chance to engage in public politics.

During the winter of 1890–91, National and Kansas Farmers' Alliance leaders laid plans to reinvigorate their organization. Members tried many strategies to relight the fire that had burned so fiercely the year before. Some disbanded suballiances and instead reconstituted strong district and county alliances, meeting monthly instead of weekly. A number of suballiances merged, carrying on as one chapter where there had been two or three. Others held more open meetings and picnics, encouraging neighbors to attend without the pressure of initiation. A few suballiances even moved their meetings to town, so that farm people could look to their "town business" before the meeting. Although some farm people may have found this change convenient, their suballiance had abandoned the ideal of congregating in a space identified as rural.[47]

By 1893, however, the Farmers' Alliance was concerned less with remaining separate from townsfolk than with simply surviving. When Mary Lease visited the State Farmers' Alliance convention that year and "ardently supported" a proposal to accept urban "producers," the delegates readily consented. Whether any urban workers actually took advantage of this is doubtful. If nothing else, they probably would have been put off by the Alliance's condescending attitude toward organizing them. Using logic reminiscent of the Woman Movement's proselytizing, delegates agreed that laborers should not be allowed to control the Alliance but rather that "the Alliance could educate and assimilate this class and receive assistance in exchange."[48] Despite the movement's desperate need to expand its base of support, the delegates were no more successful at transcending their cultural barriers than were Woman Movement activists.

For a time the Alliance's attempt to stem disintegration was successful. Members still noted attrition but also reported hopeful signs of an upturn before the 1892 election. Estimates of membership are difficult at best after 1890. However, listings of suballiances held steady in many papers, even increasing in several.[49] Correspondents writing about their suballiances conveyed a sense of excitement that replaced the listlessness found in the previous year.[50] The upsurge proved temporary, however, for while the Alliance was increasingly insistent on its separation from the Populist Party, the two organizations' fates were very much intertwined.

Alliance members were faced with the task of convincing Kansans that the organization was independent from the Populist Party. Party officials tended to assume that the Alliance would either meld into their organization or at least act as an auxiliary. The Republicans saw both groups as part of the same conspiracy to overthrow the prerogatives of reason, capital, and the G.O.P. In order to maintain a distinct identity, Alliance members set out to establish the explicit purpose of their organization. This meant promoting their vision of nonpartisanship and its place in a reform movement.

In 1892 the Farmers' Alliance state convention stated unequivocally that "everything of a partisan nature should and must be eliminated from the organization." Laura Chinn, who wrote a column for the *Industrial Free Press,* countered the idea that "because a political party has adopted our political views, our efforts should now be concentrated solely for that party. This would be a grave mistake. . . . There must be something more binding to hold us together."[51] For Chinn, the Populist Party was simply a temporary means to enact legislative reform. The Farmers' Alliance, by contrast, would always have a purpose. "We must remain a tower of strength to aid the party adopting our views," she explained, "and a terror to the party fighting them; in other words, we must remain independent of and superior to political parties. . . . In order to compel this new party to keep its promise it is necessary to follow them up." By refusing to name the particular parties, Chinn emphasized the impermanence of the Alliance's support for the Populists. Should the Populists falter or another party embrace the National Farmers' Alliance Omaha Platform, the movement's loyalties could conceivably change.

In many ways, Chinn's logic parallels Rastall's justification for supporting the national Prohibition Party during the 1880s. The WCTU, like the Farmers' Alliance, would endorse any party that supported the demands of its organization. Because the state G.O.P. had at least a theoretical commitment to prohibition and a sizeable number of prohibitionist members, it was vulnerable to pressure. Rastall could thus tempt the Republican leadership with WCTU support if the party stepped up its commitment to prohibition enforcement. Because the WCTU had been so unyielding in its commitment to enforcement, its endorsement carried a lot of weight with male prohibitionists.

Both organizations' nonpartisan policies made practical sense as long as there was another party that could make a credible claim to influence. Alliance members were certainly right to be suspicious of party functionaries and politicians, as their machinations over the fusion issue proves. Further, an independent Alliance would assure the continuation of the movement's educational, social, and economic features, which could nurture a political community if the party faltered or failed. By maintaining a commitment to the family-based Alliance, agrarian activists provided women with a political role; because it practiced citizenship independent of the franchise, women could continue to learn about and debate political issues.

The problem with this ideal of nonpartisanship was that nonmembers in Kansas did not buy the Alliance's claims. The *Industrial Free Press* declared, "The State Farmers' Alliance and Populist Party are different, and enemies of these organizations are trying to lump them together."[52] Protestations of Alliance members to the contrary, however, in the public mind the Alliance and the Populist Party were indeed one. In part, this perception came from scenes such as that recorded by the *Barton County Beacon* in 1890. On Election Day, Alliance men gathered together in the town of Sedgewick and then advanced on the polls en masse. There they received a Populist Party ticket and held it aloft until placing it in the voting box. The *Beacon* noted approvingly that this was "a novel way of telling whether the members vote for the old party or not."[53] In fact, the *Industrial Free Press* itself had argued several months before the 1892 election: "[The Alliance] is a non partisan organization, but the two old political parties are making an open war on the order, a war to the death fight. . . . The position of the regular parties is in direct opposition to the Alliance. Then how can a man be a good and true Alliance man and belong to the Republican or Democratic parties and affiliate with them in their fight against our order?"[54] Given such contradictory signals, the lumping together of the Populist Party and the Alliance was understandable.

Despite Chinn's insinuation that her organization would support only a righteous Populist Party, the Alliance never openly debated its relationship with the Populists. If its claim to influence came from keeping the Populist Party on the high road, it never took any steps to exercise it. Whereas Fanny Rastall and the WCTU could play the Republicans off against the Prohibitionists, the Alliance could look only to the Populists for meaningful change. Withdrawing support would only ensure the defeat of the Alliance's program. Yet the more the Alliance worked unquestioningly to further party prerogatives, the more precarious its independence became.

Because farm women had more to lose, they played an especially prominent role in attempting to preserve the Alliance. In response to demands to "get the order out of politics," Mrs. L. M. Furbeck told the Shawnee County Alliance, "Well, let it be so. But let me urge you, Brothers and Sisters, that you never cease from this time on to inquire, and study into questions of right and wrong, the true complements of politics."[55] For while men saw political education as a means to an informed vote, women members saw it as an end in itself.

Yet because of the Populists' new emphasis on voting, Alliance women had to be convinced that studying the "issues of the day" made a difference. One farm woman urged her sisters that it did. "Because most of the large measures upon which the betterment of farmers depends must be sought through legislation," she argued, "it does not follow that women can do nothing toward their attainment. All of the questions upon which the demands of the Alliance are based are essentially home questions. They are questions which the wives and daughters are as vitally interested in as the husbands."[56] By staying within the accepted domestic bounds, the writer hoped to reestablish the idea of the Alliance as a family-based organization. Yet in making her claim, she was admitting that its focus had indeed shifted.

Other women took a more aggressive stance, pointing to mistakes Alliance men had made at women's expense. M. C. Clark, vice president of the Alliance in 1892, told the Osage County Alliance, "The women of this country have their eyes on your actions, brothers, and look with doubt and dismay at the last election."[57] Repeating earlier criticisms that men were blind followers of political parties, she charged, "You have tried to be prudent in the matter of late, but we have not yet reached the standard that we dare to do what we know to be right." Where Alliance women in the past had castigated their men for being unable to abandon the old parties, Clark critiqued them for their acceptance of the Populists' fusion policy. An Alliance woman, she argued, would not have tolerated such a policy. "She will not . . . bring doubt or ridicule upon her party. She will scorn a bribe—scorn any system that would crowd her principles to the background. . . . How different the outcome of the last election."

Before Alliance women could vote and save the world, however, they had to have the opportunity to develop their citizenship skills. But a number of women, reviving past charges, claimed that male members' attitudes and actions often inhibited women's participation. Clark noted that a "sister" had recently written to her requesting information on how to start a separate Woman's Alliance since "the women were mere figureheads." Emma Troudner, speaking at the state convention, argued that because men had ignored their Alliance sisters, women had dropped out of local suballiances. "Then the men dropped out one by one," she concluded, "and later that suballiance was dead."[58]

Farm people could not create a mixed-gender political culture without committing a good deal of time, patience, and hard work. Simple decrees for women and men to "cooperate in all things," as Troudner suggested, could not instantly readjust years of cultural training. Bertha Utley, who wrote an Alliance column for the *Industrial Free Press,* suggested that women should learn through doing. The problem was taking that first step into the heretofore male sphere: "there are very few women but could think of something for the good of the order if she only had the courage to arise and tell it. At first, if those who are overly timid would, when anything presents itself to their minds, arise at the proper time and tell it (although they might have to clutch at their seats in order to remain standing while they speak) they would find half the battle won." Utley urged women to think of their efforts as part of a process of political education. "The second effort they would not have to hold on quite so tight," she insisted, "and finally they would find it a pleasure instead of a cross for them to arise and say anything that had a tendency for good."[59]

Although Utley took a self-help approach to women's participation in the Alliance, she did realize the unspoken pressures surrounding farm women during the meetings. She noted that women were concerned about how others, particularly men, would perceive them when speaking up: "it is not always timidity that prevents women from speaking in public. There are a great many women who have the ability to express their mind in public who would not open their mouths to speak a word although they know it is their duty to do so." Despite the Alliance's official support of women's participation in politics, farm women still feared "that awful thing of being called strong minded or masculine. I think there are a great many who will agree with me that it is not necessarily masculine to be strong minded, and surely there is no sensible woman who, (if she must be called names) would rather be called weak than strong minded." Although Alliance women did not publicly worry about issues of femininity as much as Woman Movement activists did, these concerns still shaped their approach to politics.

One way women hoped to strengthen their position in the movement was to focus on their role as social organizers. At the 1892 Farmers' Alliance state convention, women delegates demanded that their "brothers" take this role seriously:

> Inasmuch as we, the wives, mothers, and sisters of our organization feel deeply the need and importance of our order as an important factor in the great reformation, therefore we suggest the recognition of the sisters in the revival of our work. In furtherance of this work we recommend that a committee of five Alliance women be chosen by the county alliances in such counties where there is no Alliance Women's organization, whose duty it shall be to have charge of the social branch of our work.[60]

By officially laying claim to their control of social functions, women members hoped to ensure an active role in their organization. Yet in asserting their traditional place in the farm family, they risked further being ignored as political equals within the Alliance.

Although little action was taken on this resolution, some women had already chosen to formalize their role as social organizers in separate women's organizations. In Barton County, Alliance women had formed the Women's Mutual Benefit Association in 1890 "to take an active part in furthering the interests of [the Alliance]."[61] To stress its connection to the Alliance, the association changed its name to the Alliance Women's Association (AWA) several months later.[62] Its stated purpose was "to assist our fathers, our husbands, our brothers and our sons to throw off the galling yoke of tyranny."[63] Ostensibly the AWA would act as a ladies' auxiliary, providing the men with support whenever needed.

While claiming to fulfill the traditional helpmeet role, however, the AWA was also establishing a particular place for its members within the Alliance. "The institution is respected by the order, and is doing a noble work," the AWA asserted, "thus proving that the ladies of Barton County are active workers and alive to the best interests of their homes. Give the women a chance and they will take care of this world."[64] In a sense, the AWA was attempting to use the contributions of its members in the more traditional areas to establish their credentials as fellow soldiers on the political front.

The AWA was particularly adept at combining social events and fund raising, the money raised usually going to buy political literature for general distribution. These activities were nothing new for Alliance women. What made the AWA different was that it separated these activities from general Alliance work in the minds of members. Further, by taking control of particular social events, the AWA could shape the program to highlight women's contributions. It organized special picnics that featured prominent Populist and Alliance women such as Fannie McCormick and Sarah Van Emery, author of *Seven Financial Conspiracies*. For one parade, the AWA announced, "each suballiance will be under the order of a lady marshall subject to the command of the LADY MARSHALL-GENERAL, MRS. MAUD HARTMEN."[65] For Alliance women, this change of command from the usual order of things no doubt carried great symbolic weight. The *Barton County Beacon* reported the AWA's activities separately—and approvingly—from news of those of the Alliance.

The Barton County AWA remained an active and independent organization at least through 1894. Although its members encouraged Alliance women across the state to organize chapters, only a few appear to have followed its lead.[66] In part, this may have been due to the extra time and energy required to maintain a separate organization while continuing to attend local suballiance meetings. But the Barton County AWA also represented an unusual merger of town and farm women, an arrangement not found in many areas. For although most of the members were farm women, Frances Butler, a journalist from Great Bend, was the chief organizer of the AWA.

Butler's vision of the AWA combined the best features of the Alliance and the Woman Movement, of which she was an active member. The AWA brought farm women into town and established meeting places where they felt comfortable. Since farm women predominated, they did not have to be overly conscious of adhering to town ways. And while the AWA freed its members from men's influence during meetings, they could in turn declare that their actions were for the good of the farming class and the Alliance. They could thus enjoy the benefits of an all-woman organization while remaining true to their mixed-gender cause.

Not all collaborations between farm and town women worked out so neatly. In Cowley County, Populist and Alliance women joined together to create the Women's Mutual Improvement Society (WMIS). Luella Kraybill, a Populist journalist and Woman Movement activist, was the prime motivator. Unlike Butler's AWA, however, the WMIS was not an Alliance organization; rather, it attempted to position itself in the rather fuzzy area between Woman Movement–style good government issues and Populist economic reforms. The result was that the WMIS occupied a political no woman's land that seemed to inspire more confusion than commitment.

Kraybill could never quite decide the organization's agenda or focus, including its relationship with the Alliance. The most prominent officer of the WMIS was Elizabeth Clover, the only woman delegate to the National Farmers' Alliance 1889 convention and the wife of Congressman Ben Clover. Although Kraybill had presented the organization as being strictly nonpartisan, a number of potential members expressed alarm that Clover was president. Not wanting to be involved with a political organization, they requested an explanation of the WMIS's true motives. Kraybill attempted to calm their fears, portraying the organization as the equivalent to Eastern social and literary clubs.[67] Yet when organizing Alliance women, WMIS leaders stressed their group's political activities.[68]

Kraybill and other WMIS officers were no more candid about their connections to the suffrage movement than to the Alliance. After donating money to bring the KESA convention to Cowley County, the WMIS indicated its desire to remain unconnected to the suffrage organization. The WMIS treasurer, N. W. Johnson, in an article entitled "Equal Rights to All and Special Privileges to None," acknowledged that "there are a great many people rather skeptical in regard to our Woman's Mutual Improvement Society. Some have guessed that we are going to discuss the subject of women's rights. And perhaps they have not guessed altogether wrong."[69] In hoping to be all things to all women, the WMIS eventually succumbed to a case of terminal identity crisis, apparently ceasing to exist after 1892. The WMIS's attempt to define its constituency and intent continued up to its demise.[70]

Before the WMIS collapsed under the weight of its ambivalence, it did manage to bring together representatives from the local Farmers' Alliance, WCTU, and KESA chapters.[71] Although these meetings were remarked upon favorably by the *Industrial Free Press*, no further cooperation appears to have taken place. The WMIS disappeared soon after. Its fate reveals both the possibilities and the obstacles facing women who worked to bring farm and town together.

Apart from Kraybill and Butler, few urban women attempted to organize Alliance women as a separate group. Had such efforts emphasized a loyalty to the Alliance, as the AWA did, farm women would probably have been receptive. These women could then have acted as woman suffrage missionaries in the rural districts. But urban women leaders never recognized farm women's untapped potential for the cause. By 1892 Alliance women had replaced their passing comments and veiled references about the right to vote with explicit demands that the Alliance support that right. Some farm women continued the theme of men as failed voters. "Men argue that women are represented by their fathers, brothers, and sons; I know many women whose husbands misrepresented them," jibed J. C. Bare.[72] Bare also provided an interesting twist on Woman Movement activists' claim of moral superiority. "Most women have the wisdom . . . and the goodness to pursue what is right to a far greater degree than the average male citizen," she wrote. "[I do not] claim woman to be better by nature than men, but because of the special privileges the world accords to man to own all the property, to drink and smoke and chaw and be lord over the beasts of the field and of womankind, and believe his authority is divine right. The world will not allow women to commit sin and be respectable, and they never will."[73] Culture, not nature, had rendered respectable women morally superior to men. Bare reasoned that this moral superiority, coupled with the Alliance's ideological precept of "equal rights for all," would persuade Populist men to support woman suffrage.

Other Alliance women wrapped their demands in the rhetoric of domesticity but still implied that men had failed. "Will you . . . put in our hands the ballot that we may help vanquish the destroyer of our homes?" implored S. L. Ruggles. "We have grown weary of beating the air; give us the weapon to defend ourselves. . . . We voice the sentiment of thousands of earnest Alliance women and believe you are not insensible to this appeal."[74] Ruggles suggested that Alliance men had failed to protect their families. Like the fabled pioneer women who, left alone in their soddies, hoisted rifle to shoulder to drive away the wolves, women members were asking for the means to self-defense. Ruggles no doubt hoped this combination of guilt and devotion to the movement would galvanize men to support woman suffrage.

Although Alliance men had acknowledged women's contributions to the movement before the 1890 election, by 1892 these accolades were appearing far less frequently. Some women felt compelled to remind their brothers of this legacy when demanding the vote. One, writing as "one of the disenfranchised," pointed out, "The men of our party have not been afraid to allow the representative women to canvass the state, making the speeches and singing the songs, and to allow those who could not enter into the campaign to provide tons of victuals to feed the hungry multitudes at picnics and conventions; and who can say that women have not been a great moving power in the education of the public feeling in the cause of the oppressed."[75] Having laid out Alliance women's credentials for citizenship, she went on: "Certainly, brothers, there is some reward in the feeling that we have been one of the strongest factors in bringing about a great revolution in sentiment. . . . To all these hard worked sisters is due the honor of breaking down the last barriers of woman's right to political privileges." In these letters one feels a sense of betrayal, of promises made and then broken. Alliance women had proven themselves fit for citizenship—more so than the men, who had failed to thwart the schemes of fusionists. Alliance women, having experienced the thrill of effecting political change, were not willing to retreat to their homes empty handed.

The women's demands for "repayment" was based in the movement's old egalitarian vision. Alliance men did not simply owe it to women to support suffrage; adherence to the organization's motto declaring "equal rights to all" demanded it. By invoking this sacred shibboleth, women felt they had captured the highest moral ground. As "A Would Be Voter" argued, "You have pledged yourselves to support the constitution of [the Farmers' Alliance], and in thus pledging yourselves you plainly said that you endorsed the principles laid down in the Declaration of Purposes. One of these principles is, that 'we demand equal rights to all, and special privileges to none.' . . . Brethren, be consistent. Either own up that the lady members of the union have an equal right with you, or else expel them from the order, and revise your declaration, making it read, 'Equal rights to all men, and no favors whatever to the women.' "[76]

Alliance men who opposed suffrage might have found such logic powerful and difficult to refute—had they said anything. Unfortunately, men did not often argue these ideas one way or the other. Occasionally, an Alliance man might write in support of woman suffrage, as did one who stated that a woman "is just as competent to vote as the average man, and more so than a great many men who let whiskey get away with their brain."[77] The more usual male response, however, was no response.

With the formation of the Populist Party and the new focus on the voter, many Alliance men considered the real work to be in the legislative halls, the state offices, and the county conventions. They viewed the voting booth, and not the Farmers' Alliance meeting, as the place where their decisions mattered. Electoral politics remained a safe haven for Alliance men, uncomplicated by the presence of women. The reality of a mixed-gender political culture had proven more difficult than the ideal had promised.

Perhaps men's growing silence about women's concerns reflected the "brothers' " ambivalence about these newly negotiated relations in the Alliance family. Although brothers and sisters within the movement, women and men were also husbands and wives, sons and daughters. These labels came attached with long-established roles and expectations that many Alliance women were explicitly challenging. If some Alliance men silently agreed that women had indeed earned equal rights, perhaps many were afraid of the implications of woman suffrage on their families' gender relations. The number of men who had come to accept Alliance women's claims to political equality would be revealed in the 1894 election.

The real battleground for endorsing woman suffrage came not in the Alliance but in the Populist Party. Suffrage adherents included some of the most powerful men in the party. In 1891, John Davis became the first congressman to request a woman suffrage bill before a committee of Congress. Fittingly, Davis's motion was prefaced by an introduction by the *Advocate*'s Washington correspondent, who was also serving as KESA's vice president—Annie Diggs.[78]

### "ALL ARE NEEDED TO MAKE A PARTY": THE *FARMER'S WIFE* AND FARMERS' WIVES

Even as farm women struggled for recognition and respect in the Alliance, urban Populist women were fast gaining influence in their party. Diggs and Lease were the stars, but there were numerous other women working beneath them. Some, like Bina Otis and Eliza McLallin, drew on their own skills as well as familial connections to establish themselves; others came to prominence by editing or publishing reform papers. In all cases, they developed positions of power in the movement.

Urban Populist women (henceforth also referred to as "Populist women") often credited their "sisters on the farm" as political forebears and road builders. Diggs, writing in *Arena* magazine, noted that farm women had established themselves in the reform movement through their heroic deeds during the campaign of 1890. She then featured numerous "women in the Alliance," only two of whom had lived on a farm; one of these, Mary Lease, had put the experience well behind her. The structure of Diggs's article accurately, though unintentionally, reflected the changing roles of rural and urban women in the Farmers' Alliance and Populist Party. Populist women parlayed the gains made by their rural sisters into their own political capital. At the same time they helped to reduce farm women's influence in the movement.

Farm women did not disappear from the Populist Party. Newspapers occasionally remarked on their presence at rallies and meetings. One Populist man, speaking "on behalf of the mothers and sisters and children," urged local committees not to "neglect to get a lady speaker. Let us never drop any feature of our campaign meetings that will attract the ladies. All are needed to make a party."[79] Yet despite such exhortations to include the old "Alliance ways," farm women had a difficult time defining a role for themselves in the new party. When they did address Populist Party issues, they almost always did so as Alliance members.

Urban Populist women had no intention of slighting Farmers' Alliance women. In fact, Populist women hoped to aid their sisters through the publication of the *Farmer's Wife,* "a monthly Alliance journal . . . devoted to the interests of the wives and daughters of those who earn their bread by the sweat of the brow."[80] That, anyway, was their intention. The reality was a newspaper with little about farming and less about farm women. Such topics were usually contained in the column headed "For Our Agricultural Friends." Since these items were reprinted from Eastern farm journals, they were of limited use to those working the Kansas plains. Nor would farm women have found much of value from the papers' "domestic" articles. Also reprinted from Eastern sources, they discussed such concerns as the changing fashion scene and the proper serving procedures at tea parties.[81]

The opposition press immediately took notice of the difference between the paper's title and its contributors. Hoping to discredit the new Populist paper, Republican editors circulated a short notice remarking that no one editing the paper was a farmer's wife. Diggs, in her counterattack, noted sardonically, "Nothing is easier . . . for [farmers' wives] after the washing, baking, scrubbing, mending, house cleaning, churning, and a few other chores are all done, than just to up and run into town and edit a newspaper."[82] Because the economic system had rendered farm women's life so difficult, "only urban women had the opportunity to publish a paper. . . . A larger proportion of farmers' wives are in the insane asylum in this country than any other class. Possibly if the monotony of work and thought were more frequently broken by the reading of something not seen or heard in the daily round of farm life the proportion of mentally worn out farmers' wives might not be so large." By bringing a more cosmopolitan perspective to the farm, Diggs reasoned, Populist women could liberate their less fortunate sisters. Republican papers weren't edited by farm people either, she concluded, yet they claimed to be "the farmer's true friend."

In theory, urban Populist women were doing nothing wrong in writing a paper aimed at farm women. The reality, however, was reflected in Diggs's answer. Her perception of farm women as oppressed drudges was duplicated numerous times in the *Farmer's Wife*. One article, "A Frontier Farmer's Wife," by Frances Garside, was headlined "Her Burdens are Many and Her Pleasures are Few / Nothing in Her House is of Late Improvement, and at 30 She is Old and Tired of Her Lot in Life."[83] "Women in the cities cannot understand the daily work of frontier women," wrote Garside. "There are no convenient laundries, bakeries, or stores where she can buy the ready made articles she is compelled to make herself. It is unceasing work." A good deal of the blame for the farmer's wife's problem, Garside contended, lay with her husband. "Nowhere is a man so completely lord and master as on the farm." In contrast to the oppressive farmer, his wife "is a hero in a calico dress, wrinkled and stoop shouldered."[84]

Garside's comments did contain some elements of truth. Farm life on the Plains was difficult, particularly for women. Men did tend to spend extra cash on machinery rather than on home improvements. But the article, like others by urban women, was riddled with false assumptions about farm life. It ignored the satisfaction many women felt in contributing directly to the farm economy and in being as self-sufficient as possible. While farm women would have been thrilled to gain access to the labor-saving devices available in the towns and cities, they also understood many of the benefits of farm life. Like the *Farmer's Wife*'s reference to "the wives and daughters of those who earn their bread by the sweat of the brow," the article revealed its ignorance of women's participation in the farm family economy.

Garside's article also failed to understand that women's work on the farm gave them a certain leverage with their husbands. The farm family was a patriarchal institution, but then so was the urban middle-class family. Relations between women and men in the Farmers' Alliance were showing signs of strain, but only because farm men had encouraged women's political participation in the first place. The same could not be said of urban male-dominated political organizations.

When urban Populist women launched the National Woman's Alliance (NWA), they carried over their cultural blinders to their organizing strategy.[85] Although the NWA declared itself to be "composed of farmers' wives and the women of trades unions and wage workers," it was in fact dominated by middle-class urban women reformers.[86] The organization claimed that it was a national movement with affiliated groups and representatives from twenty-five states and Washington, D.C. But although the largely ceremonial positions of vice presidents included notable reformers from a number of states, the national officers were all from Kansas.[87] From the start, then, the NWA's assumptions about the viability of a national "working women's" crusade were deeply flawed.

Like the *Farmer's Wife*, the organization's official newspaper, the NWA sought to bring together the concerns of the Populist Party and the Woman Movement. The introduction to the NWA's "Declaration of Purposes" reflected the former, identifying the group as "the industrial women of America." The new organization dedicated itself to "the great social, industrial and financial revolution now dawning . . . and the universal demand of all classes of our American citizens for equal rights and privileges in every vocation of human life." The declaration itself, however, was pure Woman Movement. In advocating "the utmost harmony and unity of action among the Sisterhood, in all sections of our country," it echoed the Women's Council. The WCTU was represented by the proclamation, "to discourage in every way the use of all alcoholic liquors . . . or the habitual use of tobacco or other narcotics injurious to the human system." The declaration presented the suffragists' call for "full political equality of the sexes" and included the basic tenet of the Woman Movement, promising "to carry out into practical life the precepts of the golden rule."[88]

The NWA tried to strike a balance between loyalties to the newly emerging national Populist Party and to the Woman Movement's sisterhood. In 1891, with the WCTU's Frances Willard working to establish an all-inclusive reform army, such a strategy offered the NWA the possibility of becoming the vanguard of the crusade. All depended on the Populists and Knights of Labor endorsing woman suffrage and prohibition. The 1892 Populist convention, however, spoiled these well-laid plans.

Despite the NWA's rhetorical support of the Woman Movement's agenda, the new organization was ultimately committed to the Populist Party. When the national party followed the lead of the Cincinnatti Industrial Conference and ignored woman suffrage and prohibition in 1892, the NWA was forced to play down these issues. After the 1892 convention, the NWA tried a brief stab at establishing a place within the Populist Party that highlighted women's role as social organizers and educators. According to a *Farmer's Wife* article entitled "What Can American Women Do for the People's Party?" Populist principles "must be taught by our American mothers at American firesides. . . . The National Woman's Alliance proposes . . . the most thorough self-culture concerning political economy. Then they propose to hold neighborhood meetings at their school houses and churches, with music, dialogue, and debates. Country gatherings will follow, for the instruction of the people on the questions to be settled at the ballot box in November."[89] The NWA proposed, in effect, to take over the very same tasks that Farmers' Alliance women had been doing for several years. The urban Populist women's ignorance was further evidence of their unfamiliarity with what went on outside town limits.

Without any real connection to its supposed constituency, the NWA had no real purpose once the Populist Party chose to ignore temperance and suffrage. Following the 1892 election, the NWA quietly faded away. Kansas women Populists responded to its demise by setting their sights back on their home state. It was there, after all, that their real influence lay. In April 1893 they formed the Women's Political Progressive League and set out to establish themselves in Kansas politics.

JOINING THE PARTY: WOMAN SUFFRAGE AND PARTISANSHIP

As the NWA struggled to position itself between the Populist Party and the Woman Movement, Republican women were establishing an organization of their own. J. Ellen Foster, who had led battles over partisanship within the national WCTU, showed her true colors by establishing the National Republican Women's Association. Laura Johns was quick to organize a Kansas branch in 1891, no doubt hoping that Republican women could gain the prominence in the state G.O.P. that Kansas Populist women had achieved in their party. The male Republican leadership, however, had other ideas. The last thing that party bosses such as Cy Leland and Sol Miller wanted was "petticoat politics" interfering with their battle plans. The *Advocate,* referring to the Republican central committee's perception of the new women's association, snickered, "A WICKED Populist . . . has suggested that the Women's Republican Club might have been organized for the purpose of taking in washing to help pay the campaign expenses of the GOP."[90]

Some Republican leaders did encourage the idea of a women's role in the G.O.P., but with an important caveat: women activists would have to abandon their nonpartisan approach to municipal politics. For even as women had increased their official involvement in state partisan politics, they had remained committed to their nonpartisan local strategy. In 1891 the leading members of the capital city's WCTU and Equal Suffrage Association, headed by S. A. Thurston, had helped organize a successful campaign to defeat Quinton, the Republican mayoral candidate. The G.O.P. leadership howled that no rum-soaked Democrat could ever enforce prohibition as well as a Republican. Topeka's openly thriving "joints" and more discreet "gentlemen's clubs" spoke otherwise. Cofran, the Democratic candidate, had in fact long been a favorite reform candidate against the Topeka Republican ring. Nor was his victory unprecedented—citizens' committees had supported his victories in two of the last three elections. In 1891, however, women were for the first time prominently involved in opposing the Republican candidate.

The *Topeka Capital*'s Joseph Hudson was outraged. A prohibitionist, woman suffragist, and former Greenbacker, he was first and foremost a Republican. Although he had once bolted the G.O.P. for the Independent ticket in 1874, he now demanded complete and unquestioned loyalty to the Republican Party. To Hudson, the Topeka debacle was more personal and bitter. Here was treachery in his own backyard, fomented not by the forces of anarchy—the Populists having little support in Topeka—but by the very women he had been presenting as the most enlightened voters in Kansas. If enlightenment meant voting Democratic, Hudson was in trouble.

Hudson kept his opinions to himself until the KESA convention later that year. As luck would have it, the convention had returned to Topeka for the first time since Helen Gougar met six uncertain women in front of the Capitol in 1884. Hudson, the most prominent Republican in the city and one of the state's strongest suffrage supporters, was invited to address the convention. Determined to restore party discipline, he began his speech in a manner that the KESA secretary noted was "to be expected of an old time suffragist who for years had defended the principle."[91] The speech that followed, however, was "a most remarkable one." Hudson began by criticizing Johns's annual address, taking umbrage at her position that "Suffrage societies and woman's alliances and woman's councils should strive to teach citizenship instead of partisanship. Public service instead of party service should be inculcated and rewarded." Not so, instructed Hudson. "Fighting Joe," so nicknamed for his leadership in the prohibition crusade, now let it be known that the only thing worth fighting for in the political arena was partisanship.[92] Citizens could choose between the Republican or Democratic Party—or if they must, "they could ally themselves with the calamity party." Without partisanship, however, "they are powerless to carry out reforms. . . . The mugwump is a political egotist." Excoriating the Topeka Equal Suffrage Association and WCTU for supporting someone who, he claimed, opposed woman suffrage, Hudson placed Quinton's defeat heavily on the shoulders of the women voters. "You must have political machinery," he concluded, "and you should favor the party which favors you in its platform and shows a disposition to give you what you ask."

Although the *Capital* claimed Johns "did not feel any resentment toward the speaker for his manly exposition of his position," she was probably none too pleased at the sudden imposition of masculinist politics. Ever the diplomat, however, she simply stated that there was little support among KESA's delegates for Hudson's speech. Activists in Topeka's Woman Movement were more forthright. Affronted that Hudson had chosen to "scold the women of his own city right before the folks, as it were . . . for daring to vote their conscientious convictions," Thurston and others returned fire. Thurston, a prominent Republican, first noted that "she did not care personally what Major Hudson said." Having put the good Major in his place, she showed through careful analysis of the past three mayoral election results that women had given Quinton a two-hundred-vote majority in 1891. And in 1885, Cofran had been elected over a Republican, becoming Topeka's first Democratic mayor. But since no woman voted in 1885, Thurston pointed out, women could hardly have been responsible for Cofran's first victory.

Thurston did not use this logic to exonerate suffragists from responsibility for Quinton's defeat. In fact, she praised women activists' role in influencing men to vote for Cofran, noting that it had been Republican men who had crossed party lines in the "banner Republican city in the banner Republican state." "Viewing the election from the standpoint of a Republican partisan, and making partisanship the supreme test," she wrote, "I should reach a conclusion similar to the following: Only the people who vote my way having the inalienable right to the ballot, a few more exhibitions similar to . . . the last municipal election on the part of men voters and they will be disenfranchised, and the voting left in the hands of the women alone." Although members of the Woman Movement embraced the notion of nonpartisan municipal politics, they could not have been successful without the support of men. Men, however, did not get the blame or the lectures about the science of government through partisanship.

J. Ware Butterfield, secretary of the state Republican League, followed Hudson into the breach with another salvo against the evils of nonpartisanship. Calling women activists' role in the Topeka election "a great mistake," Butterfield insisted that "the KESA must become partisan in the near future." Realizing that if his audience took his advice they could very well endorse the Populists, "he next paid his respects to the calamity party." Since Butterfield had instructed the delegates that they should support "the only party that ever did anything for woman suffrage," he had to explain why the Populist House had voted for state suffrage while the Republican Senate had defeated it. His logic was not readily accepted, as evidenced by the recording secretary's sarcastic reporting of his remarks.

Butterfield fared little better when he attempted to use P. P. Elder's antisuffragist speech as an indictment of all Populists. The secretary reported that Butterfield claimed Elder's speech "was a disgrace to our civilization—enough to make one's blood boil with indignation, and crimson the cheek with shame and more of the same sort. He forgot, evidently, though the women who were listening to him did not, how much meaner things John J. Ingalls, Senator Buchan and many lesser lights among Kansas Republicans have said about woman suffragists than Speaker Elder did."[93] The secretary reported that Butterfield's "effort probably served to more fully establish those present in their belief in the consistency as well as wisdom of keeping the KESA what it has always been and what every distinctively woman suffrage society must be— STRICTLY NON-PARTISAN."

KESA's response to Butterfield's and Hudson's "efforts" made clear that woman suffragists refused to be bullied by their male allies, at least while as-

sembled in the safety of a KESA convention. The tone of the speakers and the
recording secretary made clear that suffrage activists were little concerned
with the political influence of the "esteemed gentlemen." When it came to the
sanctity of KESA's nonpartisan municipal suffrage stance, its leaders would
brook no interference by men. That Republican women had rebuked Hudson
and Butterfield made such a stance all the more impressive. It also compounded Hudson's personal political damage, as he was shown to be without
influence among suffragists in his own city.

Hudson and Butterfield no doubt believed that they could sway the convention toward the G.O.P. Perhaps they hoped it would repeat the pro-Republican
resolution Johns had championed following the passage of municipal woman
suffrage. The political climate had since changed, however. Had the suffragists
endorsed the G.O.P., they would have alienated a party that appeared poised
to take over state politics. Further, Populist women had achieved a much more
prominent role in KESA than Union Labor women had had in 1888. These
new alignments were making the politics of endorsement an ever trickier
business.

Following the Hudson-Butterfield imbroglio, convention delegates passed a
resolution that set an inevitable collision course between the demands of partisan politics and the ideal of political sisterhood. The delegates, after years of
holding back, finally decided to take the last, inevitable step after municipal
woman suffrage: they resolved "to petition the next legislature to grant to the
women of Kansas the right to vote for presidential electors." Perhaps the Populists' success in 1890 had given suffragists hope that the electorate was willing
to try a radical political change; perhaps they were simply tired of waiting any
longer. Whatever the case, they made the decision to enter the arena where
such a crushing blow to their cause had been delivered twenty-five years
before.

Having chosen to make their stand, woman suffragists made sure that their
resolution would not be taken lightly by the political parties. Johns planned
and executed a statewide campaign beginning in early winter 1892 which concluded just as the party conventions were beginning. In February and March,
KESA organized thirty two-day conventions in nearly one-third of the counties. Johns brought in well-known speakers from the East and from England.[94]
While Populists such as Annie Diggs and Anna Wait were involved, Johns's
contribution was extraordinary. In recounting the campaign some years later,
Diggs recalled, "Mrs. Johns arranged all of these conventions, presided one
day or more over each and spoke at every one, organizing in person twenty-
five of the thirty-one local societies which were formed as a result of these
meetings."[95] In June suffragists held a two-day convention at the Ottawa

Chautauqua Assembly for which Johns engaged Susan B. Anthony and Anna Shaw, president and vice president of the National American Woman Suffrage Association.

Having established their momentum, Johns, Anthony, and several Republican KESA officers advanced on the G.O.P. convention. With them came two towering figures of Kansas prohibition and philanthropy, Amanda Way and "Mother" Bickerdyke. Johns could not have picked a better time or a more responsive Republican audience. The convention had been hijacked by the "Young Republicans," a group of upstarts who were tired of the G.O.P.'s siege mentality. Reform-minded Republicans joined with perceptive opportunists to storm the citadel of party power, the state central committee. The coup leaders then fashioned a platform nearly as radical as the Populists'. Rather than attempting to halt the reform tide, the Young Republicans decided to throw open the floodgates in the hopes of channeling popular will toward their own ends.[96]

The Young Republicans could not have been happier with the suffragists' request, since it helped establish the G.O.P.'s reform credentials. They did, however, exercise a little caution. Rather than endorsing woman suffrage outright, they instead pledged to support a popular referendum for a woman suffrage amendment to the Constitution. The delegates then included a plank in support of prohibition, for good measure. Republican suffragists were thrilled with this turn of events. Anthony even buried her old animosity toward the Kansas G.O.P. long enough to speak from its platform during the fall campaign. Her actions signaled a truce rather than a lasting peace; in her speeches, she "simply called attention to the record of the Republican Party in the cause of human freedom, and urged them to complete it by enfranchising women, but did not take up political issues."[97]

The Republican bosses, already apoplectic over the Populist insurrection, let loose a stream of pure vitriol against the "backhanded," "villainous" traitors. Throwing caution to the winds and nasty barbs at all available targets, Sol Miller labeled the G.O.P.'s platform "Alliance rot" and "demagogue cant." It was "worded so as to catch the vote of wild-eyed lunatics," the prohibition plank was passed "to mollify a lot of cranky preachers," and the pledge to institute "Australian" (secret ballot) suffrage was "too much foreign truck." As for the support of woman suffrage, it was obviously done "to tickle a squad of women who have been travelling around to the conventions of all parties, lobbying for such a resolution."[98] Having said his piece, Miller joined the campaign in support of the upstarts, all the while plotting the return of the palace guard.

Populist suffragists nearly outdid their Republican counterparts. Diggs had fashioned a ringing endorsement of woman suffrage that appeared headed for inclusion in the Populist platform. This plan was thwarted by John Breidenthal, who was not about to let his careful fusion arrangements be derailed by a suffrage plank. Although the delegates had overwhelmingly approved the proposal, Breidenthal's parliamentary sleight of hand produced a much-watered-down document. By merely equaling the Republicans in calling for a popular referendum, Breidenthal kept the Democrats from revolting against open support of woman suffrage. At the same time, Populist suffrage supporters could claim to have matched their Republican counterparts.[99] Suffragists of all persuasions thus looked optimistically toward 1893, believing they were witnessing the coalescing of a truly nonpartisan suffrage campaign.

The WCTU looked at the upcoming suffrage drive with some relief. The prohibition issue was momentarily played out, and temperance activists needed something to galvanize their forces and reinvigorate the fight for enforcement. By focusing their resources on woman suffrage, temperance leaders could concentrate on a short-term goal that appeared to have a reasonable chance of success. More importantly, if women got the vote, the prohibition movement would clearly be the beneficiary. WCTU officers envisioned initiating a nonpartisan moral crusade at the state level parallel to the municipal strategy that had proved so effective.[100]

Rastall's departure from Kansas in 1892 had added to the WCTU's doldrums, but her continued presence would not necessarily have made much difference. When she left to manage the national WCTU's publishing business in Chicago, she did so at an opportune time for her reputation in Kansas. Her departure could thus be looked upon as the end of the Kansas WCTU's golden era. Whether it could recapture its former glory would depend in large part on the fate of the amendment that would be placed before the voters in 1894.

The results of the 1892 election in Kansas were mixed, with all sides claiming victory. Fusion gave the Populist-Democratic candidate Lorenzo Lewelling enough votes to win the governorship. Republicans also lost control of the Senate. But the House remained up for grabs, as Republicans captured ten seats by fraudulent means and were challenged by their Populist opponents. Whichever party controlled the contested seats would control the House. Both Republicans and Populists declared they would assume their offices come January.

While the Populists announced the formation of the "First People's Government on Earth," the vote totals told a different story. The Republicans had actually increased their vote from 1890. Although the Populists and Democrats together had enough votes to win the state offices, the Populists had lost some of their core support to the G.O.P. If fusion continued, those Populists who had left the Republican Party for the promise of moral politics might now abandon a party that not only appeared amoral but also looked suspiciously like the Democrats.[101]

The three years following the Populist revolt were a curious time in Kansas politics. Assumptions were no longer safe about the most basic ground rules— what group was the dominant power, who was allied with whom. Ideology tended to take a back seat to practical politics. Those who held on to their ideals were often ignored or swept aside. Activists in the Woman Movement clung tightly with one hand to their dream of a political sisterhood while reaching out to potential partisan allies with the other. Alliance members struggled desperately to maintain their independence from the Populist Party, even as political events were fast outpacing them. Alliance women attempted to fashion a place for themselves in the post-Populist Alliance which would assure them of their continued relevance within the organization. The Populists began to fracture, torn by conflicting visions of reform. And all the while the Republicans cast about for the proper strategy that would crush the Populists and redeem the state from anarchy. All stumbled onward toward the showdown in 1894, when the final consequences of the matrix of reform would be revealed.

# SEVEN

## ⥲ "AN ARMY OF WOMEN" ⥲

Immediately following the 1892 election, the *Farmer's Wife* declared war on the Woman Movement's opponents. Initiating the suffrage campaign even before the legislature had passed the amendment's enabling bill, the *Farmer's Wife* headline proclaimed:

WOMEN'S WAR

KANSAS TO BE THE NEXT BATTLE GROUND

SHE WILL JOIN WYOMING IN THE SISTERHOOD OF STATES

Sounding very much like a suffrage paper, the *Farmer's Wife* exhorted "every suffragist to gird on the armor of war to commence at once and not stop until the women of Kansas obtain the full rights of citizenship which our heavenly father vouch-safed to her from the beginning of time." Insisting it would remain nonpartisan, the newspaper declared, "The FARMER'S WIFE will be the leading factor in this fight and we invite all to give us a helping hand to place our mothers, our wives, our daughters and our sisters on equal footing with men." In the next issue, the paper implored suffrage supporters to "throw away all partisan views and let us unite in this great battle for the women of Kansas."[1]

The *Farmer's Wife*'s declaration of war trumpeted the basic assumptions of the Woman Movement—it was a monolithic, nonpartisan political sisterhood that fought on behalf of all women. Woman Movement activists had used this ideal to gain a certain amount of influence in state politics. They stood on the high ground looking down upon the promised land of state suffrage only because their vision of women's politics had energized large numbers of urban Anglo middle-class women.

By 1892, however, the Woman Movement had stretched its idealized vision to its practical limits. This "women's war" would require leaders to mobilize women beyond the safe environs of the urban middle class. Further, large numbers of committed, energetic women workers would not be enough; more importantly, suffragists would have to persuade male voters to support the amendment. Finally, they would have to fight "this great battle for suffrage" amid the partisan struggles of the Republicans, Populists, and Democrats.

## A Women's War: Suffrage Army, Partisan Divisions

The suffragists' battle lines blurred dramatically when war of another kind was declared between Kansas Populists and Republicans on 21 January 1893. Both parties had refused even to discuss a compromise over the ten challenged legislative seats. Upon entering Representative Hall to organize the House, each side had "proceeded, amid utter pandemonium," to elect its own officers. The two Houses remained in the hall together through the night, "for fear the the other might bar re-entry." After a month-long stalemate, the Republicans took the offensive. They ordered the Populist seats vacated and the chief clerk arrested; the Populists responded by rescuing the clerk, occupying Representative Hall, and posting armed guards in front. The G.O.P. legislators then stormed the hall and diverted the guards until the Republican Speaker sledgehammered the doors open; the Populists retreated in confusion. Both sides next marshaled forces and surrounded the statehouse. Partisans patrolled the capitol grounds armed with rifles and pistols, with several Gatling guns in evidence. Although the combatants eventually fashioned a truce of sorts, charges continued to fly back and forth. Mainstream newspapers across the country gave the "Legislative War" full play while depicting it as the natural outcome of Populist-inspired anarchy.[2]

Although the war had been mostly sound and fury, with no shots fired and no serious injuries, it represented the deterioration of political discourse in

Men at work: the doors of Representative Hall after they felt the wrath of a Republican sledge hammer. *Kansas State Historical Society*

Kansas. Some might have hoped that the Populists and Republicans, with similar party platforms, would be capable of enacting certain basic legislative reforms. Such visions of cooperation were dispelled by the crack of a sledge hammer. The Republicans had taken control of the House after the G.O.P.-controlled State Supreme Court ruled that the disputed seats belonged to the Republicans. The G.O.P. used the House to block reform legislation whenever it desired, which was often. And since the first legislative session of the year had been largely consumed with extralegal maneuvers, legislators had little time for introducing bills, let alone passing them.

The war disenchanted many of those who had believed the Populists would usher in the millennium. Populist leaders had promised action, but the rank and file had expected economic relief, not chaos and disorder. One immediate result of the war further disillusioned the faithful. While the electoral imbroglio remained, the House and Senate met together to elect a replacement for the late U.S. Senator Preston Plumb.[3] In order to win the election, the Populists needed Democratic support. Because of fusion arrangements, there were only three "straight" Democratic legislators. A number of fusion legislators, however, balked at an antifusion candidate. Further, because the House was not officially organized, the U.S. Senate, under Democratic control, would be the final arbiter of the Kansas senatorial election.

Fusionist Populists took advantage of the situation by maneuvering to elect John Martin, a moderate Democrat who pledged complete fealty to his party. Populists could have nominated a candidate who was unobjectionable to fusionists yet who remained loyal to the People's Party. Populist fusionists, however, were eager to reward their Democratic allies for their support in the past election and hoped to cement their relationship with the Democrats by offering them this valued prize. Thus the logic of fusion quickly worked to create more fusion.[4]

Amid all this confusion, woman suffragists managed to overcome Republican and Populist intransigence long enough to have them pass a bill mandating the submission of a constitutional woman suffrage amendment to the voters in 1894. Woman suffragists would now be able to undertake their own battle, but in a very different context from the one the *Farmer's Wife* had foreseen in November. Indeed, the men's war had an immediate effect on the women's campaign. Following the Populist rout from the capitol building, Laura Johns had given a suffrage speech to House Republicans in Representative Hall. The resulting controversy demonstrated how tenuous were the bonds that held the Kansas suffrage movement together.

Populists were quick to condemn Johns's indiscretion. The *Advocate* claimed "the dear, silly old lady hung around until 1 o'clock in the morning to make a speech," highlighting the Republican leadership's disinterest in woman suffrage. More to the point, the paper charged, "It is evident that Mrs. Johns would rather see no equal suffrage legislation than to get it from other than Republican hands." Apparently, Johns had also been deputized as a Republican sergeant at arms.[5] Populist woman suffragists were no happier with Johns than the *Advocate;* none so much as protested its condescending language toward the KESA president.

Several months later, most Populist women leaders still had not forgiven Johns. In April she wrote a letter of welcome to the newly formed Women's Political Progressive League (WPPL), successor to the National Woman's Alliance, to which WPPL President Bina Otis responded by means of an open letter published in the *Farmer's Wife.* "Dear Sister," Otis began—although the only sisterly emotion that seemed present was sibling rivalry—"It gives me great pleasure to know that you are pushing the work of this progressive period along the line of equal suffrage, even though it be under serious embarrassments, owing to the very active part you are reported to have taken in the legislative muddle of last winter. . . . Permit me to be frank and say that I think the reason that many of the People's Party folks have been led to believe that you were organizing Republican suffrage associations, is because of the active part you have taken in partisan politics while you were holding the highest office in a nonpartisan organization." She signed off, "With most friendly greeting and good wishes for the future."[6]

Unlike KESA, the WPPL was "not a 'suffrage association,' but a political club that endorses equal suffrage and temperance." For this reason, Otis explained, the WPPL would have to refuse Johns's request that they soft-pedal the prohibition issue. Johns had feared that if suffragists stressed temperance during the upcoming campaign, "wets" would make an extra effort to defeat the suffrage amendment. Otis dismissed this concern: "all anti-temperance people know full well the danger to the open saloon and the liquor traffic when women are enfranchised, and they will fight just as hard if we are silent as if we are bold and outspoken. . . . As brave and progressive women, we cannot afford to sacrifice principles upon so vital a question." Despite these differences with Johns, Otis insisted, "We stand ready to join hands in the equal suffrage cause with the women of all parties."

Otis's letter reveals the fault lines and contradictions of the Kansas Woman Movement. Johns had written a private letter in her capacity as KESA president in order to strengthen the woman suffrage network. She had included a confidential discussion about campaign strategy, hoping to get the WPPL's support for the sensitive issue of de-emphasizing prohibition. She had not expected to spark public debate. Otis, however, was more interested in scoring points.

Otis was probably right in believing that downplaying prohibition would be ineffective. But by chastising Johns in public she revealed her willingness to violate the ideal of sisterhood to gain advantage for her organization. Johns's decision to sacrifice the prohibition issue for the sake of suffrage was a difficult one. A former officer and present member of the WCTU, she had been in the front ranks of the temperance struggle for some time. Her decision was in keeping with her practical approach to moral politics, for she believed that woman suffrage would inevitably lead to strict prohibition enforcement. Otis, in revealing Johns's suggestion publicly, knew she was discrediting the KESA president in certain quarters. Yet Populist women were hardly innocent of the charge of disregarding prohibition. Most had applauded or acquiesced in the national Populist Party's refusal to endorse the issue.

Otis's objection to Johns's partisan activities was equally contradictory. Annie Diggs, KESA's second highest officer, was the most politically active and influential woman in Kansas, yet no Republican suffragist suggested that Diggs resign her KESA position. Although Johns had been active in organizing Women's Republican Clubs, as KESA president she had been remarkably even handed. Her appearance at Representative Hall was one of her few indiscretions. If KESA officers had to be somehow nonpartisan in their political activities, all, including the Populists, would have to resign. That several WPPL members besides Diggs were also KESA officers did not help Otis's case.

Otis's potshots against Johns were part of a campaign to establish the WPPL as the premier organization for women activists. By claiming to be morally purer and politically braver than Johns, the WPPL was positioning itself ahead of both the Republican Women's Club and KESA. The headline of Otis's letter—"Mrs. Otis answers Mrs. Johns"—was meant as both a response and a countercharge.

This, then, was the basic quandary of leaders of the Woman Movement as they prepared to launch the most extensive suffrage campaign in the state's history. They were aware that victory meant enormous opportunities for women's organizations. The problem was how to take advantage of those favorable circumstances without fracturing the suffrage movement and thus destroying the opportunities. Populist women seemed particularly eager to claim the mantle of a newly enfranchised Woman Movement. One WPPL member predicted the organization "will be planted in every county, township and city in the state and nation, and soon it shall be said: 'The women have their lights trimmed and burning.' They are coming from every state in the Union. The burdens they bear, the evils they endure, are common. They will join in a common defense. The lights they kindle will presently illuminate the world. The songs they sing will enthuse humanity."[7] WPPL members hoped to grab the suffrage standard and establish themselves as the vanguard. When Kansas women won the vote, the WPPL could then lead the new voters into the People's Party.

At the same time, WPPL members were sincerely committed to the Woman Movement's ideal of political sisterhood. In part, they knew that only by united action could the suffrage amendment hope to win. Further, Populist women also shared a perspective with other Woman Movement activists that most Populist men did not understand. This they held to despite all their protestations of loyalty to the party. As the Populist and woman suffrage campaigns began organizing for the final showdown in 1894, Populist women exhibited shifting loyalties that bordered on political schizophrenia.

With the cessation of the legislative war and the organization of the WPPL, Populist women added a more partisan tone to their suffrage pronouncements. The WPPL issued several unequivocal statements to the effect that "we are a People's Party organization, first, last, and all of the time, and we advocate all reforms tending to the relief of the people, including woman suffrage and control of the liquor traffic."[8] By making these pronouncements, the WPPL hoped to secure a role in the Populist Party. Apparently, they had put their plans to lead the suffrage movement on hold.

For a short time, the *Farmer's Wife* even maintained that partisanship was the only acceptable course of action for all suffragists. Sounding very much like Joseph Hudson's *Capital,* the *Farmer's Wife* insisted, "Every man that is a man and every woman that is a woman should and must arrange themselves on one side or another of these great problems that are at present agitating the public mind. The vast amount of discussion for and against these propositions leaves us no room for a neutral position."[9] The article, titled "Non Partisan Folly," seemed to agree with old party editors that "real men" were rigidly partisan; to this the article added "real women" as well. The writer, Alma B. Stryker, a WPPL organizer, issued this battle cry: "Under the discipline of the Women's Progressive Political League, we must study the art of active warfare against oppression, obeying every order of battle, taking our place among the mighty marshalled hosts of the poor and oppressed. . . . [W]e can see that only the strongest sentiments against oppression can fit our voters to meet the moral and political battles of the present day as bravely with ballots as did our union soldiers with bullets." Standing side-by-side with their men, women Populists would fight the good fight for their party.

The WPPL was emboldened by the direction of the political battles taking place within the parties. Republican bosses had easily retaken control of the central committee from the Young Republicans, who were banished in disgrace after losing the statehouse to the Populists. The restored Republican leadership purged all dissenters from inner party circles and insisted that the only issue that mattered was defeating the Populists. To underscore this strategy, only one Republican county convention in 1893 passed a resolution supporting the woman suffrage amendment. Mid-road Populists, in contrast, were attempting to wrest power away from party functionaries. With little hope of regaining the party apparatus without a base of support, the mid-roaders moved to regain control of the county conventions. One of their first volleys against the fusionists was to pass resolutions endorsing the suffrage amendment. Since many of them were suffrage supporters to begin with, these maneuvers helped both causes.

Bina Otis, in a speech in September 1893, highlighted the disparity between Populist and Republican endorsements, to score some points against her perceived rival. "Eleven Populist county conventions have adopted suffrage resolutions, and one Republican," she noted. "Permit me to say to Mrs. Johns that if the Republicans do not hustle and get on their war paint on this issue, we propose to help the Populists with our influence to whip them at the next election in the same ratio, eleven to one." Looking forward to the 1894 party conventions, Otis was weighing the pitfalls and possibilities of having the Populists alone endorse the amendment. As the *Farmer's Wife* pointedly noted, "You may talk about equal suffrage being a non-partisan movement, but if the amendment carries, which it is almost sure to do, some party will take credit for the victory. This is as sure as the sun rises and sets."[10]

Despite the WPPL's calls for party discipline, its members had too much invested in the Woman Movement to abandon the sisterhood. "There is no more important work that can be undertaken by the women of Kansas than the proposed enrollment of both men and women who will support this demand of justice," wrote Otis in June 1893. "Let every man of the state be placed on record; and when the nominating conventions meet, let no enemy of woman be placed on the ticket. If, perchance, one such should secure a nomination, let him be defeated, no matter what party he may belong to. If this is to be a war to the knife, let us have the knife to the hilt." Once again, the war was to be for the cause of women. Similarly reverting to the language of the Woman Movement, the *Farmer's Wife* stated several months later, "The women do not wish to be understood as fighting the men. They are simply fighting the miserable laws that men have made." In the same issue, the paper balanced its attacks on men with calls for women's solidarity, insisting, "While the women may differ in politics they will work together for their own enfranchisement."

Yet this transformation was not complete. Just below this announcement, the columnist asked suffragists, "In all the years the Republican Party was in power in Kansas, my sisters, what did they do for you? . . . To the women of Kansas we say stand by the party that stands by you."[11]

The Jekyll and Hyde approach of women Populists was embodied in Laura Johns's relationship with Annie Diggs and Mary Lease. Lease, whose mental stability and political influence were showing signs of erosion by 1893, focused her wrath on Johns. In a letter to the KESA president which she then distributed to Populist newspapers, "Queen Mary" imperiously attacked Johns for a number of alleged crimes and misdemeanors. Lease concluded by instructing Johns to join the Populists, because KESA was "a little one-horsed suffrage cart engaged in a futile attempt to believe [women] are non-partisan." The *Industrial Free Press* headline read:

MRS. MARY E. LEASE

SHE HOTLY SCORES MRS. JOHNS OF KANSAS

THEY DO NOT LOVE EACH OTHER[12]

No such headlines ever described Johns and Diggs's relationship. Indeed, they enjoyed what might be described as a working friendship. In part, this was due to both women's diplomatic approach to politics; yet they also developed warm regard for each other. In one letter to the *Kansas Sunflower*, Johns praised Diggs as "brave and logical and sincere." When Diggs and Johns appeared at the 1894 National American Woman Suffrage Association convention, the Boston-based *Woman's Journal* reported, "Both are small women of gentle and feminine aspect, though known as mighty workers; and when Mrs. Diggs, a soft-voiced, bright-eyed morsel of humanity, said in presenting the needs of the Kansas Equal Suffrage Association, 'Mrs. Johns is our president, and I am vice-president; she is the gentle officer, I am the savage one; my business is to frighten people'—the audience roared with laughter." The *Woman's Journal* noted approvingly that "Mrs. Johns is a strong Republican, and Mrs. Diggs an equally ardent Populist, but they were perfectly agreed in their devotion to the woman suffrage amendment."[13] Johns and Diggs provided a strong example of the possibilities of the ideal of sisterhood. The symbolism of their friendship was rendered all the more impressive given the partisan battles being fought in Kansas. The delegates responded to Johns's entreaties by donating over $2,500 to the campaign.

On September 1, 1893, leaders of the Woman Movement met to solidify their nonpartisan suffrage campaign strategy. It was a remarkable event, with more than twice as many participants as any previous KESA convention. Whereas past KESA meetings had been rather placid affairs, the "Great Suffrage Convention" was a boisterous celebration, replete with colorful streamers, exuberant speakers, and joyous song. Delegate after delegate from a wide variety of organizations—including the State Teachers Association, the Social Science Association, the Women's Relief Corps, the Kansas Women's Press Association, and the Adult Sorority PEO—marched to the podium and read their resolutions. All proclaimed support for the amendment, and most reported on the growing activity by suffragists throughout the state. S. A. Thurston declared that hundreds of Kansas newspapers had pledged to support the amendment. Emma Smith DeVoe, an Illinois suffragist, promised to raise two thousand dollars in her home state for the cause. It appeared that the Woman Movement was ready for its own "pentecost of politics."[14]

The convention passed a number of resolutions making it clear that suffrage activists wanted the amendment campaign to be nonpartisan and ecumenical, and that KESA would "confine the work for the amendment strictly to argument and propaganda for the enfranchisement of women." The campaign committee contained four Republicans, including Johns and Thurston; four Populists: Diggs, Otis, Stryker, and Eliza McLallin; and a Democrat and Prohibitionist.[15] Yet the delegates also acknowledged that women could work for their respective parties while not "under the auspices of the amendment campaign committee." As Laura Johns described the committee, "it is non partisan in its work, though ALL PARTISAN in its make up. . . . Not for one instant will these women be disloyal to their respective political or religious affiliations." Another resolution called on the various state and local party conventions to endorse the amendment. All the resolutions apparently passed with little debate and much enthusiasm.[16] No one mentioned that being simultaneously nonpartisan and all-partisan might be trickier than it appeared.

The euphoria of the convention carried over well into the next spring. During this time, the *Farmer's Wife* managed to steer away from mixing partisanship and suffrage, issuing its strongest pronouncement of sisterly solidarity when it proclaimed, "the Democrats will howl resubmission [of prohibition] and oppose the suffrage amendment. The Republicans will stake their issue on the late legislative unpleasantness and the downfall of the state under Populist rule. The Populists will hold to the issue of land, money, and transportation. They will all be drowned . . . *by the vast army of women*."[17] With this inexorable tide of support, how would anything but complete victory be possible, whether men willed it or not? Forgotten were the demands for party discipline and the sneering comments about the futility of nonpartisanship.

But within this inspiring vision of a politically transcendent women's crusade lay potential disaster. The *Farmer's Wife* might dismiss men's partisanship with a rhetorical flourish, but women activists could less easily ignore their own partisan interests. Beyond the internal fractures that might occur, how in fact was the "women's army" going to overwhelm the mainstream parties when the ground troops lacked the most important weapon in an electoral battle, the vote? The franchise would usher in a women's political millennium, its supporters argued, but this could be achieved only if men bestowed the vote on women. What would make men ignore their partisan concerns?

Anna Champe, editor of the *Kansas Sunflower,* believed she had the answer. "Organize! Organize! Organize!" she urged, "and when you get organized GO TO WORK! We can't expect a crop of equal suffragists unless we sow the seed. . . . 'As ye sow, so shall ye reap.' " The *Kansas Sunflower* was one of several suffrage newspapers established for the campaign which were strictly nonpartisan and provided a useful counterweight to the *Farmer's Wife.*[18] Champe, a Populist, issued this declaration of inclusiveness in the first issue: "The Sunflowers on our Kansas prairies bloom for all alike. They are neither partisan or sectarian. They bloom for black, white, or red, for male or female, for rich or poor."[19]

Suffragists understood the importance of moving beyond the Anglo middle class with their message. *Our Messenger* called for "the best women" to join the suffrage fight and directed them to concentrate on "departments of work among Miners, Foreigners, Railroad Men and Colored." The WCTU paper further urged that "the distribution of literature and use of the press be emphasized as being the best avenues for franchise work." The *Farmer's Wife* declared, "the WPPL does most earnestly entreat all women 'white' or 'black' who can conscientiously endorse our by-laws and constitution (and we can not see how any women would refuse to endorse them) to join us."[20]

Despite such inclusive sentiments, the WCTU intended to maintain an evangelistic approach to reaching non-middle-class Anglos. Rather than learn the lesson of Helen Gougar's Leavenworth campaign, temperance activists were determined to keep a safe distance from Kansans who were outside their class and culture. Since black and German papers could be counted on to slight the suffrage cause, the WCTU's tactic had little chance of success. The *Farmer's Wife* declaration was similarly of little practical use. Populist women expected black women to join an organization that had shown little understanding about race issues. Further, they expected their black sisters simply to organize themselves. Certainly, the WPPL made no efforts to venture into North Topeka in search of converts.

Black editors remained true to their longtime antagonism toward woman suffrage, rejecting the amendment with little debate.[21] The *Kansas Blackman* tried to ease the blow to black women by assuring them, "What man accomplishes by physical force, woman obtains from that all powerful influence resulting from the high esteem and regard in which she is held by the kings of the earth. We may never have woman suffrage, but the gentle sisters will continue to run the machinery of the world." In general, African-American papers steadfastly ignored the issue except for the occasional sneering comment about suffragists.[22]

Whether such condescendingly patriarchal tones had much effect on the African-American women suffragists is unknown. Black papers did not publish any women's letters in support of suffrage and indeed hardly published any women's letters at all. Of course, black women may have decided to beat a sudden retreat from making public commentary. A more likely scenario, however, is that black editors, never friendly toward the issue, wanted to banish any sense of dissent among the local African-American population. Instead, they attempted to use the notion of an African-American voting block to parlay favors from either the Republicans or the Populists. Although the editors were rarely successful at this, their need to present a front of unanimity was enough to keep suffrage supporters out of the black newspapers. Black suffragists, meanwhile, received little more support from their white counterparts in the Woman Movement.

If white suffragists could not transcend their cultural boundaries, they at least covered a lot of ground. Suffrage lecturers and organizers fanned out across the state to speak at county fairs, Chautauquas, assemblies, picnics, and teachers' institutes. S. A. Thurston urged suffragists to "circulate literature, hold school house meetings, present the enrollment books, give Cooper contests, in short do everything your ingenuity can devise." Helen Kimber and Ruth Dargon organized eight new Amendment Clubs in a month; Eva Corning established thirteen in two weeks. Suffrage fairs proliferated, enabling the amendment committee to run the first well-financed suffrage campaign in Kansas history.[23] In May 1894 suffragists organized special conventions in 85 of 105 Kansas counties, culminating in another rousing KESA convention at the end of the month. Meeting just before the Republican and Populist conventions, the KESA convention provided momentum for suffragists' attempts to put suffrage planks in the party platforms.

Even by modern standards such an extensive campaign would be difficult. Like the Alliance lecturers, suffrage activists kept up a grueling pace, often using primitive means of transportation. They frequently traveled by railroad but were often forced to rely on wagons and buggies to reach isolated towns.

Further, Kansas railroads were not known for their comfort, nor were the small towns that dotted the Plains famous for their amenities. Laura Johns reported from western Kansas in late 1893, "Here comes my train, and though this strong wind which breathes dust and drouth scorches everything it touches, out under a sun hot enough to blister the stone sidewalk, wearily I go on my way to urge the justice of the pending amendment. I long for the comforts of my home, and dream of enjoying them when this cruel war is over."[24] For Johns, suffragists' war metaphors had a very real component. The amendment campaign demanded tremendous physical and emotional endurance. Her melodramatic "war correspondence" had a purpose beyond self-pity: it served to motivate those suffragists left on the home front and spur them on to greater activity.

Early on, WCTU members signed up as foot soldiers for the campaign. The WCTU's 1893 "Plan of Work" declared, "[W]e recognize the opportunity which the year will bring for the advancement in every line of our work by the carrying of the suffrage amendment, therefore we recommend: That the department of Franchise receive special attention, and the best, brightest and most lovable women . . . be put in as superintendents."[25] *Our Messenger* suggested that temperance workers add the amendment committee's yellow ribbon, symbolizing the Kansas sunflower, to the WCTU's traditional white.

S. A. Thurston, who served as the WCTU's state superintendent of the Franchise Department and acting secretary for KESA's amendment committee, deftly shifted between the two as was needed. She later recalled, "The letter heads of the two organizations lay side by side on my desk at Campaign Headquarters, and I did my work under the official title that I thought would have most weight for the especial matter in hand. In towns where there was no Campaign Club, if there was a 'WCTU,' I made arrangements with it, exactly as with the other body where one existed."[26] Because the WCTU leadership had embraced suffrage as its primary goal, Thurston made use of the organization's widespread network without causing resentment among temperance workers.

While the WCTU provided many of the ground troops, it no longer assumed leadership of the suffrage battle. It is telling that Thurston spent all her time at amendment committee headquarters rather than with the WCTU. In large part, the WCTU's loss of leadership came about when KESA was at last powerful enough to take on the role. The WCTU, with its twenty-nine departments and its losing battle for prohibition enforcement, had more than enough to keep itself busy. Temperance activists graciously conceded the top ranks in the suffrage campaign to KESA.

Besides mobilizing the usual forces, the amendment committee was able to count on another group that, while not altogether new to the struggle, took a more prominent part than usual. Urban Anglo men had always had a place in the suffrage struggle but had usually remained in the background. During the amendment campaign, however, numerous men took a few steps forward; several local Amendment Clubs had some men as members and officers. Other men gave contributions to the cause and urged their peers to do the same.[27]

Perhaps most importantly, men could counter antisuffragists' objections from a male perspective. At the May 1894 KESA convention, J. Willis Gleed got to the heart of the matter with a satirical attack on men's gender assumptions. "One reason why we [men] don't want you to vote," he assured the crowd, "is because we want harmony in the home. We have it now (laughter). If the wives want tea for dinner and we want coffee, we compromise on coffee and harmony is preserved. If women get into politics our domestic life will be like dogs and cats."[28] Gleed well knew that for many men the ability to maintain the upper hand in domestic matters was of paramount importance. "Domestic strife" was thus coded language for the fear that enfranchised women would demand equality in the home as well as in the voting booth.

Mayor Harrison of Topeka, speaking several hours later, similarly unmasked one of men's favorite objections, "that . . . immoral women would control the elections. If that is so, my brothers," noted the straightlaced reformer, "then I am frank to admit that you know more about that subject than I do. Do not try to handle a keen, two-edged sword by the naked blade. You can imagine what the result would be. . . . My honest opinion is—and I give it only as an opinion, without note or comment—that the least that is said about this objection the better the showing for the masculine side in this controversy."[29] Harrison's tone and oblique commentary were calculated to sound as if he were imparting a dirty secret that men had best keep hidden. His audience, most of whom were women, already believed that prostitution existed because of men's sexual appetites and their unwillingness to allow working women adequate opportunity to make a decent living. Harrison's manner turned this assumption into an attack on men's own moral character: "How many immoral women do you suppose there would be if there were no immoral men? How many more immoral men do you suppose there are than immoral women?" Harrison and Gleed had taken men's casual observations and used them as a mirror in which men might examine their deepest fears and contradictory assumptions about gender relations.

While some men offered unreserved support, others attached a string or two. One man, writing in the *Alliant* about an amendment meeting, reported:

"The majority of the people present were gentlemen, which I think a favorable sign of success in carrying the amendment, for the men will vote upon the question this fall. They are the salvation of the Woman's Suffrage cause and it stands the ladies in hand to keep on the 'good side' of the gentlemen at least until the election."[30] This was a far cry from the *Farmer's Wife*'s declaration of independence which promised to overwhelm men's politics. Rather than currying men's favor, suffragists were more used to demonstrating men's inferiority to women. But women activists had developed this strategy as a means to galvanize women and convince political elites. With the success of the suffrage amendment in the hands of the (male) electorate, they would have at least to consider Joseph Hudson's retort to Anna Howard Shaw's speech at the May 1894 KESA convention: "Do something more than scold the men. That doesn't make the votes." Hudson, who had undergone a rather severe scolding of his own several years earlier, no doubt spoke from the heart.

Many suffragists disapproved of Hudson's imperious tone, especially as it was directed against the redoubtable National American Woman Suffrage Association vice president. His manner grated especially hard against those present who had faced off against him over the 1891 Topeka mayoral election. Hudson, however, was the editor of the most influential Republican paper in the state. Further, he had offered to press for a woman suffrage plank at the G.O.P. convention the next year. Thus no one stood up to challenge him, though perhaps more than a few bit their tongues. From the point of view of the Woman Movement, Hudson seemed to be saying that because men had immorally disenfranchised women and kept the vote to themselves, men should be accorded special favor. Such logic went against the basic ideology of the Woman Movement. But it was also good, practical politics.

## PLAYING BY THE RULES: THE SUFFRAGISTS
## AT THE PARTY CONVENTIONS

Laura Johns had long been aware that moral suasion alone, whether complimentary to or critical of men, would not sway those interested in the practical advantages of supporting suffrage. Hence suffragists added a weapon that would carry greater force in their campaign. Perhaps taking a cue from Otis's veiled threat to Johns, they warned Populist and Republican leaders that failure to endorse suffrage would mean that the opposing party would get all the credit for its passage. Annie Diggs, in a pitch for a prosuffrage resolution to a nonpartisan Cloud County convention, explained, "The suffrage movement knows no politics and we propose to go before the different conventions and ask for a plank in our favor and it will be granted to us as a matter of expediency; for don't you believe each party wants to make a bid for the vote that is sure to come."[31] By presenting the suffrage planks as being in the parties' best interest—and were not all men self-interested?—she made endorsement appear inevitable. Her logic and manner induced the great majority of men at the meeting to support the resolution, calling upon all parties to support the amendment in their platforms. Diggs's accomplishment was even more impressive considering that "most of the Populist voters were attending caucuses . . . and could not be present." Diggs's logic worked fine if all went as planned. "Don't you see," she reasoned, "that if both the Populists and Republicans declare for this, the pot cannot call the kettle black." If only one party voted in a suffrage plank, however, the expediency argument would be reversed, carrying with it the potential for disaster.

Despite the hazards, this approach had the backing of historical precedent. Suffragists could point to the 1893 Colorado amendment campaign as proof that such a strategy could be successful. In Colorado, politics was certainly as bitter and violent as in Kansas. Yet Colorado suffragists were fortunate in their timing. In 1893 each party, including the Democrats, attempted to out-liberal the others. All had endorsed the suffrage amendment, and suffragists were able to mount a truly nonpartisan campaign.[32] The result was that Colorado became only the second state to grant full enfranchisement for women, and the first to do so by direct popular vote.

In Kansas, suffragists were most concerned about gaining the endorsements of the Populists and Republicans, since the Democrats would at best refrain from opposing the amendment. Suffragists' hopes were given a boost in April 1894 when the Kansas State Editors Association passed a resolution favoring the amendment by a four-to-one margin. The *Industrial Free Press* reported that "there were no party lines drawn in the vote, members of every political party voting in favor of the amendment."[33] All seemed to be proceeding as planned.

Both the Republicans and the Populists, however, had forces organizing to avoid the woman suffrage issue. Rumblings were being heard from influential Republicans that the platform should concern itself solely with defeating the Populists. Populist fusionists were voicing similar sentiments, urging that woman suffrage and prohibition be jettisoned. "As you prize the party's existence, as you prize the life of the cause of reform, be careful, be thrice careful," warned the *Journal and Triumph*. "Woe betide us if there go into that platform planks over which any CONSIDERABLE NUMBER of people disagree. On the fundamental issues we are a unit. Adhere as closely to these as possible, and all will be well."[34] Though the paper did not say as much, all its readers knew very well that woman suffrage and prohibition would cause the greatest divisions.

As suffrage leaders began organizing their lobbying, some women activists made it clear that they wanted no part of men's political culture. In the suffrage paper *Woman's Friend,* a local KESA officer named E. A. Templins launched a scathing attack on the plan to influence the party platforms. Referring to the Kansas City resolutions, Templins charged, "The whole scheme of going to the parties was hatched under a political trickster, and the claim that it is non-partisan is as false as the trick is gauzy." Claiming that all the political parties were run by "bosses," she encouraged women to boycott the upcoming conventions. Templins's view was supported by a number of other important suffrage leaders, including one who warned, "if we owe our success to any party we are *honor bound* to support that party, no matter how obnoxious its leaders . . . may be to us." The Yates County Equal Suffrage Association passed a resolution rejecting all party platform endorsements, referring indirectly to their belief in women's moral superiority: "We all know that when partisan blood stirs in men's veins, their instincts of justice and fairness are often swept aside by the passion of the hour."[35]

Laura Johns, the obvious focus of Templins's attack, took exception to both the tone and the content of the criticism. In her response she urged a more temperate approach while generally ignoring the moral thrust of Templins's argument. Instead, she reiterated that no particular party dominated KESA and that by necessity suffragists were forced to do "whatever must be done." In fact, she carried this utilitarian argument to the extreme: "the platform will induce the men to vote for suffrage who will do anything his party tells him," thus substantiating the claims of the radical nonpartisans.[36] Johns, a product of the Woman Movement, was subverting the basic assumptions of the movement. Rather than admit the difficulty of being both "non-partisan and all-partisan," she stressed the need to gain victory on men's terms. Although Johns's position displayed political savvy in addressing those who held power, she also demonstrated considerable naïveté in not considering the possible dangers to her own organization.

Several weeks later, Johns got a hint of the consequences of her position when the Kansas Republican Women's Association (RWA) attempted to gain its party's support for a suffrage amendment plank. Party bosses, the undisputed masters of the convention, made clear that they would address just one "legitimate" issue: the "redeeming" of Kansas from the "anarchistic" Populists. Yet Republican women were optimistic: they had many longtime allies in the powerful editors of the leading Republican dailies, and they had secured the services of a number of nationally known suffragists.[37]

Their first conflict, however, was not with the party bosses—at least not directly—but among their own ranks at the association's preconvention meeting. The resolutions committee, chaired by Minnie D. Morgan, had prepared a resolution to present to the Republican convention. Tiptoeing gingerly around the issue of woman suffrage, the resolution read, "While disclaiming any desire to make it a test of party fealty, we recognize the justice of the pending suffrage amendment and ask in every Republican its just and earnest consideration."[38] It was the perfect statement for a party wishing to avoid any hint of controversy or disunity among the delegates. However this strategy might have gone over with the Republican leadership, it did not sit well with the more prominent women at the meeting. The resolution, which some claimed was written by Morgan's husband, a well-connected Republican, caused an immediate and emotional reaction. Laura Johns insisted, "It is unthinkable for women to adhere to the Republican party and not demand suffrage. I doubt if I can ever lift my head again if this resolution is adopted." Susan B. Anthony, as usual, was even more forceful. She declared that the resolution was "an insult to the women who came to Kansas in the interest of suffrage. . . . If you adopt such a resolution my work is ended in this state." J. Ellen Foster, president of the national RWA, argued for a resolution with some request for suffrage but then pointedly noted, "I care more for [R]epublican principles than woman suffrage."

In the end, Anthony's reputation and Johns's influence won out, and the RWA's resolutions committee retreated to hammer out a rather tortuous resolution: "That we, the Republican women of Kansas, having worked for the best interests of the state, using the ballot with judgement in school and municipal elections, demonstrating the benefits to be obtained, ask the Republicans in Kansas state convention assembled to testify and advocate an equal ballot and a fair count to all citizens." Anthony was little more pleased, labeling the new resolution "the veriest spaniel-like position imaginable." She also accused Foster of being "the hired emissary of Republican politicians who have determined to silence the women on this question," an accusation probably close to the truth.[39]

Anthony carried her gloomy assessment of Republican policy to the G.O.P. convention. In a short speech uncomplicated by political tact, she warned the delegates, "If you leave [the amendment] out you are dead."[40] Once again, Anthony felt compelled to bring up 1867, telling the platform committee, "I know you are not idiots, and you will put every question in your platform that interests you. . . . The same experiment of treachery in the Republican Party has become tiresome." Anthony seemed determined to create bad feeling against her, and future events would show how well she succeeded.

Unlike Anthony, Foster and Johns came to the convention with impeccable Republican credentials. Foster was particularly trusted by the Republican leadership, and she repaid that trust by prefacing her comments to the resolutions committee with the pledge, "I will stand by the Republican Party whether it does or does not" include the plank. She pushed hard for it on the grounds of expediency, urging, "Would you not like to put [the Kansas women] under obligation to you? Try, then, and see whether they would not remember you. Gentlemen, I think it would pay you as a Republican convention if you simply say 'We believe in the adoption of the woman's suffrage amendment now pending in the state.' " But she then absolved the committee members, stating, "Gentlemen, I do not impugn the conscience or the chivalry or the honesty of any man who says he will not put a plank in." The *Council Grove Courier* reported, "Her Republican utterances were applauded to the roof, but her woman suffrage sentiments met with little favor."[41] While Foster had managed not to offend anyone, she had been no more successful than Anthony in convincing the committee.

Johns's approach to the committee lay somewhere between those of Anthony and Foster. After presenting a petition with "yards and yards" of signatures supporting the amendment, she asked for and received unlimited time for the women to present their case. She too stressed Republican women's partisan efforts, declaring, "Refuse to recognize us, treat our petitions with contempt, then tell us that you can expect us to rally to the party's support."[42] Mrs. Noble Prentiss, the past president of the Western Social Science Association, put a more positive spin on this theme. Explaining that Republican women needed the plank in order to "assist the state in redeeming Kansas," she pleaded, "We can put our energy and brains against the Populist women and win." Needless to say, there was little talk of sisterhood that day.

Whether pitched hard or soft, however, none of the women's demands had any effect on the Republican delegates. Their unanimity was complete, and they rejected the woman suffrage resolution without debate and without dissent. The prosuffrage editors showed some remorse at having to sacrifice the women's cause but offered only paternalistic platitudes about patience and priorities. As for the Republican suffrage activists, "their amazement and grief was beyond expression."[43]

However traumatic their defeat, Republican women activists did nothing to reassess their strategy following the G.O.P. convention. Instead, they pushed on to the next convention in order to support the Populist women's bid for a proamendment plank. Conditions for Populist suffragists were much more favorable than those experienced by their Republican sisters. Across the state, mid-roaders had been reasserting control of the Populist county conventions, many of which had passed resolutions supporting woman suffrage while condemning cooperation with the Democrats. "We warn the members against the traitors in our camp," read one antifusionist circular, "those who have control of the People's party organization of this state."[44]

Besides having active and influential male allies, Populist women suffragists shared a political vocabulary with their male counterparts, unlike Republican women and men. Republican leaders spoke a business-oriented political language: when they talked of "redeeming Kansas," they were referring to the state's business credit and reputation, not its morals. Republican suffragists were thus limited to appeals based on expediency. Since Republican leaders had their own ideas about self-interest, they did not have to bother with countering moral arguments. Populist women, however, could challenge their party's commitment to moral politics.

Despite these advantages, Populist suffragists faced a number of obstacles. Fusionists controlled the state central committee apparatus and were able to control certain arrangements. Just as mid-roaders feared, the Populist Party chairman, John Briedenthal, and Governor Lewelling were indeed working hard to renew their arrangements with the Democrats, as mid-roaders had charged. In order to steer the Populists clear of any resolutions likely to anger the Democrats, Briedenthal had stacked the resolutions committee with anti-suffragists and profusionists. Mid-roaders demonstrated their grass-roots strength, however, by electing Ben Henderson convention chairman. Henderson, a radical antifusionist and suffrage supporter, had been actively opposed by Briedenthal.[45]

In his opening speech, Henderson set the tone of the suffragists' debate by declaring, "The women were . . . asking for nothing but their God-given right, and this Populist convention ought to give it to them." He then called upon non-Populist suffrage supporters to address the convention. Despite the sweltering heat, the hall remained packed as Carrie Chapman Catt, Susan B. Anthony, and Anna Shaw appealed to the consciences of Populist delegates. Anthony went one step farther. After repeated questioning by delegates, she acknowledged that she would campaign for the Populists if they supported suffrage. Although this was no more than Anthony had promised the Republicans, "the convention leapt to its feet in approval."[46]

The proceedings began at eight o'clock the next morning, and again the hall filled to capacity. The resolutions committee presented a platform without mentioning suffrage, which caused a good many angry murmurs. When Henderson recognized a committeeman who presented a minority report favoring the suffrage amendment, pandemonium reigned. "Fifty men were on their feet at once," reported a correspondent, "yelling for recognition from the chair at the top of their voices. . . . The chairman was pounding the table like a blacksmith would a piece of iron, and shouting 'order' that was mighty slow in coming." After quieting down to an excited buzz—and after rejecting what Annie Diggs referred to as "the milk-and-water amendment"—the convention agreed to allow all speakers five minutes each. Each side would then choose a representative to present the final argument at noon.

Populist prosuffragists knew where the strength of their argument lay. They appealed "strongly to [the delegates'] sense of fairness, consistency, justice, and right." "The opposition," by contrast, "set themselves upon the ground of policy and expediency." The prosuffragists painted their opponents as political opportunists willing to abandon their principles to gain office. Attacking their "cowardly expediency," the prosuffragists countered with references to the Populist motto, "Equal rights for all, special privileges for none." Judge Frank Doster, a Christian socialist and future State Supreme Court Chief Justice, proclaimed, "I do not want a platform . . . made for the express purpose of catching votes. I want a platform with God Almighty in it."

Delegates responded enthusiastically to such appeals for moral purity, but many were no doubt still concerned with the practical political ramifications of the plank. If the delegates who spoke were to be taken at their word, over 80 percent of them favored suffrage. Being in favor did not necessarily mean supporting the resolution, however: many delegates voiced the opinion that Populist support of suffrage would mean sure defeat for the party in November.

Fusionists were not the only ones holding such a view; some mid-roaders felt that even without fusion, a suffrage plank would alienate potential Populist supporters. One delegate, a farmer who had spoken to his wife about the question, was quoted as saying that "It was not so much a question with him or his wife whether she should have the right to vote, but the question was whether they should be able to retain their home. The People's Party had been organized and educated on the line of the paramount importance of the financial question, . . . and it was only by a reformation of this system that the people could find relief." A single second-hand source cannot provide an understanding of farm women's approach to the suffrage endorsement issue. It does, however, suggest that the perspective of an Alliance woman with a mortgaged farm might have differed from that of a middle-class Populist suffragist.

Annie Diggs, chosen to present the concluding argument, had always believed that Kansas Populists would be served well by supporting suffrage.

Whereas other Populist prosuffragists had been content to play upon the delegates' consciences, Diggs adroitly combined expediency with moral arguments. Echoing the approach of her Republican counterparts, she demanded, "Don't you want to have the leverage of having the gratitude of the women of the state?" With a clear understanding of her audience, she then mixed in the various strains of Populist campaign discourse from the past four years, insisting, "If you take a noble, manly, and courageous stand, as I am sure you will, then every cowardly republican candidate will be forced to go upon the rostrum and plead the record of his party in its defense. My friends, the thing for you now to do, from a people's party perspective, is to have the courage of your convictions." Diggs was essentially telling the Populist delegates that they could have it all—morality, manliness, and victory. Whatever the truth of this claim, it definitely struck a responsive chord in her audience. Her speech was followed by several minutes of applause and cheering.

Set against Diggs was none other than the Hon. P. P. Elder, her old foe from the 1891 suffrage bill fight. If Diggs failed to banish him from politics, as she had threatened three years earlier, her speech effectively banished him from the rostrum. Wholly unprepared for the tremendous response to Diggs's speech, Elder fumbled about for a while, admitting at one point, "I confess to you, gentlemen of the convention, that I did not dare to have a vote taken in the presence of the ladies in the committee room." Numerous delegates responded to this with loud hoots of derision. When his allotted time had elapsed, Elder gasped, "My God, is my time up?" Granted a few minutes more, he squandered that by grandly proclaiming, "Let us have a clean Repub———," and was immediately drowned out by an eruption of laughter, cheers, and jeers, followed by a wild, spontaneous demonstration. This was matched only by the outburst following the vote that established the suffrage plank shortly thereafter.[47] As for Elder, he sat down dejectedly, to be patted on the head by a gloating Susan B. Anthony.

## Taking Advantage: Partisanship and Suffrage after the Conventions

For many of the suffragists who attended the convention, this victory would be a long-remembered and significant event in their lives. For Republican women, however, the convention's outcome must have been bittersweet indeed. Despite their declarations to the contrary, they would be campaigning for the party that had coldly repudiated the suffragists' demands. It must have been galling indeed to see the "forces of anarchy" prove themselves morally courageous while their own party seemed to demonstrate the type of "bossism" and amorality that suffrage activists had criticized for years.[48]

Although the Populist convention seemed to be an exuberant kick-off for the amendment campaign, it also rekindled partisan antagonisms among suffragists. Here the Populists had the advantage, for they could support both party principles and the amendment. Some Populists even suggested that women who worked against the Populist Party were helping to defeat the suffrage amendment. Just one week after the convention, a Populist woman wrote that Republican suffragists, "being under the despotic rule of their lords and masters, may strive to undermine the foundation of the stately structure the *real* women of Kansas are now erecting. . . . Their puny efforts to destroy will only create discord in their own hearts and homes." In October the *Farmer's Wife* maintained that "the campaign made by the KESA is of small importance compared with that of the People's Party for the suffrage amendment."[49] Several times during the campaign, Populists accused Johns of favoring Republican speakers over Populists. During the winter lull in party politics, the *Farmer's Wife* could wholeheartedly declare for a nonpartisan "army of women." With the inception of the summer campaigns, however, the two parties were now engaged in the struggle to control the state's political future. Republican and Populist women found themselves caught up in the heat of the battle, often staring at each other from opposite sides of the line.[50]

The outcome of the conventions also strained relations between Kansas Republican suffragists and national suffrage leaders, particularly Susan B. Anthony. After the conventions, Anthony proceeded to fulfill her pledge to the Populists with a vengeance. No doubt still stung by the rebuffs to her cause and her reputation, as well as the Republican "treachery" in 1867, Anthony lashed out at the G.O.P. all along the campaign trail. Referring to the Republican convention, she declared, "I have read your platform thoroughly and can find nothing in it but irrigation. You seem to offer no redemption of Kansas except water, and I hope there will be enough of that to wash your dirty selves clean." While the Populist crowds greatly enjoyed Anthony's anti-Republican potshots, Republican women were horrified that the leading national suffrage activist was attacking their party. As in 1867, however, Anthony had no regrets about her actions.[51]

Despite the sporadic bickering, suffragists overcame their differences to mount a well-organized campaign. Following the convention, Laura Johns intensified the speaking tours, aided by volunteers from around the country. The speakers usually maintained the delicate balancing act between gender and party loyalties during these tours, but it was no easy task. As the Populist journalist Frances Butler related to her readers in one of her columns, "It was a pleasure to ride to and from our appointments with Mrs. Denton [district president of KESA], whom I found to be a very pleasant and agreeable companion on all occasions, yet I cannot help but feel that each of us had some real practical experience in human toleration as our . . . opinions were so widely at variance. Mrs. Denton being as radical a Republican as I am a Populist (and you all know what that means), while each tried to convert the other we parted unchanged as to our political views yet good friends."[52] As Butler's account makes clear, suffragists' adherence to particular economic and political policies was just as central to their ideological make-up as were their opinions on woman suffrage. That such passionate partisans could maintain civility—even friendship—toward each other attested to the strength of the Woman Movement's vision of a political sisterhood.

Most male Republican and Populist leaders were too concerned with the partisan war to worry much about cooperating about the suffrage issue. Joseph Hudson was quick to claim that the plank had destroyed the Populists' chance for fusion—and thus victory. "The very human result of the action of the Populists yesterday," he predicted, "will be for the press and speakers of that party to assume the pops were brave in their actions and the Republicans very cowardly. . . . Four and a half months of this sort of boasting and abuse will turn half the Republican vote against it, and the amendment will possibly go down because of partisan hostility."[53] Hudson, however, perceived a very large silver lining to the amendment's cloudy future. "If . . . the result of the action . . . on the suffrage question contributes to the complete overthrow of Populism in Kansas, it will be a source of great rejoicing for those who believe that this party . . . has too long caused the state and its citizens shame and discredit. Its riddance and extinction is the first duty of all patriotic citizens." To his suffrage allies he instructed, "Woman suffrage can come later. The first great and overshadowing work of the people is to redeem the state from Populism."

Joseph Hudson may not have been a prime exemplar of the moralist politician, but he knew his Kansas politics. No sooner had the Populist convention closed than Populist papers moved to take advantage of their moral victory. "On the suffrage question, the people endeared their party to every one in the state who desires to see the amendment carried," trumpeted the *Industrial Free Press*. "No matter what may be their political views, the women must recognize that the Populist Party has stood by their cause." A number of Populist papers printed names of Republicans who would now vote Populist because of the suffrage plank.[54] The *Journal and Triumph* printed a cartoon showing the

Republican gubernatorial candidate, Edward Morrill, steaming upon hearing that the Populists had included a suffrage plank. The cartoon implied that the plank would enable the Populists to reap the inevitable benefits. Since the *Journal and Triumph* had vigorously opposed including the plank before the convention, its sudden conversion may be seen as whistling in the dark. In private, Populist editors were perhaps less sanguine about the fate of the amendment and its affect on their party.

Populists had good reason to worry. Their party would have the opportunity to gain women's thanks only if the amendment carried. Many Republican editors, in fact, declared they would vote against the amendment because it had become "a Populist measure." In July the *Great Bend Register* intoned darkly, "when a lot of old women get together and resolve to make the question a political one and swear . . . that they will work for the election of a certain political party that saw fit to endorse suffrage, then we quit trying to solve the matter. . . . Since they foolishly sold the suffragists to the pops, we desire to not be considered in that deal."[55] Clearly, Anthony's barbs had found their targets. But the editor's comments also display antagonisms toward suffrage activists beyond the partisan issues. As in 1867, Anthony's attacks on the G.O.P. had given those Republicans already ambivalent or hostile to woman suffrage the excuse—in fact, the imperative—to attack it.

Several months after the conventions, Republican leaders were routinely equating the amendment with the Populists. In late September, Laura Johns obliquely criticized those Republicans who advocated this policy, by reasoning, "Judge Doster talked in convention about putting God in the Populist platform. Suppose it had been done; certain absurd politicians of other parties, in order to be 'logical,' would be compelled to turn atheists."[56] Because these men were so blindly partisan, argued Johns, they would reject anything that the Populists supported. Republicans, however, had followed that course since 1890, and saw no reason to change now. To Johns, such amorality was reprehensible, although it did not stop her from remaining true to the G.O.P. Her continued belief in moral politics and the Republican leaderships' disdain of it underscore women's difficulty in gaining influence in the G.O.P. as long as they embraced the Woman Movement's political culture.

Once both parties had positioned themselves in relation to the amendment, most party papers ignored the issue entirely. Given the Republicans' ruthless slash-and-burn campaign strategy, this policy is not so surprising. More startling is that Populist newspapers soon became little more attentive toward the issue than their Republican counterparts. The best that Populist suffrage activists could hope for was the occasional pieces submitted by women; relegated to "Women's Columns," they were kept discreetly away from the din and roar of the "real" war.[57] "Probably we editors will be too much engaged in the work of the campaign to pay attention to Woman's Rights the subject deserves," explained the Norton *Liberator,* "the attention of the Populist editors being directed to the maintenance of what few rights we now have."[58] Populist newspapers had a duty to support the suffrage cause, both because it was in the platform and because the Populists were supposedly a party that eschewed the amoral politics of the G.O.P. But as the *Liberator* explained, the Populist Party was principally concerned with issues of economic justice.

Slighting social issues, even ones that a majority of the membership supported, was nothing new for Populists. In 1890 the party had resisted Republican efforts to bait it with the prohibition issue despite farm people's overwhelming support for the cause. Similarly, the 1892 national Populist Party convention, with its large Kansas contingent, had suppressed an attempt to place woman suffrage in its platform. Populist editors reasoned that woman suffrage was not the issue that would bring swing voters into the Populist camp. Hence they stuck to the issues of "land, money, and transportation," leaving woman suffrage to the WPPL and the *Farmer's Wife.*

Populist leaders' attitudes toward woman suffrage shifted as the political context changed. The Populist convention had passed the suffrage plank under extremely favorable circumstances. Mid-roaders were determined to use the issue to sidetrack the fusionists. Whereas Anthony had been a hindrance to the suffragists' cause at the G.O.P. convention, her offer to campaign for the Populists had electrified the convention. Prosuffrage forces included far more Populist stars—including Frank Doster, John Otis, Ben Henderson, Annie Diggs, and Mary Lease—than the fusionists had. Finally, the suffragists' appeals to delegates' sense of morality had worked well at the emotionally charged convention. During the fall campaign, however, these conditions were either irrelevant or invisible to Populist editors. They accepted or ignored the amendment according to its perceived usefulness at the time.

Populist editors, like their Republican counterparts, had demonstrated their support for suffrage in the past. No doubt they continued to support the amendment, but in private. The *Liberator's* justification sounds very much like a kinder, gentler version of Hudson's postconvention statements. For most liberal Republican politicians, such a conclusion was in keeping with their basic political ideology: that without economic progress, moral progress was impossible. Before issues such as woman suffrage could even be considered, the Populists had to be defeated and the state returned to sound business principles. The Populist leadership had to work a little harder to justify ignoring the amendment, but the results were largely the same. With all the deep divisions between Populist and Republican editors, they had at last found common ground—the shared assumption that the cause of woman suffrage must be sacrificed to the demands of partisan politics.

## The Last Battle: The Populist Party
## and the Alliance in the Fall Campaign

Populist editors had good reason to fear any issue that might lose votes. As the fall campaign began, the Populist Party was in the process of disintegrating. Republican politicians and editors had pulled out all the stops in their effort to redeem Kansas, committing nearly every kind of fraud and dirty trick available. These tactics included inventing damaging "interviews" with prominent Populists, and paying Populists to declare publicly for the Republicans and denounce their own party.[59] The Republican disinformation campaign merely exacerbated the Populists' problems, however. Most of the G.O.P.'s basic material was provided by the Populists themselves.

Fusion lay at the root of most Populist problems, for while mid-roaders had won the battle for the woman suffrage plank, they had essentially lost the convention war. The 1894 ticket replicated the 1892 fusion arrangement, except that the new slate replaced two Republicans with Democrats. Despite this extra bait dangled in front of the Democrats, the Populists' erstwhile partners refused to bite. "Stalwarts," headed by David Overmeyer, now controlled the Democratic Party; they wanted no part of the Populists' "socialistic schemes." "Democrats today in Kansas," proclaimed the *Wichita Beacon*, "do not believe in paternalism. They are not greenbackers. They oppose every form of government aid."[60]

Nor had Democrats waited for the Populist convention to repudiate fusion; party bosses had made their sentiments known early on. Just to make sure their intentions were clear, however, the Democratic convention countered the Populists, declaring, "We oppose woman suffrage as tending to destroy the home and the family, the true basis of political safety, and express hope that the helpmeet and guardian of the family sanctuary may not be dragged from the modest purity of self-imposed seclusion to be thrown unwillingly into the unfeminine place of political strife."[61] The rest of the platform was in the same vein of curmudgeonly conservatism.

Although Democratic bosses rejected fusion, local Democrats, with the aid of the Briedenthal machine, were still able to make a few "arrangements" with Populists. The Populists had a fusionist state ticket and some fusionist congressional nominees but no official support from the Democrats.[62] The Populist Party thus alienated mid-roaders and Republican-Populists while gaining few benefits for the party.

Radical antifusionists, led by Cyrus Corning's *New Era,* began a campaign that directed its fire not against the G.O.P. but against the Lewelling administration. Radical antifusionists justified their tactics by claiming that Populist fusionists had committed treason against the true reform movement. Through the *New Era* and other papers, antifusionists urged the rejection of the Populist ticket because "defeat . . . is the only thing that will open the eyes of an honest membership and cause them to rise as men and patriots and rescue the principles of the party from the hands of incompetents and traitors."[63] Whereas once, farmers could redeem their manhood through voting the Populist ticket, antifusionists now argued that redemption could come only by cleansing the party's soul.

Several radical antifusionists made good their threats against the Populists by deserting the party amid maximum publicity. Ben Henderson wrote a widely published letter repudiating the Lewelling administration. Ben Clover, a former Populist congressman and Farmers' Alliance president, published a similar letter charging that Populism no longer adhered to the ideals of 1890. John Willits, still an officer of the National Farmers' Alliance, similarly abandoned the party. All rejoined the Republican Party, whose press, of course, gave these events front-page treatment. Populists charged that the defectors had sold out for positions in the G.O.P.[64] Whether such charges were true or not, the mass exile of so many early heros of Populism clearly damaged the party.

Mary Lease, never shy about placing herself in the spotlight, created the biggest stir. She had an almost pathological hatred of Democrats, two brothers and her father having been killed by "the rebels." Following the election of U.S. Sen. John Martin, Lease had declared, "I respect and esteem Mr. Martin as a man, as a lawyer and as a gentleman . . . but he is a Democrat, and you know I HATE DEMOCRATS. I AM DONE WITH DEMOCRATS AND FUSION."[65] Governor Lewelling, perhaps hoping to regain her allegiance, appointed Lease to the Board of Charities. When she increased her attacks on fusionists in general and Lewelling in particular, he dismissed her.

Lewelling's reaction was not unlike tossing cold water on very hot oil. Lease sued the governor for wrongful discharge and made ever wilder accusations. Indeed, her actions and statements were fast crossing the threshold of mental stability. At one point she claimed that Lewelling tried to blackmail her by threatening to spread a rumor that she had slept with James B. Weaver, the

245

1892 Populist presidential candidate. One Populist official retorted, "I am no longer surprised at anything she says. The woman is crazy. Her reference to the supposed story about J. B. Weaver and herself is new to me and new to everybody at the statehouse." He then added, demonstrating both the Lewelling administration's hardball tactics and Lease's vulnerability as a woman, "If she wants to advertise her own shame that's her business, not ours. The story I heard about Mrs. Lease does not drag in the name of Weaver."[66]

Despite all this mud being splattered, Lease continued to campaign for the Populists. Her appearances caused more damage than benefit, however, as she praised Populism in general while slighting the Lewelling administration. Her political vertigo sent her crashing about the state, causing confusion wherever she went. Eventually she found herself attacking the woman who had been paired with her during that fateful summer of 1890, so very long ago.

On July 12, at a rally featuring the Colorado Populist Governor Waite, she faced off against Annie Diggs in a confrontation the *State Journal* billed as "TWO WOMEN AT WAR."[67] It was an ironic counterpoint to the *Farmer's Wife*'s declaration of a women's war twenty months before. After Waite's speech, the crowd called for Diggs to speak. Diggs began by taking up a collection for striking Pullman railroad car workers and praising the suffrage amendment and "that good man, Gov. Lewelling." She then noted, "People who opposed him and fought him bitterly were traitors to the cause and unworthy to be called Populists, but they are now in line again." She then continued about the railroad conditions. Diggs had fired the first volley at Lease but probably expected the matter to end there. Lease had not been invited to speak, but as the *Journal* reported, "she had come to talk and no man on the committee was big enough to stop her." Once again, Lease was gleefully defying convention. Yet this time, while the crowd was "spellbound," it was also "dumbfounded, astonished out of utterance, and amazed at Mrs. Lease's attack."

"I am glad that certain individuals are now . . . praising the administration," stated Lease, "who one short year ago knew nothing outside of one little ism—prohibition—who called me an anarchist, and who telegraphed over the country that the governor was a traitor." As there was nothing remotely truthful in Lease's claim, Diggs "walked calmly to the front of the platform . . . and said, 'That is false. Please take it back.'" But as the *State Journal* reported, "Mrs. Lease was not there to take anything back. Looking straight over the little woman's head, she waved her arms and swung her body and declared in her deep orotund, 'I believe I have the floor for a few moments.'" Diggs opted for a tactical retreat: announcing, "It's a lie all the same," she took her place on the platform. "I almost got myself into it," she confided to friends who came to offer support.

Lease was far from finished. After a voice from the crowd shouted, "Please keep from personalities then," Lease responded, "Those people who said that Mrs. Lease would not talk to the people of Kansas here today have found out their mistake, and will find out if they attempt to stop me that they will have a bigger war on their hands than Pullman has." After speaking of national politics for a time while studiously avoiding mention of the Kansas Populist ticket, she suddenly interjected: "This is no time for personal wrangling. This is no time for one woman who calls herself a reformer and claims to be working for the party's good to stand upon a platform and brand another as a liar." Asked if she had joined the Prohibitionist Party, she replied, "I wish we could prohibit narrow minded, weak brained women who called themselves reformers from running at large to call other women liars." After the speech, Lease was asked about the alleged telegram sent by Diggs, and responded, "I did not say it was Mrs. Diggs. If the coat fits her, let her put it on. She admits it doesn't she in taking it upon herself."[68]

Lease's performance naturally made the front page of Republican dailies. For Populists, it was a cruel reversal of the summer of 1890, when so much seemed possible. Now the farmers' "Queen Mary" was aiming her oratorical missiles not at the Money Power but at their beloved "Little Annie." As the antifusionist but pro-Lewelling *Barton Beacon* had noted earlier in the year: "If Mrs. Lease would spend more of her valuable powers against public enemies and less time against the Populist administration she would be doing better work for the cause of humanity in these poverty stricken days. She seems to be working more for herself than for all other purposes combined."[69] Lease had been instrumental in converting the self-confidence that farm people had gained in the Alliance into a belief that they could control state politics. If she helped build a boom mentality that sent Populism's fate skyrocketing, she also contributed to shaking the confidence necessary to maintain the movement.

Lease's wild attack lent credence to her critics' claims that she had indeed gone crazy. In fact, most prominent antifusionists in general exhibited either rabid zealotry or a talent for chicanery. Their tactics tended toward the destructive rather than the constructive; they themselves had largely lost faith in the Populist mission. Yet whatever their personal and tactical failings, their claims against the Lewelling administration and Briedenthal's central committee were largely valid. Besides the Sen. Martin fiasco and the election of other "straight Democrats" to Populist positions, the Lewelling administration had been mired in scandal. Lewelling had granted Democrats patronage jobs in exchange for their party's support in 1892. Many of these cared far less about purifying politics than about lining their own pockets with the spoils of office, further discrediting the Populist administration.[70]

Populists were also saddled with the old problem of accomplishing reform without complete control of all branches of state government. With the House in Republican hands, Populists were still unable to pass significant legislation, accomplishing little even as the depression, now national in scope, grew more severe. President Grover Cleveland, a Democrat, had made things worse for Kansas farmers by demonetizing silver. Although Cleveland hoped to restore confidence in the gold standard, his monetary policy served only to tighten credit. Cleveland had been elected in part because G.O.P. states such as Kansas had supported the Populist ticket. Republicans pinned much of the blame for the Cleveland administration's policies on the Populists and urged ex-Republicans not to make this mistake twice.[71]

The ongoing Populist scandals and ineffectiveness were taking their toll on the Farmers' Alliance. As Alliance members lost faith in the Populist Party, they found themselves with no political alternatives. The *Alliant* asked, "What about the Alliance? Is it dead, or is it only sleeping?" The answer depended on where one looked. By 1893 the Alliance was effectively gone from a number of counties, yet some suballiances continued to undergo revival campaigns, sending out evangelists to renew farm people's faith. In Barton County, local suballiances reported increases in membership, and several new alliances were formed.[72] In Cloud County, home of the *Alliant,* the county alliance answered the paper's query on its health by stating, "[We] are certain that this noble order is alive and kicking" and cited increased membership as proof. Yet many of the alliances were concerning themselves less with politics and the Populist Party and more with general questions of agricultural reform and farming practices.

Even as evidence surfaced that the Alliance was still active, the organization's presence shrank in the newspapers. Even the most supportive papers began to delete Alliance columns and directories, despite the fact that its correspondents continued to write to the paper.[73] While members fought to resurrect their cause, the newspapers that had played such a prominent role as the organization's voice abandoned it. Instead the papers looked to the electoral campaign, hoping to salvage something from the constant setbacks confronting the Populists.

Although Farmers' Alliance women were ever more evident as local officers, they were writing far fewer letters to newspapers by 1894. Even the suffrage amendment did not generate much correspondence, in part because most local alliances did not discuss the issue; perhaps they assumed that there was general agreement among members in favor of it. Indeed, one of the few debates among correspondents was initiated by an antisuffragist Alliance man who encouraged responses to his argument. Apparently uncomfortable with challenging the Alliance's unofficial support for woman suffrage, he asserted, "I am a full-fledged hayseed." Eppie Winter, a prominent Alliance correspondent, replied, "My friend, you are not a full fledged hayseed or you would not need the woman suffrage question agitated."[74] Over the next month, there followed a lively discussion among a number of writers, most of whom supported the amendment. The election would prove to what degree Alliance men needed to hear the "suffrage question agitated."

Eppie Winter was not alone in believing that "true hayseeds" would vote for the amendment. The *Farmer's Wife* agreed, arguing that farm women "are almost unanimously in favor of their enfranchisement. . . . The country is all right, and when we say that we make no idle boast. The *Farmer's Wife* is in close communication with these sisters and knows how their men will vote." Because of this knowledge, the paper felt confident in urging suffragists: "Look after the votes in the towns and cities. . . . Give your attention almost wholly to the city people. . . . [Even then], the farming vote will far exceed that of the cities and towns."[75] Yet just before these statements, the *Farmer's Wife* was promising a "school-house campaign" that would be more thorough than that of the Farmers' Alliance in 1890.

As things turned out, suffragists apparently followed their plan to concentrate on the urban areas. Although Laura Johns once again urged a schoolhouse meeting in every voting district, suffragists did not initiate an official campaign to organize farm folk. A few women activists proved notable exceptions. Frances Butler continued her work among farm people, urging "sisters of the Alliance" to wear and distribute yellow ribbons to willing Alliance men. She often visited suballiance meetings and "talked suffrage" among the farm people. Other times, she organized nonpartisan country meetings with her carriage mate, Mrs. Denton.[76] Rachel Childs, the state lecturer of the Iowa Equal Suffrage Association, also seems to have been committed to organizing "country clubs." Beyond these individual efforts, however, suffragists did "leave the country alone." Much would depend, then, on whether the country really was "all right."

As suffragists approached Election Day, they believed they had done all that was possible. Despite the many obstacles that activists faced during the campaign, their optimism seemed to grow stronger as November 6th—Election

Day—approached. With no opinion polls available, the women could rely only on the impressions they received while organizing and campaigning. All the suffrage newspapers seemed absolutely confident of victory and looked forward to celebrating what was expected to be the second "Great Suffrage Convention" in December. Leaders of the Woman Movement had given hundreds of speeches, traveled thousands of miles, and spoken to hundreds of thousands of people. They had exhorted cheering crowds, challenged skeptics, and through it all had proven that women could organize a massive political campaign. Further, they had managed to maintain their political sisterhood despite enormous provocations and temptations from all sides. Surely, they believed, politics in Kansas would be redeemed at last.

## A KANSAS RECESSIONAL

Several days after the election, Kansans awoke to find their state's politics had undergone yet another upheaval.[77] Unlike that of 1890, however, this political earthquake had restored the shaken foundations of the status quo. Republicans had redeemed Kansas in no uncertain terms, gaining control of the statehouse, the lower house of the legislature, and all but one congressional seat. They had garnered over 148,000 votes (51%), to the Populists' 115,000 (38%). The woman suffrage amendment suffered an equally devastating defeat, 139,000 to 95,000; suffragists would have had to search their newspapers to find this information among the mass of stories concerning the party elections—few papers even recorded the results.[78]

Kansas voters, like the newspapers, were more concerned with party politics than woman suffrage. One-quarter of the electorate ignored the amendment question entirely. A Populist paper suggested that voters had failed to notice the amendment because of its position at the bottom of the ballot, although this had never caused problems before.[79] More to the point, the amendment's place at the bottom of the ticket represented the priorities of many voters in the election.

Some Republicans—and a few historians—claimed that the Populists lost because of the woman suffrage plank in their platform. A more likely analysis is that voters rejected the Populists because of their past fusion efforts, legislative ineffectiveness, the ever worsening depression, and administrative corruption, aided by additional Republican smears.[80] If the suffrage amendment had a hand in the Populists' defeat, it joined a long line of causes.

Some suffrage activists pointed to "party endorsements" as the primary reason for the amendment's overwhelming defeat.[81] However, the endorsement strategy might have worked if both Populists and Republicans had included a suffrage plank. The suffragists' mistake was not in appealing to the parties but in attempting to gain the support of one party after failing with the other. The contradictions between the movement's nonpartisan local and partisan state strategy, between its vision of political sisterhood and quest for political power and legitimacy, had been laid bare.

Had the Kansas suffrage campaign taken place in 1892 instead of two years later, perhaps the outcome would have been different. Sarah Thurston was able to tabulate the returns from 71 of 105 counties. Her figures, while not official, do suggest some intriguing conclusions concerning voting behavior and partisan concerns. Thurston calculated that of those who voted on the amendment, 14 percent of the Democrats, 38.5 percent of the Republicans, 54 percent of the Populists, and 80 percent of the Prohibitionists voted yes.[82] Apparently, the numerous Republican editors and politicians who had denounced the amendment as a Populist measure had demonstrated their influence at the polling booth. Had the Republican Party endorsed woman suffrage and had the Democrats at least refrained from denouncing it, the amendment would have gained considerable support. A year earlier in Colorado all three parties had supported the suffrage amendment and it had passed easily.

The endorsement strategy of Kansas suffragists does not explain away the lopsided vote. The average Kansas voter in 1894 did not hold a particularly optimistic opinion about promises to purify politics. That talk had been largely discredited by the legislative war and the Populists' fusion experiments. Each party, when in power, had proven itself equally capable of corruption and incompetence. Little wonder, then, that not a few Kansas men decided that woman suffrage was simply not worth the risk of upsetting politics any further. Municipal woman suffrage had been passed when change meant economic progress, moral reform, expansion, and optimism; state suffrage was defeated when voters equated change with economic depression, political disillusionment, and political anarchy.

Suffragists had ridiculed men's "objections" to woman suffrage on the grounds that worries about domestic harmony and who would rock the baby were completely unfounded. These objections were not merely chimerical, however. They represented men's worst fears about the basic relations between women and men. Women had tried to assuage these fears by insisting that municipal suffrage had not compromised their "womanliness," a code word meant to connote that domestic arrangements would stay the same. But the election votes show that many men simply were not ready to give women an equal political voice.

There was a political as well as a cultural component to men's uncertainty about woman suffrage. Both Republicans and Populists had expressed concern that women did not vote as men expected them to. Many Republicans based their objections to the amendment on the fear that grateful women would support the Populists if the amendment passed. The Woman Movement's nonpartisan approach to municipal elections should have lessened the G.O.P.'s fears on that score. Republican leaders wanted it both ways, however; they criticized women activists if their nonpartisanship meant abandoning Republican candidates who did not measure up to the Woman Movement's high moral standards. Essentially, the G.O.P. leadership was opposed to any strategy, partisan or nonpartisan, which challenged Republican officeholders. Populist papers, meanwhile, had commented disparagingly on women's likelihood of voting Republican in city elections, claiming that women owed their allegiance to Republicans because they had passed the municipal woman suffrage bill.

Men of all parties wondered what would happen if enfranchised, nonpartisan women entered men's political culture. Annie Diggs, writing six years after the amendment's defeat, observed: "Politicians have been annoyed by interference with their schemes. Men have learned that women command influence in politics, and the party machine has become hostile to further extension of woman's opportunity and power to demand cleaner morals and nobler standards."[83] The Woman Movement's very success at maintaining a political sisterhood may have contributed to its defeat.

Men's assumptions and Republican policy assured that suffragists would face an uphill battle for the amendment. Yet suffragists added to their troubles by concentrating their campaign on the urban Anglo middle class. Perhaps the greatest mistake was in ignoring farm women and men. The relatively low Populist vote for the amendment belies the *Farmer's Wife*'s assumption that "the country is all right." The country was in fact very much in need of some active organizing. Had suffragists made the effort, they could have connected with the many Farmers' Alliance women who had demonstrated their passion for political participation. Further, suffragists might have been able to confront farm men's hidden doubts that lay buried beneath the Alliance's official endorsement of the issue.

The 1893 Colorado campaign again provides a telling comparison. Colorado suffragists reached out to working-class women, employing many as organizers, and enlisted the services of Leonora Barry, the Knights of Labor general investigator for women's work. The Woman Movement was also fortunate to connect with a strong union and socialist movement in Colorado, both of which had previously shown support for woman suffrage. Organized labor in Kansas, by comparison, was much weaker, and a viable socialist movement was still several years away. Colorado suffragists had proven that it was possible to transcend cultural barriers, at least for the duration of the campaign, and be well rewarded for their efforts.[84] When one includes the other groups of women and men left out of the Kansas suffragists' strategy—blacks, Catholic immigrants, and the working class—then the "Grand Suffrage Campaign," impressive as it was in miles covered, appears much narrower in scope.

However the suffrage activists' endorsement strategy may have influenced the vote on the amendment, their partisan activity had a far more devastating effect on their movement. After the November election, the *Farmer's Wife* folded without so much as a parting message. One participant later wrote, "No one except those who have gone through with [the amendment campaign] can realize the bitter, cruel and humiliating disappointment endured by the women workers of the day." Laura Johns, using language similar to a mother who has lost a child, confided to a friend, "I have mourned and mourned and mourned, and I don't deny that I am almost heart broken. I didn't believe this could come. . . . Every morning I wake with a sense of a burden of disappointment and grey missing." Johns recollected of the progress made during the summer. "You should have seen my big meetings," wrote Johns, wistfully recalling the summer campaign. "Such crowds and enthusiasm."[85] This sense of loss and betrayal pervaded suffragists' involvement with state politics for many years to come.

In December, suffragists' frustration and past rivalries transformed the second "Great Suffrage Convention" into a vicious struggle. The *Kansas City Times* gleefully proclaimed, "The women KNOW IT ALL—Kansas Equal Suffragists Lobby Like Old Politicians," and in many ways the convention did resemble those of the male political culture. There were bitter floor fights, parliamentary maneuvers, and free-swinging accusations. The *Times* reported that delegates "watch every move of the enemy with distrust and imagine all sorts of deep schemes are being laid," and tut-tutted that some women delegates "started the pernicious habit of calling each other by their last names."[86] To suffrage opponents, the convention was proof that political activity inevitably unsexed women.

The main struggle at the convention was Johns's renomination, which was opposed by an alliance of certain Populists, Democrats, and nonpartisan radicals. The delegates also battled over whether KESA should work for resubmission of the amendment, which Johns opposed. She was well aware of the plans of the dissident faction, led by the WPPL's Eva Harding, Alma Stryker, and Bina Otis. "I am informed that the Topeka tomahawks are after my scalp," Johns wrote Lucy Johnston, a Republican activist in the Woman Movement, alluding to the core of WPPL members who opposed Johns.[87] To counter the dissidents, Johns got the Winfield Equal Suffrage Association to host the convention, because "We have no other invitation except Topeka and I don't want to go *there*. . . . They are always in a squabble there, and they'll get up a row as sure as the world if we go there, and then we—the state organization—will get the credit of it. . . . I simply have a horror of that sort of thing." Despite her efforts, the convention proved the undoing of the Kansas Woman Movement.

Johns had in fact planned to step down after the amendment's defeat. She wrote Johnston, however, that while she did not want to lead KESA, she was determined to stop the Populist suffragists' reported plan to install Mary Lease as president. Since Lease had by this time discredited herself with most Populists—it would certainly be difficult to imagine Annie Diggs accepting Lease's nomination—Johns may have been reacting more to rumor than to reality. The following year, Johns indicated that there had been more than politics at stake: there had been personal pride as well. In July 1895, Johns wrote Johnston: "I need to be *free*. My health is far from robust. I didn't get strong, and I wish to lay down this burden. I am sorry I didn't do so last year, but I thought that I couldn't afford to permit Dr. Harding to *kick* me out after my years of hard work to build up that organization."[88]

Johns eventually won re-election, but the constant battles shattered the movement. Almost all the women who attended the convention were demoralized and angry with one or another faction. At one point the dissidents bolted the assembly hall and recaucused elsewhere. Harding claimed that Johns had "packed the convention" with her own supporters, thus making a fair election impossible. Johns protested against "the base suspicions and preposterous charges with which the air is filled," but the dissidents continued their attacks after the convention. Several weeks later, Otis wrote in the *Advocate*: "[Johns], who is a Republican first and a suffragist second, had practiced some sharp trickery, by issuing a circular admitting new members to vote on payment of a dollar, and thus she was able to pack the convention. All this was as the Republican politicians wanted it and the real friends of suffrage did not want it."[89] Otis's reference to "real suffragists" recalls her earlier attempts to discredit Johns. As in the past, Otis and other WPPL activists were positioning themselves to gain control of the suffrage movement. By pushing for the resubmission of the suffrage amendment over Johns's objections, the Populist women could appear to be taking the lead from the overly timid KESA president.

Johns and other suffragists' objection to resubmission arose from their belief that Kansans—both women and men—had proved themselves unready for woman suffrage. "It amuses me to see the women sitting here clapping their hands when resubmission is recommended," wrote one who had been active in the previous campaign. "It costs too much . . . money and sacrifice. I believe we had better go home and educate, agitate, and organize." S. A. Thurston reported that the election had cost the state over ten thousand dollars and that the legislature would balk at spending that kind of money so soon after the amendment's resounding defeat. Lucy Johnston noted that legislators would not be very likely to vote for resubmission if their districts had voted against the amendment, as the majority had.

In reflecting on her reasons for opposing resubmission, Johns admitted to a startling conversion. The amendment's overwhelming defeat had caused her to reflect on the basic contradiction of all-partisan nonpartisanship. "I do not doubt that I will shock you," she told the convention, "that I wish the women of this State and of all other States would enlist under one political banner, and in such organizations study the history and philosophy of political parties and learn practical politics. Permit me to say that suffrage associations do not make women into suffragists half as fast as political organizations do."[90] Women needed to create their own political party, Johns argued, if they hoped to establish a lasting political presence. Such a suggestion had little appeal to most in the Woman Movement since it would have meant abandoning one-half of their political identity. It does suggest that Johns had at least come to accept the validity of the radical antipartisans' arguments against involvement in "men's" parties.

WPPL members had learned no such lesson. Indeed, Stryker even proposed that KESA endorse the Populists for two years if the party promised to promote the suffrage cause actively. Given the political climate and the exhaustion of suffrage workers, the dissidents' resubmissionist strategy seems politically naïve at best. But the dissidents were less concerned with winning another amendment drive than with attempting to embarrass the Republican Party. Eva Harding argued at the convention that "she would like to be spared the time and expense of another campaign, but she wanted the Republicans put on record as doing one thing or another."[91] Because the WPPL activists seemed again more concerned with advancing their own organization's agenda over that of KESA, their claim to being "the real friends of suffrage" rang hollow.

Susan B. Anthony had similarly shown that she had another agenda besides winning state suffrage for Kansas, and this resurfaced after the election. In a pamphlet that lambasted the Kansas Republican Party and the Republican Women's Association, Anthony used the Kansas election to prove the futility of state suffrage campaigns. Upon reading Anthony's "Topeka Resolutions," Johns asked Johnston, "Weren't you *sorry?*" "I could have *cried.*" The Kansas historian Elizabeth Barr perhaps put it best: Anthony had "forgotten the 'Kansas language.' "[92]

Others took Anthony's criticisms with less sorrow and more anger. Helen Kimber, one of KESA's rising stars in 1894, had opposed Anthony's habit of lambasting the Republicans during the amendment campaign. Six years later, she wrote to Alice Stone Blackwell: "The truth is Mrs. Anthony, Mrs. [Rachel] Avery and Mrs. [Anna] Shaw are fighting Mrs. Catt like they fought Mrs. Johns, and they are still fighting me because of what I said in '94. . . . I am not sorry for a word I said in '94, I only wish I could have said it strong enough and in time to have prevented the disaster."[93] Kimber's exact words to Anthony in 1894 have not been preserved. However, her retort in 1900—"I'll bet you I'll sit on Anna Shaw until she won't want to be resurrected. . . . You watch in the paper for four bloody nosed women!!!"—gives some idea of the tenor of her remarks.

A decade and a half after the 1894 debacle, Kansas suffragists had still not forgotten their disagreements with Eastern suffrage leaders. Johns, writing from California, advised Kansans to avoid using speakers or donations from the national office for the 1911 amendment campaign. She also noted that, since Western women had been far more successful than Easterners in gaining suffrage, the latter should heed the advice of their more effective sisters.[94] Johns even blamed many of the troubles of the 1894 campaign on Anthony and Shaw. Lila D. Monroe, president of KESA in 1911, agreed with Johns and turned down the national organization's offer of assistance. This declaration of independence was yet another lesson learned from the 1894 campaign. The price of such knowledge was high, however.

KESA suffered a dramatic loss of faith following the twin blows of overwhelming defeat and internal dissension. Even those who remained in the organization demonstrated nothing like the spirit of the 1887–94 period. The 1895 convention drew only a fraction of the previous year's delegates, and the number continued to decrease steadily. The organization did not fully recover until many years later. Kansas suffragists returned as a political force in state politics only after Carrie Chapman Catt revived the state-by-state strategy and the KESA leadership gained a new generation of leaders. By that time, the new century was ten years old, and the term *Woman Movement* had given way to *feminism.*[95] The "vast army of women" did not "drown" the dominant male political culture in 1894. Instead, Woman Movement activists were themselves caught up in mainstream politics and overwhelmed by it.

One week after the 1894 election, Republicans staged an elaborate funeral parade that celebrated the death of Populism. Marching, cheering, and singing through the streets of Topeka, G.O.P. supporters believed their party's decisive electoral victory had provided a sudden death blow to the Populist Party. The Republican celebrants were wrong on at least two counts. The Populist Party, after fusing with the Democrats in 1896, would again control state politics for several years. But it had become a very different party from the one that arose suddenly in the heady summer of 1890. The new version was a practical, business-oriented organization. Although positioning itself to the left of the conservative administration of Republican Governor Morrill, it eschewed the radical ideology and democratic politics that Populists had inherited from the Farmers' Alliance. Populism had not been suddenly transformed by the 1894 election, however. The roots of the Populists' demise went much deeper than that one event.[96]

While most Populist Party leaders abandoned the Farmers' Alliance's principles after 1894, so too did the Alliance finally abandon the Populist Party. The Alliance made no official announcement of this policy; suballiances simply stopped talking about the Populist Party. In fact, there was much less talk about politics in general at Alliance meetings. Instead, discussion topics concentrated on issues such as cooperative ventures and agricultural problems.[97] The Alliance's shift in focus was the natural outcome of its determination to support the Populist Party only so long as the party remained true to its "first principles." After 1894, it was obvious that it had not.

Remarkably, a number of alliances continued to thrive for several years. Barton County listed six active suballiances in 1896. The *Advocate* reported on the organization's ongoing activities throughout 1895 in its "Alliance Column." However, after Stephen McLallin quit the editorship at the end of the year, the column did not reappear. In general, fewer and fewer Populist newspapers carried news about the Alliance, even though proof of its existence continued to appear.[98] Populist papers were themselves disappearing, as their readers lost faith in the movement.

The Populist Party was now different from the two old parties in name only; its structure and approach to politics were nearly indistinguishable. In 1896, the Populists fused at both the state and the national levels with the Democrats. Delegates abandoned the Omaha Platform in exchange for a single plank promising that the remonetization of silver would cure all the country's ills. After the new Kansas Populist-Democrat governor, John Leedy, gave his inauguration speech, the *Capital* noted, "The address of the new Governor was well chosen in words and sentiment, and met the approval of his audience without regard to political affiliation."[99] William Allen White provided perhaps the best epitaph for his old nemesis when he surveyed the Populist leadership and observed:

> There is nothing of the old Alliance Puritan cry for reform in these men. Has not the whole fabric of the reform party, its heros, its aspirations, its ambitions, its lofty desires fallen among thieves on the Jericho Road? Where is the Alliance man with the courage to deny that his party that was going to reform the world has made a "deal" that would have been hissed out of the first farmers convention in the year of our Lord 1890?[100]

White had not mentioned Alliance women, but then they had not been much in evidence at the 1890 Populist convention. Instead, they had populated the picnics, rallies, and meetings, bringing with them a perspective that had helped create the Alliance's mixed-gender political culture. By 1895, however, Alliance women were no longer a visible presence. Although the number of women officers in the State Farmers' Alliance continued to increase—by 1895 there were four—suballiances were no longer encouraging women to join, nor were they featuring women as speakers.

One exception, the Sherman Alliance, proved the rule. After noting that his suballiance had gone from twenty-two to forty-eight members because of the addition of "ladies and young people," the correspondent advised, "Is your sub-alliance dead? Is the attendance light and little interest manifested? Take your wives to the next meeting and ask their advice about what to do. Take an interest in getting the ladies interested in the meetings and within a month your school house will not hold the people who will come to your meetings."[101] Apparently, Emma Troudner had been correct in warning that women would leave the Alliance if ignored by men. Recognizing this, the Sherman Alliance correspondent encouraged Alliance men not only to "take your wives to the meeting" but to listen to them as well. Only then would the Alliance community be made whole again. Without women's participation, the Alliance goal of creating a political culture based on the farm family was doomed.

The WPPL similarly slipped out of the public eye. Although individual women probably continued to work for the Populists, urban women no longer maintained an organized presence within the party. Indeed, with the new fusion arrangements, women's participation was becoming an embarrassment to Populist leaders. In 1900, when Annie Diggs proposed organizing farm women to rekindle the spirit of the "old Alliance victories," the Democrats protested and the Populists bowed to their wishes.[102] One Democrat explained his party's reaction by noting, "Germans . . . abhor petticoat politics." While German men might have objected, the Democratic leaders themselves resented Diggs's influence among the Populists. The Democrats grudgingly admitted her ability but complained about the indignity of "a great party being whipped by a small woman."

That Diggs could have retained her influence for so long and in such adverse conditions attests to her skill in negotiating the cultural constraints imposed on her as a woman. Her achievements are also a testament to the Woman Movement and the Farmers' Alliance. Their efforts to legitimize women's political participation had made Diggs's political ascent possible, while enabling thousands of women and men to become engaged and informed citizens. If activists had failed in their immediate goals, they had for a number of years given their lives new meaning through their political participation.

Looking back at the Populist movement in 1906, Diggs wrote, "For the first time in the life of the great republic, there was a political organization which grappled directly and fundamentally with the growing injustice which marked the dealings between Exploiters and the Exploited in the realm of industrialism."[103] Diggs valued the movement not so much for its accomplishments as for its attempt to transform a nation that had been structured to resist fundamental change. For Diggs, victory was always dreamed of, but fighting the good fight was what made life worthwhile.

# Conclusion

## THE BOUNDARIES OF CULTURE

In 1889, as organizers from the Southern Farmers' Alliance moved in earnest into Kansas, few could have predicted the outcome of their efforts seven years later. The same may be said of the Woman Movement as it stood proudly triumphant in 1887. Both movements were operating within particular cultures, framed by a larger national culture that dictated certain constraints. Within these boundaries, Kansas reformers faced a series of difficult choices that were not always readily apparent to them. Reformers' ideas about gender shaped their day-to-day actions, ideas, speeches, and writings. But because so much of gender discourse appeared to be "common sense" and unremarkable, activists had difficulty negotiating its ever shifting meanings. Once these gendered assumptions were put into play, few understood how they would affect Kansas politics.

Because reformers drew on the cultural resources at hand, their use of gendered discourse made particular sense to their core constituencies. Middle-class women readily embraced the Woman Movement's idealized vision of a monolithic, morally superior political sisterhood that would transform male political culture; farm people flocked to the Alliance's call for a nonpartisan, moralistic "family" that would challenge the urban moneyed elite. Both movements believed they could redeem the soul of the Republic and bring about the political and moral millennium.

But once activists moved beyond their own subcultures, they had difficulty adjusting to the new contexts and the new meanings. Woman Movement leaders struggled to balance notions of respectability with the need for inclusiveness. Alliance members failed to understand the contradiction between the ideal of the egalitarian political family and the reality of gender relations in the farm family. Both challenged male notions about party politics only to find that their need to attain power overwhelmed their nonpartisan stance. Even Republican leaders could not be sure of the effect of labeling Mary Lease a "man-wife" or Alliance men "hayseeds."

The story of the Woman Movement activists, Populists, and Republican leaders suggests that understanding the way gender operates in politics is much easier in hindsight. Gender discourse, dynamic, ever shifting, and yet superficially immutable, was both a minefield of potential disasters and a treasure trove of possibilities. Political activists in Kansas, caught up in frenetic battles, had little time to survey carefully the cultural lands that lay before them before setting out. And even if they had had the time, the landscape would have changed by the time they arrived.

One need only look at today's political battles to appreciate the difficulties that Gilded Age activists faced. An update of the puzzle presented by Sen. Patty Murray's 1992 "Mom in Tennis Shoes" campaign, with which I began this study, suggests the slippery nature of the problem. Like the Woman Movement and the Populists, Murray struck a chord with her core constituencies by her canny use of gender discourse. By energizing liberal Democrats and moderate Republican women, she became the poster senator for the "Year of the Woman" media campaign, and pundits celebrated women's newly flexed political muscle.

When I wrote the introduction to this book in the summer of 1994, I noted that resurgent Republicans had brought issues of immigration, crime, and deficits to the foreground. By November the "Republican Revolution" had made the "Year of the Woman" seem a distant memory, as political strategists and pundits beat the drums about the newly resurgent "Angry White Male." The prototypical angry white male was, we were told, tired of affirmative action, gay rights, big government, and welfare cheats, all of which he believed were leading to stagnant wages and job insecurity. Right-wing talk radio, whose commentators and listeners were overwhelmingly White, Male, and Angry, became the masculinist cultural icon as well as an important organizational tool of the revolution. Women voters, particularly moderate white women, stayed away from the polls in record numbers. Political experts spoke sagely about the "Bubba factor," integrating the necessary class (working and lower-middle) and regional (Southern) signifiers into the mix of gender and race. The Democrats, many believed, were doomed unless they lured Bubba away from the G.O.P. They had, the experts diagnosed, a "gender gap problem."

It is now the autumn of 1996, and the gender gap is still around. Now, however, the experts are pinning the problem on the Republicans. The numbers have not changed much from those of 1994: the difference between women's and men's support of the Democrats and Republicans is still around 12 percent. What has changed is the context. For the past six months, Democrat Bill Clinton has enjoyed a double-digit lead over Republican Bob Dole in the presidential campaign. Suddenly the G.O.P. is desperate to solve their "woman problem" (no one seems overly concerned about Bubba at the moment). Republican leaders have been rethinking some policies that might win back moderate women voters, but they have spent more energy on symbolic gestures, such as the prominent display of prime-time prochoice women speakers at their nominating convention. But these "soccer moms" (to use the latest signifying label for the prototypical suburban white woman with a career, family, and minivan) may not be reacting as the G.O.P. strategists have planned. Antiabortion forces at the convention obliterated any language meant to assuage prochoice Republican women, while Dole nominated the former American Football League quarterback Jack Kemp to be his running mate. The two reveled in their use of football metaphors to the point of absurdity, helped along by the press, until Kemp's wife, Joann, reportedly put a stop to it.

How both men and women voters interpret these various mixed messages is, of course, anybody's guess. And as the context continues to shift, the messages from both the Democrats and Republicans (and Perot's Reform Party) will become ever more mixed, and prognostication ever more dicey. If Dole retakes the lead or the G.O.P. gains in Congress, will Democrats show a renewed concern for Bubba? Will professional women come to see Elizabeth Dole as a kinder, gentler version of Hillary Clinton and switch their loyalties?

By the time this book is published, some of these questions will be answered, but the larger issues about gender and politics will remain. The ever shifting cultural context, the deeply embedded quality of gender discourse, and the dynamic relationship between gender and politics ensures this. If the political activists of Kansas had a difficult time accurately perceiving their cultural boundaries, their modern-day equivalents do not seem to have a much better handle.

Those who care about politics today might do well to contemplate this humbling lesson. Even with the current hypersensitivity about gender, it remains, along with race and class, a deeply ingrained, somewhat mysterious, but highly effective part of our political discourse. We continue to draw on it as a resource, but it seems no more stable today than it did one hundred years ago. Washington Sen. Patty Murray's "Mom in Tennis Shoes" image worked brilliantly in 1992. How it plays out in 1998 will tell us a lot about how the cultural context of Washington and the nation has shifted and what has remained unchanged.

# NOTES

## INTRODUCTION: GENDER, POLITICS, AND POWER

1. *Time,* 16 November 1992; *New York Times,* 17 September 1992, 12 February 1993; *Wall Street Journal,* 23 August 1993.

2. *Newsweek,* 19 October 1987, p. 28.

3. For stylistic purposes, I refer throughout this book to the National Farmers' Alliance and Industrial Union as the National Farmers' Alliance.

4. All historiographical commentary may be found in the "Note on Historiography and Sources."

5. Scott G. McNall, *The Road to Rebellion: Class Formation and Kansas Populism, 1865–1900* (Chicago, 1988), 63.

6. Contrary to its detractors' claims, the *Light Bearer*'s editor asserted that the name referred not to the devil but to the paper's agnostic principles.

7. This phrase comes from journalist Elizabeth Barr's oft quoted description of the 1890 campaign. Elizabeth Barr, "The Populist Uprising," in William Connelly, ed., *History of Kansas* (New York, 1928), 2:1128.

8. Nancy F. Cott, *The Bonds of Womanhood: "Women's Sphere" in New England, 1780–1835* (New Haven, 1977), 2, argues that those who helped create these ideas were responding to public attitudes about gender. The ideas were developed

by a complex interaction between those with power and a specific agenda, and the beliefs of the general public.

9. Ibid., 8–9; Barbara Welter, "The Cult of True Womanhood," *American Quarterly* 18 (1966), 151–74.

10. Robert Griswold, "Anglo Women and Domestic Ideology in the American West in the Nineteenth and Twentieth Centuries," in Lillian Schlissel, Vicki Ruiz, and Janice Monk, eds., *Western Women* (Albuquerque, 1988), 15.

11. *Farmer's Wife*, November 1892.

12. *Industrial Free Press*, 10 November 1892.

13. *Farmer's Wife*, December 1893. Italics added.

14. Nancy F. Cott, *The Grounding of Modern Feminism* (New Haven, 1987), 3, 16–20; Mari Jo Buhle, *Women and American Socialism, 1870–1920* (Urbana, Ill., 1981), 49–94.

## CHAPTER ONE. MYTHS AND REALITIES: THE CULTURAL ORIGINS OF KANSAS POLITICS

1. Thomas R. Hietala, *Manifest Design: Anxious Aggrandizement in Late Jacksonian America* (Ithaca, N.Y., 1985); Richard Slotkin, *The Fatal Environment: The Myth of the Frontier in the Age of Industrialization, 1800–1890* (New York, 1985); Henry Nash Smith, *Virgin Land: The American West as Symbol and Myth* (Cambridge, Mass., 1970).

2. Glenda Riley, *The Female Frontier: A Comparative View of Women on the Prairie and the Plains* (Lawrence, Kans., 1988), 8–10.

3. As Patricia Limerick points out in *Legacy of Conquest* (New York, 1987), 323–24, this metaphor still holds a great deal of force.

4. Robert Johannson, "Stephen A. Douglas, Harper's Magazine, and Popular Sovereignty," *Mississippi Valley History Review* 45 (March 1959); Roy F. Nichols, "The Kansas-Nebraska Act: A Century of Historiography," *Mississippi Valley Historical Review* 43 (September 1956).

5. Kenneth A. Davis, *Kansas* (New York, 1984), 37–41.

6. Although New Englanders were not numerous, they founded Topeka and Lawrence, soon to be the site of the capital and the state university respectively. Their ability to secure these institutions, which ensured their cities' importance and influence, demonstrates their power in the legislature. Prominent New Englanders included Charles Robinson, the first governor; Cyrus Holliday, who headed the Santa Fe Railroad; Clarina Nichols, the state's leading women's rights activist; and Samuel Pomeroy, the first U.S. senator. Robert W. Richmond, *Kansas: A Land of Contrasts* (St. Charles, 1974), 37–38.

7. There were also antislavery Missourians who settled in Kansas and then became Free Staters, but their existence was largely ignored by the media's attempt to portray a stark, simplistic sectional conflict. Ibid., 63.

8. Beecher's congregation contributed a rifle to every member of the Free State Party who eventually settled the town of Wabaunsee. The town became known as "Beecher's Bible and Rifle Church." Davis, *Kansas,* 46.

9. The suffragist Susan B. Anthony used the phrase *martyred state* when considering whether to settle in Kansas after the war. Katherine Anthony, *Susan B. Anthony: Her Personal History and Era* (Garden City, N.Y., 1954), 186. For a discussion of Kansas's "moral" image, see Richmond, *Kansas,* 63–78.

10. Thomas Cox, *Blacks in Topeka, 1865–1915* (Baton Rouge, La., 1982), 10.

11. Ibid., 9–12. Davis, *Kansas,* 54, highlights the differences between New Englanders and Midwesterners in the "anti-Negro" resolution debate.

12. Richmond, *Kansas,* 83–84. For a vivid firsthand account see John M. Patterson, "Letters of Edward and Sarah Fitch, Lawrence, Kansas, 1855–1863," *Kansas History* 12 (Spring 1989), 95–96.

13. Southerners had their own tales of Yankee depredations to recall, including the raids on Missouri border towns by Kansas Jayhawkers. Union officials had countered Quantrill's raid with some inhumanity of their own, ordering the forced resettlement of Missourians living along part of the Kansas border. Richmond, *Kansas,* 86.

14. On bloody shirt politics across the country, see Lawrence Goodwyn, *Democratic Promise: The Populist Moment in America* (New York, 1976), 4–24. For Kansas see Peter H. Argersinger, *Populism and Politics: William Alfred Peffer and the People's Party* (Lexington, Ky., 1974), 43–45.

15. Scott G. McNall, *The Road to Rebellion: Class Formation and Kansas Populism, 1865–1900* (Chicago, 1988), 38–39, 85.

16. These women's rights laws were similar to those Nichols had helped pass in New York State. Nichols came to Kansas with a group sponsored by the New England Emigrant Aid Society, and she was a frequent contributor to numerous Free State newspapers in Kansas. Edward T. James, ed., *Notable American Women* (Cambridge, Mass., 1971), 2:625–26. For activity to secure women's rights at the 1859 convention, see Susan B. Anthony and Elizabeth Cady Stanton, eds., *The History of Woman Suffrage* (New York: 1969), 3:704; Wilda M. Smith, "A Half Century of Struggle: Gaining Woman Suffrage in Kansas," *Kansas History* 4 (Summer 1981), 75–76.

17. June O. Underwood, "Civilizing Kansas: Women's Organizations, 1880–1920," *Kansas History* 7 (Winter 1984), 300–301.

18. W. Smith, "Half Century of Struggle," 89; Anthony and Stanton, *History of Woman Suffrage,* 2:704.

19. William Frank Zornow, *Kansas: A History of the Jayhawk State* (Norman, Okla., 1957), 73, 124; Richmond, *Kansas,* 110; Patterson, "Letters of Edward and Sarah Fitch," 53, 63.

20. Ellen DuBois, *Feminism and Suffrage: The Emergence of an Independent Women's Movement in America, 1848–1869* (Ithaca, N.Y., 1978), 89.

21. Ibid., 53–64. The Radicals did little for the cause of Northern blacks, who endured an equally virulent racism—though not as violent—as did their Southern counterparts. See Eric Foner, *Reconstruction: America's Unfinished Revolution, 1863–1877* (New York, 1988), 309–16.

22. Anthony and Stanton, *History of Woman Suffrage,* 2:229–30; K. Anthony, *Susan B. Anthony,* 186–87.

23. DuBois, *Feminism and Suffrage,* 94–95.

24. Ibid., 95–97.

25. Ibid., 97–98; Anthony and Stanton, *History of Woman Suffrage,* 2:267–68.

26. DuBois, *Feminism and Suffrage,* 96. This point is made more strongly by Bettina Aptheker, *Women's Legacy: Essays on Race, Sex, and Class in American History* (Amherst, Mass., 1982), who views the Kansas campaign and Stanton and Anthony's subsequent efforts to defeat the Fifteenth Amendment as a negative benchmark in the history of women's rights.

27. Aptheker, *Women's Legacy,* 51.

28. DuBois, *Feminism and Suffrage,* 102–4, 162–202. The Kansas legislature, again demonstrating that it was a step ahead of popular opinion, was the first in the nation to pass the Fifteenth Amendment to the Constitution, which was meant to guarantee blacks the right to vote.

29. Ironically, the same may be said of activists in the Kansas Equal Suffrage Association, most of whom were part of the small minority of the state's abolitionists from the Free State struggles.

30. DuBois, *Feminism and Suffrage,* 95.

31. One of the major policy disagreements between the American and National Suffrage associations was whether to pursue a state-by-state or national constitutional approach. Not surprisingly, Stanton and Anthony's organization followed the national approach. To underscore the differences between the two associations, the National held its conventions in Washington, D.C., whereas the American convention was held in a different state every year.

32. H. Smith, *Virgin Land,* 128.

33. John Hicks, *The Populist Revolt* (Lincoln, Neb., 1961), 1–35. See also Everett Dick, *The Sod House Frontier, 1854–1890: A Social History of the Northern Plains* (New York, 1937), 118–19; Richard Hofstadter, *The Age of Reform: From Bryan to FDR* (New York, 1955), 23–59. For a discussion of the ideological and symbolic importance of the Homestead Act, see Alan Trachtenberg, *The Incorporation of America: Culture and Society in the Gilded Age* (New York, 1982), 21–22; Hofstadter, *Age of Reform,* 54–55.

34. Seventeen million acres of Indian land went to special interests, and over one-quarter of the public lands went to the railroads. Railroads received twenty acres in alternate blocks along both sides of the proposed route. Since the routes usually followed river valleys, this was often the most productive land in central and western Kansas. Lands farther away from the railroad were less expensive but

often less profitable because of the difficulty and expense involved in transporting goods over great distances. Paul Wallace Gates, *Fifty Million Acres: Conflicts of Kansas Land Policy, 1854–1890* (Ithaca, N.Y., 1954), 2–8; McNall, *Road to Rebellion,* 71.

35. Hicks, *Populist Revolt,* 13; McNall, *Road to Rebellion,* 43–47; Gilbert Fite, *The Farmer's Last Frontier, 1865–1890* (New York, 1966), 17.

36. Fite, *Farmer's Last Frontier,* 11–13; Craig Miner, *West of Wichita: Settling the High Plains of Kansas, 1865–1890* (Lawrence, Kans., 1986), 26–37; Gates, *Fifty Million Acres,* 249–94; Fite, *Farmer's Last Frontier,* 26–33.

37. Kansas propagandists were quite effective: Kansas received the greatest number of settlers following the war. Miner, *West of Wichita,* 32–33. See also David Emmons, *Garden in the Grass Lands: Boomer Literature of the Central Plains* (Lincoln, 1971), 25–46.

38. The quotation is from the National Land Company, cited in Andrew Bingham, "The Significance of Settler Confidence in Kansas as a Cause of Populist Revolt" (B.A. thesis, Harvard College, 1957), 39.

39. James C. Duram and Eleanor A. Duram, "Letters from Paradise," *Kansas History* 9 (Spring 1986), 10; Miner, *West of Wichita,* 46–47.

40. Duram and Duram, "Letters from Paradise," 10–11.

41. Scott G. McNall and Sally Allen McNall, *Plains Families: Exploring Sociology through Social History* (New York, 1983), 42. On the ethos of success and Western settlement, see Eric Foner, *Free Soil, Free Labor, Free Men: The Ideology of the Republican Party before the Civil War* (New York, 1971), 13–15; John Cawelti, *Apostles of the Self-Made Man* (New York, 1965), 167–99.

42. On economic pressures on Old Northwest farmers during this time, see Alan Bogue, *From Prairie to Cornbelt: Farming on the Illinois and Iowa Frontier* (Chicago, 1963), 169–92. On small business failures see McNall, *Road to Rebellion,* 107–18.

43. On rural women's networks back East, see Joan Jensen, *Loosening the Bonds: Mid-Atlantic Farm Women, 1750–1850* (New Haven, 1986), 145–204; John Mack Faragher, *Sugar Creek: Life on the Illinois Prairie* (New Haven, 1986), 151–55; Faragher, *Women and Men on the Overland Trail* (New Haven, 1979). In *Women and Men,* 120–28, Faragher notes the difference between the rough-and-tumble social gatherings of men and the quieter networking of women. These social events were recreated on the Plains, though they seem largely to have lost their sex-segregated nature and to have been correspondingly more "domestic."

44. The exception is the case of single women who came West hoping to find greater economic and individual freedom. Riley, *Female Frontier,* 18–23; Dick, *Sod House Frontier,* 129. On women's reasons for not wanting to initiate emigration, see Elizabeth Jameson, "Women as Workers, Women as Civilizers," in Elizabeth Jameson, ed., *The Women's West* (Norman, Okla., 1987), 149–50.

45. Miner, *West of Wichita,* 154; Joanna L. Stratton, *Pioneer Women: Voices*

*from the Kansas Frontier* (New York, 1981), 55; Walter Hart Blumenthal, "Back Soon—Gone to Get a Wife," *New York Posse Brand Book* 7 (1960), 6–7. Often men went to Kansas first and "batched" for a few years, developing a claim and (hopefully) saving up money before returning East. Howard Ruede, *Sod House Days: Letters from a Kansas Homesteader, 1877–1888* (Lawrence, Kans., 1983); Dick, *Sod House Frontier*, 121; Blumenthal, "Back Soon," 4–8.

46. Miner, *West of Wichita*, 7–13. "It can be argued that western Kansas was *the* most frustrating representative of the general frustration of agrarian civilization on the Great Plains." Ibid., 11. Italics in original.

47. Blumenthal, "Back Soon," 6–7. Italics in original.

48. Collecting these petrified chunks of bison dung was considered a woman's job, as was collecting bison bones, which were shipped back East to be made into fertilizer.

49. Walter Prescott Webb, *The Great Plains* (Boston, 1936); James Malin, "Factors in Grassland Equilibrium," and "Rural Life and Subhumid Environment during the Decade of the Seventies: 'The Clean Shirt and Good Living,'" in Robert Swierenga, ed., *History and Ecology: Studies of the Grassland* (Lincoln, 1984).

50. Miner, *West of Wichita*, 38–40; McNall, *Road to Rebellion*, 66–69.

51. Miner, *West of Wichita*, 131; Paul Travis, "Changing Climate in Kansas: A Late Nineteenth-Century Myth," *Kansas History* 1 (Spring 1978).

52. *Chase County Historical Sketches* (n.p., 1940), 1:82, Sterling Memorial Library, Yale University.

53. Stratton, *Pioneer Women*, 60.

54. Hoppers had descended on various sections of the Plains in the past, but never had they been so numerous or destructive. The national media tended to focus on Kansas, which had the largest population of the affected states. Miner, *West of Wichita*, 54–55.

55. Ibid., 52–66; McNall, *Road to Rebellion*, 69; Dick, *Sod House Frontier*, 202–12; Charles C. Howes, *This Place Called Kansas* (Norman, Okla., 1952), 165–71.

56. Miner, *West of Wichita*, 121–22.

57. Trachtenberg, *Incorporation of America*, 85.

58. Ibid., 70–88; Glenn Porter, *The Rise of Big Business, 1860–1910* (Arlington Heights, Ill., 1973); McNall, *Road to Rebellion*, 44–45.

59. Porter, *Rise of Big Business*, 9–11; Bruce Palmer, *"Man over Money": The Southern Populist Critique of American Capitalism* (Chapel Hill, N.C., 1980), 81–95; Goodwyn, *Democratic Promise*, 10–23; Alan Bogue, *Money at Interest: The Farm Mortgage on the Middle Border* (Ithaca, N.Y., 1955). For a more extensive discussion of mortgage rates, see Michael Goldberg, "Army of Women" (Ph.D. diss.), 40, nn. 84, 86.

60. Hicks, *Populist Revolt*, 55–78; William Cronon, *Chicago and the Great West* (New York, 1991), 122–37.

61. Hicks, *Populist Revolt*, 60–64. For a more extensive discussion of railroad rates, see Goldberg, "Army of Women," 39 n. 80.

62. Hicks, *Populist Revolt*, 65–69, 83.

63. McNall, *Road to Rebellion*, 45–47; Miner, *West of Wichita*, 142–44; Dick, *Sod House Frontier*, 95–97; John Ise, *Sod and Stubble: The Story of a Kansas Homestead* (New York, 1938), 221.

64. James Malin, *Winter Wheat in the Golden Belt of Kansas: A Study in Adaptation to Subhumid Geographical Environment* (New York, 1973), 268. Alan Bogue, *Money at Interest*, 105–6, found that in one Kansas township during the 1870s, 55% of the farms on public land and 79% of those on the more expensive railroad lands were mortgaged.

65. Cornelia Butler Flora and Jan L. Flora, "Structure of Agriculture and Women's Culture in the Great Plains," *Great Plains Quarterly* 8 (Fall 1988), 200–202.

66. *Kansas Farmer*, 11 December 1890.

67. Miner, *West of Wichita*, 143–44. Miner does not explicitly employ gender analysis, but it is no accident that all his examples are from men speaking in very "male" tones about the draw of machines and "mastery" of the land. Annette Kolodny, *The Lay of the Land: Metaphor as Experience in American Life and Letters* (Chapel Hill, N.C., 1975). On the connection between machinery and optimism, see Dick, *Sod House Frontier*, 288–89. As Dick and others have noted, this optimism was not without basis. Technological improvements had helped create a revolution in U.S. farmers' productivity. In order for productivity to equal profitability, however, investments in new technology had to be made carefully.

68. Anne Mayhew, "A Reappraisal of the Causes of Farm Protest in the United States, 1870–1900," *Journal of Economic History* 32 (1972), 470–74. Examples of this philosophy may be found in Ise, *Sod and Stubble*, 139–42; McNall and McNall, *Plains Families*, 23–25.

69. Flora and Flora, "Agriculture and Women's Culture," 204; Miner, *West of Wichita*, 155; Dick, *Sod House Frontier*, 303; *Kansas Farmer*, 16 February 1887, 7 March 1889.

70. *Western Farmer*, 26 October 1889.

71. Gertrude Macaulay Zimmerman, *A Pint of Pearls* (Kansas City, Mo., 1967), 104. Fite, *Farmer's Last Frontier*, 47–48; McNall and McNall, *Plains Families*, 23; Riley, *Female Frontier*, 85–90.

72. This arrangement was particularly common before large harvesting machinery required a crew to be hired. But the new technology did not prove labor-saving for women: they were expected to spend most of their time cooking, cleaning, and washing for these temporary workers.

73. Flora Moorman Heston, "I Think I Shall Like Kansas: The Letters of Flora Moorman Heston, 1885–1886," *Kansas History* 6 (Summer 1983).

74. John Mack Faragher, "History from the Inside Out: Writing the History of Women in Rural America," *American Quarterly* 33 (Winter 1987). For a historiographical discussion of empowerment and the settlement process, see Goldberg, "Army of Women," 44 n. 98.

75. Blumenthal, "Back Soon," 4–6; Miner, *West of Wichita,* 154; Flora and Flora, "Agriculture and Women's Culture," 200–203; McNall and McNall, *Plains Families,* 25; Allen County Historical Society, *Life Is So Daily: Changing Views of Housework* (n.p., n.d.), Sterling Memorial Library, Yale University; Julie Roy Jeffrey, *Frontier Women: The Trans-Mississippi West, 1840–1880* (New York, 1979), xvi.

76. Stratton, *Pioneer Women,* 133; Ise, *Sod and Stubble,* 22; *Chase County History,* 82; Riley, *Female Frontier,* 97.

77. Miner, *West of Wichita,* 104.

78. *Story of a Kansas Pioneer,* 33.

79. Peter H. Argersinger, "Pentecostal Politics in Kansas: Religion, the Farmers' Alliance, and the Gospel of Populism," *Kansas History* 1 (1969), 24–35. Ironically, many of these same organizations were busy "saving the heathen" in Africa through missionary societies with extensive fund-raising networks.

80. Stratton, *Pioneer Women,* 179.

81. McNall, *Road to Rebellion,* 72.

82. John Stitz, "A Study of Family Farm Culture in Ellis County, Kansas and the Relationship of That Culture to Trends in Farming" (Ph.D. diss., University of Kansas, 1983); John Stitz and Jan L. Flora, "Ethnicity, Persistence, and Capitalization of Agriculture in the Great Plains during the Settlement Period: Wheat Production and Risk Avoidance," *Rural Sociology* 50 (Fall 1985), 201–4; Hofstadter, *Age of Reform,* 43–44; Ise, *Sod and Stubble,* 13.

83. Flora and Flora, "Agriculture and Women's Culture," 203.

84. Daniel Scott Smith, "Family Limitation, Sexual Control, and Domestic Feminism in Victorian America," in Cott and Peck, *Heritage of Her Own;* McNall and McNall, *Plains Families,* 19, 54.

85. Flora and Flora, "Agriculture and Women's Culture," 202.

86. Ibid.; for a literary treatment of this subject, see Willa Cather, *My Antonia* (New York, 1979).

87. Miner, *West of Wichita,* 83.

88. McNall and McNall, *Plains Families,* 59; Zimmerman, *Pint of Pearls,* 103; Robert Hine, *Community on the American Frontier: Separate but Not Alone* (Norman, Okla., 1980), 118–19, 175; Miner, *West of Wichita,* 82, 155. Immigrant German settlers arrived in Kansas with a number of advantages over most of their Anglo counterparts. Many of the German-Russian groups possessed a fair amount of capital and were able to purchase good land, usually from the railroads, free and clear of any mortgage. Additionally, many had been farmers in the semiarid Russian steppes and were thus familiar with many of the skills and crops needed to succeed in central Kansas.

89. Miner, *West of Wichita,* 79; Fife, *Farmer's Last Frontier,* 48; Flora and Flora, "Agriculture and Women's Culture," 201–4.

90. Robert Swierenga, "Agriculture and Rural Life: The New Rural History," in

James Gardner and George Rollie, eds., *Ordinary People in Everyday Life* (Nashville, 1983), 94.

91. Dick, *Sod House Frontier*, 240–41; June Underwood, "The Ladies' Lounge," sound cassette, Kansas Center for the Humanities, 1987.

92. *Kansas Farmer*, 4 March 1889, 17 May 1890; *Advocate*, 12 February 1891.

93. The term *hayseed* was derived from the debris left in a farmer's beard after spending the night in the livery stable in town. *Clodhopper* refers to the farmer's need to jump over large clumps of soil while plowing the tough Prairie ground. Dick, *Sod House Frontier*, 246.

94. Slotkin, *Fatal Environment*, 70–71, 306–9; Trachtenberg, *Incorporation of America*, 22–25; Hofstadter, *Age of Reform*, 23–36.

95. Trachtenberg, *Incorporation of America*, 81–84; Paula C. Baker, *The Moral Frameworks of Public Life: Gender, Politics, and the State in Rural New York, 1870–1930* (New York, 1991), 26–27; *Register*, 31 March 1887; *Sentinel*, 3 April 1888.

96. Cited in McNall, *Road to Rebellion*, 94. The poem was published on 4 July 1876, probably to honor the Centennial. Presumably Ware was more successful as a businessman than as a poet. Additional background information on Ware from James Malin, *Doctors, Devils, and the Woman: Fort Scott, 1870–1890* (Lawrence, Kans., 1965), 60–61.

97. Dick, *Sod House Frontier*, 41, 360; Stratton, *Pioneer Woman*, 189.

98. Stanley Parsons, *The Populist Context: Rural versus Urban Power on a Great Plains Frontier* (Westport, Conn., 1973), 41; Miner, *West of Wichita*, 96.

99. Parsons, *Populist Context*, 46; Dick, *Sod House Frontier*, 361.

100. Of the over one thousand railroads chartered in the state, fewer than two hundred even laid down track. Richmond, *Kansas*, 110.

101. Miner, *West of Wichita*, 31.

102. McNall, *Road to Rebellion*, 107–11.

103. For example, Fort Scott, with a population of ten thousand, had forty-five grocery stores, ten shoe stores, nine dry goods stores, and seven general stores, most of them established during the 1880s boom. When the boom collapsed, so did many of these businesses. Ibid., 107–8.

104. Tellingly, journalists rarely noted women who publicly complained about economic or environmental conditions. Historians who have concerned themselves with whether women settlers were generally content or miserable might ask the same about the men. McNall, *Road to Rebellion*, 169, presents a poem from the Kingsly *Mercury* with a representative use of the kicker figure: "Oh, kickers all, / Both great and small, / No longer stand aloof, / If you can't join the throng, / And help things along / You'd better 'come off' the roof."

105. Anthony Rotundo, *American Manhood: Transformations in Masculinity from the Revolution to the Modern Era* (New York, 1993), 227, 232.

106. In cash-poor Kansas control of tax resources was especially important to

one's economic well-being. On state and local benefits of officeholding in Kansas, see *Kansas Weekly Chief,* 16 December 1886; Osage City *Republican,* 14 July 1882; McNall, *Road to Rebellion,* 85–86; Dick, *Sod House Frontier,* 459–60.

107. Miner, *West of Wichita,* 58–60.

108. Ibid., 56–60.

109. Ironically, the legislature's refusal to accept reality was duplicated by most farmers during better times.

110. Miner, *West of Wichita,* 56.

111. Solon Buck, *The Granger Movement: A Study of Agricultural Organization and Its Political, Economic, and Social Manifestations, 1870–1880* (New York, 1920), 40–42.

112. Ibid., 50–93; Dick, *Sod House Frontier,* 305–11.

113. Buck, *Granger Movement,* 63, 280–81, 299; Underwood, "Civilizing Kansas," 294; Dragoon Grange Minutes, 1 January 1873, KSHS.

114. Kansas Patrons of Husbandry, "List of Charter Members," lists a number of granges by male and female members: 99 members are identified as men and 46 as women. The following sources list officers of local granges, none of which contain a woman's name: *Farmer's Advocate,* 3 March 1876; *Sickle and Sheaf,* 7 July 1874, 18 October 1873. "List of Charter Members," Kansas Patrons of Husbandry Collection, KSHS. See also Hiawatha Grange Minutes, 28 March 1872, KSHS.

115. McNall, *Road to Rebellion,* 50.

116. Argersinger, *Populism and Politics,* 2.

117. Ibid., 2–3; Gene O. Clanton, *Kansas Populism: Ideas and Men* (Lawrence, Kans., 1969), 8.

118. C. S. Finder to Ware, "Correspondence," Edward Ware Papers, 1 March 1890 (Kansas State Historical Society). See also E. D. Thomas to Ware, 3 July 1890; Lyman Humphrey to Ware, 16 July 1890; L. Sharpe to Ware, 29 March 1884; Delos Walker to Ware, 14 April 1884; Gov. George Glick to Ware, 18 January 1884.

119. *Advocate,* 30 April 1890, cited in Clanton, *Kansas Populism,* 57.

120. Baker, *Moral Frameworks;* Michael McGerr, *The Decline of Popular Politics: The American North, 1865–1928* (New York, 1986); Paula Baker, "The Domestication of Politics: Women and American Political Society, 1870–1920," *American Historical Review* 89 (June 1984), 626–29.

121. Nancy Cott, *The Bonds of Womanhood* (New Haven, 1977); Mary Ryan, *Cradle of the Middle Class: The Family in Oneida, New York, 1790–1865* (Cambridge, Mass., 1981); Carol Smith-Rosenberg, "The Female World of Love and Ritual: Relations between Women in Nineteenth-Century America," *Signs* 1 (Autumn 1975), 1–29. For analysis of how these "female worlds" were transformed into women's public participation, see Nancy Hewitt, *Women's Activism and Social Change: Rochester, N.Y., 1822–1872* (Ithaca, N.Y., 1984); Barbara Berg, *The Remembered Gate: Origins of American Feminism* (New York, 1978).

122. Underwood, "Civilizing Kansas," 294.

123. Jeffrey, *Frontier Women*, 95; Robert J. Griswold, "Anglo Women and Domestic Ideology in the Nineteenth and Early Twentieth Centuries," in *Western Women*, 24; *Kansas Farmer*, 14 August 1889.

124. Mark C. Carnes, *Secret Ritual and Manhood in Victorian America* (New Haven, 1989), 74–77.

125. Underwood, "Civilizing Kansas," 294; Griswold, "Anglo Women," 23–24.

126. Jeffrey, *Frontier Women*, 183–84.

127. To argue for the difference in middle-class women's and men's political priorities is not to claim that all men are heartless and all women altruistic. There were many men who performed great acts of selfless charity during the grasshopper crises, and there were women who condemned charity as a blow to self-reliance. See, e.g., Miner, *West of Wichita*, 58–61. Further, while women's organizations sought to alleviate people's miseries during periods of extreme deprivation, most of these same women supported the social and economic inequalities that helped create such problems.

128. This ideology is readily apparent in the pages of the *American Citizen*, the *Historic Times*, the *Kansas Blackman*, and other Kansas black newspapers. See also Cox, *Blacks in Topeka*, 105–8.

129. Leavenworth *Advocate*, 4 May 1889; *Colored Citizen*, 3 May 1879, cited in Cox, *Blacks in Topeka*, 48.

130. Cox, *Blacks in Topeka*, 44–48.

131. Ibid., 108. Some papers were worse at reporting about black women than others. The *Afro-American Advocate* made no mention of black women's politics whereas the *American Citizen* was more receptive.

132. *American Citizen*, 11 January 1889, 2 January 1888, 22 June 1888; *Kansas Blackman*, 4 May 1894.

133. See, e.g., *Baptist Headlight*, 1 November 1889; *Kansas Blackman*, 25 May 1894.

134. For background of Kansas radicals see Clanton, *Kansas Populism*, 33–46.

135. Robert Smith Bader, *Prohibition in Kansas* (Lawrence, Kans., 1986), 27, 40.

136. Ibid., 1–12.

137. Ibid., 1–2. Despite these grand hopes, Bader reports the crowds were mostly from Kansas.

138. Ibid., 29; *1892 Prohibition Party Platform*, Prohibition Party Pamphlets, KSHS.

139. Bader, *Prohibition in Kansas*, 33–34, notes that even if these numbers were exaggerated, the campaign's success was still impressive.

140. Ibid., 43.

141. Agnes Hayes, *The White Ribboners in the Sunflower State* (Topeka, Kans., 1953), 47.

142. Bader, *Prohibition in Kansas*, 43.

143. Ibid., 50.

144. Ibid., 59–60. Bader believes it would have been more beneficial to the fledgling WCTU if Wilson had spent less time on the road and more building the organization. However, as I note, the rural vote was crucial to the amendment's passage.

145. Ibid., 58.

146. Ibid., 63.

147. Ibid., 66–68; Leon Fink, *Workingman's Democracy: The Knights of Labor and American Politics* (Urbana, Ill., 1983), 122–23.

148. Fink, *Workingman's Democracy,* 115; Bader, *Prohibition in Kansas,* 74–89.

149. Bader, *Prohibition in Kansas,* 79–82; Fink, *Workingman's Democracy,* 122–23.

150. This loophole caused the phenomenon during the eighties of a not-so-mysterious malady that struck at the otherwise healthy male population of small-town Kansas. In some towns, 95% of "prescriptions" were ordered by men. Whiskey was by far the most popular nostrum, at 70% of the purchases, with beer a distant second. Bader, *Prohibition in Kansas,* 85.

151. Ibid., 110–11; see also *Kansas City Journal,* 1 September 1891.

152. Background information on the boom derived from Raymond Miller, "The Economic Background of Populism," *Mississippi Valley Historical Review* 11 (March 1925), 470; Miner, *West of Wichita,* 202–5; McNall, *Road to Rebellion,* 78; Fite, *Farmer's Last Frontier,* 116–17; James Malin, "The Kinsley Boom of the Late Eighties," *Kansas Historical Quarterly* 4 (1935), 164–87.

153. McNall and McNall, *Plains Families,* 46; Miller, "Background of Populism," 470–71; Hicks, *Populist Revolt,* 56.

154. Fite, *Farmer's Last Frontier,* 119–21; Miner, *West of Wichita,* 137; Hicks, *Populist Revolt,* 23–24; Bogue, *Money at Interest,* 7.

155. *Belle Plains News,* 27 February 1886. Quotation compiled from Hicks, *Populist Revolt,* 28, and McNall, *Road to Rebellion,* 75; originally cited in Miller, "Background of Populism," 470.

156. Miner, *West of Wichita,* 27, 207–8.

157. KESA Minutes, 1–4: 117, KSHS.


CHAPTER TWO. "AT HOME AMONG YOU":
THE RISE OF THE KANSAS WOMAN MOVEMENT

1. Here I am largely borrowing from Sara M. Evans and Harry C. Boyte, "Schools for Action: Radical Uses for Social Space," *Democracy* 3 (Fall 1982), 60–61. Evans and Boyte are paraphrasing Nancy F. Cott, *The Bonds of Womanhood: "Women's Sphere" in New England, 1780–1835* (New Haven, 1977).

2. James Green, "Populism, Socialism, and the Promise of Democracy," *Radical History Review* 24 (Fall 1980), makes this point about the strictures of free social

spaces when critiquing Lawrence Goodwyn, *Democratic Promise: The Populist Moment in America* (New York, 1976).

3. Cott, *Bonds of Womanhood*, 154.

4. This term obviously owes much to *paternalism*, but that word seems rather inappropriate here. *Maternalism* is meant to imply a mother-daughter relationship, at least as Woman Movement activists saw it. Reformers hoped to mold women who were outside the mainstream gently but sternly into respectable women, while shielding them from the corrupting influence of men. Finally, *maternalism* is meant to connote the ideal of "making the world homelike," in Frances Willard's words: to bring the qualities of the middle-class home to the political arena.

5. *Kansas Suffrage,* August 1893.

6. KESA Minutes to the Annual Meeting, 1887, 53 (Kansas State Historical Society).

7. Ibid., 1890, 13.

8. Ibid., 1889, 34.

9. Ibid., 1891, n.p.

10. *Topeka Daily Capital,* 16 May 1890, *Woman Suffrage Clippings,* vol. 3, n.p. The source of the quotation is Sen. John J. Ingalls, never a popular man with woman suffragists.

11. *Topeka Capital,* 15 November 1888, *Woman Suffrage Clippings,* 5:31; Wilda M. Smith, "A Half Century of Struggle: Gaining Woman Suffrage in Kansas," *Kansas History* 4 (Summer 1981), 79.

12. Ruth Bordin, *Woman and Temperance: The Quest for Power and Liberty, 1873–1900* (Philadelphia, 1981), 86, found that the national WCTU also favored proselytizing over organizing the foreign born.

13. *Our Messenger,* February 1892. Italics in original.

14. Ibid., March 1883.

15. Ibid., December 1891.

16. Ibid., January 1886, February 1894. Italics in original.

17. Ibid., February 1887, July 1891, August 1890.

18. WCTU Minutes to the Annual Meeting, June 1886, 92 (KSHS); June 1888, 89.

19. Background on Harper from Edward T. James, ed., *Notable American Women* (Cambridge, Mass., 1971), 2:137–39. On Harper's appearances in Kansas see *Our Messenger,* July 1891.

20. Thomas Cox, *Blacks in Topeka, 1865–1915* (Baton Rouge, La., 1982), 105–8.

21. See, e.g., "Temperance Notes" in the *American Citizen,* 15 June 1888.

22. *Baptist Headlight,* 28 March 1894.

23. *Historic Times,* 25 July 1891.

24. *American Citizen,* 13 April 1888, 22 June 1888.

25. Ibid., 30 March 1888.

26. Barbara Hilkert Andolson, *"Daughters of Jefferson, Daughters of Boot-blacks": Racism and American Feminism* (Macon, Ga., 1986), 38.

27. KESA Minutes, 1887, 56. See also ibid., 1884, 73–74; *Our Messenger,* April 1887.

28. KESA Minutes, 1887, 57.

29. Ibid., 1890, 10–11.

30. WCTU Minutes, 1887, 48.

31. KESA Minutes, 1889, 35.

32. Ibid., 11.

33. Ibid., 1887, 54. Italics in original.

34. Robert Smith Bader, *Prohibition in Kansas* (Lawrence, Kans., 1986), 94.

35. See, e.g., *Our Messenger,* January 1886.

36. Ibid., February 1887.

37. Ibid., April 1887; W. M. Smith, "Half Century of Struggle," 79; Katherine Anthony, *Susan B. Anthony: Her Personal History and Era* (Garden City, N.Y., 1954), 377.

38. These impressions drawn from surveying the KESA's and WCTU's *Minutes to the Annual Meeting.* See also Bader, *Prohibition in Kansas,* 85. Bordin, *Women and Temperance,* 70, describes the ever more elaborate conventions organized by the national WCTU. The Kansas WCTU appears to have remained a bit more understated.

39. WCTU Minutes, 1882, 9; *Our Messenger,* 1 January 1891.

40. KESA Minutes, 1886, 17.

41. Ibid., 1887, 33; WCTU Minutes, 1887, 13; KESA Minutes, 1886, 17 (italics in original).

42. KESA Minutes, 1886, 17.

43. Bader, *Prohibition in Kansas,* 100.

44. Ibid., 85–90.

45. Jack S. Blocker, "The Politics of Reform: Populists, Prohibition, and Woman Suffrage, 1891–1892," *Historian* 34 (August 1972), 14–15.

46. Bordin, *Women and Temperance,* 67, 69.

47. Bader, *Prohibition in Kansas,* 93. Italics in original.

48. WCTU Minutes, 1890, 4.

49. *Topeka Capital,* 1 March 1894; *Our Messenger,* February 1891.

50. *Our Messenger,* May 1893.

51. These characteristics would become especially apparent during the 1894 campaign. On Anthony's relations with Republican leaders, see Smith, "Half Century of Struggle," 94.

52. On Anthony's commitment to a long-term, national struggle, see Eleanor Flexnor, *Century of Struggle: The Woman's Rights Movement in the United States* (Cambridge, Mass., 1958), 176–77.

53. Kansas WCTU members demonstrated the same antagonism toward male culture that Barbara Epstein found in the national WCTU. Barbara Epstein, *The Politics of Domesticity: Women, Evangelism, and Temperance in Nineteenth-Century America* (Middletown, Conn., 1981), 114–15.

54. WCTU Minutes, 1886, 11.

55. *Kansas Suffrage,* August 1893.

56. WCTU Minutes, 1887, 41.

57. KESA Minutes, 1890, 11.

58. Ibid., 27–28.

59. Bader, *Prohibition in Kansas,* 96.

60. WCTU Minutes, 1888, 43.

61. Bader, *Prohibition in Kansas,* 81.

62. *Our Messenger,* June 1887.

63. Ibid., June 1887.

64. Ibid., July 1890.

65. Joseph Gusfield, *Symbolic Crusade: Status Politics and the American Temperance Movement* (Urbana, 1963).

66. Bordin, *Women and Temperance,* 7–8.

67. Ibid., 6–7.

68. Farnsworth, *Plainswoman,* 60–119. Italics in original.

69. WCTU Minutes, 1888, 40.

70. On national WCTU leaders, see Bordin, *Women and Temperance,* 107.

71. Quoted in Bader, *Prohibition in Kansas,* 100.

72. WCTU Minutes, 1887, 44.

73. WCTU Minutes, 1885, 41.

74. Historians have found the presence of God a tough phenomenon to prove empirically and so have usually depended on functionalist arguments about the social reasons why women became religious to explain religiosity. My argument is that whether God existed or not, Woman Movement activists believed that He did. One need not be a believer to accept the idea of spiritual power.

75. KESA Minutes, 1888, 32.

76. Ibid., 1891, n.p.

77. See, in particular, Annie Diggs, "Women under the Rule of Church and Law," WSC, v. 2–3, n.p.

78. On Diggs's relations with the WCTU, see *Farmer's Wife,* 28 January 1893.

## Chapter Three. The Woman Movement Triumphant

1. Edward T. James, ed., *Notable American Women, 1607–1950* (Cambridge, Mass., 1971), 2:69–70; Susan B. Anthony and Elizabeth Cady Stanton, *History of Woman Suffrage,* 3:543.

2. KESA Minutes to the Annual Meeting, 1–4:8–10.

3. Gougar had first worked for her husband in his law firm, where she gained extensive knowledge of the law. James, *Notable American Women,* 2:69.

4. KESA Minutes, 1–4:18.

5. Ibid., 95–97.

6. Ibid. Robert Smith Bader, *Prohibition in Kansas* (Lawrence, Kans., 1986), 102–3.

7. Bader, *Prohibition in Kansas,* 71–72.

8. Ibid., 73. Whereas Bader reports that many Germans "shut their eyes and voted Democratic," Leon Fink, *Workingman's Democracy: The Knights of Labor and American Politics* (Urbana, Ill., 1983), 118, notes that Germans in Kansas City retained their traditional Republican loyalties. It may thus be assumed that Kansas City's notoriously lax enforcement policy was a significant factor for Germans there.

9. Bader, *Prohibition in Kansas,* 73.

10. Ibid., 71–74.

11. Ibid., 76–78; WCTU Minutes, 1885, 110 (KSHS). For Kansas Republicans the third-party threat of the 1880s came from the Prohibitionists, and not the Greenbackers, whose economic reforms would serve as the basis for the Populist platforms of the next decade. The Prohibitionists' influence would shift dramatically at the end of the 1880s in direct proportion to the rise of the Populist threat to Republicans.

12. Bader, *Prohibition in Kansas,* 78–80.

13. KESA Minutes, 1–4:94–95.

14. F. G. Adams and C. R. Carruth, *Woman Suffrage in Kansas* (Topeka, Kans., 1888), 14 (hereafter cited as WSK). This work was a collection of representative quotations from every newspaper in Kansas which reported on municipal woman suffrage.

15. Mr. Carroll, Democrat of Leavenworth, complained obliquely about "the blind following of party," to which Mr. Hatfield, a Republican, replied that "the grand old party is taking up this movement just as they took up the prohibition movement—because there seems to be a popular clamor for it." These are the only references to party issues during the debate. KESA Minutes, 1–4:116–18.

16. Ibid., 105, 114, 115.

17. Ibid., 115–17.

18. Ibid., 115.

19. Ibid., 119.

20. Sarah B. Hall to Martin, 9 February 1887, Gov. John Martin Papers (KSHS). See also Elizabeth Saxon to Martin, 7 February 1887, and Mrs. C. B. Hoffman to Martin, 9 February 1887.

21. KESA Minutes, 1–4:121; *Our Messenger,* April 1987; Adams and Carruth, WSK, 13–14.

22. Adams and Carruth, WSK, 13–14.

23. Ibid., 14. Italics in original.

24. Ibid., 29, 31, 57, 72, 75, among others. Twenty-two women gained local office. For a more in-depth look at one of the all-women city councils, see Rosalind Urbach Moss, "The Girls from Syracuse: Sex Role Negotiations of Kansas Women, 1876–1893," in Susan Armitage and Elizabeth Jameson, eds., *The Women's West* (Norman, Okla., 1987).

25. Women activists were credited with defeating or challenging Republican candidates in as many as sixteen local elections in 1887, including Atchison, Garden City, Argonia, and Arkansas City. Candidates appeared before special women's caucuses in at least nine different towns. Adams and Carruth, WSK, 33–36; KESA Minutes, 1887, 65, 87.

26. *Fort Scott Daily Monitor,* 6 April 1887, cited in WSK, 31.

27. Ibid.

28. *Garden City Daily Sentinel,* 6 April 1887, cited in WSK, 58.

29. *Gaslight,* 8 April 1887, cited in WSK, 77.

30. *Emporia Evening News,* 7 April 1887, cited in WSK, 73.

31. Ibid.

32. WCTU Minutes, 1885, 59.

33. *Our Messenger,* 2 February 1889.

34. *Iola Register,* 15 April 1887, cited in WSK, 24.

35. *Meade Globe,* 9 April 1887, cited in WSK, 76.

36. *Garden City Daily Sentinel,* 6 April 1887, cited in WSK, 58.

37. The constant reference to degraded women seems to have been a perjorative term not for working-class women (since it was often employed by Democrats who had a working-class constituency) but rather probably for prostitutes and other "fallen" women. Such fears of a block of "degraded" women storming the polls appears a bit preposterous.

38. *Ashland Republican-Herald,* 14 April 1887, cited in WSK, 37. This statement is representative of many about women's purity.

39. *Burlington Independent,* 25 March 1887, cited in WSK, 44.

40. *Lawrence Tribune,* 25 March 1887, cited in WSK, 56.

41. *Garnett Eagle,* 25 March 1887, cited in WSK, 24.

42. Bader, *Prohibition in Kansas,* 269–70. Although Bader does not attempt to quantify prohibition supporters, the fact that many small towns elected pro-enforcement legislators and managed to close down most saloons by the late eighties demonstrates that their influence must have been substantial.

43. *Index* (Medicine Lodge), 1 April 1887, cited in WSK, 28.

44. *Chapman Courier,* 14 April 1887, cited in WSK, 37.

45. *Prohibitionist,* 4 April 1887.

46. See, e.g., *News,* 1 April 1887; KESA Minutes, 4:115. A number of husbands did in fact physically abuse their wives for voting (and were subsequently jailed or fined for their actions). In these cases, however, the reports indicate that the

men had a history of violent behavior and that they had committed similar assaults before. Tellingly, they were usually convicted of interfering with election law rather than assault. *Sun,* 31 March 1887; *Globe,* 9 April 1887, cited in WSK, 25, 64.

47. See, e.g., *Lawrence Tribune,* 25 March 1887; *Ottawa News,* 6 April 1887, cited in WSK, 55–56.

48. Bader, *Prohibition in Kansas,* 66–68; *Leavenworth Times,* 21 February 1887, 3 March 1887.

49. The Metropolitan Police Act authorized a state police force to crack down on recalcitrant localities.

50. KESA Minutes, 1–4:101.

51. *Leavenworth Times,* 6 February 1887.

52. Ibid.

53. Ibid., 3 April 1887.

54. *Standard,* 4 April 1887.

55. *Osage City Republican,* 7 June 1882.

56. *Leavenworth Times,* 3 April 1887.

57. Ibid.

58. *Our Messenger,* March 1887.

59. *Leavenworth Times,* 8 April 1887.

60. *Standard,* 4 April 1887.

61. Ibid., 2 April 1887.

62. Ibid., 21 March 1887.

63. *Leavenworth Times,* 13 February 1887, 20 February 1887.

64. Ibid., 20 February 1887.

65. *Our Messenger,* March 1887; *Leavenworth Times,* 3 April 1887.

66. *Standard,* 6 April 1887; *Leavenworth Times,* 6 April 1887.

67. *Standard,* 3 April 1887, 6 April 1887.

68. *Leavenworth Times,* 7 April 1887.

69. *Daily Capital,* 30 April 1887.

70. *Leavenworth Times,* 7 April 1887.

71. *Standard,* 7 April 1887.

72. The women's vote in 1887 was 37 percent of men's vote; in 1888, it was 31 percent of men's vote. Adams and Carruth, WSK, 109–10.

73. Ibid., 108.

74. KESA Minutes, 1887, 11–12.

75. *Our Messenger,* February 1888.

76. F. R. Southwick to Martin, 28 May 1887, Gov. John Martin Papers. Martin received similar requests from Iowa and Mississippi. W. A. Ellis to Martin, 28 November 1887; [illegible name] to Martin, 2 December 1887.

77. KESA Minutes, 1889, 12.

78. Ibid., 50–51.

79. *Kansas Chief,* 6 December 1889.

80. *Our Messenger,* March 1888; *Afro-American Citizen,* 10 April 1888; *Advocate* (Leavenworth), 9 March 1889.

81. Fink, *Workingman's Democracy,* 118–19, 123–24; Thomas Cox, *Blacks in Topeka, 1865–1915* (Baton Rouge, La., 1982), 120–22.

82. Fink, *Workingman's Democracy,* 148, n. 64.

83. *American Citizen,* 2 January 1888.

84. Ruth Bordin, *Woman and Temperance: The Quest for Power and Liberty, 1873–1900* (Philadelphia, 1981), 124–25.

85. *Capital-Commonwealth,* 23 December 1888, WCTU Clippings, KSHS.

86. On partisan positions within the WCTU, see WCTU Minutes, 1886, 43; *Capital,* 26 September 1885, WCTU Clippings, n.p.

87. WCTU Minutes, 1886, 43.

88. *Rising Sun,* 14 October 1885.

89. *Kansas Lever,* 1 November 1887.

90. WCTU Minutes, 1885, 44.

91. WCTU Clippings, 131–32.

92. Bader, *Prohibition in Kansas,* 93.

93. Foster would show her true colors in the 1894 Kansas suffrage campaign, as well as at various points in her career. For Foster's zealous support of the Republican Party, see James, *Notable American Women,* 1:652.

94. *Capital,* 29 September 1885, Woman Suffrage Clippings (hereafter cited as WSC), v. 2–3, n.p.

95. Bader, *Prohibition in Kansas,* 93.

96. WCTU Minutes, 1889, 48.

97. Bader, *Prohibition in Kansas,* 116.

98. *Capital,* 16 November 1888, WSC, v. 5, n.p.

99. KESA Minutes, 1887, 55.

100. *Daily Commonwealth,* 26 September 1885, WCTU Clippings, n.p.

101. *Capital,* 27 September 1885, WCTU Clippings, n.p.

102. *Our Messenger,* December 1890.

103. KESA Minutes, 1891, 52.

104. Cited in June O. Underwood, "Civilizing Kansas: Women's Organizations, 1880–1920," *Kansas History* 7 (Winter 1984), 293.

105. *Journal and Triumph,* 15 May 1890.

106. Ibid., 17 May 1894. Whether this single-sex membership was by choice or circumstance, however, is not clear.

107. *Capital,* 8 May 1889.

108. WSC, 5:16. On Jane Croly and Sorosis, see Karen Blair, *The Club Woman as Feminist: True Womanhood Redefined, 1868–1914* (New York, 1980), esp. 15–31.

109. On Kansas clubs see Underwood, "Civilizing Kansas."

110. KESA Minutes, 1890, 10.

111. *Capital-Commonwealth*, 17 November 1888, WSC, 5:41.
112. *Our Messenger*, December 1888.
113. Bader, *Prohibition in Kansas*, 98.

CHAPTER FOUR. LIKE A FAMILY:
BUILDING THE ALLIANCE COMMUNITY

1. Craig Miner, *West of Wichita: Settling the High Plains of Kansas, 1865–1890* (Lawrence, Kans., 1986), 212–13; James Malin, "The Kinsley Boom of the Late Eighties," *Kansas Historical Quarterly* 4 (1935), 164–87; Raymond Miller, "The Economic Background of Populism in Kansas," *Mississippi Valley Historical Review* 11 (March 1925), 481–86.
2. Miner, *West of Wichita*, 213; Miller, "Background of Populism," 485.
3. Robert C. McMath, "Preface to Populism: The Origin and Economic Development of the Southern Farmers' Alliance in Kansas," 53–54; *Advocate* (Topeka), 23 April 1890, 9 July 1890; *Kansas Farmer*, 2 May 1889, 30 October 1889, 7 May 1890; *Free Press*, 28 June 1890; *Alliant*, 19 July 1890, 26 July 1890. For a fuller discussion about Alliance membership numbers and organizing tactics, see Michael Goldberg, "An Army of Women: Gender Relations and Politics in Kansas Populism, the Woman Movement, and the Republican Party, 1879–1896" (Ph.D. diss., Yale University, 1992), 199 n. 7. The best source for the tactics of Kansas Alliance organizers is S. M. Scott, *Champion Organizer of the Northwest* (McPherson, Kans., 1890), as well as numerous accounts in the state and local reform press (see, e.g., *Advocate* (Topeka), 2 January 1890; *Kansas Farmer*, 27 November 1889).
4. John Hicks, *The Populist Revolt* (Lincoln, Neb., 1961), 84; Peter H. Argersinger, *Populism and Politics: William Alfred Peffer and the People's Party* (Lexington, 1974), 62–66. For a more extensive discussion of the causes of the Populist uprising, see Goldberg, "Army of Women," 197–98 n. 6.
5. Goodwyn, *Democratic Promise*, ii.
6. Ibid. Basic demands taken from the 1889 "St. Louis demands" of the Southern Farmers' Alliance in Hicks, *Populist Revolt*, 427–28.
7. Bruce Palmer, *"Man over Money": The Southern Populist Critique of American Capitalism* (Chapel Hill, N.C., 1980), 31.
8. *Kansas Farmer*, 21 October 1891.
9. Ibid., 4 September 1889.
10. An Alliance member explaining the purpose of Alliance meetings and gatherings. *El Dorado Republican*, 18 September 1890.
11. *Advocate*, 25 June 1890.
12. Ibid., 7 May 1890.
13. Agendas of meetings drawn largely from Lone Tree Farmers' Alliance, no. 2005, Jewell County, Minutes of Meetings, 1890–1892, KSHS, a well as numerous

newspaper accounts including *Advocate,* 26 March 1890, and *Free Press,* 7 June 1890.

14. Mary Jo Wagner, "Farms, Families, and Reform: Women in the Farmers' Alliance and Populist Party" (Ph.D. diss., University of Oregon, 1986), 159–86, contains a very useful section on children's place in the Kansas Farmers' Alliance.

15. *Barton County Beacon,* 23 April 1891.

16. McMath, *Populist Vanguard,* 69, claims that Alliance women in the South were more likely to express feelings about religion than men. I have not found this to be the case in Kansas.

17. Peter H. Argersinger, "Pentecostal Politics in Kansas' Religion, the Farmers' Alliance, and the Gospel of Populism," *Kansas History* 1 (1969), 24–25.

18. One wonders what Jefferson the committed deist would have thought of such a combination. Palmer, *"Man over Money,"* 26–27.

19. *Advocate,* 23 September 1891.

20. Palmer, *"Man over Money,"* 126–29.

21. *Advocate,* 28 May 1890.

22. *Industrial Free Press,* 31 December 1892.

23. Ibid., 16 January 1891.

24. *Farmer's Wife,* April 1892.

25. Elizabeth Barr, "The Populist Uprising," in William Connelly, ed., *History of Kansas* (New York, 1928), 2:1159.

26. S. M. Scott, "The Great Sub-Treasury Plan," KSHS, n.d., n.p.; S. S. King, "Seed Time and Harvest," KSHS, n.d., n.p.

27. See, e.g., *Populist Hand-Book for Kansas: A Compilation from Official Sources of Some Facts for Use in the Succeeding Campaign* (Indianapolis, 1891).

28. *Industrial Advocate,* 31 December 1891. On libraries see *Industrial Free Press,* 11 February 1892.

29. *Advocate,* 13 March 1890; *Alliant,* 26 November 1891.

30. *Kansas Farmer,* 25 February 1891; Lone Tree Minutes; *Industrial Free Press,* 19 March 1891.

31. *Industrial Free Press,* 24 March 1890.

32. Lone Tree Minutes.

33. *Advocate* Topeka, 23 July 1890.

34. Ibid., 7 May 1890.

35. Ibid., 13 April 1892.

36. Scott, *Champion Organizer,* 21.

37. Annie Diggs, "Women in the Alliance Movement," *Arena* 6 (July 1892), 162–63.

38. Lone Tree Minutes.

39. *Advocate* 6 January 1890, 21 May 1890.

40. Ibid., 13 January 1890.

41. Ibid., 22 July 1892.

42. *Kansas Farmer,* 2 May 1889; *Industrial Free Press,* 2 February 1892.

43. *Industrial Advocate,* 7 August 1890; *Alliant,* 27 September 1890; *Industrial Free Press,* 19 March 1891; *Barton County Beacon,* 12 February 1891; *Advocate* (Topeka), 16 April 1890, 20 August 1890, 19 July 1891, 1 May 1892, 2 July 1894, among many others.

44. Cited in Scott G. McNall, *The Road to Rebellion: Class Formation and Kansas Populism, 1865–1900* (Chicago, 1988), 192–93.

45. *Advocate,* 16 July 1890.

46. *Farmer's Wife,* August 1891.

47. *Advocate,* 22 July 1891.

48. Ibid., 26 March 1890. See also ibid., 13 February 1890; *Western Farmer,* 25 June 1890; *Free Press,* 25 May 1890.

49. *Barton Beacon,* 11 January 1894.

50. *Barton County Beacon,* 2 October 1890; *Industrial Advocate,* 31 December 1891.

51. *Advocate,* 28 May 1890.

52. *Alliant,* 22 October 1891; *Barton County Beacon,* 2 October 1890; Alliance Woman's Association, Minutes, 1–3, KSHS.

53. *Advocate,* 25 June 1890.

54. Ibid., 28 May 1890.

55. Ibid., 20 May 1891.

56. Ibid., 19 October 1889; *Free Press,* 3 May 1890; *Barton County Beacon,* 4 September 90.

57. Goodwyn, *Populist Movement,* 135.

58. McNall, *Road to Rebellion,* 193.

59. *Advocate* Topeka, 18 June 1890.

60. Ibid., 19 October 1889.

61. Ibid., 18 June 1890.

62. Ibid.; *Free Press,* 7 June 1890.

63. *Advocate,* 14 May 1890, 28 May 1890.

64. Barr, "Populist Uprising," 1128. The selection originally appeared in 1913.

65. *Advocate,* 3 September 1890.

66. Although James Malin does not label them as such, his short study of a Farmers' Institute chapter demonstrates the general background and activities of progressive farmers. James C. Malin, "The Adaptation of the Agricultural System to Subhumid Environment: Illustrated by the Activities of the Wayne Township Farmers' Club of Edwards County, Kansas, 1886–1893," *Agricultural History* 10 (July 1936), 118–41. The basic public forum for progressive farmers was the *Kansas Farmer,* and their frequent contributions in the late 1880s to the early 1890s provides the reader with a good sense of their general philosophy.

67. *Kansas Farmer,* 26 April 1889.

68. Ibid., 31 December 1890, 19 November 1890; *Western Farmer,* 18 April 1889.

69. *Advocate* Topeka, 16 January 1890.

70. Hicks, *Populist Revolt*, 129.

71. *Advocate* Topeka, 29 February 1890.

72. *Kansas Farmer*, 11 March 1891.

73. Richard Hofstadter, *The Age of Reform: From Bryan to FDR* (New York, 1955), 23–59.

74. *Advocate*, 19 April 1890.

75. Cited in Goodwyn, *Democratic Promise*, 193.

76. *Advocate* Topeka, 30 April 1890.

77. Ibid., 6 March 1890.

78. *Kansas Farmer*, 28 March 1889.

79. *Advocate* Topeka, 7 June 1890.

80. *Kansas Farmer*, 16 February 1890.

81. Ibid.

82. *Our State*, 15 February 1890.

83. Cited in Miller, "Background of Populism," 92.

84. Cited in McNall, *Road to Rebellion*, 213.

85. Alliance editors also made the comparison between the Alliance and trade associations. See *Advocate*, 13 August 1890.

86. *Great Bend Register*, 17 April 1890. See also *Kansas Farmer*, 1 January 1890.

87. It is thus ironic that Diggs, who held a position of real influence in the Alliance and who championed women's place in politics and business, utilized this language unselfconsciously.

88. *Industrial Free Press*, 23 January 1891.

89. Cited in McNall, *Road to Rebellion*, 194–95.

90. *Advocate*, 25 June 1890.

91. *Kansas Farmer*, 13 October 1889.

## CHAPTER FIVE. "FOR BETSY AND BABIES": FROM FARMERS' ALLIANCE TO POPULIST PARTY

1. Peter H. Argersinger, *Populism and Politics: William Alfred Peffer and the People's Party* (Lexington, Ky., 1974), 23–24.

2. For a more extensive narrative on the creation of the Kansas Populist Party, see O. Gene Clanton, *Kansas Populism: Ideas and Men* (Lawrence, 1969), 50–61.

3. Ibid., 57.

4. John Hicks, *The Populist Revolt* (Lincoln, Neb., 1961), 128.

5. *Winfield Courier*, 17 April 1890.

6. *El Dorado Republican*, 31 January 1890; *Great Bend Register*, 15 May 1890.

7. Argersinger, *Populism and Politics*, 43–46.

8. Cited in Lawrence Goodwyn, *Democratic Promise: The Populist Moment in America* (New York, 1976), 186.

9. Clanton, *Kansas Populism,* 55–56.

10. *Great Bend Republican,* 29 August 1890.

11. Cited in Goodwyn, *Democratic Promise,* 187.

12. *Advocate,* 23 July 1890, 13 August 1890. See also Argersinger, *Populism and Politics,* 41.

13. *Alliant,* 13 September 1890.

14. The concerns of Republican Alliance members have been largely ignored by historians. An important exception is Scott G. McNall, *The Road to Rebellion: Class Formation and Kansas Populism, 1865–1900* (Chicago: 1988), 199–200.

15. Hicks, *Populist Revolt,* 155.

16. *Republican Plaindealer,* 31 October 1890.

17. *Kansas Farmer,* 29 April 1890, cited in McNall, *Road to Rebellion,* 199.

18. While such estimates must be considered carefully, the ever higher number of suballiances reporting to the *Advocate* testifies to the Alliance's continuing success in organizing new members.

19. *Alliant,* 15 November 1890.

20. "To the Polls," by J. C. Ruppenthal, from *Songs for the Toiler,* KSHS.

21. *Journal and Triumph,* 17 April 1890.

22. See the invitation of the *Western Farmer,* 28 August 1888, to women to join the local Union Labor club. (Despite its title, the *Western Farmer* was affiliated with the Union Labor Party rather than the Alliance.) See also the Ottawa *Journal and Triumph*'s acknowledgment of women at the Union Labor convention (6 September 1888) and its remarks about women and politics (15 August 1889).

23. Ibid., 16 August 1888. See also ibid., 15 August 1889; *Western Farmer,* 21 June 1888.

24. *Industrial Educator,* 9 May 1890; *Advocate,* 30 January 1890, 6 July 1890, 23 July 1890; *Kansas Farmer,* 26 November 1890.

25. *Advocate,* 30 January 1890.

26. Cited in Hicks, *Populist Revolt,* 168. See also the song "Goodbye, My Party, Goodbye," ibid., 169.

27. This phrase, representative of the idea of alliance men as protectors of their families, was often used by Populists. See particularly *Kansas Farmer,* 26 November 1890.

28. *Advocate,* 25 June 1890, 4 June 1890.

29. Ibid., 27 August 1890.

30. Ibid., 30 January 1890. Italics in original.

31. Ibid., 4 June 1890. See also ibid., 4 July 1890.

32. Cited in McNall, *Road to Rebellion,* 176.

33. Clanton writes in *Kansas Populism,* 266, "Mrs. Lease later denied having originated the statement, but she said she let it stand because she thought 'it was a right good bit of advice.'"

34. Background on Lease from Clanton, *Kansas Populism,* 73–78; Edward T. James, ed., *Notable American Women* (Cambridge, Mass., 1971), 2:380–82.

35. Cited in Clanton, *Kansas Populism,* 74–75.
36. *Kansas Sunflower,* 31 October 1894.
37. *Monitor,* 3 October 1890, cited in Clanton, *Kansas Populism,* 76.
38. Cited in Mary Jo Wagner, "Farms, Families, and Reform: Women in the Farmers' Alliance and Populist Party" (Ph.D. diss., University of Oregon, 1986), 23–24.
39. The characterization of White as a "pudgy little editor" comes from Clanton, *Kansas Populism,* 75, and precedes White's description of Lease. Though Clanton has no explicit gender analysis here, his juxtaposition of White's appearance with his judgment of Lease makes for a subtle comment on the era's double standard.
40. *Kansas City Star,* 1 April 1891, cited in Clanton, *Kansas Populism,* 265.
41. The term *man-wife* is cited in Wagner, "Farms, Families, and Reform" and is attributed to the *Leavenworth Post.*
42. *Advocate,* 27 August 1890.
43. *Journal and Triumph,* 10 July 1890.
44. *Capital,* 11 July 1891, 15 July 1891.
45. *Advocate,* 20 July 1892.
46. *Kansas City Star,* 5 August 1900, cited in Clanton, *Kansas Populism,* 79. Other background information from James, *Notable American Women,* 1:481–82.
47. Clanton, *Kansas Populism,* 79; *Advocate,* 4 June 1890.
48. *State Journal,* 5 August 1892; *Kansas City Star,* 1 April 1891, cited in Clanton, *Kansas Populism,* 75.
49. Cited in James, *Notable American Women,* 1:481.
50. *Barton County Beacon,* 12 March 1891.
51. *Topeka Daily Capital,* 6 November 1890, cited in Clanton, *Kansas Populism,* 87.

## CHAPTER SIX. THE MATRIX OF REFORM

1. The Democrats had wisely chosen the popular Free State governor, Charles Robinson, to make it easier for resubmissionist Republicans to abandon their party. The resubmissionists hoped to have the prohibition amendment resubmitted to the voters.
2. O. Gene Clanton, *Kansas Populism: Ideas and Men* (Lawrence, Kans., 1969), 87–88.
3. Peter H. Argersinger, *Populism and Politics: William Alfred Peffer and the People's Party* (Lexington, Ky., 1974), 73–75.
4. Robert Smith Bader, *Prohibition in Kansas* (Lawrence, Kans., 1986), 106–32, portrays the 1890s as a frustrating period for prohibitionists.
5. *Daily Capital,* 11 November 1890, cited in Clanton, *Kansas Populism,* 88.
6. Ibid., 91–92.

7. Susan B. Anthony and Elizabeth Cady Stanton, eds., *The History of Woman Suffrage* (New York, 1969), 4:653.

8. Ibid.

9. Cited in Clanton, *Kansas Populism*, 94–95.

10. Anthony and Stanton, *History of Woman Suffrage*, 4:653–54.

11. Clanton, *Kansas Populism*, 87.

12. *Daily Capital*, 14 August 1890.

13. *Our Messenger*, February 1892.

14. *Kansas Farmer*, 11 June 1890, 18 June 1890.

15. *Advocate*, 18 June 1890, 2 July 1890.

16. Ibid., 19 October 1889.

17. Ibid., 2 March 1892, cited in Jack S. Blocker, "The Politics of Reform: Populists, Prohibition, and Woman Suffrage, 1891–1892," *Historian* 34 (August 1972), 624–25.

18. *Journal and Triumph*, 26 June 1890.

19. *Alliant*, 30 August 1890.

20. On Ives and the impact of the 1890 election on Kansas prohibition, see Bader, *Prohibition in Kansas*, 113–16.

21. *Farmer's Wife*, December 1891.

22. Blocker, "Politics of Reform," 623–29; Clanton, *Kansas Populism*, 100; Bader, *Prohibition in Kansas*, 108.

23. Hicks, *The Populist Revolt*, 165; Clanton, *Kansas Populism*, 100.

24. Clanton, *Kansas Populism*, 100.

25. *Advocate*, 27 May 1891. Italics in original.

26. Ibid., 20 April 1892.

27. Ibid., 6 April 1892.

28. Argersinger, *Populism and Politics*, 127–29.

29. Ibid., 116.

30. Clanton, *Kansas Populism*, 65.

31. Argersinger, *Populism and Politics*, 140. Biographical information on Briedenthal from Clanton, *Kansas Populism*, 121–22.

32. The one exception was Congressman Jerry Simpson, who had been a Union Labor–Democratic fusion candidate in 1888. Simpson enjoyed wide Democratic support in the Seventh District, which included the Democratic stronghold of Wichita.

33. Argersinger, *Populism and Politics*, 123.

34. Ibid., 134.

35. Ibid., 133.

36. Ibid., 150–51.

37. Ibid., 136.

38. *Kiowa Times*, 16 December 1892. See also Argersinger, *Populism and Politics*, 141.

39. *Industrial Free Press*, 14 July 1892.

40. *Advocate*, 14 December 1892.

41. *Kansas Agitator*, 1 September 1892, cited in Argersinger, *Populism and Politics*, 141.

42. *Advocate*, 14 December 1892.

43. McNall, *Road to Rebellion*, 274–75.

44. Robert C. McMath, *Populist Vanguard: A History of the Southern Farmers' Alliance*, (Chapel Hill, N.C., 1975), 104.

45. *Kansas Farmer*, 16 March 1891.

46. Clanton, *Kansas Populism*, 102. Some Alliance leaders, according to Clanton, "did not particularly care about graduating." Men such as S. M. Scott remained committed to the Alliance's mission despite the opportunity to seek public office. Clanton claims that these new leaders were more conservative than their Populist brethren. Alliance members continued to support the radical demands of the Omaha Platform, however. My argument is that Alliance leaders were not so much politically conservative as radically nonpartisan.

47. *Industrial Free Press*, 8 December 1892, 5 January 1893, 12 March 1893, 27 April 1893; *Advocate*, 1 February 1893. McMath, *Populist Vanguard*, 139, notes a similar pattern for suballiances in the South.

48. *Advocate*, 13 December 1893.

49. See *Industrial Free Press, Barton Beacon, Liberator, Alliant*, and *Kansas Agitator* during this period.

50. *Advocate*, 22 July 1891, 28 August 1891; *Industrial Advocate*, 14 April 1892; *Alliant*, 26 November 1891.

51. *Industrial Free Press*, 10 November 1892.

52. Ibid., 23 April 1891.

53. *Barton County Beacon*, 14 September 1890.

54. *Industrial Free Press*, 14 July 1892. See also *Alliant*, 25 May 1893.

55. *Farmer's Wife*, May 1893. See also ibid., November 1892.

56. *Industrial Free Press*, 20 February 1891.

57. *Farmer's Wife*, May 1893.

58. *Advocate*, 12 December 1893.

59. *Industrial Free Press*, 29 December 1892.

60. *Advocate*, 16 November 1892.

61. *Barton County Beacon*, 4 September 1890.

62. Proceedings, Alliance Women's Association of Barton County, Kansas (Great Bend, Kans., 1891), 3.

63. Ibid., 4.

64. *Barton County Beacon*, 4 September 1890.

65. Ibid., 9 October 1890, 16 October 1890. Italics in original.

66. *Advocate*, 11 April 1894.

67. *Industrial Free Press*, 13 February 1891.

68. Ibid., 4 February 1892.

69. Ibid., 7 May 1890.

70. Ibid., 26 March 1891, 14 April 1892.

71. Ibid., 14 April 1892, 11 August 1892.

72. *Advocate,* 29 March 1893.

73. Ibid.

74. Ibid., 30 March 1892.

75. Ibid., 3 February 1892.

76. Ibid., 16 March 1892. For others who used the "equal rights to all" argument, see ibid., 17 February 1892; *Industrial Free Press,* 30 April 1891, 4 February 1892; *Barton Beacon,* 12 April 1894.

77. *Alliant,* 15 November 1890.

78. Petitions to Congress to consider woman suffrage had in the past been made by nonpoliticians, both women and men. *Advocate,* 17 June 1891.

79. Ibid.

80. Ibid., 1 July 1891.

81. See Marilyn Dell Brady, "Populism and Feminism in a Newspaper by and for Women of the Kansas Farmers' Alliance, 1891–1894," *Kansas History* 7 (Winter 1894/95). Despite the article's title, Brady notes the inappropriateness of the paper's contents and the nonagrarian agenda of its writers.

82. *Farmer's Wife,* October 1891.

83. Ibid., January 1893.

84. Ibid., September 1891.

85. The NWA did include several Farmers' Alliance officers, including Bina Otis and M. C. Clark. Both were among a small group of Alliance women who moved easily between the Woman Movement and the Alliance. For list of officers see *Farmer's Wife,* October 1891.

86. Cited in Brady, "Populism and Feminism," 284.

87. Ibid., 284; Wagner, "Farms, Families, and Reform," 317.

88. Cited in Mari Jo Buhle, *Women and American Socialism,* 88.

89. *Farmer's Wife,* September 1892.

90. *Advocate,* 9 August 1893.

91. KESA Minutes, 1891, n.p.

92. Bader, *Prohibition in Kansas,* 107.

93. KESA Minutes, 1891, n.p.

94. These included Rev. Anna Shaw of the National American Woman Suffrage Association and the British suffragette Florence Balgarnie. Anthony and Stanton, *History of Woman Suffrage,* 4:642.

95. Ibid.

96. Clanton, *Kansas Populism,* 122; Republican State Central Committee, *Proceedings of the Republican State Convention* (KSHS, n.p., 1982).

97. Anthony and Stanton, *History of Woman Suffrage,* 4:643.

98. *Kansas Chief,* in Republican Party Clippings, 1, KSHS. See also Argersinger, *Populism and Politics,* 146.

99. Argersinger, *Populism and Politics,* 163.

100. WCTU Minutes, 1892, 41.

101. Argersinger *Populism and Politics,* 149–50.

## CHAPTER SEVEN. "AN ARMY OF WOMEN"

1. *Farmer's Wife,* November 1892, December 1892.

2. O. Gene Clanton, *Kansas Populism: Ideas and Men* (Lawrence, Kans., 1969), 131–35; Peter H. Argersinger, *Populism and Politics: William Alfred Peffer and the People's Party* (Lexington, Ky., 1974), 154–55; Scott G. McNall, *The Road to Rebellion: Class Formation and Kansas Populism, 1865–1900* (Chicago, 1988), 280–81.

3. Plumb had been one of the few Republicans to have any sympathy for the plight of the farmer.

4. Argersinger, *Populism and Politics,* 155–57.

5. *Advocate,* 15 February 1893; Mary Jo Wagner, "Farms, Families, and Reform: Women in the Farmers' Alliance and Populist Party" (Ph.D. diss., University of Oregon, 1986), 333.

6. *Farmer's Wife,* May 1893.

7. *New Era,* 2 September 1893.

8. *Kansas Suffrage,* August 1893.

9. *Farmer's Wife,* January 1893.

10. Ibid., October 1893, December 1893.

11. *Advocate,* 23 June 1893; *Farmer's Wife,* October 1893.

12. Johns's transgressions included using Lease's name to attract a crowd when Johns supposedly knew that Lease would not be in attendance.

13. Susan B. Anthony and Elizabeth Cady Stanton, eds., *The History of Woman Suffrage* (New York, 1969), 4:222.

14. *Advocate,* 6 September 1893. See also Anthony and Stanton, *History of Woman Suffrage* 4:644.

15. Carrie Chapman Catt, Rachel Foster Avery, and Alice Stone Blackwell served as representatives of the National American Woman Suffrage Association.

16. *Kansas Suffrage,* November 1893; *Advocate,* 6 July 1893.

17. *Farmer's Wife,* December 1893. Italics added.

18. *Kansas Sunflower,* September 1893; these newspapers also included *Kansas Suffrage* and *Woman's Friend.*

19. *Kansas Sunflower,* August 1893.

20. WCTU Minutes of the Annual Meeting, 1893, 37; *Farmer's Wife,* May 1893.

21. *Blade,* 10 October 1894.

22. *Kansas Blackman,* 18 May 1894; *Blade,* 7 July 1894.

23. *Our Messenger,* May 1894; Anthony and Stanton, *History of Woman Suffrage,* 4:645; *Farmer's Wife,* April 1894; Wilda M. Smith, "A Half Century of Struggle: Gaining Woman Suffrage in Kansas," *Kansas History* 4 (Summer, 1981), 79.

24. *Kansas Sunflower,* September 1893.

25. WCTU Minutes, 1893, 37.

26. Mary Couper, "History of Woman Suffrage in Kansas," 32 (KSHS). The source is a letter from Thurston to Couper.

27. *Advocate,* 9 May 1894; *Kansas Suffrage,* August 1893; *Barton Beacon,* 31 May 1894.

28. *Farmer's Wife,* May 1894.

29. Ibid., May 1894.

30. *Alliant,* 19 April 1894.

31. Ibid., 7 June 1894.

32. On Colorado Populism see James Wright, *The Politics of Populism: Dissent in Colorado* (New Haven, 1974). On the Colorado campaign see Carolyn Stefanco, "Networking on the Frontier: The Colorado Woman Suffrage Movement, 1876–1893," in Susan Armitage and Elizabeth Jameson, eds., *The Women's West* (Norman, Okla., 1987), 272–73; and Anthony and Stanton, *History of Woman Suffrage,* 4:511–13.

33. *Industrial Free Press,* 15 April 1894.

34. *Record,* 25 May 1893; Clanton, *Kansas Populism,* 151; *Journal and Triumph,* 7 June 1894.

35. *Woman's Friend,* May 1894; *Journal and Triumph,* 19 May 1894, Woman Suffrage Clippings, v. 1 (hereafter cited as WSC).

36. *Woman's Friend,* May 1894.

37. Clanton, *Kansas Populism,* 151; *Kansas Suffrage,* May 1894.

38. *State Journal,* 6 June 1894, WSC, v. 1.

39. Foster had worked for Republican interests in other women's and reformers' conventions. WCTU Clippings, 123–24, KSHS; Edward T. James, ed., *Notable American Women* (Cambridge, Mass., 1971), 2:651–52.

40. Republican Party Clippings, 1:45 KSHS.

41. Ibid.; *Courier* (Council Grove), 15 June 1894.

42. Republican Party Clippings, 1:45.

43. Anthony and Stanton, *History of Woman Suffrage,* 4:645.

44. Argersinger, *Populism and Politics,* 171.

45. Ibid., 166–73.

46. *Journal and Triumph,* 21 June 1894. All quotations from the Populist convention are from this source.

47. The final vote was 333–269.

48. Carrie Chapman Catt and Nettie Rogers, *Woman Suffrage and Politics: The Inner Story of the Suffrage Movement* (Seattle, 1969); *Barton Beacon,* 21 June 1894.

49. WSC, 1:7 (italics in original); *Farmer's Wife,* October 1894.

50. A comprehensive account of tensions between Populist and Republican suffragists may be found in Wagner, "Farmers, Families, and Reform," 338–41.

51. *Barton Beacon,* 28 June 1894; W. Smith, "A Half-Century of Struggle," 90–92.

52. *Barton Beacon,* 23 August 1894.

53. *Daily Capital,* 14 June 1894.

54. *Industrial Free Press,* 22 June 1894; *Barton Beacon,* 12 July 1894; *Council Grove Courier,* 22 June 1894.

55. *Great Bend Register,* 7 July 1894.

56. *Kansas Sunflower* (Clyde), 3 October 1894; *Osborne County News,* 21 June 1894; *Barton Beacon,* 27 September 1894.

57. These observations are based on a survey of numerous Populist papers, including the *Barton Beacon,* the *Opinion,* the *Liberator,* the *Advocate,* the *Industrial Advocate,* the *Kansas Agitator,* and the *Industrial Free Press.*

58. *Liberator,* 22 June 1894.

59. Clanton, *Kansas Populism,* 166–67.

60. Argersinger, *Populism and Politics,* 175–76.

61. McNall, *Road to Rebellion,* 284.

62. Argersinger, *Populism and Politics,* 176–77.

63. *New Era,* 3 June 1894, cited in Argersinger, *Populism and Politics,* 179.

64. Clanton, *Kansas Populism,* 166; *Industrial Free Press,* 9 August 1894, 6 September 1894.

65. Lease had been particularly disturbed by her father's death in the infamous Confederate prison camp at Andersonville. Argersinger, *Populism and Politics,* 168–69.

66. Cited in Clanton, *Kansas Populism,* 144.

67. *State Journal,* 13 July 1894. All quotations about the Lease-Diggs imbroglio are from this source unless otherwise noted.

68. *Capital,* 13 July 1894.

69. *Barton Beacon,* 4 January 1894.

70. Argersinger, *Populism and Politics,* 161–62.

71. John Hicks, *The Populist Revolt,* 281, 310–11.

72. *Alliant,* 25 May 1893; *Barton Beacon,* 8 February 1894.

73. See, e.g., *Industrial Free Press* after May 1894; *Industrial Advocate* after June 1894.

74. *Alliant,* 5 May 1894, 3 June 1894, 12 May 1894.

75. *Farmer's Wife,* October 1893.

76. *Barton Beacon,* 16 August 1894, 12 April 1894, 26 April 1894; *Advocate,* 13 September 1893.

77. The title of this section is taken from Willa Cather, "Eldorado: A Kansas Recessional," *New England Magazine* 24 (1901). The story describes the cycle of boom and bust in Kansas.

78. Clanton, *Kansas Populism,* 167–68. Papers surveyed include *Barton Bea-*

*con, Opinion, Liberator, Advocate, Industrial Advocate, Kansas Agitator, Industrial Free Press, Smith County Journal, Daily Capital, Register,* and *Republican Plaindealer.*

79. *Smith County Journal,* 5 November 1894.

80. Argersinger, *Populism and Politics,* 151–91. For a more extensive discussion of the historiography of the 1894 election, see Michael Goldberg, "An Army of Women: Gender Relations and Politics in Kansas Populism, the Woman Movement, and the Republican Party, 1879–1896" (Ph. D. diss., Yale University, 1992), 372 n. 5.

81. See, e.g., "Women's Column," *Industrial Advocate,* 11 December 1894; Laura Johns to Lucy Johnston, 11 November 1894, Lucy Browne Johnston Collection, KSHS.

82. Thurston, secretary of the amendment campaign committee, was able to gain access to the ballots after the election and then "carefully tabulated" the results. Anthony and Stanton, *History of Woman Suffrage,* 4:647. For a vote count of the amendment, see Clanton, *Kansas Populism,* 168–69.

83. Anthony and Stanton, *History of Woman Suffrage,* 4:662.

84. Stefanco, "Networking," 272–73; Anthony and Stanton, *History of Woman Suffrage,* 4:511–13.

85. Lucy Johnston, "History of the Kansas Woman Suffrage Movement," manuscript; and Johns to Johnston, 11 November 1894, Lucy Browne Johnston Collection.

86. *Kansas City Times,* 6 December 1894, 7 December 1894, WSC, v. 1.

87. Johns to Johnston, 11 November 1894, Lucy Browne Johnston Collection. All quotations in this paragraph are from this source. Annie Diggs was in Colorado and did not participate in the struggles between KESA factions.

88. Ibid., 15 July 1895.

89. *Kansas City Times,* 7 December 1894; *Advocate,* 19 December 1894.

90. *Kansas City Times,* 7 December 1894.

91. *Advocate,* 20 February 1895; Johns to Johnston, 15 July 1895, Lucy Browne Johnston Collection.

92. Johns to Johnston, 15 July 1895, Lucy Browne Johnston Collection; Barr, cited in Wagner, "Farms, Families, and Reform," 342.

93. Lucy Kimber to Alice Stone Blackwell, Woman Suffrage Collection, KSHS. Alice Stone Blackwell was the daughter of Lucy Stone and Henry Blackwell, who had opposed Stanton and Anthony's anti-Republican strategy in the 1867 campaign.

94. W. Smith, "Half-Century of Struggle," 84.

95. On the eclipse of the Woman Movement and the emergence of feminism, see Nancy F. Cott, *The Grounding of Modern Feminism* (New Haven, 1987), 3–10.

96. On the new business orientation of post-1894 Populist leaders, see Clanton, *Kansas Populism,* 182–83.

97. *Advocate*, 30 October 1895, 11 December 1895.

98. See, e.g., *Industrial Free Press*, *Kiowa County Times*, and the *Barton Beacon* for 1895.

99. Cited in Clanton, *Kansas Populism*, 197.

100. Cited in Argersinger, *Populism and Politics*, 232.

101. *Barton Beacon*, 19 April 1895.

102. Kansas City *Star*, 25 July 1900, in Populist Party Clippings, v. 2, KSHS. All quotations in this paragraph are from this source.

103. Cited in James, *Notable American Women*, 1:482.

# NOTE ON HISTORIOGRAPHY AND SOURCES

In this study I have tried to make subjects that are well known to historians appear in a new light. Rather than create a whole new picture of the Populists, Woman Movement activists, and Republican Party leaders, I hoped to expose different shadings of meaning. Traditional political historians will no doubt notice that I have done little new research on such subjects as voting patterns, party structure, legislative histories, and economic conditions. Instead, I have integrated the findings of others into my study to demonstrate that although such topics are not usually associated with an understanding of gender relations, much can be learned by incorporating this new perspective.

Beyond my broader intention to integrate gender and politics into our understanding of the Gilded Age, I have sought to fill in certain historiographical holes. Although scholars have become increasingly aware of women in the Populist movement, no one has yet published a full-scale account of the way women specifically, and gender more generally, shaped both the Farmers' Alliance and the Populist Party. Similarly, no historian has yet produced an extended study of the Woman Movement's involvement with state party politics and the way that involvement influenced the political history of the state. Finally, historians have not yet examined how the cultural assumptions of Woman Movement activists molded their political culture and their political fortunes. I have sought to fill these

299

historiographical gaps not simply by inserting women into the picture but by stressing that gender is relational (between women and men, among different cultural groups), integrated with different causative factors, and dynamic.

In the interest of writing a more compact, readable book, I have largely stayed away from discussions of specific historiographical debates, such as the role of cooperatives in the formation of the Populist movement. Rather, I have directed interested readers to appropriate places in my dissertation where I discuss these debates more fully. In most instances, I have found myself borrowing from different sides in the debates. My understanding of Gilded Age politics has been enriched by the complexity provided by these multiple perspectives.

Because the historiography of women's and men's political culture is well known, I have not included an extended discussion of these texts here. However, I should point out those works whose analytical insights I found particularly helpful: Richard Slotkin, *The Fatal Environment: The Myth of the Frontier in the Age of Industrialization, 1800–1890* (New York, 1985); Alan Trachtenberg, *The Incorporation of America: Culture and Society in the Gilded Age* (New York, 1982); Paula Baker, "The Domestication of Politics: Women and American Political Society, 1780–1920," *American Historical Review* 89 (June 1984); Paula Baker, *The Moral Frameworks of Public Life: Gender, Politics, and the State in Rural New York, 1870–1930* (New York, 1991); Michael McGerr, *The Decline of Popular Politics: The American North, 1865–1928* (New York, 1986); John Hicks, *The Populist Revolt* (Lincoln, Nebr., 1961); Lawrence Goodwyn, *Democratic Promise: The Populist Moment in America* (New York, 1976); Robert C. McMath Jr., *Populist Vanguard: A History of the Southern Farmers' Alliance* (Chapel Hill, N.C., 1975); Richard Hofstadter, *The Age of Reform: From Bryan to FDR* (New York, 1955); Ruth Bordin, *Woman and Temperance: The Quest for Power and Liberty, 1873–1900* (Philadelphia, 1981); Ellen DuBois, *Feminism and Suffrage: The Emergence of an Independent Women's Movement in America, 1848–1869* (Ithaca, N.Y., 1978); and Mari Jo Buhle, *Women and American Socialism, 1870–1920* (Urbana, 1981). I have made good use of the rich historiography of Kansas Populism, but I found two books particularly helpful: O. Gene Clanton, *Kansas Populism: Ideas and Men* (Lawrence, Kans., 1969); and Peter H. Argersinger, *Populism and Politics: William Alfred Peffer and the People's Party* (Lexington, 1974). Robert Bader, *Prohibition in Kansas* (Lawrence, Kans., 1986), was an invaluable source for both prohibitionist politics and the strategies of the WCTU.

I was especially dependent on other historians when constructing a portrait of daily life in Gilded Age Kansas. Although much has been made of the split between "old" and "new" Western historians, I felt equally comfortable borrowing from both. In this study I have benefited especially from the work of Everett Dick, *The Sod House Frontier, 1854–1890: A Social History of the Northern Plains* (New York, 1937); Gilbert Fite, *The Farmer's Last Frontier, 1865–1890* (New York, 1966); Craig Miner, *West of Wichita: Settling the High Plains of Kansas, 1865–1890*

(Lawrence, 1986); Glenda Riley, *The Female Frontier: A Comparative View of Women on the Prairie and the Plains* (Lawrence, Kans., 1988); and Cornelia Butler Flora and Jan L. Flora, "Structure of Agriculture and Women's Culture in the Great Plains," *Great Plains Quarterly* 8 (Fall 1988). Two books that do not bear directly on my topic but influenced my thinking about women's intercultural relations in the West are Sarah Deutsch, *No Separate Refuge: Culture, Class, and Gender on the Anglo-Hispanic Frontier in the American Southwest, 1880–1940* (New York, 1987); and Peggy Pascoe, *Relations of Rescue: The Search for Female Moral Authority in the American West, 1874–1939* (New York, 1990).

While I have not included any explicit theoretical discussions in the text, feminist, gender, and cultural theorists have shaped many of the questions I have brought to this study. The major influences on my understanding of gender relations include Joan W. Scott, *Gender and the Politics of History* (New York, 1988); Judith Butler, *Gender Trouble: Feminism and the Subversion of Identity;* the essays in Juliet Mitchell and Ann Oakley, eds., *What Is Feminism?: A Re-Examination* (New York, 1986), especially those by Juliet Mitchell, "Reflections on Twenty Years of Feminism," and Nancy Cott, "Feminist Theory and Feminist Movements"; Anthony Rotundo, *American Manhood: Transformations in Masculinity from the Revolution to the Modern Era* (New York, 1993); Mark C. Carnes, *Secret Ritual and Manhood in Victorian America* (New Haven, 1989); Harry Brod, ed., *The Making of Masculinities: The New Men's Studies* (New York, 1987); and Judith Lorber and Susan A. Farrell, eds., *The Social Construction of Gender* (Newbury Park, 1991).

I have made my way through the vast and often unnecessarily dense landscape of cultural theory as something of a tourist rather than as a resident. My choice of destinations has been random at times, but it has rarely failed to expand my thinking about power relations, discourse, and cultural boundaries. Some of the most useful works include Clifford Geertz, *Local Knowledge: Further Essays in Interpretive Anthropology* (New York, 1983); Marshall Blonsky, ed., *On Signs* (Baltimore, 1985); Michel Foucault, *The History of Sexuality* (New York, 1980); Irene Diamond and Lee Quinby, eds., *Feminism and Foucault: Reflections on Resistance* (Boston, 1988); Stuart Hall, ed., *Culture, Media, Language: Working Papers in Cultural Studies, 1972–1979* (London, 1980); Dick Hebdige, *Subculture: The Meaning of Style* (London, 1979); Mikhail Bakhtin, *The Dialogic Imagination: Four Essays,* edited and translated by Caryl Emerson and Michael Holquist (Austin, 1981); and Hayden White, *Tropics of Discourse: Essays in Cultural Criticism* (Baltimore, 1978).

As a cultural historian of politics, I am primarily concerned with the way individuals, groups, and movements negotiate systems of meaning—how political activists use language and symbols to make sense of their world and effect political change and how these discourses define their options. I have therefore largely employed those primary sources which provide access to activists' public discourse.

In my work I have not gone far beyond the massive collections of the Kansas State Historical Society used by other historians of Kansas Populism, the Woman Movement, and the Republican Party.

Although I benefited a great deal from organizational records, personal letters, campaign literature, and collections of prominent politicians, I spent most of my time scouring through the Kansas State Historical Society's rich collection of newspapers from the period: *Advocate* (Topeka); *Advocate* (Leavenworth); *Afro-American Advocate* (Coffeyville); *Alliant* (Concordia); *American Citizen* (Topeka); *Baptist Headlight* (Topeka); *Barton Beacon* (Great Bend); *Barton County Beacon* (Great Bend); *Parsons Weekly Blade; Topeka Capital; Topeka Capital-Commonwealth; Chapman Courier; Council Grove Courier; Winfield Courier; Topeka Daily Capital; Farmer's Advocate* (Salina); *Farmer's Wife* (Topeka); *Free Press* (Hays); *Meade Globe; Historic Times* (Lawrence); *Industrial Advocate* (Augusta); *Industrial Educator* (Winfield); *Industrial Free Press* (Winfield); *Journal and Triumph* (Ottawa); *Kansas Agitator* (Garnett); *Kansas Blackman* (North Topeka); *Kansas City Star; Kansas Farmer* (Topeka); *Kansas Lever* (Ottawa); *Kansas Suffrage* (Topeka); *Kansas Sunflower* (Clyde); *Kansas Sunflower* (Garnett); *Kansas Weekly Chief* (Troy); *Kiowa Times; Lawrence Tribune; Leavenworth Times; Liberator* (Norton); *Lucifer the Light Bearer* (Valley Falls); *New Era* (Valley Falls); *Lindsborg News; McPherson Opinion; Osborne County News* (Osborne); *Ottawa News; Our Messenger* (Topeka); *Our State* (Topeka); *Prohibitionist* (Lyons); *Great Bend Register; El Dorado Republican; Osage City Republican; Republican Plaindealer* (Garnett); *Rising Sun* (Salina); *Sickle and Sheaf* (Oskaloosa); *Smith County Journal* (Smith Centre); *Garden City Sentinel; Standard* (Leavenworth); *State Journal* (Topeka); *Suffrage Advocate* (Lawrence); *Sun* (Parsons); *Western Advocate* (Burr Oak); *Western Farmer* (Farmer City); and *Woman's Friend* (Yates Center).

# INDEX

*Advocate, The,* 136, 257; support of women's participation, 141; attacks on Republican Party, 152; agitates for new political party, 161; and Women's Republican Club, 211; and Laura Johns, 221–22. *See also* McLallin, Stephen

AERA. *See* American Equal Rights Association

African-American leaders, ideology, 44; support of Republican Party, 44–45; and KESA, 64; and the WCTU, 64, 113–14; and African-American women, 64, 114, 229; and woman suffrage, 64, 228–29

African-Americans, and 1887 Leavenworth election, 106, 108–9

African-American women: relationship with African-American leadership, 45; and Woman Movement, 60; and the WCTU, 62–63; and African-American leadership, 64; commonalties with Anglo middle-class women, 65–66; and anti-immigrant comments, 65–66; and woman suffrage, 65, 229

Alliance Women's Association, (AWA), 202–3

*Alliant* (Concordia), 248

American Equal Rights Association (AERA), 15, 17

Anderson, Naomi, 63

"Angry White Male," 261–62

Anthony, D. R., 15, 105, 106

Anthony, Susan B., 14–17; compared to Frances Willard, 77; and Republicans, 77, 236, 240, 242, 255–56; and municipal woman suffrage bill, 88,

tion, 207; and Alliance women, 207; and state woman suffrage amendment campaigns, 214, 232; and 1892 Populist convention, 215–16; symbolism of relationship with Laura Johns, 226; and 1894 Populist convention, 238–39; maintains influence, 259. *See also* Farmers' Alliance; KESA; Populist Party; Woman Movement
Dole, Bob, 262
Douglas, Stephen, 11
Doster, Frank, 238, 242

economic conditions, and effect of farmers, 23–25
editors, Populists: and state woman suffrage amendment, 242–43; similarity to Republican editors, 244; and reporting of Farmers' Alliance, 248
editors, Republicans: reaction to municipal suffrage, 96–103; reaction to Farmers' Alliance's politicization, 164–66; recognition of farm women's role in Alliance, 175; criticize *Farmer's Wife,* 208; similarity to Populist editors, 244
Elder, Peter Percival, 213; and state woman suffrage, 187–89; and 1894 Populist convention, 239
*El Dorado Republican,* 164–65
elections: 1890 state election, 182–83, 184; 1891 state election, 194; 1891 Topeka mayoral election, 211; 1892 state election, 216–17; 1894 state election, 250
elevator operators, 24
Ellsworth, Bertha, 71–73, 88
Emery, Sarah Van, 203

farm children, 33
"Farmer is the Man, The," 156–57

Farmers' Alliance, Kansas, 128; and gendered political discourse, 6, 136, 145, 155–56; and farm family ideal, 7, 129–30, 132, 142, 148; political ideology, 129; compared with Woman Movement, 129, 198; compared to mainstream parties, 130; and gender relations, 130–31, 141, 201, 205–6; mixed-gender political culture, 130, 132, 142; and political education, 131, 136–37; roots in Anglo farm culture, 133; children's role in, 133–34; and religion, 134–35; members' relations with townspeople, 135, 147, 153–54, 155–59, 197–98, 202–5; and democratic process of organization, 137; suspicion of politicians, 137–38, 196; and non-partisanship, 138; women as percentage of membership and leadership, 139–42; women as participants, 139, 143–44, 148, 161, 165–66, 196–203, 248–49, 258; 1890 campaign, 145–48; debates about farming practices, 148–51; and the economy, 148–52; and cooperatives, 153–54; and definitions of manliness, 156–59; transformation into Populist Party, 161–63, 291n. 46; new party as extension of Alliance political community, 166; objections within Alliance to partisanship, 166–68, 198–200; male ethos of success as organizing tool, 171–72; women members' criticism of male members as voters, 172–75, 200–201, 204–6; influence on 1890 election, 185; women members' need for Alliance, 185; and prohibition, 189–91; reinvigorated, 197–98; relationship to Populist Party, 198–200; compared to the WCTU, 200; separate women's organizations, 202–4; and

toward women, 39–40, 66; and partisan politics, 40–41, 167
*Great Bend Register,* changing attitude toward Alliance, 164–65
Greenback Party, 40

Harding, Eva, 254
Harper, Frances, 63, 64, 65–66
"hayseeds," as putdown, 33; Farmers' Alliance use of term, 156
"Hayseed, The," 171–72
Henderson, Ben, 237, 245
Home for the Aged and the Orphaned, African-American, 63
Homestead Act, 18, 37
Hudson, Joseph: and WCTU's partisanship, 119; reaction to Farmers' Alliance's politicization, 164–65; double-standard on women's political participation, 180; and 1890 election, 182–83, 187; and Woman Movement's non-partisanship, 211–14; critique of Anna Shaw, 232; and state woman suffrage amendment, 241. See also *Topeka Capital*

"If It Wasn't for the Mortgage" (Egan), 150
Industrial Conference of 1891, 191–92, 210
Ingalls, John J.: and comments about moral politics, 41; attacked by Farmers' Alliance, 162
Ives, John, 185, 191

Jefferson, Thomas, 17–18
Johns, Laura, 60, 61, 72, 180, 225; and farm women, 66, 249; and women's clubs, 69, 123; attitude towards men's political culture, 69, 79, 98; and rise of KESA, 73–74; and municipal woman suffrage, 88, 112, 113;

and elitism, 109; and Republican Party, 119, 212, 215, 221, 242; and partisanship, 119, 227, 234; as temperance activist, 121; call for Kansas Council of Women, 123; and state woman suffrage legislation, 188; and Kansas Republican Women's Club, 211, 235; response to Joseph Hudson, 212; and state woman suffrage amendment campaigns, 214–15, 230, 240–41; rebuked by Bina Otis, 222–23; relationship with Annie Diggs, 226; reaction to amendment loss, 253; renomination of, 253–54; need for women's party, 255; and Eastern suffragists, 256. See also KESA; WCTU; Woman Movement
Johnston, Lucy, 254

Kansas: and Eastern press, 4; and frontier myth, 9; as "martyred state," 12; myth of liberal, 13, 16, 17, 88, 193; economic booms, 19–20, 54–56; and economic busts, 23, 127–28
Kansas City, Kans., 52
Kansas Council of Women, 123–24
*Kansas Farmer,* 136; critiques farming practices, 149
"Kansas fever," 19–20
Kansas legislature: and reaction to grasshopper invasion, 38; and prohibition amendment, 49; and age of consent controversy, 124; and passage of reform legislation, 187; and woman suffrage, 187–88; and "Legislative War," 219–21
Kansas-Nebraska Act, 11
Kansas State Editors Association, 233
Kansas State Farmers' Alliance. *See* Farmers' Alliance, Kansas

Kansas State Teachers Association,
123, 227
Kansas State Temperance Union, 50,
80
*Kansas Sunflower:* as counterweight to
*Farmer's Wife,* 228
Kansas Supreme Court, 188, 221
Kansas Women's Press Association,
227
Kellogg, Lyman, 191
Kemp, Jack, 262
Kemp, Joann, 262
KESA (Kansas Equal Suffrage Association), 6, 226; and racism, 59–60;
and African-American women, 60;
and elitism, 60–61, 252–53; concern
about femininity, 61; and farm
women, 66–67, 249, 252; rise of, 73–
74; and attitudes toward men, 79;
and religiosity, 84; formation of, 88;
and municipal woman suffrage bill,
88–89; and partisanship, 119, 234,
253–56; state woman suffrage and
political parties, 185, 234; and
Topeka mayoral election, 211–13;
and non-partisanship, 213–14, 233,
234; and 1894 state woman suffrage
amendment, 214–15, 229–32; and
"Great Suffrage Convention," 226–
27; amendment campaign strategy
and tactics, 229–33; 250–53; KESA
1894 convention, 253–54; and post–
1894 decline, 256–57. *See also*
Diggs, Annie; Johns, Laura;
WCTU; Woman Movement
Kimber, Helen, 229, 256
Knights of Labor: and 1887 Leavenworth municipal election, 106, 109;
compared to Farmers' Alliance, 132;
and formation of Populist Party,
162–63
Kraybill, Luella, 203–4

Law and Order League, 106–8
Lawrence, Kans., 4; and Quantrill's
raid, 13; and women's anti-saloon
actions, 48
Lease, Mary Elizabeth, 197, 254; background, 176; and lack of feminine
qualities, 177–78; flaunts gender
norms, 178–79, 246; mothering
qualities defended, 179–80; and
Annie Diggs, 181, 182, 246–48; and
Laura Johns, 226; mental condition
of, 226, 245–48; and fusion, 245
Leavenworth: as focus of Republican
hatred, 52, 104–5; as proslavery
stronghold, 104; resistance to prohibition enforcement, 104–5; as mid-
roader, 194
Leedy, John, 258
"Legislative War," 219–21
Leland, Cy, 195
Lewelling, Lorenzo: as fusion candidate, 195; fusion efforts of, 237; and
Mary Lease, 245; administration of,
247–48
Lone Tree Alliance, 137, 139

Manifest Destiny, 11
Martin, John (Kansas governor), 93–
94, 112
Martin, John (U.S. senator), 221, 245
"maternalism," 60, 277n. 4
McCormick, Fannie, 203; and Populist
support for prohibition, 190–91
McLallin, Eliza, 207
McLallin, Stephen, 161; and defense of
merchants, 154–55; as mid-roader,
194; resigns, 257. See also *Advocate,
The*
men: fear of women in politics, 7, 98–
104, 251–52, 281n. 37; benefits of
male political culture, 99; violence
against wives, 103, 281n. 46; and

Library of Congress Cataloging-in-Publication Data

Goldberg, Michael L., 1959–
    An army of women : gender and politics in gilded age Kansas / Michael Lewis Goldberg.
    p.    cm. — (Reconfiguring American political history)
Includes bibliographical references and index.
ISBN 0-8018-5562-4 (alk. paper)
    1. Women in politics—Kansas—History—19th century.    2. Populism—Kansas—
History—19th century.    3. Kansas—Politics and government—1865–1950.
I. Title.    II. Series.
HQ1236.5.U6G65      1997
306.2—DC21          96-53208
                          CIP